D1434548

16

I NS

1 2 0534444 3

EYEWITNESS COMPANIONS

Opera

ALAN RIDING &
LESLIE DUNTON-DOWNER

LONDON, NEW YORK,
MUNICH, MELBOURNE, AND DELHI

Project Editor Sam Atkinson
Project Designer Victoria Clark
DTP Designer Laragh Kedwell
Production Controller Melanie Dowland

Managing Editor Debra Wolter
Managing Art Editor Karen Self
Publisher Jonathan Metcalf
Art Director Bryn Walls

Picture Researcher Sarah Smithies
Editorial Assistant Oussama Zahr
Indexer Hilary Bird

Produced for Dorling Kindersley by

studio **cactus** ltd **C**

13 SOUTHGATE STREET WINCHESTER HAMPSHIRE SO23 9DZ UK
TEL 00 44 1962 878600 EMAIL MAIL@STUDIOCACTUS.CO.UK WEBSITE WWW.STUDIOCACTUS.CO.UK

Project Editor Jennifer Close
Project Designer Dawn Terrey
Designers Sharon Cluett, Claire Moore, Sharon Rudd
Editorial Assistance Jane Baldock, Aaron Brown, Rob Walker

First published in 2006 by Dorling Kindersley Limited
80 Strand, London WC2R 0RL

A Penguin Company

2 4 6 8 10 9 7 5 3 1

A CIP catalogue record for this book
is available from the British Library

ISBN-13: 978-1-40531-279-0
ISBN-10: 1-40531-279-3

Colour reproduction by GRB, Italy
Printed and bound in China by Leo

See our complete catalogue at
www.dk.com

CONTENTS

EVEN PASSIONATE MUSIC FANS MAY BE FORGIVEN FOR CONSIDERING OPERA OVER-THE-TOP. AFTER ALL, HOW BETTER TO DESCRIBE AN ART FORM THAT FLAUNTS CONVOLUTED PLOTS, INCOMPREHENSIBLE LYRICS, STORMY ORCHESTRATION, HYPERBOLIC ACTING, EXOTIC STAGING, AND TEMPERAMENTAL SINGERS? ANOTHER WORD MIGHT BE "OPERATIC".

And yet, to its legions of worshipful followers, opera continually adds new converts. It may first touch the unsuspecting soul through a diva's charisma on television, a haunting chorus on the radio, or the thrill of a live performance. Whatever the impetus may be, people have a way of remembering the moment when opera began to change their lives.

We both came to opera along different paths. But it has since led us to see the world – and ourselves – with fresh eyes. It has taken us on imaginary journeys and has accompanied us on our travels. And now, through this book, we hope to share the many pleasures that opera has afforded us.

Opera is, of course, an emotional, even intimate experience. Its dramatic essence cannot be overlooked: story, lyrics, and music come together to express powerful feelings. The words themselves may be sung in any number of languages – those we address here are in Italian, German, French, Russian, Czech, Hungarian, and English – but the music itself requires no translation.

It may be tempting to think of opera as an artificial, even contrived form of art. Barely four centuries old, it was born in the European land that provided its name and many of its greatest composers: Italy. Yet, in reality, singing – of love, betrayal, suffering, or joy – is older than recorded history, inseparable from human passion itself. Thus, what opera's earliest creators did was to give age-old emotional truths a new lyrical and dramatic form.

Successive generations of composers and librettists have captured the operatic sentiments of their own times. And as opera grew in popularity, spawning theatres designed around its needs, it also became an international art form. Singers, composers, poets,

Crowds arrive for *La traviata* at the "old" Metropolitan Opera in New York in 1961, five years before it was replaced by today's larger Met at Lincoln Center.

Thousands of fans brave the damp weather as the great Italian tenor Luciano Pavarotti celebrates 30 years in opera with a free concert in Hyde Park, London, in July 1991.

and designers criss-crossed Europe and soon they carried opera to the New World and beyond.

No single book could cover every surviving opera: they number in the thousands. Instead, we have chosen those of enduring popularity, as well as those that played a crucial role in opera's evolution. Thus, while highlighting some 165 works and their composers, the book also aims to tell the story of opera itself.

This is a story of how the artform appeared and changed over the centuries. But it is also a story of composers who were worshipped like gods and others who died in misery; of operas banned as subversive and others that became patriotic banners; of arias, duets, and choruses that became popular hits; of electrifying

singers and dazzling stagecraft; of opera houses burned to the ground and lovingly rebuilt; and, not least, of the devoted audiences who make opera what it is.

As authors, we too have been on a voyage. We both began with our own favourite operas, composers, and musical periods. But in selecting works for detailed examination, our research led us to discover new operatic treasures, and to admire the extraordinary variety and continuity of opera through the ages.

Opera is a richly rewarding world and it can be entered through myriad doors. We trust that this book will serve as a welcome companion to anyone exploring the unique realm of opera.

ALAN RIDING
LESLIE DUNTON-DOWNER
May 2006

Introducing Opera

WHAT IS OPERA?

Four centuries ago, music, theatre, and dance came together in Italy to create a new art form called opera. It soon caught on and, by 1700, it was entertaining commoners and royalty alike across Europe. Over time, the sound of its music would change, yet the essence of opera has not: accompanied by an orchestra, with scenery, costumes, and light adding drama, singers tell a story.

MUSIC'S UNIQUE POWER to move people is no secret, but opera's special appeal lies in the voice, arguably the most affecting of all instruments. It conveys emotion even when the lyrics are not understood, while talented voices can enliven the most familiar of scores and plots. Indeed, the pleasure of revisiting beloved operas explains how an entire art form can rest on the genius of Mozart, Verdi, and Wagner and a core repertoire of some 150 works.

Still, it remains a mystery why relatively few operas have survived and many thousands are forgotten. Some operas, sell-outs in their day, are now never performed. Others, heckled at their premieres, have become firm favourites. There are also fashions: once considered the summit of the art, French *grand opéra* has vanished; in contrast, Renaissance and Baroque opera has been rediscovered with enthusiasm. Today, contemporary opera is a minority taste, yet works are continually being composed and a few have entered the repertoire.

Opera's stories also matter. Its scores can be recorded in studios or presented in concert version, yet opera was born as music theatre, that is, music set to a libretto for the stage. True, most people only remember the name of the opera's composer, yet even the greatest composers have always valued a good libretto. It may borrow its plot from Greek mythology or Roman history, from Shakespeare or Schiller, from historical epics, romantic dramas, or the occasional farce of life. More importantly, it should use the poetry of language to express a spectrum of emptions. The composer taps onto all these ingredients of human drama. Thus, the greatest operas can be about violence, greed, ambition, intrigue, betrayal, reconciliation, and death, but they may also be shaped by humour, joy, passion, and love.

A POSSESSIVE PUBLIC

Score and libretto become an opera through the voices of soloists and chorus, supported by orchestra and staging. And when all work together, the opera's creators can feel satisfied. Except, of course, they are rarely alive. Instead the role of judge and jury is played by the public, some newcomers to opera, others veterans of myriad productions, all with opinions flowing from strong passions. Indeed, if opera audiences often proclaim their verdicts with loud cheers or boos, it is because they feel deeply possessive about opera.

Yet rare is the opera devotee who likes all operas. In fact, some verge on the sectarian, worshipping one composer, disdaining another. Wagner lovers, for instance, resemble a cult. Then there are those who prefer Verdi's dramatic operas, while others yearn for the *bel canto* – "beautiful singing" – of, say, Bellini. Russian and Czech audiences are strongly loyal to their own national operas, while the French have led the revival of Baroque opera.

At the same time, an art form once mocked by Samuel Johnson as "an exotick and irrational entertainment" continues to win converts. In this, glamorous stars make a difference.

At the 100th anniversary of the Metropolitan Opera in New York on 22 October 1983, performers at a gala evening filled the stage to receive a standing ovation from an ecstatic audience.

And even in the absence of mega-divas like Maria Callas, stars keep appearing: with Renée Fleming or Bryn Terfel on a bill, a full house can be assured. Spectacles like *The Three Tenors* also attract new audiences. To satisfy this demand, opera houses are renovated and new ones are built. Opera festivals keep multiplying, while crowds watch live performances on screens in squares and parks. Four centuries after its inception, opera is alive and well.

GENRES OF OPERA

In the 18th century, *opera seria* – and its comic cousin, *opera buffa* – were the dominant models, with sung recitatives and strict aria structures. Many other types were also popular. Gluck's *Orfeo ed Euridice* was a *tragédie opéra*. The German Singspiel and the French *opéra comique* both used spoken dialogue, while French *grand opéra* required five acts and ballet. But many composers named their operas as they wished. Mozart's *Don Giovanni* was called a *dramma giocoso* ("jocose" opera). Verdi often chose *melodramma*, Wagner varied the description of his operas and Mussorgsky came up with "national music drama" for *Khovanshchina*.

HOW IT ALL BEGAN

Opera was yet another fruit of the Italian Renaissance. And, as such, it is no accident that its roots lie in the creative exuberance of Florence. In the final decade of the 16th century, a group of artists, musicians, and poets, calling themselves the "Camerata" met there to promote a revival of Greek drama. What they came up with instead was the idea that these stories could be told as an *opera in musica* – "a work in music".

Michele Marieschi's view of the courtyard of the Palazzo Ducale in Venice, where for the first time opera was staged in public theatres for paying audiences.

Claudio Monteverdi is considered the father of opera because he took the Florentine experiment a step further: with *L'Orfeo*, presented in Mantua in 1607, he absorbed his audience in a lyrical drama. The new art quickly spread to other courts and soon arrived in Venice. There, with the opening of the city's first opera house in 1637, opera reached a new public. By the end of the century, Venice boasted 17 opera houses and the Italian love for opera was sealed.

The city was never short of composers, with Antonio Vivaldi its early 18th-century star. Europe's royal courts also wanted the new *divertimento*, or entertainment and Italians often provided it, with Jean-Baptiste Lully introducing opera to France as Louis XIV's official composer. George Frideric Handel, a

German, made opera popular in 18th-century London, although the first opera in English, Henry Purcell's *Dido and Aeneas*, was performed as early as 1689.

OPERA'S REFORM

The prevailing model for much of the 17th and 18th centuries was *opera seria*, with the narrative recounted in sung dialogue called recitatives and moments

The artist Thomas Rowlandson captures the social dimension of opera-going in the 18th century in this lively and crowded scene.

of high emotion provided by arias, which allowed soloists – frequently *castratoes*, men castrated before puberty to preserve their high voices – to show off their virtuosity. Neapolitan opera broke with this solemnity by introducing humorous *opera buffa*, but this too demanded great technical prowess of singers.

In the late 18th century, two figures broke the mould. The Viennese-based composer Christoph Willibald Gluck emerged as the key figure in a so-named *reforma* by moving opera away from vocal exhibitionism towards expression of the drama. His *Orfeo ed Euridice*, in particular, paved the way for opera's first undisputed genius, Wolfgang Amadeus Mozart.

Mozart inherited a legacy of *opera seria* and *opera buffa* as well as German Singspiel, a form of opera with spoken dialogue instead of sung recitative. But while he exploited these genres, he also transformed them, responding to

In the 18th century, the operas of Christoph Willibald Gluck (1714–1787) increased the dramatic aspect of the art form.

the audacity of his librettists with music of rare inspiration. Today his reputation rests on four late masterpieces: *Le nozze di Figaro*, *Don Giovanni*, *Così fan tutte*, and *Die Zauberflöte*. In practice, opera history can be divided into pre-Mozart and post-Mozart.

THE RISE OF NATIONAL OPERAS

The clearest way of tracking what followed is through space rather than time. The 19th century, for instance, was an era when Italy, Germany, and the Czech region were forging themselves as nation states, while Tsarist Russia was opening itself up to Europe. At the same time, travel also encouraged cross-fertilization. With so much change in the air, opera was inevitably affected.

Influenced by Gluck and Mozart, and with its instinct for melody, Italian music spawned five monumental 19th-century composers. Gioacchino Rossini wrote 39 operas between the ages of 17 and 37, then

---

TYPES OF VOICES

Voices are defined by their tessitura, a palette of notes which for professional singers usually covers two octaves. However, while composers write roles to fit these tessituras, the singer's range may be expected to surpass them, above all when sopranos and tenors are assigned exceptionally high notes. The tonal ranges of the six different voice types are shown to the right, from soprano (the highest) to bass (the lowest). There are also subdivisions of each type that define whether they are light or heavy, lyric or dramatic. For instance, there are at least six categories of sopranos and tenors. A Wagnerian tenor is thus unlikely to sing a Mozartian tenor aria.

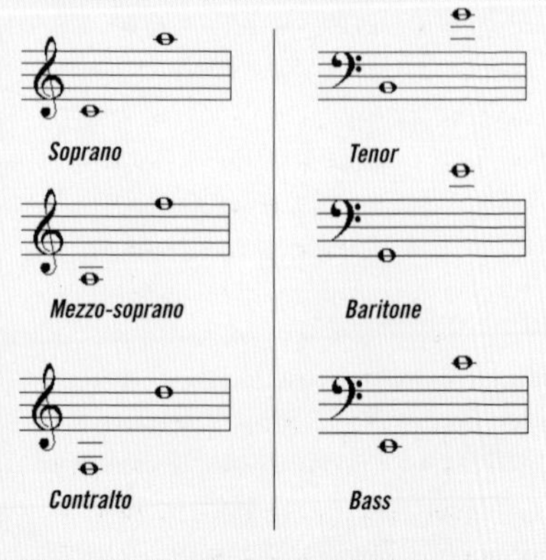

Soprano

Mezzo-soprano

Contralto

Tenor

Baritone

Bass

An 1826 stage design for the port of Damiata (now Dumyat) in Egypt, the setting of Act I of Giacomo Meyerbeer's crusader opera, *Il crociato in Egitto*, shows the elaborate sets that are so often a feature of opera.

abandoned composition. In comic operas like *Il barbiere di Siviglia* and *La Cenerentola*, he refined *bel canto*, a florid and virtuoso form of singing which was adopted by his successors, Vincenzo Bellini and Gaetano Donizetti.

A still greater opera composer followed. Giuseppe Verdi not only created a stream of memorable works but also came to personify the *risorgimento*, Italy's revolt against Austrian occupation. Several of his operas, notably *Nabucco*, were metaphors for this struggle, although his most popular works, *Rigoletto*, *Il trovatore*, and *La traviata*, are deeply romantic. His successor, Giacomo Puccini, was no less drawn to tragic love stories. Rich in memorable tunes, his greatest operas, *Manon Lescaut*, *La bohème*, *Tosca*, and *Madama Butterfly*, all portray ill-fated heroines.

THE PARIS CROSSROADS

Although Italian opera held its own, from the 1820s Paris became Europe's opera capital, drawing composers from across Europe. Their influence was considerable. Rossini, Donizetti, and Verdi all worked there. A German expatriate, Giacomo Meyerbeer, created the spectacle known as *grand opéra*, comprising five-act operas with historical librettos, rich décor, and lengthy ballet interludes. Another German, Jacques Offenbach, invented the operetta, or *opéra-bouffe*, which earned him great popularity in Paris and a following across Europe.

French opera as such had to carve its own path. Hector Berlioz turned away from *grand opéra* for his few lyrical works. Charles Gounod and Jules Massenet, who both studied in Rome, made their names with melodious Italianate operas. Georges Bizet was less prolific, yet his *Carmen*, with its exotic setting, fiery love story, and catchy tunes, carried his name around the world. However, it was another maverick, Claude Debussy, whose work *Pelléas et Mélisande* would be considered the most revolutionary French opera of its time.

GERMAN ROMANTICISM

Puzzlingly, of the great 19th-century Germanic composers of instrumental music, only Beethoven was drawn to opera and he wrote just one, *Fidelio*. Richard Wagner, in contrast, was interested only in opera and, by the mid-century, he was transforming the art form with through-composed music, expressionist orchestration, unorthodox harmonies, and grand "arches" of melody. Seeking inspiration for his librettos in German Romanticism, he embraced Teutonic

Wagner's Valkyries have long been caricatured as symbols of opera's otherworldliness. Today, with Wagner's *Ring* Cycle ever more popular, these female warriors often appear in modern dress.

story material with almost religious fervour. With his early operas, *Tannhäuser* and *Lohengrin*, he forged a Romantic style that reached its apex with *Tristan und Isolde*. But he is most revered for his monumental four-opera cycle known as *Der Ring des Nibelungen*.

Wagner's influence was such that two generations of composers wrestled to escape his shadow. One of the first to do so successfully was Richard Strauss. He took Wagner's radicalism to a new plane in his early operas. He then built on Wagner's Romanticism and even tapped Mozart in his ever-popular *Der Rosenkavalier*, *Arabella*, *Capriccio*, and *Ariadne auf Naxos*.

The 19th century also saw the rise of other national "sounds". In Russia, Mikhail Ivanovich Glinka tapped Slavic folk music, while Modest Mussorgsky brought Russian history to the stage with *Boris Godunov*. But it was the Romantic composer, Piotr Ilyich Tchaikovsky, who entered the Western repertoire with *Yevgeny Onegin* and *The Queen of Spades*. Similarly, in the Czech lands, while Bedřich Smetana is hailed as the father of nationalist opera, Leoš Janáček wrote works of greater sophistication, such as *Jenůfa* and *Kát'a Kabonová*, which are now performed alongside the works of Mozart.

MUSICALS

Musical comedy is an American invention, but its roots are in Europe. Just as *opera buffa* inspired Offenbach, Lehár, and Gilbert and Sullivan to write operettas, when the operetta met American jazz, music hall, and folk music, the musical was born. George Gershwin, Cole Porter, Irving Berlin, and Richard Rodgers were drawn to it and landmark musicals followed, from *Show Boat* to *West Side Story*. Then, after London adopted the genre, Andrew Lloyd Webber created global hits like *Cats* and *Phantom of the Opera*. Today, musicals dominate both Broadway and the West End, yet they can also serve as a gateway to opera.

The link between popular musicals and opera was underlined by the hit show *Rent*, which borrowed its story from Puccini's opera *La bohème*.

MODERN OPERA'S MANY FACES

The notion that different opera movements can exist simultaneously was never clearer than in the 20th century. Richard Strauss's *Salome* and *Elektra* sent shock waves through the opera world. Soon afterwards, Arnold Schoenberg broke with traditional ideas about music by rejecting harmony in favour of atonality (music organized without reference to a musical key). He and Alban Berg then brought dissonance (unresolved notes or chords) to opera in the 1920s, Schoenberg with *Erwartung* and *Moses und Aron*, and Berg with *Wozzeck* and *Lulu*. Yet while they were redefining modern music, more conventional operas were still being composed.

Since the end of World War II, however, opera has resembled a laboratory, with composers like

Karlheinz Stockhausen, Luciano Berio, and Philip Glass testing different idioms, from serialism (in which tones, tempos, and other variables are set in sequences) and minimalism (characterized by the repetition of musical elements) to electronic music and even explorations of silence and noise. Yet, so far, among post-war composers, only Benjamin Britten is regularly performed across the globe. With *Peter Grimes* and *Billy Budd*, he successfully achieved the ideal of setting powerful librettos to deeply stirring music.

Today, as in the past, it remains the composer's challenge to keep opera moving forward with verve and originality. Encouragingly, some opera houses are assuring opera's future by commissioning new works, even at the risk of losing audiences who prefer old favourites over experimentation. After all, opera history proves that amid today's strangest sights and sounds may lie tomorrow's masterpieces.

Kaija Saariaho's *Adriana Mater*, which premiered in Paris in 2006, sets a story of maternal love in a conflict reminiscent of the Bosnian war of the 1990s.

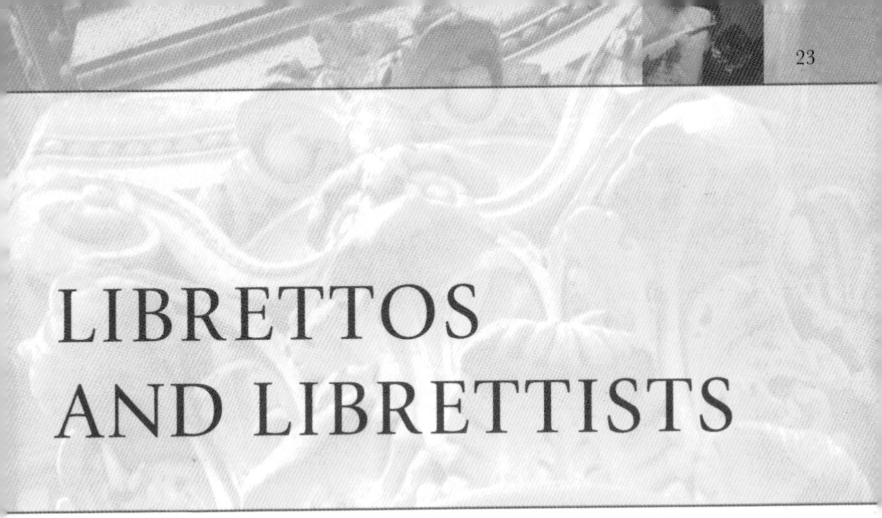

LIBRETTOS AND LIBRETTISTS

"First words, then music", is the old Italian opera credo. Some composers have objected to the claim, yet every great opera starts with a strong libretto. Whatever the story being told, the librettist inspires the music that will make the opera memorable. Fictional or factual, comic or tragic, the most successful librettos trigger passionate music and powerful emotions.

OPERA COMPOSERS HAVE always valued talented librettists. Wagner and Janáček wrote their own librettos, but masterworks by Mozart, Bellini, Verdi, Puccini, Richard Strauss, and Britten all resulted from close collaborations with gifted librettists. Yet librettists are often the unsung heroes of opera. Once their stories are set to music, the opera is remembered for its composer. Worse, a failed opera is often blamed on a weak libretto. At the birth of opera, there was no such dispute. In Monteverdi's *L'Orfeo*, scored to a poetic libretto by Alessandro Striggio, words formed the centre of gravity: music served the text by expressing the musical qualities of the language and the action.

Yet, whether an opera was to draw on such timeless story-tellers as Aeschylus, Ovid, Shakespeare, or Goethe; on beloved playwrights such as France's Beaumarchais, or national poets, such as Russia's Pushkin; on history or folklore, or any other source, the raw material had to be shaped to suit the conventions – and possibilities – of the opera's historical moment. When the courtly, quasi-academic operas of Mantua and Florence led to the rise of commercial opera, top librettists needed to hold the attention of a new, mixed public. Giovanni Faustini ruled the day in mid-17th-century Venice, where his librettos, such as *La Calisto* for composer Francesco Cavalli, featured pastoral love and comical or satirical action, often spiced with erotic tension. Giovanni Francesco Busenello took a new tack in 1643, when he was the first to use history, rather than fiction, as his source. The result was Monteverdi's absorbing *L'incoronazione di Poppea*, which invited Venetians to see the past through the new prism of music theatre.

When opera travelled beyond Italian courts and cities, librettists adapted the form to suit indigenous languages, stories, and theatre traditions. Like the early librettists of Venice, some wrote for public opera houses, where the key to success was to unleash the greatest passions of paying opera-goers. Others wrote for court productions, where the task was to please the sovereign who commissioned the opera. In either case, the opera's subject had to be worthy of emotional and theatrical grandeur. Costly to mount, operas also required an unusual mix of talents and energies to stage. Already in 1627, the Spanish court tested Florentine ideas in the nascent art of *recitar cantando*, or "sung recitative", in *La selva sin amor*, with

The first opera to draw its story from historical chronicles was Monteverdi's *L'incoronazione di Poppea*, with a plot set in Emperor Nero's ancient Rome.

"Orpheus, Leading Eurydice Out of Hell, Looks Back Upon her and Loses her Forever", a 1731 engraving by Bernard Picart, captures a mythological moment of interest to librettists since opera's earliest days.

text by Spain's great dramatist Lope de Vega. Lully's long-time librettist, Philippe Quinault, drew on the heroic French epic for *Roland*, given at Versailles in 1685. Composing for a more hybrid London theatre audience, Henry Purcell set John Dryden's

libretto for *King Arthur* in 1691, and the next year adapted Shakespeare's *A Midsummer Night's Dream* for *The Fairy Queen*. As opera proliferated, its librettos gained new languages, forms, and stories.

THE 18TH CENTURY

Many librettists collaborated closely with composers to shape words and music into opera. But the most famous librettist of the 18th century was a stranger to most of the composers who set his words. Metastasio, a Roman who served as poet to the court theatre of Vienna, wrote dozens of librettos used by composers including Vivaldi, Handel, Gluck, Mozart, and even the 19th-century Meyerbeer. *Artaserse*, a libretto about the Persian Emperor Xerxes, was so popular that it was put to music some 50 times by various composers. Through his influential librettos, Metastasio defined the contours of *opera seria*, a form that dominated the 18th century until the momentous arrival of Mozart.

The Italian Lorenzo da Ponte collaborated with fellow countryman Antonio Salieri, as well as with Spain's Vicente Martín y Soler and the German Peter Winter. But da Ponte's legendary collaboration – indeed, one of the greatest in opera history – was with the Austrian Mozart. Da Ponte's fresh-sounding language and vibrant dramatic action inspired Mozart's best opera music, beginning with *Le nozze di Figaro*. It was called an *opera buffa*, but its characters and story were far from mere farce. For *Don Giovanni*, da Ponte went even further in mixing serious

Pietro Metastasio, who perfected the *opera seria* form, was the 18th century's most important librettist.

and comical strains. These and *Così fan tutte* possessed a new lyricism and energy, dynamic characterizations, and lively dramatic structure and pacing – all perfectly suited to Mozart's musical palette. In the wake of these operas, the old Metastasian categories of *opera seria* and *opera buffa* no longer held up. As Europe's old social order crumbled following the French Revolution, a new kind of audience called for more relevant stories. Plots derived from mythical antiquity suddenly seemed distant and stale, and gave way to stories about more recognizable people struggling to achieve glory, or to find love.

CARLO GOLDONI

Carlo Goldoni (1707–1793) was the greatest Italian comic stage writer of his era. As a theatre reformer, he rejected stereotypes to create life-like characters. Goldoni ran away from school as a boy to join a touring acting company. He became a lawyer, but at age 40 left the bar for the stage. He wrote for theatres in Venice until 1762, when he became director of the Comédie Italienne in Paris. Later, he tutored Louis XV's daughters in Italian, only to die in poverty after the French Revolution. He wrote over 150 plays and 80 opera librettos, some set by Mozart and Haydn.

As well as being a sought-after librettist, Carlo Goldoni (shown centre, with a company of travelling actors) was also an accomplished playwright.

THE 19TH CENTURY

In France, the leading librettist was Eugène Scribe, who wrote almost 60 librettos for operas appealing to the expanding middle classes of Paris. For 30 years, a libretto by Scribe, whose stories often explored heroism of historical magnitude, served as a passport for composers seeking sure entry into the venerable Paris Opéra. Daniel Auber and Giacomo Meyerbeer turned to him repeatedly, but Scribe also wrote librettos for Rossini, Donizetti, Bellini, and even Verdi. Verdi's most important librettists, though, were Francesco Maria Piave and Arrigo Boito. Piave wrote *Macbeth*, *Rigoletto*, and *La traviata*, among many other works for Verdi, while Boito was the librettist for *Otello* and *Falstaff*. As the 19th century waned, Wagner

Arguably the greatest composer–librettist duo of all time was Richard Strauss (seated left in this 1922 drawing) and Hugo von Hofmannsthal.

changed the course of opera history in part by serving as his own librettist. With his grand vision of opera as *Gesamtkunstwerk*, or "total art form", Wagner could only have realized his masterpiece, the cycle *Der Ring des Nibelungen*, by fusing his music to his own words and action. By the end of the century, Giuseppe Giacosa and Luigi Illica co-authored librettos in the Romantic Italian mould for Puccini's *La bohème*, *Tosca*, and *Madama Butterfly*. And though Puccini constantly hounded his librettists, together they created some of the world's best-loved operas.

THE MODERN LIBRETTO

Some remarkable librettist–composer collaborations played a large role in keeping opera alive in the 20th century. The Austrian Hugo von Hofmannsthal supplied Richard Strauss with exquisite librettos for a string of masterpieces beginning with *Elektra* and including *Der Rosenkavalier*. Germany's Bertolt Brecht teamed up with Kurt Weill to make opera history with original librettos for *Aufstieg und Fall der Stadt Mahagonny* and *Die Dreigroschenoper*. And the American Gertrude Stein penned original librettos for Virgil Thomson, whose musical voice came alive

Giacomo Puccini (*left*) collaborated with Giuseppe Giacosa (*centre*) and Luigi Illica on several major operas at the turn of the 20th century.

FAUST

Some stories are so operatic that they have spawned more than a handful of operas. One of these is the legend of Doctor Faust, who sold his soul to the devil to gain forbidden knowledge of the earthly world. Faust inspired literary works by Christopher Marlowe, Johann Wolfgang Goethe, and Thomas Mann, and held enduring appeal for librettists. Operas based on the legend include Hector Berlioz's *La damnation de Faust*; Charles Gounod's *Faust*; Arrigo Boito's *Mephistopheles*, and Feruccio Busoni's *Doktor Faust*. The many Faustian operas of the 21st century include *Faust, The Last Night* by the French Pascal Dusapin.

The devil who lures Faust, shown on the cover of a score for La damnation de Faust, *the 1846 opera by Hector Berlioz.*

through her rhythmic and flowing verses for *Four Saints in Three Acts* and *The Mother of Us All*. But the librettist of widest influence from the time of World War II was the English-born American poet WH Auden. His lyrical ear and keen sense of dramatic action placed him in high demand for three decades. Initially writing *Paul Bunyan* for Britten, Auden – with Chester Kallman – was later librettist to Hans Werner Henze for *Elegy for Young Lovers* and *The Bassarids*, and to Igor Stravinsky for *The Rake's Progress*. He even contributed to *Un re in ascolto*, Luciano Berio's avant-garde opera inspired by

Shakespeare's *The Tempest*. By the end of the 20th century, new kinds of story-telling had found their way into opera. Robert Wilson's visual approach led him to use artwork instead of words to inspire Philip Glass's *Einstein on the Beach*. And Alice Goodman's libretto for John Adams's *Nixon in China* took its cues from television news. Yet, whatever its source material, what really counts is whether the libretto inspires a composer to weave musical magic that will take audiences on an operatic journey.

US president Richard Nixon's state visit in 1972 inspired Adams's *Nixon in China*, which in the late 20th century set new trends for operas based on news events.

STAGING OPERA

Opera can be enjoyed in recordings, but it only truly comes alive when music and words meet interpretation, décor, lighting, and costumes. It is then that the audience decides if the alchemy has succeeded. For conductor and singers no less than director and designers, staging an opera is the moment of truth. And when the curtain falls on opening night, they face the public's verdict.

From OPERA's earliest days, audiences wanted spectacle along with music and drama. In Venice, with its rich experience of *commedia dell'arte* (a form of popular theatre), public theatres soon found ingenious ways of conveying the magic of the stories being told. Louis XIV's court at Versailles then borrowed from Venice to embellish its own productions. In the strange, unreal world of opera, it seems, imaginative new machinery made everything possible. Scenes were rapidly changed between acts; gods would "fly" on and off stage on invisible wires; mountains, storms, and monsters appeared unexpectedly; flames would engulf assorted scoundrels.

Then, once Mozart had brought a fresh naturalism to operatic characters in, say, *Le nozze di Figaro*, the Paris Opéra was free to step further towards realism with historical epics. Crowds – peasants, soldiers, courtiers – were represented by large choruses and armies of extras.

Scenery became more complicated, while period costumes used velvets and silks for authenticity. Acrobats and fire-eaters peopled the stage, while real animals joined hunt scenes and royal processions. *Grand opéra*'s trademark was opulence, and Paris being Paris, opera houses in Vienna, Milan, London, and St Petersburg followed its example.

Lighting also played a central role in shaping the aesthetics of opera. In the 17th and 18th centuries, candlelight prevailed despite the accompanying risk of fire, with metal screens sometimes masking candles placed directly in front of the stage. In the 19th century, gaslight was introduced to theatres and, here again, techniques were developed to create mysterious colour effects. Finally, from the 1880s, electricity began to reach major opera houses, allowing the auditorium to be darkened, while events on stage were transformed by spotlights, colours, and shadows.

ENTER THE AGE OF ARTISTS AND DIRECTORS

In the early 20th century, as Modernism swept both music and art, what opera audiences saw and heard also changed. The new art was as revolutionary as the new music of Schoenberg and Stravinsky. Diaghilev's Ballets Russes took the lead in showing it. Among the artists recruited to design décor and costumes were Pablo Picasso, Natalya Goncharova, Henri Matisse, Jean Cocteau, and Salvador Dalì. The staging of opera also mirrored new art movements, like Constructivism, Cubism, and Surrealism.

But the rise of Fascism in the 1930s drove avant-garde art from German and Italian stages. Across Europe and the United States, opera came under the sway of musicians, personified by the composer Richard Strauss and Arturo Toscanini, opera's reigning *maestro* until the 1950s. In fact, conductors ruled the roost, among them Wilhelm Furtwängler, Herbert von Karajan, Carlos Kleiber, Leonard Bernstein, Karl Böhm, and Georg Solti.

In the late 1960s, however, yet another era began in opera, prompted less by the creation of new operas than by a perceived need make the standard opera repertory seem relevant to modern audiences. Following the example of post-war playwrights and theatre directors, the idea now was to focus not on physical staging, but on interpretation. This might be supported by décor and costumes, but the approach was principally

Arturo Toscanini, pictured conducting at Milan's Teatro alla Scala, was an inspirational figure in 20th-century opera.

Giorgio Strehler (*right*), a theatre director who also turned his hand to opera, marks out stage positions for *Fidelio* at the Théâtre du Châtelet, Paris, in 1999.

PUTTING ON AN OPERA

An opera house must book top singers years ahead of an engagement, but its most important decision involves picking the director of a new production. Once named, he or she chooses set, lighting, and costume designers and, together, they give form to the director's concept of the opera. Next, theatre workshops start building scenery, computerizing lighting plans, and making costumes and wigs. Then, several weeks before opening night, rehearsals begin. Soloists and chorus should know their parts, but the director must define how they act. The conductor then shapes the sound of the opera, but its look is already fixed.

Making the scenery for Offenbach's Orphée aux Enfers at the workshop of the Paris National Opera.

Peter Stein, Stéphane Braunschweig, and Luc Bondy, theatre's influence on opera continues to this day.

SINGERS AS ACTORS

The most important result has been to turn singers into actors. Since the birth of opera, singers have provided most of the electricity that draws crowds to opera. From *castratoes* like Farinelli, through tenors like Enrico Caruso, to soprano divas like Maria Callas, their voices and charisma have literally provoked hysteria. But with the new generation of directors, more was wanted of singers: now they were expected to bend to a coherent dramatic vision of an opera. The two leading tenors of the late 20th century illustrate the change. Luciano Pavarotti represented the old school of singers who relied on the magic of their voices, while Plácido Domingo, a true actor-singer, set the theatrical standard now required of opera.

Today, singers must learn to live their roles, to convey emotion through physical and facial expression as well as through voice, to interact intensely with friends and foes alike, to sing in seemingly impossible positions, occasionally to bare themselves, and even to feign death convincingly.

intellectual. Productions in modern dress became fashionable, while 19th-century operas were portrayed as 20th-century political struggles. It was to prove a watershed: the rise to operatic power of stage directors.

Unsurprisingly, the theatre world supplied many influential opera directors. Patrice Chéreau was already a theatre star when he directed a famous centenary production of Wagner's *Ring* cycle at the Bayreuth Festival between 1976 and 1980. Acclaimed theatre directors like Peter Brook, Giorgio Strehler, and Harry Kupfer also engaged in opera with notable success, as did Ingmar Bergman, the Swedish movie and theatre director. And, with directors like Richard Eyre, Deborah Warner,

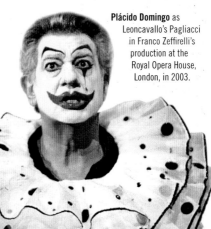

Plácido Domingo as Leoncavallo's Pagliacci in Franco Zeffirelli's production at the Royal Opera House, London, in 2003.

STAGE FASHIONS

Until the 20th century, costumes evoked the era in which an opera was set. Today, costumes are used to define the mood of a production: period costumes announce a traditional approach; modern dress anticipates a social or political message. And yet stage characters may also be clothed in a peculiarly operatic *mélange*: heroines in bejewelled gowns opposite heroes in martial Roman-style uniforms, women in brightly-coloured chiffon with men in black leather. Still, since costumes are expensive to tailor, they are never an afterthought. In practice, while they may fit no exact period, they form an intrinsic part of every production.

Ornate costumes, like these at the Palais Garnier in Paris, help maintain the mystique of opera.

At times, they complain that a theatre director has little understanding of their need to breathe properly as well as to act. And on such occasions, conductors and costume designers may come to their rescue.

Still, appearance is more important than ever: singers are expected to look their parts so that, say, a hefty soprano is unlikely to be cast as a tragic heroine dying of consumption. Thus, soloists who are handsome or beautiful and can act well are avidly courted by opera houses. And opera "couples" – such as Roberto Alagna and Angela

The live performers look tiny in this massive, quasi-Surrealist set for Puccini's *La bohème* at the Bregenz Festival in Austria in 2001.

Gheorghiu or, more recently, Rolando Villazón and Anna Netrebko – are in particular demand for romantic roles.

NEW LOOKS ON STAGE

As a crossroads of the arts, opera has also drawn other outsiders. Some film directors – notably Joseph Losey with *Don Giovanni* and Francesco Rosi with *Carmen* – have adapted operas to the screen. Many more – Roman Polanski, Baz Luhrmann, Julie Taymor, Anthony Minghella, and Michael Haneke among them – have brought the pace of cinema to the opera stage. Their show business aura has helped to attract a younger public to opera.

Leading choreographers have also turned to directing opera, with the lengthy musical interludes in 17th- and 18th-century works offering the best opportunity to combine song and dance. Trisha Brown's first venture into opera led her to Monteverdi's *L'Orfeo*, but she then applied her modern

dance vocabulary to a new opera, Salvatore Sciarrino's *Luci mie traditrici*. For her magical production of Gluck's *Orfeo ed Euridice*, Pina Bausch doubled singers and dancers in the three main roles, while the chorus sang from the orchestra pit. Mark Morris, who also directed *Orfeo ed Euridice*, chose to place the singers in theatre boxes, leaving the stage entirely to dancers.

Still, some directors are known principally for their opera productions. Franco Zeffirelli's visual extravagance is identified with the Metropolitan Opera in New York. Other directors have been more daring, and three Americans stand out. Peter Sellars, who presented Mozart's *Così fan tutte* as a contemporary story, invariably approaches opera with a fresh eye:

for Wagner's *Tristan und Isolde*, he incorporated large-screen videos by the American artist Bill Viola. Robert Wilson's minimalist productions in turn blend the stylized gestures of Japan's Kabuki theatre with remarkable lighting effects, while Francesca Zambello exploits the technical wizardry of modern stages.

Then there are opera directors, led by the Catalan Calixto Bieito, who set out to shock audiences with sex and gore. They often draw full houses and loud protests, but their antics can also distract from the music, leading many conductors to feel that their authority has been further eroded. More than ever, then, the opera stage is an arena in which different artistic elements vie for dominance. It is a high-risk business in which many directors become unstuck. Yet when music, story, interpretation, décor, and costumes come together with a certain flair, opera blossoms in many colours.

OPERA HOUSES AND FESTIVALS

Opera houses are more than just theatres. Their imposing façades suggest temples to a pagan cult, their ornate interiors reinforce the mystique for those who pass through their doors, and their stages present beauty in the form of ritual. Still more critically, they keep the art of opera alive by commissioning new works and bringing cherished classics to new audiences.

OPERA HOUSES can also be troublesome. Enormously costly to run, they live off government subsidies or private patronage. They are often arenas for fierce political struggles and are themselves variously attacked as elitist or populist. They are vulnerable to last-minute strikes by the unseen technicians who make every performance happen. And they can present productions that send audiences into paroxysms of rage. Yet for all the headaches they cause, opera houses are loved with a passion.

A typical opera house is still one built in the late 18th or 19th century, its exterior Neoclassical, a marble foyer leading to a red and gold horseshoe auditorium, with boxes which originally offered perfect view of the presiding monarch or nobles in the royal box. Indeed, for a long time, the social life of the opera house was as important as what occurred on stage. Dressed in their finery, the wealthy went to the opera to observe each other, while the less prosperous crowded the highest gallery, waited in a nearby bar, or stood below, eating and talking, until some stirring aria demanded their attention.

Certainly, the earliest opera houses, built in 17th-century Venice, reached out to all classes. It was this accessibility that quickly turned opera into popular entertainment across the Italian peninsula and beyond. First in Venice, soon in Bologna, Naples, and Milan, and later in London, Vienna, and Paris, opera houses multiplied and competed for audiences. Of these, few survive. But by the 19th century, notably in the Italian states and German principalities, every self-respecting European city boasted an opera house as a symbol of status. Then, to these were added opera festivals, starting with Wagner's Bayreuth Festival in Bavaria in 1876, followed by Austria's Salzburg Festival in 1920 and the Glyndebourne Festival in England in 1934.

ITALY'S OPERA SHRINES

In Italy, three opera houses stand as monuments to the golden age of Italian opera. The Teatro di San Carlo in Naples, arguably Italy's most beautiful theatre, was inaugurated in 1737 and, while destroyed by fire in 1816, was rebuilt in just six months: operas by Rossini, Bellini, Donizetti, and Verdi all had their premieres there. The Teatro La Fenice in Venice, a jewel squeezed among the city's canals, opened in 1792 and, though ravaged by fire in 1836 and again in 1996, it was twice rebuilt, living up to its name of The Phoenix. Verdi premiered operas at La Fenice, as did Igor Stravinsky and Benjamin Britten in the 20th century. To this day, Venetians walk through its doors with a sense of pride.

Venice's glorious Teatro La Fenice burned down in 1996, allegedly the result of arson, but it was rebuilt and reopened with a larger backstage in 2003.

Inaugurated in 1778, Milan's world-famous Teatro alla Scala was at the heart of the city's social and political life throughout the 19th century.

Milan's Teatro alla Scala, however, has long been the true home of opera in Italy. Every 19th-century Italian composer wanted his opera to premiere there, with none more present than Verdi. For rising soloists, consecration at La Scala also became a vital rite of passage. Badly damaged by Allied bombing in 1943, the theatre opened

anew in 1946. Then, in 2001, it was closed for three years to undergo modernization of its backstage, but its glorious auditorium remains much as when Austria's Empress Maria Theresia inaugurated it in 1778.

Elsewhere in Europe, the history of opera houses is no less a record of fires and war damage. Before the Paris Opéra occupied the seemingly impregnable Palais Garnier in 1875, no fewer than six of its previous homes were razed by fire. In Vienna, several opera houses preceded the opening of the grand Hofopernhaus in 1869. In 1918, with the collapse of the Habsburg monarchy, the Hofopernhaus became the Staatsoper Wien. Then, while it functioned under the Nazi occupation, it too was damaged by Allied bombers in 1945 and only reopened in 1955.

THE GERMAN OPERATIC MOTOR

Inevitably, German opera houses suffered most during World War II, with those of Berlin, Cologne, Dresden, Hamburg, Leipzig, and Stuttgart among dozens destroyed. The elegant 18th-century Staatsoper Unter den Linden in Berlin and the Bayerische Staatsoper in Munich were reconstructed, but in most cases new buildings were necessary. What was not affected was Germany's devotion to opera. To this day, no country has more opera houses than Germany, most working on a repertory system: singers

> ### THE OPERA BOSS
>
> Opera houses only prosper when they have strong leaders. In 18th-century London, Handel managed his own theatres, while Domenico Barbaia shaped 19th-century Italian opera at both La Scala in Milan and the San Carlo in Naples. Sometimes, the drive comes from conductors, such as Gustav Mahler at Vienna's Staatsoper, Arturo Toscanini at La Scala, and, more recently, James Levine at the Metropolitan Opera in New York. In the 1970s, it was the theatre manager and composer Rolf Liebermann who brought innovation to the Paris Opéra. Whether a theatre presents top singers, exciting productions, and new operas depends on who is in charge.

from around the world head to sing in Germany, the only country where they can quickly build up a roster of roles.

In England too, war disrupted opera, with the Royal Opera House at Covent Garden used as a dance-hall and the Sadler's Wells Theatre as a shelter for homeless Londoners. Inaugurated in 1858, the Royal Opera House survived the war and was finally modernized and expanded in the late 1990s. The Sadler's Wells Opera moved in 1968 to the London Coliseum, where in 1974 it was renamed the English National Opera. The Welsh National Opera, founded in 1946, was in turn given a new home at the Wales Millennium Centre in Cardiff Bay in 2004.

The Staatsoper Unter den Linden, Berlin's oldest opera house, has recovered its former glory since reunification.

Built on the orders of Napoleon III and inaugurated after his overthrow in 1875, the Palais Garnier in Paris has long been considered the pinnacle of operatic opulence.

Many singers find the 3,800-seat Metropolitan Opera of New York intimidatingly large, but a Met début remains an essential stepping stone for any budding star hoping for a major career.

Until World War II, it was traditional for operas to be sung in the language of the audience. For instance, while Paris had a Théâtre-Italien, even Donizetti and Verdi had to use French librettos to gain access to the Paris Opéra. In fact, audiences everywhere wanted to hear words sung in their own language. It was also easier for the singers, who were usually employed by opera houses. Today, however, operas are performed in their original language almost everywhere: the English National Opera, the Komische Oper in Berlin, and the Opera Theatre in St Louis, Missouri, are among the few exceptions. The reason for the change was practical. Opera has become so internationalized that major stages now present singers from all over the world. And peripatetic soloists have no time to learn the same role in several languages. The preferred solution, then, is to provide translation, either above the proscenium stage or on the backs of seats.

OPERA'S LONG REACH

Opera itself had no trouble travelling, spawning opera houses in Prague – its Estates Theatre premiered Mozart's *Don Giovanni* in 1787 – and across Eastern Europe. Russia's tsars also wanted opera, building the Mariinsky Theatre in St Petersburg and the Bolshoi Theatre in Moscow. The opera fad spread still further afield: the Cairo Opera House opened in 1869, the Teatro Colón in Buenos Aires in 1892, the Manaus Opera House in the heart of the Amazon in 1896, and the Hanoi Opera in French Indochina in 1911.

With its large European immigrant population, the United States also quickly embraced opera: gold and silver boom towns in the South-West were among the first to build opera houses. But the turning-point came in New York in 1883 with the opening of the Metropolitan Opera, which was soon

FOREVER SALZBURG

In a calendar crowded with summer festivals, one held in Mozart's birthplace clearly has special appeal. With Richard Strauss among its founders in 1920, the Salzburg Festival flourished until the Nazis occupied Austria in 1938. Then, in the post-war era, with the Vienna Philharmonic again its resident orchestra, it became the fiefdom of Herbert von Karajan who, in 1967, added the Salzburg Easter Festival. Today, with top conductors, orchestras, and singers on their programmes, the festivals remain among Europe's most prestigious.

A busy night in the Festival Quarter in Salzburg.

presenting top soloists in the best European operas. And it preserved its reputation for offering star singers after it moved to its far larger current home in Lincoln Center in 1966.

Meanwhile, most American cities presented opera. In 1875, Philadelphia's Academy of Music auditorium was modelled on La Scala. San Francisco, which lost many theatres in the 1906 earthquake, moved its new opera

The Glyndebourne Festival in England is famous for the picnics in its elegant gardens during the interval of evening operatic performances.

company into the War Memorial Opera House in 1932. Today, opera houses flourish across America, from Seattle to Washington, Los Angeles to Miami, Chicago to Houston.

For the Soviet Union too, opera represented status and political power and, by the mid-20th century, the capital of every Soviet republic, from Kiev to Tashkent, had its own opera house. And elsewhere, pride continues to generate opera houses. None is more iconic than the Sydney Opera House, which opened in 1973. But Paris now also has the Opéra Bastille, while Copenhagen and Valencia have new opera houses. Festivals have also multiplied, with Aldeburgh in England, Aix-en-Provence in France, Verona in Italy, and Santa Fé in the United States among the most popular. The greatest novelty, though, is Asia's growing interest in the art, with opera houses opening in Tokyo in 1997, Shanghai in 1998, and Beijing in 2008, and plans for one in Seoul.

The festival of Les Chorégies d'Orange in southern France is held in a Roman theatre well-suited to opera spectacles such as Verdi's *Aïda*.

IDOLS OF OPERA

Opera is inseparable from diva worship. Over the centuries, a small number of singers with exceptional voices and powerful personalities have come to personify all the passion and drama of opera. And opera fans have always responded to them – with excitement, adulation, even hysteria. Onstage and off, opera's idols fuel the entire art form with their love of high drama.

LARGER-THAN-LIFE opera stars are almost always sopranos, literally *divas*, or "goddesses" in Italian; but they can also be tenors and, in an earlier age, they were often castratos. Together, they have played a central role in perpetuating the mysterious appeal of opera. What is their secret?

A talent for reaching extraordinarily high notes is almost a must: a high C, well sung and long held by a soprano or a tenor, electrifies audiences. The reigning opera vocalists are also gifted actors, bringing roles to life with the conviction of their singing. Yet just as important are their glamorous and volatile personalities. It is little wonder that many divas became muses to the best opera composers and conductors.

But it is among opera lovers that diva addiction thrives. They follow their favourite singers around the world; they toss bouquets of flowers at curtain-calls; and they collect the minutiae of divas' lives, from lovers to pets, to hairstyles and diets. The reigning diva, or *diva assoluta*, can even acquire a telling alias. The ultra-revered 20th-century Greek–American soprano Maria Callas was known as *La Divina* ("The Divine One"), while her rival Renata Tebaldi was dubbed *La Regina* ("The Queen").

Certainly, top singers can be moody and demanding, and many have been infamously capricious and narcissistic. But they can afford to be: their mere presence sells out an opera house. So, along with enduring weighty costumes, itchy wigs, ungainly props, and bizarre special effects, they carry heavy commercial responsibilities. And, since the early period of public opera houses in Venice, they have commanded exorbitant fees. Even today, they are often paid in cash in their dressing-rooms during the first interval of an opera performance.

CASTRATOS

The entire diva saga can be traced back to opera's castratos, whose voices evolved out of sacred choir music, and whose techniques were passed down to future vocalists through the Italian tradition of *bel canto* singing. Castratos were the first opera stars, and established the rules for the divas who followed. For some castratos, special treatment began with vocal training. Even before opera emerged, promising boy singers schooled in Italian conservatories were fed richer foods, and lodged more comfortably than other classmates, all in the name of enhancing their voices. With females in the Papal Roman states forbidden to sing in church or in public over the first 200 years of opera, castratos were highly prized.

Castration involved the severing of a duct, and not the removal of an organ. Officially banned, it was nonetheless practised since medieval times in order to supply church choirs with glorious, high male voices. When opera appeared in the 17th century, castratos readily sang male as well as female roles. The most popular dazzled fans far and wide, among

Farinelli, whose real name was Carlo Broschi (1705–1782), travelled throughout Europe. For a time, he appeared with the Opera of the Nobility in London.

them Carlo Broschi, who débuted in Naples in 1720. Under the name Farinelli, he earned cult followings in opera houses and courts throughout Europe. Another 18th-century castrato, Luigi Marchesi, had such a following that opera houses accepted his outrageous demands: he was to enter the stage sporting a plumed helmet, riding a horse, and singing any aria his heart desired, even if it was not in the opera he was performing.

Castratos also bequeathed to divas their often stormy natures. Gaetano Majorano riveted audiences under the name Caffarelli in the 18th century,

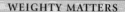

WEIGHTY MATTERS

In 2003, London's Royal Opera House revived an old question when it broke a contract with 220-pound soprano Deborah Voigt: does sight matter more than sound? Marietta Alboni (1824–1894) stopped performing only when her girth prevented her from standing long enough, while Luisa Tetrazzini famously breakfasted on whole chickens, unconcerned about weight. Maria Callas dropped 100 pounds (45kg) over one summer to please the eye, but her voice consequently suffered. The real nightmare for divas is audience rejection. Creating the emaciated Violetta in Verdi's *La traviata* at La Fenice in Venice in 1853, the 287-pound Fanny Salvini-Donatelli barely endured the heckling and laughter.

Deborah Voigt singing at Avery Fisher Hall *in New York in 1998, prior to surgery that drastically reduced her weight.*

but he also skipped rehearsals, cancelled appearances on a whim, loudly criticized other singers during performances, and even physically attacked fellow artists.

PRIMA DONNAS

Where women were allowed to appear on stage in the 17th and 18th centuries, prima donnas were cherished. Venice anointed Anna Renzi, the first female singer to fill opera houses; her roles included Ottavia in Monteverdi's 1643 *L'incoronazione di Poppea*. By Handel's era, the Italians Faustina Bordoni and Francesca Cuzzoni were known throughout Europe as much for combustible tempers as for vocal fireworks. By the end of the 18th century, Caterina Gabrielli had also spread diva joy – and wreaked diva havoc – from Russia to Sicily. Like her castrato compatriot Caffarelli, the headstrong Gabrielli served a brief prison sentence for outrageous conduct while performing.

The Romantic era ushered out the castrato, but welcomed new voice types and divas to go with them. Soprano Angelica Catalani drove Europe wild with her voice and stage presence, even as her high fees and defiance scandalized imperial leaders from Catherine the Great to Napoleon. Roles scored by Rossini produced mezzo-soprano divas,

such as the legendary Maria Malibran. And in the 1830s, soprano Giuditta Pasta shook La Scala with her creations of Bellini roles, including Norma.

But the Golden Age for divas arrived with Verdi. Any pretender to the title of reigning diva had to leave her mark on Violetta of *La traviata*, or the title role of *Aïda*. And with opera houses and conservatories opening

Renata Scotto's vocal daring made her the Puccini interpreter *par excellence*, in roles such as Musetta (*right*), Mimì, Cio-Cio-San, and the three heroines of *Il Trittico*.

across the world in his era, Verdi was the first to score roles that instantly spoke to international audiences. Puccini's touching prima donnas – Tosca, Manon Lescaut, Cio-Cio-San, Mimì – would gain a place of their own in the pantheon of diva-making roles. Glamorous Czech soprano Emmy Destinn was among the first of many to bring Puccini's suffering ladies fame on a global scale.

Wagnerian opera demanded more stamina and distinct vocal technique. The controversial *vibrato*, with the voice seeming to wobble, allowed voices to be heard over a more sonorous and sizeable orchestra. The noted Wagnerian soprano diva Lilli Lehmann blazed trails, inspiring generations of Sieglindes and Brünnhildes in her wake. Operas by Richard Strauss called for yet another kind of prima donna to set singing on a new course over the 20th century. But with few exceptions, the modern-day diva prefers dramatic characters of former eras over the more abstract roles of contemporary opera.

For the last 100 years, too, star singers have gained still greater notoriety as recording artists. German soprano Elisabeth Schwarzkopf, *diva assoluta* Maria Callas, Italian mezzo-soprano Cecilia Bartoli, and American soprano Renée Fleming are among them. But even fine recordings of top singers fail to capture the thrill of a live performance in an opera house.

TENORS

Since the wane of the castrato, noted male voices have mainly been tenors. Early divos – although the term is rarely used – were passionate romantic lovers or historical saviours; later, the Wagnerian Heldentenor (literally "heroic tenor") produced a more forceful sound suited to mythical themes and larger orchestras.

In the 1820s, the Italian Giovanni-Battista Rubini amazed opera houses with a high voice modelled on florid castrato effects. And the French tenor

Russia's soprano Anna Netrebko, with her blend vocal magic and off-stage glamour, is opera's latest diva. She fills each of her roles, from Mozart to *bel canto* to Verdi, with an irresistible charm.

Adolphe Nourrit made audiences swoon and scream in the 1820s and 1830s, especially at the Paris Opéra, where he created countless roles. But the sensuous voice of Frenchman Gilbert-Louis Duprez, who in 1836 became the first tenor to float up to high C from the chest, is credited with setting off a tenor craze that continues to this day.

The Three Tenors sang their début concert on the eve of the 1990 World Cup in Rome. Their signature song is "Nessun dorma" from Puccini's *Turandot*, with its climactic moment on the word *vincerò* ("I will win").

Venerated as opera performers and recording stars alike were Enrico Caruso, the Italian whose glorious voice brought new audiences to opera, and Danish Wagnerian Heldentenor Lauritz Melchior, whose performances and recordings of the early half of the 20th century remain legendary.

Unusually for the history of opera, the biggest stars of the late 20th century were tenors: Luciano Pavarotti and Plácido Domingo, who not only stirred frenzies among opera-goers but also, with José Carreras, took opera's most popular tunes to a mass audience as The Three Tenors. Such was their importance to opera houses, recording companies, and fans, that expectations rise every time an impressive young tenor – and potential successor – appears on stage. And the same applies to striking new sopranos who show promise.

Certainly, it is hard to imagine that opera would have survived 400 years without its beloved vocalists. Indeed, they inspire composers, excite audiences , and fill theatres far and wide. They also stir the deep passions that continue to assure opera's future.

DIVA vs. DIVA

In 1727, the Italian sopranos Faustina Bordoni and Francesca Cuzzoni broke into fisticuffs while singing on stage in London. Bookings for both ladies soared, and John Gay immortalized the duo in *The Beggar's Opera* (1728). Paris in the 1840s saw rival mezzo-sopranos: Rosine Stoltz, mistress of the director of the Opéra, drove the threatening Julie Dorus-Gras from the company; Stoltz was ejected herself when Paris tired of her diva tyranny. Methods differed at London's Covent Garden, where Australian soprano Nellie Melba barred Luisa Tetrazzini. But their rivalry exploded in 1907, when Melba returned from a trip to learn that her nemesis had taken 20 curtain calls as Violetta in Verdi's *La traviata*. The Verdi role unleashed diva fury again in 1951, when Maria Callas told Renata Tebaldi that her Violetta was deficient. Tebaldi, who refused to appear at Milan's La Scala whenever Callas did, snapped that "a chicken coop doesn't hold two roosters". Callas, the Greek-American diva, had recently declared her own voice champagne to Tebaldi's Coca-Cola in a 1956 cover story for *Time*.

Tetrazzini and Melba, aptly caricatured as duelling gramophones in Punch *magazine, 1908.*

Monteverdi
to Mozart

WHEN MONTEVERDI fashioned a new kind of entertainment for a court in Mantua at the dawn of the 17th century, few could have foreseen its rapid rise and far reach. From Sicily to St Petersburg, over 1,000 operas were created before Mozart's birth in 1756. With its mix of music, drama, and spectacle, opera awakened powerful new appetites for a new art form.

OPERA BEFORE MOZART

Once considered formal, even rigid, operas from the period between 1600 and 1750 have returned to vogue. With early opera's seeming restraint came contrasting expressions of overwhelming love and raging jealousy, aesthetic bliss and moral torment, or potent desires to live and even to die. Indeed, opera dramatized emotions so extreme as to resemble sacred passions. Great roles of the day portrayed larger-than-life figures in dramas adapted from mythology or chivalric romances. They wielded supernatural powers and magic charms. Roman emperors and Persian princesses were among the storied high-born stars of opera before Mozart. Their emotional turmoil was amplified through beautiful music, stunning costumes and scenery, and pyrotechnical stagecraft. Immortal heroes and heroines

Sets for a 1650 operatic version of Pierre Corneille's *Andromède* in Paris were designed by Giacomo Torelli, who had revolutionized stagecraft in Venice opera houses.

transported the sentiments of human opera-goers into glorious realms of timelessness and divinity.

VENICE

Opera dawned in northern Italian Renaissance courts, but swiftly gained new ground. In the dynamic business world of Venice, entrepreneurs were quick to respond to popular interest. The first theatre to welcome a

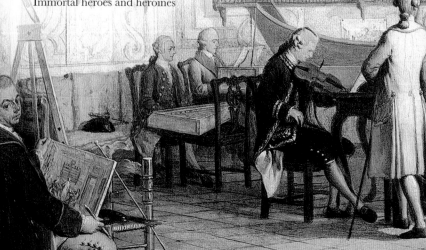

paying public opened in 1637, and other theatres soon offered vigorous competition. By the end of the century, some 200 operas were created to satisfy the public's burgeoning demands. Already in the 1640s, theatres teemed with innovation. For his Teatro Novissimo, Giacomo Torelli invented a revolving stage, flying machines, and technology to change scenery in mere seconds. Monteverdi drew audiences to a rival theatre with *L'incoronazione di Poppea*; set in the time of Emperor Nero, and in the steamy bedchamber of his mistress, this was the first opera to take history, rather than mythology, as its source. The sensual music of Francesco Cavalli, often to risqué librettos by Giovanni Faustini, captivated decades of opera-

A contemporary design for the god Apollo in *Phaëton*, Jean-Baptiste Lully's 1683 opera, demonstrates the striking costumes used.

goers in works like *La Calisto*. The 18th century brought Antonio Vivaldi, who claimed to have written over 90 operas. Many, including *Orlando furioso*, used orchestral resources to sublime effect. But this strength was weakened in later operas. Venice in the 1730s was besotted with new sounds arriving from Naples, and with such intoxicating castrato singers as Farinelli. The "Neapolitan style" was all about vocal virtuosity and, to Vivaldi's detriment, it became all the rage in his home town.

NAPLES

A major centre of sacred music training since the medieval period, Naples boasted four conservatories, top music masters, and a steady supply of budding talents who readily adapted to the growing demand for opera singers. Most prized in Naples was the gifted and studious young castrato whose exquisite high voice would be preserved in adulthood. In principle sacrilegious, castration was performed on boys, usually by people in their families dreaming of lucrative careers. The castrato's moment of operatic glory came in the 18th century, with the da capo aria; its first section was repeated with elaborate improvisation and vocal ornaments, such as trills. Indeed, in the 18th century, Neapolitans such as Nicola

A mid-18th-century painting of music-makers by Pietro Fabris depicts the vibrant cultural life of an aristocratic household in Naples.

OPERA BUFFA

Students in the conservatories of 18th-century Naples lampooned the gravity of *opera seria*, the speciality of their music masters. Drawing on stock figures and comical action from the earthy theatrical tradition known as *commedia dell'arte*, they created ludicrous works of music theatre.
Young composers including Giovanni Battista Pergolesi first wrote *intermezzos*, works performed between acts of solemn operas. The *opera buffa* ("comic opera") followed in works by Giovanni Paisiello and Domenico Cimarosa. But Mozart later combined elements of *opera seria* and *opera buffa* to create his own brand of opera.

Porpora and Niccolò Jommelli played to the skills of top castratos by filling their operas with da capo arias, often from librettos by Rome's brilliant poet, Metastasio. Like the castratos, whose voices were relished from the steppes of Russia to the tip of Spain, Neapolitan composers and librettists often served foreign courts and theatres. Porpora led a commercial opera company in London, and Metastasio became Court Poet to the theatre in Vienna.

LONDON
England's Civil War in the mid-17th century shut down theatres, which only reopened after the Restoration of 1660. The native composer Henry Purcell, influenced by musical productions of Shakespeare plays

and pageant-like masques, then wrote numerous "semi-operas". But the sole true opera in English, and indeed the only great opera in English before the 20th century, was Purcell's *Dido and Aeneas* of 1689. Eighteenth-century London would welcome the prolific German George Frideric Handel, in whose hands the *opera seria*, or "serious opera", reached its zenith. His Baroque masterpieces, *Giulio Cesare* and *Tamerlano*, sung in Italian, were both given in 1724, when he ran the Royal Academy of Music. But competition for audiences was stiff. *The Beggar's Opera* (1728), a ground-

King ARTHUR:
OR,
The British Worthy.
A Dramatick
OPERA.
Perform'd at the *QUEENS* Theatre
By Their MAJESTIES Servants.
Written by Mr. DRYDEN.

London, Printed for Jacob Tonson, at the Judge's-Head in Chancery-Lane near Fleetstreet, 169.

The 1694 title page of Henry Purcell's popular semi-opera *King Arthur, or The British Worthy*, with text written by Purcell's famous collaborator, John Dryden.

MONTEVERDI TO MOZART

1607 Monteverdi's *L'Orfeo* is given in Mantua	**1643** Monteverdi's *L'incoronazione di Poppea* is the first historical opera	**1689** Purcell's *Dido and Aeneas* is given by schoolgirls in Chelsea
1600	**1650**	**1675**

1598 Jacopo Peri's *Daphne* is given in Florence	**1637** First opera house opens in Venice	**1660** English Restoration, theatres reopen for first time since Civil War	**1671** Cambert's *Pomone*, the first opera in French, rivets Paris	**1672** Lully heads L'Académie Royale de la Musique; begins composing operas

breaking "ballad opera" by John Gay, laced familiar tunes and new lyrics into a spoken drama that sparkled with satirical irreverence in English. Handel, by then managing his own opera company, entered into a fierce rivalry with the Opera of the Nobility, an Italian company led by the Neapolitan Nicola Porpora. But by 1741, the time of Handel's last opera, London opera-goers had had their fill of *opera seria* sung in Italian.

PARIS

Spectacular entertainments were integral to the court politics of the French King Louis XIV. But Lully, the court's reigning composer, would not conceive of a French opera until the triumph of Robert Cambert's *Pomone* of 1671 to the first libretto in French, by Pierre Perrin. Lully at once began a long-term collaboration with librettist Philippe Quinault. His love of dance, shared by his monarch, left a strong mark on French opera. For three decades of the 18th century, Lullian dance elements animated the operas of Jean-Philippe Rameau. Rameau's operas were initially attacked for being too unlike Lully's. But Parisian circles were

Philosopher, writer, music theorist, and opera composer Jean-Jacques Rousseau (1712–1778) sparked opera reform in Paris.

soon engulfed in other debates. In 1752, Neapolitans descended on Paris with Pergolesi's rollicking *La serva padrona* and other farcical works of Italian *opera buffa* or "comic opera". Jean-Jacques Rousseau hailed the Italians; attacked the unnaturalness of French music theatre; and called for reform. His pleas would be answered in Vienna, where Christoph Willibald von Gluck and librettist Raniero da Calzabigi viewed words not as a verbal skeleton to be fleshed out by diverting dances and fanciful scenery, but rather as opera's blood and guts, the dramatic source of each aspect of its expression.

In a sense, Gluck returned the focus of opera to its roots in Monteverdi, whose recitative-driven lyric dramas were also built on the bedrock of words. But Gluck's fresh approach to language and orchestration sounded the arrival of Classical opera when his works were heard in Paris in the 1770s. Seeds of the French Revolution were then taking root, and so was the signature sound of another Viennese composer who would take opera in an entirely new direction: Wolfgang Amadeus Mozart.

1700		1719 Handel co-founds the Royal Academy of Music in London		1750	1756 Mozart is born in Salzburg	1762 Gluck's *Orfeo ed Euridice* is given in Vienna	1775	
	1711 *Rinaldo*, Handel's first opera for London, opens	1720 Farinelli débuts in Naples and begins to tour widely	1752 Pergolesi's *La serva padrona* introduces Paris to Italian *opera buffa*	1753 Rousseau's essay on French music theatre sparks heated debate		1786 Mozart's *Le nozze di Figaro* opens in Vienna	1789 The French Revolution begins	

"How can I move the passions?"
Claudio Monteverdi

CLAUDIO
MONTEVERDI

Born: 15 May 1567, Cremona (Italy)
Died: 29 November 1643, Venice (Italy)

Claudio Monteverdi is regarded as opera's founding father. His *L'Orfeo*, first performed in 1607, was the first work to unite opera's basic ingredients in an enduring manner. Monteverdi's early lyric dramas were the fruits of courtly Mantua, while his late operatic masterpieces were for public audiences in Venice. No other opera composer made such a leap.

When Monteverdi arrived in Mantua in 1590 as a young string-player for Duke Vincenzo Gonzaga, the court was bubbling with cultural innovation. The setting was ideal for a rising composer with an ear for polyphony and a keen sense of dramatic action. Following studies in Cremona, Monteverdi composed madrigals popular across Europe.

But Mantua offered new musical horizons. By the late 15th century, the court had assembled musicians, poets, dancers, and painters to stage heroic and pastoral stories. A century later, Monteverdi performed as a musician in the latest of these, and by 1602 became Mantua's music director. There, in 1607, his momentous *L'Orfeo* premiered.

In 1613, Monteverdi became the music director at the Basilica of St Mark in Venice. In 1637, Venice saw the opening of the first commercial opera house. Until then, operas addressed the noble and mythological themes preferred by their commissioners. But success was now in the hands of paying audiences. They wanted marvellous sets, gripping dramas, and exhilarating arias delivered by virtuoso singers. At first, Monteverdi failed to appreciate this, offering a revision of his ill-suited *Arianna*, an opera originally composed for Mantua's court. But he struck Venetian gold with *Il ritorno d'Ulisse in patria* (1640) and *L'incoronazione di Poppea* (1643).

English soprano Joanne Lunn sings the role of Fortuna in Monteverdi's *L'incoronazione di Poppea* for the English National Opera production of 2000 at the London Coliseum.

FIRST PERFORMANCES

1600

1607 L'Orfeo
1608 Arianna (only a lament survives)
Ballo delle ingrate

1610

1620

1624 Combattimento di Tancredi e Clorinda

1630

1640 Il ritorno d'Ulisse in patria

1640

1641 Le nozze d'Enea con Lavinia (lost)
1643 L'incoronazione di Poppea

1650

L'ORFEO

(Orpheus)

🎼 Favola in musica in a prologue and five acts,
1¾ hours
📅 c.1607

🏛 24 February 1607, Palazzo Ducale, Mantua
📖 Alessandro Striggio Jr, after *Euridice* (1600)
by Ottavio Rinuccini

L'Orfeo is often called the first opera, but opera's evolution was in fact too gradual to support such a pat claim. Still, *L'Orfeo* presents the earliest successful synthesis of elements that define opera: sung words, dramatic impersonation, scenery, and, music. The opera opens in joy, and passes through shock and grief before descending further, into regions of Hell. Indeed, the work oscillates between hope and despair, praise and lament. Immortalized, Orfeo finally transcends his extreme passions. Following Monteverdi, strong emotions would remain the essence of great opera.

> ⚜ The Mantuan courtier Carlo Magno wrote on the day before *L'Orfeo*'s premiere that the work was unusual because "all the actors sing their parts". He also worried that the hall would be too crowded for him to attend. ⚜

✦ PRINCIPAL ROLES ✦

La Musica *soprano*
Music personified

Orfeo *tenor*
Shepherd and musician

Euridice *soprano*
Wife to Orfeo

Silvia *soprano*
Member of Euridice's
entourage

Speranza ("Hope") *soprano*
Orfeo's escort
to Hades

Caronte *bass*
Ferryman
of the River Styx

Plutone *bass*
God of the underworld

PLOT SYNOPSIS

Hades, the heavens, and places in between including Thrace, in mythological Antiquity

PROLOGUE La Musica celebrates the power of music to "incline men's souls to heaven".

ACT ONE On the open fields of Thrace, shepherds and nymphs celebrate the union of Orfeo and Euridice, and the end of Orfeo's lovesickness 🎵. Orfeo invites the "Rose of Heaven", the sun, to witness his joy, and sings to Euridice of his love for her. Euridice returns his love, and all prepare to pray that the gods preserve her life. Nymphs and shepherds note that joy is all the greater following its absence, and Orfeo's laments have given way to rousing praise.

"Lasciate i monti"

ACT TWO Orfeo addresses the groves of trees, reminding them how his laments had extracted pity even from stones. He sings of the former suffering that makes present joy all the more blissful. Suddenly, Silvia reports horrifying news: Euridice, bitten by a snake, died in her arms 🎵. Orfeo is determined to use the power of song to soften the hard heart of Plutone, the ruler of Hades, and thus either return Euridice to life on earth, or else remain in hell himself 🎵.

"In un fiorito prato"

"Tu se' morta"

At the English National Opera in 1996, physical contact among chorus members in the underworld suggests Orfeo's desire to be reunited with Euridice.

ACT THREE Speranza ("Hope") escorts Orfeo to the threshold of Hades, where he is warned by Caronte, ferryman of the River Styx, to proceed no further ♪. Orfeo attempts to gain access with his music ♪, but Caronte is unmoved. When a new tune lulls the ferryman to sleep, Orfeo passes unnoticed into hell. Underworld spirits sing of human success achieved through courageous defiance of obstacles.

"O tu ch'innanzi morte"

"Possente spirto"

ACT FOUR In Hades, Proserpina appeals to her husband Plutone to grant Orfeo's prayers. Moved, Plutone agrees that Euridice may regain life on the condition that Orfeo does not behold her during their return journey from hell. Spirits note Plutone's orders, while Orfeo praises his lyre for bringing him success. Yet, unsure that Euridice follows him, Orfeo turns to behold his beloved. He briefly sees her before she disappears, then cries out in song for losing what he loved too much. Orfeo is drawn back into daylight as Spirits note that he is defeated by his own affections.

Simon Keenlyside interprets the role of Orfeo in a production conducted by René Jacobs and choreographed by Trisha Brown for the Festival d'Aix-en-Provence, France, in 1998.

ORPHEUS AND OPERA

With its immortal singer-hero, tragic love story, and emotional intensity, the Orpheus myth has inspired operas through the ages, beginning with Jacopo Peri's 1600 *Euridice*. Christoph Willibald Gluck used the story for his Classical *Orfeo ed Euridice* (1762) and revised *Orphée* (1770). With *Orphée aux enfers* (1858), Jacques Offenbach set the myth as operetta. In the 1990s, Jean Cocteau's films inspired American Philip Glass to compose an Orpheus opera trilogy.

A film poster by Jean Cocteau for his Le Testament d'Orphée.

ACT FIVE Back in the fields of Thrace, the stricken Orfeo vows to lament always amidst Nature's hills and stones. Echo, the signal voice of bereavement, returns his words. Orfeo praises Euridice's soul and body, but sings angrily of all other women. His father, the god Apollo, descends from heaven to discourage ignoble excess of both joy and grief. Virtue is rewarded as father and son ascend into the heavens ♪.

"Saliam cantando al cielo"

IL RITORNO D'ULISSE IN PATRIA

(The Return of Ulysses)

⏃ Opera in a prologue and five acts, 3 hours
🔊 Unknown
♔ Carnival in February 1640, Teatro San

Cassiano, Venice (Italy)
📖 Giacomo Badoaro, based on Books 12–23 of Homer's *The Odyssey* (8th century BCE)

Il ritorno d'Ulisse in patria, Monteverdi's first opera for the public theatre world of Venice, premiered when he was 73. Even so, he adapted to the tastes of his new audience, introducing comic figures, such as the glutton Iro, and stage effects, including those that would deliver the goddess Minerva from the heavens. The opera was successful enough to be given in Bologna the same year as its Venice premiere, and to return to Venice the following year. Monteverdi's first opera, *L'Orfeo*, composed over 30 years earlier, was built of more rigid recitatives and arias. But *Il ritorno d'Ulisse in patria* uses another approach, freeing orchestra and voices to explore a more fluid palette of expression.

> ✧ **PRINCIPAL ROLES** ✧
>
> **Ulisse** *tenor*
> King of Ithaca
>
> **Penelope** *soprano*
> Faithful wife to Ulisse
>
> **Telemaco** *tenor*
> Son to Ulisse and Penelope
>
> **Ericlea** *mezzo-soprano*
> Childhood nurse to Ulisse
>
> **Melanto** *soprano*
> Servant to Penelope
>
> **Eumete** *tenor*
> A poor old shepherd
>
> **Iro** *tenor*
> A gluttonous nobleman

⇥ Opera's first great tragic heroine, Penelope sings exclusively in grief-stricken recitative until the opera's last scene. Then, when she recognizes her husband, Ulisse, she joins him in a glorious duet. ⇤

PLOT SYNOPSIS

In and near the Royal Palace of Ithaca, in mythological Antiquity

PROLOGUE L'Humana Fragilità (Human Frailty) deplores Time, Fortune, and Love.

ACT ONE Penelope bitterly awaits her husband's return following the Trojan War. Her servant, Melanto, hopes that Penelope will choose one of her many suitors. At sea, Nymphs quiet the winds so that Ulisse may sleep through his return to Ithaca, but the sea god Nettuno, angry at Ulisse, turns the ship to stone. Ulisse awakens confused on shore ⚓. But he soon recognizes his protector goddess, Minerva, who has taken the form of a shepherd. She gives Ulisse the appearance of an old man so he may face his rivals incognito. Learning that his servant Eumete awaits him, and that his son Telemaco will arrive, he rejoices in the strength that allows mortals to bear joy and torment.

"Dormo ancora"

GIACOMO TORELLI

Rich in special effects, *Il ritorno d'Ulisse in patria* responded to popular set designs by a former military engineer, Giacomo Torelli, at his Teatro Novissimo in Venice. He invented stage technology allowing elaborate scenes to change in mere seconds. His theatrical illusions, which earned him the title of "The Great Wizard" ("Il gran stregone"), so astonished audiences that many went to operas just to marvel at the sight of them.

Anthony Rolfe Johnson was Ulisse at the English National Opera in 1992. Reunited with his powerful bow, Ulisse uses the weapons to slay his rivals.

ACT TWO In the palace, Penelope rejects the idea of accepting a suitor. At a nearby fountain, Eumete chases the gluttonous Iro from his flock, and offers refuge to Ulisse, whom he takes to be a beggar. From her chariot, Minerva presents Telemaco. He watches in awe as the earth appears to swallow up the "beggar" and regurgitate his father ♫. Reunited, Telemaco and Ulisse weep with joy.

"Che veggio, ohimé"

ACT THREE In the palace, Melanto and Eurimaco celebrate love while suitors fail to amuse Penelope with songs and dances. Eumete announces Telemaco's return and, when he suggests that Ulisse may follow, suitors brace for vengeance ♫. In a wood, Minerva instructs Ulisse: she will assure his victory in a game to avenge him against his rivals.

"Amor è un'armonia"

ACT FOUR Telemaco tells his mother that Helen of Troy was worth warring for ♫. Eumete ushers in a "beggar", who defeats Iro in a wrestling match. Governed by Minerva's power, Penelope proposes that whoever best shoots an arrow from Ulisse's bow will win wife

"Del mio lungo viaggio"

and kingdom. All suitors fail even to bend the bow. But the "beggar" sends an arrow flying. Minerva guides the arrow to slay the suitors.

ACT FIVE The slain Iro prepares for his well-fed body to feed worms ♫. The suitors' ghosts departed, Penelope refuses to believe that the bowman is Ulisse. In heaven, Nettuno finally agrees to forgive Ulisse. Within the palace, Penelope at first suspects sorcery when she sees the undisguised Ulisse. Ulisse reminds his wife of images of Diana that she wove into their bed sheets. Penelope begs his forgiveness and the couple rejoices.

"Oh dolor"

L'INCORONAZIONE DI POPPEA

(The Coronation of Poppea)

⚏ Opera in a prologue and three acts, 3½ hours
🔊 Unknown
♇ Carnival in 1643, Teatro Santi Giovanni e

Paolo, Venice (Italy)
📖 Giovanni Francesco Busenello, after Tacitus, Suetonius, and perhaps Seneca

L'incoronazione di Poppea, an early masterpiece, is the first opera to be based on a historical rather than a mythological or fictional subject. The libretto draws on spicy Ancient Roman biographical portraits of Emperor Nero to explore adultery, lust, and ambition. The opera premiered during Carnival, when licence to push moral boundaries was freer than usual. More than other Monteverdi operas, *L'incoronazione di Poppea* relies on the strengths of vocalists in its many commanding lead roles. The opera's authorship has been questioned, and the hands of other composers, including Cavalli, have been detected in the score.

⚐ The notoriously decadent Emperor Nero inspired Busenello to write scenes that sizzle with erotic energy. A line of Nero's to Poppea: "As I behold you, my eyes take back the flaming spirit that I spent inside you." ⚐

✦ PRINCIPAL ROLES ✦

Nerone *soprano*
Roman Emperor

Ottavia *mezzo-soprano*
Roman Empress

Poppea *soprano*
Lover to Nerone

Drusilla *soprano*
Servant to Ottavia

Ottone *male soprano*
In love with Poppea

Arnalta *alto*
Confidante to Poppea

Seneca *bass*
Adviser to Nerone

Lucano *tenor*
Poet serving Nerone

Venere (Venus) *soprano*
Goddess of Beauty

PLOT SYNOPSIS

Rome, Italy, and environs under Emperor Nero, 64 BCE

PROLOGUE On clouds, Fortuna, Virtù, and Amore ("Fortune", "Virtue", and "Love") debate which of them is sovereign. All agree: Love commands the world.

ACT ONE Ottone stands before his beloved Poppea's home near Rome, crushed that she is sharing her bed with

"E pur io torno qui" | Emperor Nerone ♂. Inside, Poppea learns

with joy that Nerone plans to divorce his wife, Empress Ottavia. Arnalta, Poppea's confidante, warns against her affair with Nerone, but Poppea dreams

"Disprezzata regina" | of becoming empress. In Rome, Ottavia laments the lot of women ♂. Her nurse

Malena Ernman's Nerone receives a steamy kiss from Carmen Giannattasio's Poppea at Berlin's Staatsoper in 2006.

urges her to forget Nerone's infidelity, but she cannot. Seneca notes the virtuous strength her fate has given her. Alone, he considers the sufferings of the crowned, and greets Athena, who descends from heaven to forewarn him of his death. Then, Nerone tells Seneca that Poppea will be empress, and is enraged when Seneca questions the wisdom of this. During their next tryst, Poppea provokes Nerone to order Seneca's death. Ottone talks himself out of his love for Poppea and welcomes the attentions of his former lover Drusilla, serving Ottavia. But in his heart he knows that he still belongs to Poppea.

ACT TWO Seneca receives Nerone's death sentence. Once it is carried out, Nerone requests a love song from Lucano. Ottone realizes he is still deeply in love with Poppea, but Ottavia commands him on pain of death to disguise himself as a woman and slay Poppea. He confides in Drusilla, who offers clothes for his disguise. In her garden, Poppea rejoices at news of Seneca's death, then sleeps as her nurse, Arnalta, sings a lullaby ♫. Disguised as Drusilla, Ottone enters the garden to commit murder. But Amore blocks him; Poppea awakens to see "Drusilla" poised over her with a knife, and Ottone escapes.

"Addaggiati, Poppea"

ACT THREE Drusilla awaits news of her rival's death. Instead, she is arrested for attempted murder and presented to Nerone. To protect Ottone, she admits to the crime, and is removed for execution. But Ottone confesses, explaining that Ottavia ordered the murder. Nerone

sends the three plotters into exile, and renews his bond of love with Poppea ♫. Ottavia touchingly bids Rome farewell ♫. In Rome, Consuls and Tribunes crown Poppea empress. And, with the blessing of Venere, goddess of beauty in heaven, Amore crowns Poppea goddess of beauty on earth. Finally, Poppea and Nerone love and idolize one another ♫.

"Ne più s'interporrà noia o dimora"

"A Dio, Roma! a Dio, patria"

"Pur ti miro, pur ti godo"

Jacek Laszczkowski, as Nerone, and Anna Caterina Antonacci, as Poppea, perform in the coronation scene staged by David Alden at the Opéra Bastille, Paris, 2005.

FRANCESCO
CAVALLI

Born: 14 February 1602, Crema (Italy)
Died: 14 January 1676, Venice (Italy)

Francesco Cavalli was the most important opera composer from the early days of the opera houses in Venice. Among his dozens of engaging operas are *L'Egisto* (1643), *L'Ormindo* (1644), *Giasone* (1649), *Xerse* (1655), and *Scipione Affricano* (1664), to a libretto by frequent collaborator Niccolo Minato, perhaps the first librettist to distinguish arias from recitatives. Cavalli's father, named Caletti, was *maestro di cappella* (director of music) of Crema Cathedral. Caletti's son was taken to Venice by a patron named Cavalli, whose name he kept. Cavalli sang in the choir of the Basilica of St Mark under *maestro di cappella* Monteverdi, and in 1668 assumed the post himself.

LA CALISTO
(Callisto)

⚏ Dramma per musica in a prologue and three acts, 2½ hours
☏ c.1651

♔ 28 November 1651, Teatro San Apollinare, Venice (Italy)
📖 Giovanni Faustini

La Calisto was the ninth of ten operas written by Cavalli to librettos by Giovanni Faustini. They offered Venice well-mixed cocktails of romantic love, silliness, and a dash of outrage. Here, Faustini combined two Greek myths about sexual love between gods and mortals: one of Jove seducing Calisto, and another of Diana falling for Endymion. The subject is doubly racy when Giove (Jove), disguised as the goddess Diana, enjoys erotic meetings with Calisto. As a musician of the Basilica of St Mark, Cavalli may seem an improbable composer for such a work, but, like the unfettered Calisto of this opera, the Republic of Venice enjoyed unusual freedom from religious and moral strictures. Cavalli responded to the story with his uniquely sensuous and sweetly varied music.

✦ PRINCIPAL ROLES ✦

Calisto *soprano*
Follower of Diana

Giove (Jove) *baritone*
God

Giunone (Juno) *soprano*
Goddess, wife of Giove

Mercurio (Mercury) *tenor*
Messenger god

Diana *soprano*
Goddess

Endimione *alto*
Shepherd in love with Diana

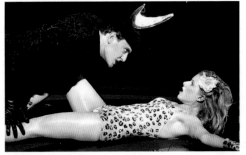

◅ The role of Giove is set for a baritone voice. Disguised as "Diana" to enjoy sex with Calisto, Giove sings in falsetto. Some Gioves enjoy this rare onstage chance to mock singers with higher voices, imitating their excesses or vanity. ▻

Umberto Chiummo plays an aggressive Giove to Sally Mathews's surprised Calisto for a production at Munich's Bayerische Staatsoper in 2005.

PLOT SYNOPSIS

On and around Mt Lycaeus, in mythological Antiquity

PROLOGUE Fate asks Nature to immortalize Diana's follower Calisto as a new constellation in the heavens. The reasons for the request are secret. Calisto joins the firmament (as Ursa Major).

ACT ONE In a barren forest, Giove falls in love with Calisto, a chaste follower of the goddess Diana. When Calisto suffers in the drought afflicting Nature, Giove conjures ambrosia from a fountain for her to drink. He came to heal earth's burning, but confesses he is instead ablaze for her. A confirmed virgin, Calisto rejects the liquid, and his lust. Mercurio counsels Giove to take the form of Diana, whom the girl clearly adores, and is sure to embrace freely. Alone, Calisto celebrates her life of freedom ♫. She crosses paths with "Diana", who proposes exchanging kisses in a remoter location. The shepherd Endimione rejoices to see water flowing again, but his heart still burns for Diana. He finds her out hunting, and they confess their love to one another, but the goddess refuses to break her vows of chastity. Diana is then surprised to hear from a blissful Calisto tales of their recent kissing session. Outraged, she banishes Calisto ♫.
Pan, who is also in love with Diana, considers a scheme to kill his rival.

"Non è maggior piacere"

"Taci lasiva, taci"

ACT TWO At night on Mt Lycaeus, Endimione falls asleep admiring Diana's star ♫. Diana descends from heaven to lie beside him as he dreams of embracing her. When he awakens to discover her in his arms, he rejoices, but one of Pan's impish satyrs is watching. Giunone descends to earth, sure that Giove is up to mischief, and jealously observes as "Diana" offers Calisto another kissing date. Endimione suffers lovesickness. Jealousy consumes him when "Diana" introduces "her" secret lover, Mercurio. Pan and his followers ambush "Diana" and Endimione. The former flees, but Endimione is captured.

"Lucidissima face"

ACT THREE Calisto aches with love for Diana ♫. Jealous, Giunone transforms her into a bear. But Giove promises his beloved Calisto immortality. When she dies, she is to remain beside him forever in the firmament ♫. Diana rescues Endimione and they depart for Ionia as lovers. Calisto returns joyfully to her forest, and Giove remains in heaven to await her return.

"Restino imbalsamate"

"Mio foco fatale"

Mezzo-soprano Louise Winter interprets the love-struck goddess Diana at the Staatsoper Unter den Linden in Berlin in 2002.

JEAN-BAPTISTE
LULLY

Born: 28 November 1632, Florence (Italy)
Died: 22 March 1687, Paris, France

Jean-Baptiste Lully ruled 17th-century French opera with an authority as absolute as that of his sovereign, Louis XIV. As politically cunning as he was musically gifted, Lully composed regal operas enhanced by dances and *divertissements*. They remained a reference point for French opera through the dawn of the French Revolution.

Born in Florence, Lully arrived in Paris at 13. At age 20, he was a noted violin player in the court ensemble of the young monarch, Louis XIV. As the king flourished, so did Lully. The budding composer rose to prominent posts, and earned acclaim as a musician and exceptional dancer. With Molière in the 1660s, he introduced music to plays to create a new dramatic genre, the *comédie-ballet*. Having insisted that the French language was unsuitable for opera, Lully was taken aback in 1671 by the success of Robert Cambert's *Pomone*, the first opera in French; he began attending plays to study cadences of French speech, and to fashion a recitative style adapted to the language. Cambert's financial problems soon allowed Lully to seize his royal rights to stage operas. After that, virtually no music theatre could be staged in the kingdom without Lully's blessing, which from 1672 to 1686 he bestowed almost exclusively on himself. Librettos by long-term collaborator Philippe Quinault treated heroic myths and medieval chivalric exploits; Lully responded with music of refined precision and glorious pomp.

FIRST PERFORMANCES

1670 —
1672
Les fêtes de l'Amour et de Bacchus

1673
Cadmus et Hermione

1674
Alceste, ou Le triomphe d'Alcide

1675
Thésée

1676
Atys

1677
Isis

1678
Psyché

1679
Bellérophon

1680 —
1680
Proserpine

1682
Persée

1683
Phaëton

1684
Amadis

1685
Roland

1686
Armide
Acis et Galathée

1687
Polixène (co-written with Pascal Colasse)

1690 —

A costume design for Lully's *Armide* places typical emphasis on lavish textiles, ornate headwear, and shoes designed for onstage dancing.

ALCESTE, OU LE TRIOMPHE D'ALCIDE
Alceste, or The Triumph of Hercules

🎭 Tragédie in a prologue and five acts, 2½ hours
🗓 c.1673–1674
🎭 19 January 1674, Jeu de Paume du Bel-Air,

Paris, France
📖 Philippe Quinault, after the tragedy *Alceste*
(438 BCE) by Euripides

Lully and his librettist Philippe Quinault marshalled all resources to make *Alceste* a spectacle pleasing to Louis XIV, their Sun King. The opera is framed by the personage of the king, whose absence is lamented in the prologue, and whose symbolic double, the sun god Apollo, glorifies celebrations in the final act. Sets and dazzling special effects by Carlo Vigarani, to be Lully's decades-long collaborator, added further majesty.

⚜ For the king's pleasure, the opera was rehearsed at Versailles. But when it opened in Paris, Lully's enemies gathered in the theatre, a converted tennis court, and attempted to disrupt the show. Still, Paris was won over. ⚜

✦ PRINCIPAL ROLES ✦

Alceste (Alcestis) *soprano*
Betrothed to Admète

Admète (Admetus) *tenor*
Betrothed to Alceste

Alcide (Hercules) *baritone*
In love with Alceste

Lycomède (Lycomedes) *bass*
Ruler of an island kingdom

Proserpine *soprano*
Goddess of Hades

Apollo *haute-contre*
God of the sun

PLOT SYNOPSIS

On earth and in Hades, in mythological Antiquity

PROLOGUE The Nymph of the River Seine awaits the return of a Hero (King Louis XIV) ⚜. Glory announces his return.

"L'héros que j'attends ne reviendra-t-il pas"

ACT ONE Alcide confesses that he loves Alceste, who is betrothed to Admète. But during a fête, Lycomède kidnaps Alceste to take her to his island.

ACT TWO On the island, Alceste despairs until Alcide and Admète arrive and slay Lycomède. Alcide rescues her, but Admète is fatally wounded ⚜. Apollo announces that Admète's life will be spared if another dies in his stead.

"Alceste, vous pleurez! Admète, vous mourrez"

Dramatic staging marked a 1991 production of Lully's opera directed by Jean Louis Martinoty for the Opéra Royal in Versailles, France.

ACT THREE Admète suddenly revives to see Alceste enshrined in a monument, and he realizes that she has given her life for his. Alcide offers to return Alceste from Hades if he can then keep her for himself. When Admète is moved by love to accept this proposal, the goddess Diana helps Alcide.

ACT FOUR Alcide reaches the throne room of Hades, where the god Pluton is entertaining Alceste. Finally, with Proserpine's intervention, Alcide and Alceste depart in Pluton's winged chariot.

ACT FIVE Alceste must leave Admète in order to fulfil the promise made to Alcide, but the lovers are distraught with grief. Touched by their devotion, Alcide returns Alceste to her beloved. The god Apollo descends from the heavens to preside over a grand celebration of love and of the generosity of Alcide.

ATYS

❧ Tragédie en musique in a prologue and five acts, 2¼ hours
☙ 1675–1676

♜ 10 January 1676, Saint-Germain-en-Laye, France
📖 Philippe Quinault, after Book IV of Ovid's *Fasti* (1–4 CE)

Atys is an exquisitely sensuous and, by French Baroque standards, even erotic opera. Quinault's libretto builds tension scene by scene with themes of denial, secrecy, betrayal, and the dangers of succumbing to love. The opera abounds in highlights, from solo and choral vocal passages to gorgeous orchestral music, notably in Atys's famous dream sequence of Act II. Atypical of Lullian opera, *Atys* concludes with the tragic deaths of its lovers.

⊲ The opera was known during the reign of Louis XIV as "the King's opera" because it was his favourite. He was said to recognize himself in the tragic hero Atys, and to see his wife in Cybèle and his mistress in Sangaride. ⊳

✦ PRINCIPAL ROLES ✦

Atys *haute-contre*
Shepherd who loves Sangaride

Sangaride *soprano*
Daughter to a river god, in love with Atys

Celenus *baritone*
King of Phrygia, betrothed to Sangaride

Cybèle *soprano*
Goddess in love with Atys

Mélisse *soprano*
Confidante to Cybèle

PLOT SYNOPSIS

Phrygia (now Turkey), in mythological Antiquity

PROLOGUE Time assures that none will outlast the most brilliant of heroes (Louis XIV). Preparing for his war campaign, the Hero attends the story of Atys.

ACT ONE Atys awakens the Phrygians to receive the goddess Cybèle. He reluctantly reveals to a fellow Phrygian that he is in love, but to Sangaride denies that love is of interest to him. Alone, Sangaride laments that she

At the Opéra Comique in Paris in 1989, the jealous goddess Cybèle (Jennifer Smith, *top*) uses magic to destroy Atys and his beloved Sangaride.

must marry King Celenus even as she loves Atys. Finally, Atys reveals his feelings to Sangaride.

ACT TWO In her temple, Cybèle selects Atys to be her high priest. She reveals to her confidante Mélisse that, while she thought herself above such things, she has fallen for the mortal Atys.

ACT THREE In Cybèle's palace, Atys falls into a sleep filled at first with dreams 🜨. He awakens from nightmares to discover a fawning Cybèle. Her mood darkens as she realizes he loves Sangaride.
    "Dormons, dormons tous"

ACT FOUR Abusing his post as Cybèle's high priest, Atys outlaws the marriage of Sangaride to Celenus.

ACT FIVE To punish Atys for his betrayal, Cybèle causes him to see Sangaride as a monster, and even to stab her. His senses regained, Atys attempts suicide. But Cybèle changes him into a pine tree, and laments his death with her nymphs 🜨.
    "Ah! Quel malheur!"

ARMIDE

🎵 Tragédie en musique in a prologue and five acts, 2½ hours

🗓 1685–1686

🏛 15 February 1686, Palais-Royal, Paris, France

📖 Philippe Quinault, after Cantos II, V, X, and XIV of Torquato Tasso's poem *Gerusalemme liberata* (1575)

Armide responded to new developments in the French court. Marie-Thérèse, the fun-loving first wife of Louis XIV, had died in 1683. His new wife, Madame de Maintenon, cast a more pious shadow over royal entertainments. Pyrotechnical stagecraft and fanciful *divertissements* were not banned, but a moralistic tone is established in the prologue. Highlights include Armide's famous Act II solo *"Enfin il est en ma puissance"*.

⇥ Lully and his librettist Philippe Quinault had created 14 operas before this one, their last collaboration. It was the Lully opera most frequently given in Paris in the 18th century, when Rameau considered it Lully's masterpiece. ⇤

→ **PRINCIPAL ROLES** ←

Armide *soprano*
A sorceress, niece of Hidraot

Hidraot *bass*
Magician, King of Damascus

Renaud *haute-contre*
Heroic Christian knight

Phénice *soprano*
Confidante to Armide

Sidone *soprano*
Confidante to Armide

La Haine (Hatred) *baritone*

PLOT SYNOPSIS

Fictional Jerusalem, at the end of the First Crusade (1099)

PROLOGUE Wisdom and Glory exchange views on the triumph of Love.

ACT ONE Below an Arch of Triumph, the sorceress Armide and her army celebrate victory over Christian Crusaders. All pay her homage save one: Renaud. Armide is incensed. Her uncle Hidraot urges her to select a husband, but Armide vows to marry only the man who defeats Renaud.

Stephanie Novacek as Armide and Curtis Sullivan as La Haine at Opera Atelier, Toronto, Canada in 2005.

ACT TWO On Armide's island, Renaud is held captive, and Armide uses magic music to bring him under her sway ♂. Unable to kill him, Armide orders spirits to take him to her palace.

"Enfin il est en ma puissance"

ACT THREE Renaud and Armide are now in love, but she is unhappy that his love for her is purely the result of magic. She invokes La Haine ("Hatred") to expel the love in her heart, then changes her mind.

ACT FOUR Ubalde and the Danish knight search for Renaud, their missing companion. Ubalde uses a magic diamond shield to vanquish monsters and block spells cast by Armide.

ACT FIVE Renaud's companions arrive with their shield to break Armide's spell on him. She tries many tactics to detain her beloved Renaud ♂. When he finally leaves, she invokes evil spirits. As she departs in her chariot, her palace crumbles and burns.

"Le perfide Renaud me fuit"

MARC-ANTOINE
CHARPENTIER

Born: 1643, Paris, France
Died: 24 February 1704, Paris, France

The French composer Marc-Antoine Charpentier studied in
Rome before returning to Paris, where he had the misfortune
of practising his art under the Sun King, Louis XIV, and under the court's no-
less-absolute composer, Jean-Baptiste Lully. Such was Lully's sway that Charpentier
was unable to present an opera on a public stage before Lully's death in 1687.
Until then, his projects were restricted to music for plays, notably Molière's
Le malade imaginaire (1673); for private entertainments; and for court functions,
including the unveiling of a statue of Louis XIV. He also set works on biblical
themes for a Jesuit college, where Lully's sphere of influence did not quite reach.

MÉDÉE
(Medea)

✍ Tragédie en musique in a prologue and five acts,
3 hours
☎ c.1693

🏛 4 December 1693, Paris Opéra, France
📖 Thomas Corneille

The Ancient Greek story of Medea,
the sorceress whose passion drove her to
infanticide, is inherently operatic. Indeed,
a century after Charpentier's opera, it
was the subject of a second masterpiece
in French, Luigi Cherubini's *Médée*.
Charpentier's *Médée* was a failure in Paris
in 1693, possibly because

> ✦   **PRINCIPAL ROLES**   ✦
>
> **Médée** *soprano* Foreign sorceress
> **Jason** *haute-contre* Husband to Médée
> **Créon** *bass* King of Corinth
> **Créuse** *soprano* Princess of Corinth
> **Oronte** *bass* King of Argos
> **Nérine** *soprano* Servant to Médée

rabid supporters of the late Lully assured a negative
response to any opera that was not by him. *Médée*
bears heavy marks of the reign of Louis XIV, who
is overtly flattered in its prologue. But the opera
possesses a timeless brilliance. *Lullistes* would
have been outraged to discover that *Médée*,
with its breathtaking harmonic palette, is
now widely considered to be the greatest
opera of 17th-century France.

⊰ The librettist Thomas Corneille was the brother of famous
playwright Pierre Corneille, who had written *Médée* (1635),
a tragedy on the same subject. Inspired by his brother's
work, Thomas even used some lines from it. ⊱

Sumptuously costumed by Patrice Cauchetier,
American mezzo-soprano Lorraine Hunt interprets
Médée in Caen, France, in 1993.

PLOT SYNOPSIS

Corinth, Greece, in mythological Antiquity

PROLOGUE Shepherds and rustics praise King Louis. Personifications of Victory and Fame glorify France.

ACT ONE Médée laments. She has sacrificed much for her husband Jason, yet he is ungrateful. Her servant, Nérine, notes that Princess Créuse can help. But Médée vows to unleash her sorcery if Jason consorts with Créuse 🔔. Jason assures Médée he befriends Créuse purely to protect their children in wartime, and asks that she makes Créuse a gift of her shining robe. King Créon rejoices when Oronte and his warriors arrive from Argos to defend Corinth against Thessaly, but Jason is envious: Oronte acts for love of Créuse. Argians and Corinthians join in dancing and mock battling devoted to Victory.

"Qu'il le cherche"

ACT TWO King Créon orders Médée into exile for the duration of the war. Alone, Jason and Créuse savour their love 🔔. Oronte joins them and adds his declaration of love for Créuse. Then, Amour ("Love") descends from the sky in his chariot, which is drawn by his captives from different nations of the world. The chariot lifts Oronte, Jason, and

"Goutons l'heureux plaisir"

Créuse into the air, where Amour ceremoniously instructs Créuse to choose a lover who assures Victory.

ACT THREE Betrayed by their beloveds, Oronte and Médée join forces. Jason is moved by Médée's grief, but insists on defending Corinth 🔔. Learning that Jason loves Créuse, Médée calls upon spirits from Hell to cast poison spells on the shining robe that she will give to her rival.

"Quel prix de mon amour"

ACT FOUR Créuse revels in her new robe, while Médée tells Créon she refuses to leave Corinth until Créuse marries Oronte. Outraged, he orders her arrest. But Médée uses magic to control the guards, and to drive Créon into madness 🔔.

"Noires divinitez"

ACT FIVE Corinthians mourn Créon, who has committed suicide 🔔. Suddenly, the poison from Médée's robe burns into Créuse, who is "borne away". With his beloved Créuse dead, Jason can imagine nothing worse. Yet, mounted on an aerial dragon, Médée invites him to avenge their children, whom she has slain. She orders him to mourn forever the woes released by the flames of his passion.

"Ah! Funeste revers"

With this, the palaces become a blaze of ruins inhabited by monsters, and fire hails down on Corinth.

Stephanie Novacek's Médée in the arms of dancer Patrick Lavoie at the Elgin Theatre, Toronto, Canada, 2002.

HENRY
PURCELL

Born: 1658 or 1659, London, England
Died: 21 November 1695, London, England

Henry Purcell wrote only one true opera, *Dido and Aeneas*. And with this single short work, he became the most important composer of opera in English for a period of over two hundred years. Purcell's unsurpassed musical responses to language made him a model for Benjamin Britten and other modern composers setting works in English.

Purcell turned to opera only in the last years of his life. He had studied music in London and his early posts led him to compose mainly for the court. In 1678, he succeeded the celebrated John Blow as organist of Westminster Abbey. But in 1689, when the reign of William and Mary brought hard times for artists, he began accepting commissions. Apart from *Dido and Aeneas* (1689), possibly composed at the request of a schoolmaster, other works were "semi-operas" for the Dorset Garden Theatre in London. The first of these popular plays featuring elaborate musical segments was *The Prophetess, or The History of Dioclesian* (1690), for which the famous Shakespearean actor Thomas Betterton provided the libretto. Purcell's next librettist was the great writer John Dryden, who had worked as a playwright in London before being appointed Poet Laureate of England in 1668. Dryden penned the libretto for Purcell's semi-opera *King Arthur, or The British Worthy* of 1691. To an anonymous libretto, *The Fairy Queen* followed in 1692, based on Shakespeare's popular comedy *A Midsummer Night's Dream*. In 1695, Purcell was composing *The Indian Queen* to a libretto inspired by John Dryden and Sir Robert Howard's tragedy. He died while writing this tragic semi-opera, but his younger brother, Daniel Purcell, completed the score.

SEMI-OPERAS

Semi-operas gained popularity in London in the late 17th century, not least through successful works by Purcell. They were essentially plays in which non-singing actors interpreted the lead roles. But dramatic action was rather spare, and shaped to absorb interspersed musical episodes and lively masques, which were performed by singers and dancers. Purcell's semi-operas – *Dioclesian*, *King Arthur*, *The Fairy Queen*, and *The Indian Queen* – premiered in London over the first half of the 1690s. Their colourful plots and mixed casts were popular with the audiences of the day.

Purcell's semi-operas premiered in London at the Dorset Garden Theatre (*below*) in the 1690s.

THE FAIRY QUEEN

❧ Semi-opera in a prologue and five acts,
3½ hours (2 hours of music)
🕮 1691–1692 (rev. 1693)

♔ 2 May 1692, Dorset Garden Theatre, London
📖 Anonymous adaptation of Shakespeare's
A Midsummer Night's Dream (1595–1596)

In this traditional semi-opera, the principal actors carry the story with Shakespeare's spoken dialogue, while Purcell adds unrelated, but enchanting, musical set pieces. Audiences of the period were weary of wordplay and desired spectacle (as in Act V's Chinese Garden of Eden). Purcell's rich yet frolicsome diversions, or masques, do not appear in Shakespeare's text, but they illuminate its personality. The score was lost, then neglected, for 200 years before its rediscovery in 1903.

> ❧ **PRINCIPAL ROLES** ❧
>
> **Oberon** *spoken*
> King of Fairies
> **Titania** *spoken*
> His wife
> **Coridon** *bass baritone*
> A shepherd
> **Fairy** *soprano*
> Attendant to Titania

⚔ Focusing on Titania, Purcell eliminated some of the most popular scenes from the Shakespeare play. Instead, he added ravishing if rather arbitrary songs, like "The Plaint" of Act V. ⚔

PLOT SYNOPSIS

A palace in Athens, Greece, and nearby wood

ACT ONE Hermia's father attempts to force her engagement to Demetrius despite her love for Lysander. MUSICAL SCENE In the forest, Titania's fairies pinch and torment three drunken poets, one of whom stutters terribly and confesses to writing doggerel verse.

ACT TWO Oberon and Titania quarrel. The fairies entertain Titania until she asks for a lullaby. Oberon sprinkles a love potion over her eyes. MUSICAL SCENE The fairies Night, Mystery ♫, Secresie, and Sleep sing a cycle of airs to lull Titania into sleep.

"I am come to lock all fast"

ACT THREE Puck accidentally makes both Lysander and Demetrius fall in love with Helena. Titania falls in love with Bottom and conjures a bucolic scene to court him. MUSICAL SCENE Coridon the shepherd pleads with Mopsa, who refuses him kisses.

ACT FOUR Oberon corrects Puck's folly and wakes Titania and Bottom from the spells on them. He requests music from Titania. MUSICAL SCENE The fairies present the four seasons.

ACT FIVE The two pairs of lovers marry. MUSICAL SCENE Oberon gives entertainments, such as an exquisite garden ♫.

"Hark, now the Echoing Air"

Scottish soprano Janis Kelly performs in the English National Opera's quirky 1995 production of Purcell's semi-opera directed by David Pountney.

DIDO AND AENEAS

🎭 Tragic opera in three acts, 1 hour
📅 1689
🏛 Spring 1689, Mr Josias Priest's Boarding

School for Girls, Chelsea, England
📖 Nahum Tate, based on his play *Brutus of Alba* (1678), after Virgil's *Aeneid* (29–19 BCE)

Dido and Aeneas is England's operatic crowning glory. It is the only major work of music theatre in English before the operas of Benjamin Britten, in the 20th century. Purcell integrated the dances favoured in French opera, and followed Italian fashion by dwelling on arias. But he broke new ground with his treatment of lyrics and action. The opera was publicly given in 1700, but only entered the repertoire in 1895.

⊰ The earliest known performance of the opera dates from 1689, when girls performed it at their school in Chelsea under headmaster Josias Priest, also choreographer to the Theatre Royal in London. ⊱

✦ PRINCIPAL ROLES ✦

Dido *soprano*
Queen of Carthage

Belinda *soprano*
Dido's sister

Aeneas *tenor*
Prince of Troy

Sorceress *mezzo-soprano*

First Witch *soprano*

Spirit *mezzo-soprano*

Second Woman *soprano*

Sailor *soprano*

PLOT SYNOPSIS

In and near Queen Dido's palace in Carthage, Tunisia, in mythological Antiquity

ACT ONE In the palace of Carthage, Belinda urges her sister Dido to be joyful, but the lovesick queen suffers "Ah, Belinda" because her anguish is concealed 🎵. Belinda encourages Dido to express her love for the Trojan prince Aeneas, and courtiers

Dancers Mark Morris and Guillermo Resto as Dido and Aeneas in a 2000 production by the Mark Morris Dance Group for the English National Opera, London.

praise their political union. As Dido's torment mounts, Belinda is moved to pity. Aeneas asks Dido when he will be blessed with her love. She replies that fate forbids her to love him. He begs Dido to pity him, if not for his own sake, then for the sake of Empire-building – he is destined to found a new Troy, and her rejection would spell failure. With fresh energy,

Belinda and the people of Carthage encourage Aeneas's bid for love . A dance celebrates love's triumph.

"To the hills and the vales"

ACT TWO A Sorceress beckons witches to a cave to help her deprive Dido of "fame, of life, and love!" The witches scheme: Aeneas and Dido are hunting, but a conjured storm will lure Aeneas to their cave, where a Spirit resembling the god Mercury will order him to leave Carthage. Their voices echoing in the cavern, the witches enjoy their wicked plot in song and dance.

"In our deep vaulted cells"

In a remote grove favoured by the goddess Diana, Belinda and a Second Woman recall Actaeon, devoured by his hunting dogs when he happened on Diana bathing naked. The tragic mood endures, and Dido's women dance for their Trojan guest. Aeneas presents the fruits of his hunt, a boar's head. But all scatter when Dido notes a storm's arrival. Aeneas is lured to the witches'

"Haste, haste to town"

cave, where the disguised Spirit says Jove orders his departure. Aeneas agrees to obey, but laments his loss of Dido.

ACT THREE A sailor with Aeneas's fleet urges preparation for departure. Fellow sailors respond in song and dance. The witches rejoice in Dido's demise with their own song and dance. Dido complains to Belinda that her advice on love matters has failed. Belinda finds comfort in Aeneas's heartfelt sorrow, but Dido does not believe him. She urges him to depart and found the new Empire, while she dies. Aeneas proposes to stay instead. But Dido will not hear of his remaining. When Aeneas leaves, Dido welcomes her new guest, Death. She then begs Belinda to remember her, but to forget her fate. The people of Carthage solemnly invite Cupids to watch eternally over Dido's tomb.

"When I am laid in earth"

DIDO'S LAMENT

Dido's final aria is among the greatest opera laments ever composed. Music alternately caresses and resists lyrics, illustrating their sense, or conveying their expressive limits. As the opera opens, Dido is isolated by inner turmoil. But the action switches to a hurried exterior world, as a storm requires the lovers to seek shelter. Dido's lament finally returns her to emotional turbulence, but this time so strong as to be fatal.

ANTONIO
VIVALDI

Born: 4 March 1678, Venice (Italy)
Died: 27 or 28 July 1741, Vienna (Austria)

Vivaldi is first remembered for his instrumental *Four Seasons*, but the ordained red-headed composer known as "the Red Priest" also wrote some 50 operas. While only 16 complete operas survive, partial scores continue to be discovered. Vivaldi's vibrant opera music is readily recognized by its often maverick instrumentation.

Like his father, Antonio Vivaldi was a celebrated violinist. From his native Venice, he also became the reigning Italian concerto composer. His first opera, *Ottone in villa*, already captures distinctive instrumentation. Like his contemporary, Handel, the prolific Vivaldi also struggled as an impresario. *L'incoronazione di Dario* was his first opera for a theatre he managed, the Teatro Sant'Angelo. Following a period in Mantua, he returned to Venice in 1720, but only briefly; his operas were attacked in a satirical essay by Benedetto Marcello. Five years later he was back, but then to contend with the new fervour for Neapolitan opera, in which the orchestra mainly served virtuoso vocalists. *Orlando furioso* and *L'Olimpiade* date from this dynamic period, 1725 to 1728. At the end of the decade, Prague proved more welcoming to the Red Priest. Then, in the 1730s, he donned his impresario hat for the last time, to tour operas through the Italian provinces. Vivaldi travelled in 1740 to Vienna, where he died penniless.

FIRST PERFORMANCES

1710

1713
Ottone in villa

1717
L'incoronazione di Dario

1719
Tito Manlio

1720

1720
La verità in cimento

1724
Il Giustino

1726
Dorilla in Tempe

1727
Farnace
Orlando furioso

1730

1732
La fida ninfa

1734
L'Olimpiade

1735
La Griselda
Il Tamerlano

1740

Vivaldi's room at the Ospedale della Pietà, a convent orphanage and music conservatory where he taught violin from 1704 to 1740

ORLANDO FURIOSO
(Orlando Enraged)

🎵 Dramma per musica in three acts, 4 hours
⏳ c.1727
🎭 Autumn 1727, Teatro Sant'Angelo, Venice

📖 Grazio Braccioli, loosely taken from part of the epic poem *Orlando furioso* (1516) by Ludovico Ariosto

Vivaldi had contributed to an earlier Venice opera about the wildly jealous Orlando in 1713, but in 1727 he and librettist Grazio Braccioli returned to the material. Exquisite roles, vibrant music, and luminous vocal lines form a far-fetched yet coherent drama. Highlights include Alcina's role; Orlando's "mad scene" of Act II; and Ruggiero's velvety aria *"Da te, mio dolce amore"*, where voice and flute flutter about one another like magic love birds.

⚜ In 1726, grenadiers threatened to arrest the diva contralto Maria Caterina Negri in her Prague home for breaking a singing contract. She went on to create Bradamante both in this opera, and in Handel's *Alcina* (1735). ⚜

> ✦ PRINCIPAL ROLES ✦
>
> **Orlando** *contralto*
> A knight jealous of Medoro
>
> **Alcina** *contralto*
> Enchantress
>
> **Medoro** *contralto*
> Prince betrothed to Angelica
>
> **Angelica** *soprano*
> Beloved of Medoro
>
> **Ruggiero** *contralto*
> A knight following Orlando
>
> **Bradamante** *contralto*
> Female warrior, beloved of Ruggiero

PLOT SYNOPSIS

The island of the enchantress Alcina

ACT ONE The enchantress Alcina promises to unite Angelica with her lost Medoro and to protect her from Orlando, who is violently jealous of Medoro. The female warrior Bradamante counts on a magic ring to block Alcina's powers over her beloved Ruggiero. Alone, Orlando resolves to uncover the source of Alcina's magic: the sorcerer Merlin's ashes. Alcina finds Medoro shipwrecked on the shore. Then, when she uses a potion, Ruggiero falls for her ♦. Bradamante despairs when Ruggiero fails to recognize her.

"Sol da te, mio dolce amore"

ACT TWO Bradamante breaks the spell on Ruggiero, but when she deserts him Orlando offers consolation ♦. Angelica cruelly sends the worshipful Orlando on a mission that traps him. Bradamante and Ruggiero reunite,

"Sorge l'irato nembo"

and Angelica and Medoro celebrate their wedding. Escaped, Orlando loses his senses when he sees the newly-weds.

ACT THREE Bradamante and Ruggiero believe Orlando is dead. They thwart Alcina's magic and, in a temple, find a statue of Merlin. Orlando, demented, arrives to mistake "Merlin" for Angelica. Lifting the statue, he destroys Alcina's power. Her island now deserted, she departs vowing revenge. Orlando comes to his senses, reconciles with Angelica, and approves her marriage to Medoro.

Choreographer Zuzana Dostálová modernized Baroque dance for the Czech premiere of *Orlando Furioso* in 2001 at Prague's State Opera.

GIOVANNI BATTISTA PERGOLESI

Born: 4 January 1710, Jesi, near Ancona (Italy)
Died: 16 March 1736, Pozzuoli, near Naples (Italy)

Giovanni Battista Pergolesi had the good fortune of studying in Naples, where music training in his day was unsurpassed. He wrote masterful sacred music and oratorios in his teens and, at 22, presented his first *opera seria* and first comedy. His fame came almost accidentally when he added a humorous *intermezzo* to the *opera seria*, *Il prigionier superbo*. This *intermezzo*, *La serva padrona*, gained huge popularity and is now considered the archetypal *opera buffa*. Pergolesi used fashionable librettos by Metastasio for *Adriano in Siria* – given with a new *intermezzo* – and for *L'Olimpiade*. Having completed a final comedy and *Stabat Mater*, his instrumental masterpiece, he died near Naples aged 26.

LA SERVA PADRONA
(The Maid Turned Mistress)

✍ Intermezzo in two parts, 1 hour   (Italy)
☛ 1733   🛏 Gennaro Antonio Federico
♇ 5 September 1733, Teatro San Bartolomeo, Naples

La serva padrona has been an audience-pleaser ever since its premiere in 1733. It then served as a literal *intermezzo*: it provided diversion "between the acts" of a more solemn main attraction. *La serva padrona* was sandwiched into *Il prigionier superbo*, an *opera seria* also by Pergolesi, and was the first *intermezzo* to be performed independently. Within 20 years, its revolutionary portrayal of a man in love with his servant enthralled audiences in Florence, Venice, Dresden, Hamburg, Prague, Paris, Vienna, Copenhagen, London, and Barcelona. In 1752, it ignited Paris's *querelle des bouffons*: a politically-charged "war" over the relative merits of reverent French and irreverent Italian music theatre. *La serva padrona* sparked reforms that led to Gluck's operas, and opened the way for those of Mozart. Given in Baltimore, Maryland, in 1790, it is also among the earliest operas performed in the United States.

> ⇥   **PRINCIPAL ROLES**   ⇤
>
> **Uberto** *bass* An elderly bachelor
> **Serpina** *soprano* Tyrannical maid to Uberto
> **Vespone** *silent role* Mute servant to Uberto

⇥ Pergolesi was not the first to employ this plot in an *intermezzo* drawing on a popular comic tradition born in Naples. Georg Philipp Telemann's *Pimpinone* took the same plot for a Hamburg premiere eight years earlier. ⇤

The title page of an early edition of Pergolesi's *opera buffa*, published in Paris.

PLOT SYNOPSIS

Uberto's dressing room, in the morning

PART ONE The elderly bachelor Uberto complains to his mute servant, Vespone, about the bossy maid, Serpina. He has been waiting for three hours, and she has yet to bring him hot chocolate. Serpina finally enters, without the hot chocolate, to beat Vespone. She asks Uberto for respect, but her every word only adds to his despair. He would dearly

"Sempre in contrasti" | like to put an end to his misery 🔔. Uberto asks Serpina to bring his clothes so that he can
"Stizzoso, mio stizzoso" | leave the house. Instead, she demands attention 🔔.

Uberto then begs Vespone to find him a wife, even if she resembles a monster. Serpina suggests he should marry her instead. Uberto erupts in protest. She asks if he does not find her attractive. Uberto says no over and over, while Serpina counters with yes.

PART TWO Serpina coaches Vespone: they will play a great prank, persuading their master to marry Serpina. Uberto enters, dressed to go out, and trusts that the "mistress" of the house will grant him permission to leave. Serpina tells Uberto that a "Captain Tempesta" wishes to marry her. She apologizes for her past behaviour, but informs him that she will be departing now to live with her new husband 🔔. She leaves a confused Uberto, who is unsure whether he feels love or pity 🔔. Serpina returns with the disguised Vespone, explaining that he, her suitor, requires her dowry: 4,000 crowns. Uberto is shocked by the sum, but learns that the alternative is to marry Serpina himself. When Uberto accepts this solution, Vespone's false moustache is removed, and Serpina owns up to the hoax. But Uberto is by now sure he adores her, and wishes to marry anyway. They celebrate their love, and Serpina notes that she is "a maid turned mistress" 🔔.

"A Serpina penserete"

"Son imbrogliato io già"

"Caro. Gioia. Oh Dio!"

Anna Maria Panzarella (Serpina) and Angelo Romero (Uberto) at the Théâtre des Champs-Élysées, Paris, in 2002.

"*True music speaks in the language of the heart*"

Jean-Philippe Rameau

JEAN-PHILIPPE
RAMEAU

Baptized: 25 September 1683, Dijon, France
Died: 12 September 1764, Paris, France

The first great composer of French birth, Jean-Philippe Rameau was 50 years old when his first opera, *Hippolyte et Aricie*, shook Paris. Reactions were extreme, but far from harmonious. Some derided Rameau's sound as "baroque", "turbulent", and "a lot of noise". Others, including luminaries of the day, heard his music as ageless, and posterity was to prove them right.

Before Rameau's birth, Jean-Baptiste Lully was the reigning composer in the court of Louis XIV. In 1733, when Rameau made his operatic début, Lully's ghost still haunted the Paris opera world. War was instantly declared: *Lullistes* attacked Rameau's work, and *Ramistes* hailed it the music of France's new Orpheus. Tension mounted with each successive opera until, in 1739, *Dardanus* so enraged the *Lulliste* librettist Charles-Pierre Roy that he and the composer traded punches.

Rameau grew up in Dijon and studied under his father, an organist. From 1702, he was also an organist, mainly in provincial cathedrals. But publication in 1722 of his book, *A Treatise on Harmony*, brought Rameau to Paris. Influential even into the 20th century, Rameau's new understanding of harmony also distinguished his own music. Voltaire and Jean-Jacques Rousseau collaborated on his librettos, while Louis XV's court extended commissions. *Les Indes galantes* and *Castor et Pollux* premiered at the Paris Opéra. But from 1745, the king requested pieces ranging from the comical *Platée* to the sumptuous *Les Boréades*, which, for unknown reasons, was rehearsed but never given in Rameau's lifetime. Like Lully, Rameau composed glorious music for dances, a vital element in French opera.

Nathan Berg as the Inca priest Huascar and Jaël Azaretti as the Peruvian princess Phani in Rameau's colourful *Les Indes galantes*, directed in 2003 by Andrei Serban for Les Arts Florissants at the Palais Garnier in Paris.

FIRST PERFORMANCES

1730	**1733** Hippolyte et Aricie
	1735 Les Indes galantes
1735	**1737** Castor et Pollux
	1739 Les fêtes d'Hébé, ou Les talents lyriques
	Dardanus
1740	**1745** La princesse de Navarre
	Platée
	Les fêtes de Polymnie
1745	Le temple de la Gloire
	1748 Zaïs
	Pygmalion
1750	**1749** Naïs
	Zoroastre
	1751 La guirlande, ou Les fleurs enchantées
1755	Acante et Céphise, ou La sympathie
1760	
	1763 Les Boréades (rehearsal; no performance given)
1765	

LES INDES GALANTES

(The Amorous Indies)

🎵 Opéra-ballet in a prologue and four entrées, 2½ hours
🎭 Unknown

🏆 10 March 1736, Paris Opéra, France (complete form)
📖 Louis Fuzelier

Les Indes galantes was so successful in 1735 that within 40 years it was given in various forms over 300 times in Paris. The opera presents a sequence of four independent lyrical dramas linked by a theme established in its prologue: that Love unites distinct cultures. Louis Fuzelier turned for his libretto to documents and eye-witness accounts of "the Indies", by which he understood exotic places: Turkey, Peru, Persia, and North America. Rejecting standard Baroque gods, goddesses, and enchanters, Fuzelier favoured "average" people who fall in love. Rameau responded with highly varied music for each *entrée*. Melodic lines, rhythms, and his signature wealth of harmonic invention present a mosaic of worlds united by love, and by music.

⚜ In 1725, two Native Americans demonstrated traditional dances in Paris. Rameau drew from their exhibition to compose *Les sauvages*, a work for the harpsichord, which he revised for the fourth *entrée* of this opera. ⚜

PLOT SYNOPSIS

In the "amorous Indies", exotic locations

PROLOGUE IN THE GARDEN OF HÉBÉ
Four men of the allied nations of France, Spain, Italy and Poland abandon Hébé, god of marriage, to carry out a war campaign. Cupids who are followers of Hébé note that, with Europe having forsaken them, they will depart for exotic lands, "the Indies".

FIRST ENTRÉE LE TURC GÉNÉREUX/THE GENEROUS TURK
Emilie, a French girl from Provence, is enslaved to the pasha Osman on his Turkish island. He is in love with the Christian girl ♂, but she remains true to her beloved Valère, an officer in the French marines; she has not seen him since the day of their wedding, when pirates

"Il faut que l'amour s'envole"

Colourful costumes and sets are used to explore the exotic settings of the "amorous Indies" of Rameau's opera in a visually-arresting Zurich production staged in 2004.

DANCE

The wild dancing in this opera suited its exotic themes. But from the time of Lully, dance or ballet interludes were essential in French opera. Rameau perpetuated this tradition, which continued well into the 19th century. The Paris Opéra would then insist that even guest composers like Donizetti and Verdi include ballet segments in French productions of their operas. Lully's legacy remains strong even today in France, where an acclaimed ballet corps forms part of the Opéra National de Paris.

abducted her. By chance, a storm shipwrecks Valère on the pasha's island. There, Osman recognizes the Frenchman as the person who once freed him from slavery, and generously releases the lovers from captivity 🎵.

"Partez! On languit sur le rivage"

SECOND ENTRÉE LES INCAS DU PÉROU/THE INCA OF PERU Below an active volcano, Don Carlos, a Spanish officer, and Phani, a Peruvian princess, vow mutual love. Huascar, the High Priest of the Sun, is also in love with Phani. When the volcano erupts during a festival worshipping the Sun god, Huascar tries to persuade Phani that the god protests her love for the enemy officer. But Carlos discovers that Huascar cast rocks into the volcano's crater to set off the eruption 🎵. A real eruption finally engulfs Huascar in lava.

"Pour jamais l'amour nous engage"

THIRD ENTRÉE LES FLEURS, FÊTE PERSANE/A PERSIAN FLOWER FESTIVAL Tacmas, a Persian prince, is in love with Zaïre, the slave girl serving his confidant, Ali. Tacmas disguises himself as a woman to sneak into Ali's garden and discover Zaïre's feelings. There, Fatima, the slave girl serving

Tacmas, also enters the garden, but disguised as a man; she is in love with Ali. When Tacmas mistakes Fatima for a rival lover of Zaïre, he nearly kills her with his dagger before recognizing her. Tacmas and Ali exchange slaves to form two contented couples. Love is celebrated with a Festival of Flowers 🎵.

"L'éclat des roses les plus belles"

FOURTH ENTRÉE LES SAUVAGES/THE SAVAGES In a North American forest, Zima, daughter of the tribal chief, is wooed by two officers: Don Alvar of Spain, who is possessive, and Damon of France, who advocates freer love. Zima finds each too extreme 🎵. Instead, she gives her hand to Adario, an Indian brave. The ceremony of the Great Pipe of Peace marks reconciliation between Indians and Europeans, and celebrates the union of Zima and Adario.

"Le coeur change à son gré"

PLATÉE
(Plataea)

❦

✍ Ballet bouffon in three acts, 2 hours
☎ c.1744–1745
⚜ 31 March 1745, La Grande Écurie,

Versailles, France
📖 Adrien-Joseph Le Valois d'Orville from Jacques Autreau's play, *Platée, ou Junon jalouse* (1745)

Platée is a farcical opera about a hideous and conceited marsh nymph who is ridiculed in a mock marriage to the god Jupiter. It was written for the Dauphin Louis's marriage in 1745 to the Spanish princess Maria Teresa, herself of legendary ugliness. Still, while a risky venture, the piece was well-received. Revised for the Paris Opéra in 1749, *Platée* enjoyed popular success, and has since been acclaimed a masterwork of French comic opera.

⚅ The role of Platée was created by Pierre de Jelyotte, an idolized French singer who had risen to fame in other Rameau roles. Cross-dressed as the ugly and vain marsh nymph, Jelyotte held his royal audience spellbound. ⚅

→ PRINCIPAL ROLES ←

Platée *tenor (haute-contre)*
A marsh nymph

Jupiter *bass*
King of the Gods

Cithéron *bass*
King of Greece

Momus *bass*
God of Ridicule

Mercure (Mercury) *tenor (haute-contre)*
Messenger to the Gods

Junon (Juno) *soprano*
Queen of the Gods

PLOT SYNOPSIS

A field and marshland below Mount Cithaeron, in mythological Antiquity

PROLOGUE As the inventor of Comedy, a drunken Thespis conspires with Love, the god of Ridicule, and Comedy's Muse to present a "new spectacle" demonstrating how Jupiter cured his wife of jealousy.

ACT ONE Mercure tells Cithéron, the King of Greece, of his plan to cure the goddess Junon of jealousy: Jupiter, her husband, will feign love for the ugly marsh nymph, Platée. When Mercure informs Platée that Jupiter loves her, she swells with pride and impatience ♂.

"Quittez, Nymphes, quittez vos demeures profondes "

ACT TWO Jupiter and Momus, god of Ridicule, descend from the heavens. While Cithéron and Mercure watch, Jupiter transforms into an ass to enchant Platée. When Jupiter turns into an owl and is frightened off by birds, Platée laments. Jupiter finally reveals himself to his "fiancée", and Platée is fêted with a concert led by Folly.

ACT THREE Platée enjoys her "nuptial" festivities ♋. Jealous, Junon rips the veil from the face of Jupiter's "bride" and, seeing the hideous Platée, bursts into laughter. The ridiculed Platée vents her anger, and then runs off to fling herself back into her marsh home.

"Chantons, célébrons en ce jour le pouvoir de l'Amour"

English tenor Mark Padmore embodied the ugly swamp nymph at the Edinburgh Festival in Scotland in 1997.

LES BORÉADES

(The Sons of Boreas)

⛵ Tragédie en musique in five acts, 3 hours
🎵 c.1763
🏛 21 July 1982, Théâtre de l'Archevêché,

Aix-en-Provence, France
📖 Attributed to Louis de Cahusac

Mystery surrounds *Les Boréades*, Rameau's last great opera: the librettist's identity is uncertain and, while it was rehearsed in 1763, it was not staged until 1982. Some experts have gleaned Masonic themes, and believe that the work was barred as subversive. The music responds to the quick pace of its fairy-tale story with brilliant harmonic innovation and forceful rhythms. It also contains gorgeous vocal parts and a stunning array of spirited dances.

✻ According to popular lore, Rameau walked out of the Paris Opéra during a rehearsal of the opera on 12 September 1764, only to disappear forever. ✻

✧ PRINCIPAL ROLES ✧

Alphise *soprano*
Queen of Bactria
Abaris *tenor (haute-contre)*
Foreigner
Borilée *baritone*
Prince descended from Boréas
Calisis *tenor (haute-contre)*
Prince descended from Boréas
Adamas *bass*
The High Priest of Apollo
Boréas *bass*
God of the North wind

PLOT SYNOPSIS

The kingdom of Bactria, in fictional Antiquity

ACT ONE Queen Alphise of Bactria is in love with the foreigner Abaris. A confidante warns that Boréas, god of the North wind, will be angry if Alphise fails to uphold tradition and marry into his family. Two descendants of Boréas, Borilée and Calisis, woo Alphise, but she determines to consult the god Apollo.

ACT TWO In the temple of Apollo, Alphise asks Adamas, the High Priest, to seek the god's approval of her beloved. Abaris celebrates their love 🎵, and Cupid presents Alphise with an enchanted arrow.

"Charmes trop dangereux"

Paul Agnew interpreting the role of Abaris receives Cupid's bow at the Opéra Garnier in Paris in 2003. William Christie led musicians of his ensemble, Les Arts Florissants in this production.

ACT THREE When gives Abaris Cupid's arrow, her subjects approve of him. Seeking revenge, Borilée and Calisis appeal to Boréas, whose unleashed winds sweep Alphise away.

ACT FOUR As Boréas's tempest rages, the priest Adamas exhorts Abaris to abandon his love for Alphise. Abaris prays to Apollo, and resolves to love Alphise.

ACT FIVE Boréas orders winds to strike the earth 🎵. He threatens Alphise with slavery if she does not marry according to tradition. Alphise is presented in chains, and Abaris uses his magic arrow to calm his rivals. But Apollo arrives to enlighten all: Abaris is his own son, born to a nymph of Boréas's bloodline. Alphise and Abaris are finally united.

"Obéissez, quittez vos cavernes obscures"

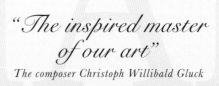

"*The inspired master of our art*"

The composer Christoph Willibald Gluck

GEORGE FRIDERIC
HANDEL

Born: 23 February 1685, Halle an der Saale (Germany)
Died: 14 April 1759, London, England

George Frideric Handel is best known today for the *Messiah* and other oratorios, but he is also the uncontested master of 18th-century *opera seria*. Born and raised in Germanic Saxony, he set operas in Italian for London audiences speaking English. Together, his extraordinary works and vibrant career establish him as the first truly European composer.

Handel studied under a church organist in Halle and, at age 17, was made organist of the town's Domkirche. At 19, he played violin for the opera in Hamburg, where he became its harpsichordist. His first two operas premiered in Hamburg in 1705, but only the first, *Almira*, set to a libretto in German, survives. The composer then travelled to Florence, which saw the premiere of *Rodrigo*, his first opera in Italian, and Venice, where *Agrippina* brought success. At age 25, he was appointed Kappelmeister to the House of Hanover, whose Elector became George I of England in 1714. By then, Handel was residing in London. His first opera for an English audience, *Rinaldo*, was given in 1711. It was a phenomenal success, and it served to fire up entrepreneurial spirits at the Haymarket Theatre, which was in the risky business of presenting Italian operas to English patrons.

In 1719, Handel helped found the Royal Academy of Music, and became its "Master of the Orchestra". The Haymarket was renamed The King's Theatre, and Handel's operatic masterpieces, including *Giulio Cesare*, *Tamerlano*, *Rodelinda*, and *Orlando*, then premiered on its stage. Acclaimed casts were led by prima donnas Faustina Bordoni and Francesca Cuzzoni, and by the alto castrato Senesino. In 1728, the Academy went bankrupt (today's

The English mezzo-soprano Sarah Connolly in the title role of Handel's *Giulio Cesare* for the Glyndebourne production of 2005.

FIRST
PERFORMANCES

1705 — **1705**
Almira

1711
Rinaldo

1715 —

1720
Radamisto
1724
Giulio Cesare
Tamerlano
1725 — **1725**
Rodelinda

1733
Orlando

1735
1735 — Ariodante
Alcina
1737
Berenice
1738
Serse
1741
Deidamia

1745 —

Royal Academy was founded in 1822), leaving Handel with the challenge of managing his own company.

A RIVAL OPERA COMPANY

New problems arose in 1733, when Handel's carefully-assembled star singers were lured to a rival company, the Opera of the Nobility, which was run by the influential Italian composer Nicola Porpora. Under these trying circumstances, Handel was forced to cede The King's Theatre to Porpora, and to set up his own company in Covent Garden. Bolstered by newly-recruited singers, he then waged a sporadically successful opera war on Porpora. When Porpora gained the upper hand, fresh ideas kept Handel's company in the game of enticing London audiences to attend operas sung in Italian. Two operas from this period, *Ariodante* and *Alcina*, even offered the curiosity of a French ballet troupe.

OPERAS AND ORATORIOS

The Opera of the Nobility closed in 1737, and audiences began to lose interest in Italian operas. Still, Handel wrote several more, including the magnificent *Serse*. But his last opera, *Deidamia*, was given in London the same year that his *Messiah* premiered in Dublin, Ireland: 1741. Handel

The King's Theatre, London, was destroyed by a fire in 1789, although it was later rebuilt. Handel's greatest operas, including *Giulio Cesare* and *Tamerlano,* premiered on its stage.

then abandoned opera to inject opera-like qualities into the oratorio, a non-dramatic form of vocal music employing religious themes. Indeed, whether closer to opera or oratorio, his great works of this era, including *Samson, Semele, Judas Maccabeus,* and *Jeptha,* defied neat classification. Yet through powerful music and story-telling, they continue to win devoted listeners today.

THE BEGGAR'S OPERA

In 1728, London audiences applauded *The Beggar's Opera* by John Gay who was also the librettist for Handel's *Acis and Galatea* (1718). Gay used existing songs — some traditional and some by composers including Purcell and Handel — but added his own lyrics satirizing life and Handel's opera company in London. Spoken dialogue and nearly 70 numbers advance the action. The first of its kind, this "ballad opera" was to set the stage for the French *opéra comique*, the German Singspiel, and the American musical.

The climactic scene from The Beggar's Opera is set in Newgate Prison, and shown here in a 1729 painting by William Hogarth.

RINALDO

🖋 Dramma per musica in three acts, 3 hours
🎭 1710–1711; rev. 1731
🏛 24 February 1711, Queen's Theatre, Haymarket,

London, England
📖 Giacomo Rossi, after *Gerusalemme liberata* (1575), by Torquato Tasso

Rinaldo was the first of Handel's operas for a London audience. With its love story set amid pageantry in magical realms, it calls for elaborate stagecraft. Indeed, the London *Spectator* applauded its "Thunder, Lightning, Illuminations, and Fireworks". Handel scored the opera in mere weeks, but he also borrowed music, including the much-loved march for Crusade forces in the closing act, from some of his earlier work still unknown in London.

◁ The first Rinaldo was the singer-actor Nicolino (1673–1732), a castrato whose career began in Naples at age 12. Popular in London before Handel first arrived in 1710, his star appearances added to the success of *Rinaldo*. ▷

> ⇥ PRINCIPAL ROLES ⇤
>
> Rinaldo *alto (castrato)*
> Christian soldier
>
> Goffredo *alto (castrato)*
> Captain of the Christian army
>
> Eustazio *alto (castrato)*
> Brother to Goffredo
>
> Almirena *soprano*
> Daughter to Goffredo
>
> Argante *bass*
> King of Jerusalem
>
> Armida *soprano*
> Enchantress Queen
> of Damascus

PLOT SYNOPSIS

Fictional Jerusalem, at the end of the First Crusade (1099)

ACT ONE The Christian leader Goffredo has offered the hand of his daughter, Almirena, to Rinaldo if he can take Jerusalem from King Argante. But as the sweethearts vow love, the enchantress Armida, Argante's mistress, uses magic to kidnap Almirena. Rinaldo despairs ♪. But his spirits lift when Goffredo and Eustazio tell him of a Christian hermit.

"Cara sposa, amante cara"

ACT TWO Journeying to the hermit, Rinaldo is lured into a magic boat, which carries him to Armida's palace. There, Argante tries to seduce the captive Almirena, who rejects him ♪. When Rinaldo arrives, Armida falls in love and, using magic to appear as Almirena, woos him. Still seeming to be Almirena, Armida attracts Argante's lust. Furious, she changes out of her disguise to declare war on Argante.

"Lascia ch'io pianga"

ACT THREE Goffredo and Eustazio visit the hermit, who gives them a magic wand. In the palace, Rinaldo saves Almirena from Armida. Goffredo and Eustazio use the wand to transform Armida's palace into the battle zone before Jerusalem. There, Armida and Argante end their personal quarrel and prepare for battle. But Rinaldo takes them captive. Christians celebrate their victory and welcome the now-married Rinaldo and Almirena.

Soprano Emma Bell performs as Almirena in a *Rinaldo* of 2000 directed and co-designed by David Fielding for the Grange Park Opera in Hampshire, England.

GIULIO CESARE

(Julius Caesar)

🎵 Dramma per musica in three acts, 3¼ hours
🎭 1723–1724
🎼 20 February 1724, King's Theatre, Haymarket,

London, England
📖 Nicola Francesco Haym, after a 17th-century libretto by Giacomo Francesco Bussani

Giulio Cesare has been called the quintessential *opera seria*. With grand themes of historical warfare and passionate love, of heroic action and inner turmoil, it offers lyric drama on a truly epic scale. Its wide scope is matched by its prodigious number of arias, with Cleopatra and Cesare alone allotted eight each. Along with *Tamerlano*, also premiering in 1724, and *Rodelinda* of 1725, *Giulio Cesare* shows Handel at the height of his powers while leading England's Royal Academy of Music. The opera enjoyed an initial run of 13 performances, and Handel revived it twice in London with continued success. Today, it is the most often-performed Handel opera. And, with its many strongly drawn principal roles, it is also a favourite among singers of Baroque repertoire.

→ PRINCIPAL ROLES ←

Giulio Cesare *alto (castrato)*
Roman emperor

Curio *bass* Roman tribune

Cornelia *contralto*
Wife of Pompeo, Cesare's foe

Sesto Pompeo *soprano*
Son of Pompeo

Cleopatra *soprano*
Queen of Egypt

Nireno *alto (castrato)*
Eunuch to Cleopatra

Tolomeo *alto (castrato)*
Half-brother to Cleopatra

Achilla *bass*
In service to Tolomeo

⚜ Handel broke new ground in the opening scene of Act II: Cleopatra arranges a set piece of nine Muses atop Mount Parnassus to help her to seduce Cesare, and the Muses are accompanied by onstage musicians. ⚜

PLOT SYNOPSIS

Egypt, just after Caesar's victory over Pompey in Greece, 48 BCE

ACT ONE On a plain near Alexandria, Egyptians praise Cesare, who arrives victorious from battle against Pompeo. Cesare accepts a peace agreement offered by Pompeo's wife and son, Cornelia and Sesto. But Achilla arrives on behalf of Tolomeo, Queen Cleopatra's half-brother, to present Pompeo's severed head. Cornelia curses Tolomeo's barbarity, but Achilla falls in love with her. The Roman tribune Curio offers to make Cornelia his wife and to avenge Pompeo. Alone, Sesto resolves to be the man to avenge his father. In the palace, Cleopatra learns that Tolomeo has decapitated

Pompeo, and she angers him by asserting that she alone is Egypt's ruler. Achilla offers to kill Cesare if Tolomeo will give Cornelia as a reward. In his camp, Cesare honours Pompeo, grieving over his coffin ♪. Cleopatra arrives disguised as the servant "Lidia", and Cesare falls in love with her. When "Lidia" laments the usurping Tolomeo ♪, Cesare vows to exact justice. Cleopatra observes as Cornelia grieves her husband's death.

"Alma del gran Pompeo"

"Piangerò la sorte mia"

Soprano Kathleen Battle sang Cleopatra in sumptuous costumes for a *Giulio Cesare* of 1998 at the Metropolitan Opera, New York.

Cornelia takes up a blade to avenge Pompeo, but her son Sesto stops her: this is his task. Still incognito, Cleopatra offers to lead them to Tolomeo. Tolomeo warmly welcomes Cesare, who detects the scheme to murder him. When Cornelia appears with Sesto, Tolomeo also falls in love with her, and plans to betray his promise to Achilla. Meanwhile, Cornelia rejects Achilla's offer of freedom in exchange for marriage, and is heart-

"Ah, sempre piangerò" | broken to be separated from her son ♪.

ACT TWO As "Lidia", Cleopatra seduces Cesare with enchanting music ♪. In the palace harem garden, Achilla and Tolomeo successively fail to seduce Cornelia. Sesto arrives just in time to prevent her suicide. Cleopatra's eunuch, Nireno, summons Cornelia to Tolomeo's harem, promising Sesto a chance to avenge his father at last. Meanwhile, "Lidia" has agreed to be Cesare's wife. But Curio reports that conspirators are calling for Cesare's death. Cleopatra reveals her identity, and as Cesare

"V'adoro, pupille"

"Se pietà di me non senti" | leaves to confront the conspirators, she prays for him ♪.

ACT THREE After Tolomeo's forces defeat Cleopatra, he imprisons her. Sesto and Nireno discover the wounded Achilla, now eager for Tolomeo's downfall. Before dying, Achilla hands over a seal that commands a secret army. Using the seal, Cesare leads the secret army to rescue Cleopatra, and then to complete the conquest of Egypt. The

"Da tempeste il legno infranto" | enamoured Cleopatra is ecstatic ♪. In the palace, Tolomeo is

about to rape Cornelia when Sesto kills him. In Alexandria, Egyptians rejoice at the tidings of Tolomeo's death. After embracing Sesto and Cornelia in mutual friendship, Cesare and Cleopatra declare their everlasting love for each other.

SENESINO

The charismatic and versatile Italian castrato Francesco Bernardi (*below left*), better known as "Senesino", riveted London audiences in Handel operas for 13 seasons. The composer wrote eight captivating arias for him to deliver as Giulio Cesare, one of Handel's most demanding roles. In 1733, having created the love-struck Medoro in *Orlando*, Senesino moved to the rival Opera of the Nobility. There, composer Nicola Porpora set his contralto voice to maximum effect in operas co-starring the younger castrato sensation Farinelli, a soprano.

The costumes worn by Giulio Cesare (Kate Aldrich, *right*) and Tolomeo (Martin Wölfel) throw new light on Handel's *Giulio Cesare* at the Staatsoper in Hamburg in 2005.

TAMERLANO
(Tamerlane)

🎭 Dramma per musica in three acts, 3 hours
📅 1724
🏛 31 October 1724, King's Theatre, Haymarket,

London, England
📖 Nicola Francesco Haym, after works based on a 1675 play by Jacques Pradon

Tamerlano joins *Giulio Cesare* and *Rodelinda* as one of the great operas Handel composed in the early 1720s. It pits love against duty in a troubled political context. The historical Asian conqueror Tamerlane, a popular stage subject at the time, is treated dramatically, not factually. Noted for its brilliant structure, the opera opens with captive emperor Bajazete attempting suicide, and ends only when his renewed attempt succeeds.

⊰ With Francesco Borosini, the first Bajazete, it was a rarity for a tenor to sing a lead role in an *opera seria* of the 18th century. The higher, more ornamented voices of women and castratos were deemed more beautiful. ⊱

⇾ PRINCIPAL ROLES ⇽

Tamerlano *alto (castrato)*
Tartar Emperor

Bajazete *tenor*
Conquered Turkish Emperor

Asteria *soprano*
Daughter to Bajazete

Andronico *alto (castrato)*
Greek prince

Irene *contralto*
Princess of Trebizond

Leone *bass*
Friend to Andronico

PLOT SYNOPSIS

The Turkish city of Prusa (now Bursa), the capital of Bithynia, occupied by Tamerlane in 1403

A spare set – two bronze folding screens and a throne – directs attention to the lavishly-costumed characters in Jonathan Miller's 2001 staging.

ACT ONE Imprisoned, the defeated Turkish emperor Bajazete contemplates suicide ♫. In love with

"Forte e lieto" | Bajazete's daughter, Asteria, Andronico arranges for her to appeal to the conquering emperor Tamerlano to spare Bajazete. Betrothed to Irene, Tamerlano falls in love with Asteria and insists Irene marry Andronico

"S'ei non mi vuol amar" | instead. Asteria laments her beloved Andronico's betrayal ♫. Irene is shocked that she is to marry Andronico, who agonizes over his situation.

ACT TWO Disguised as a messenger, Irene enters the Imperial Hall, where Bajazete is made to prostrate himself before Tamerlano's throne. Tamerlano tells Asteria to walk over her father to take her place as his empress. She refuses, and Bajazete defies orders to rise. Finally mounting the throne, Asteria places a dagger at Tamerlano's feet, declaring that she married him only to take revenge. Outraged, Tamerlano orders the executions of Asteria and Bajazete.

ACT THREE Tamerlano still loves Asteria, who renews love bonds with Andronico. Tamerlano has Bajazete brought into the Imperial Hall to be humiliated by banquet splendours. When the disguised Irene sees Asteria poisoning Tamerlano's cup, she warns him, revealing her identity. But Bajazete poisons himself, cursing Tamerlano as he expires. With Bajazete's death, an appeased Tamerlano approves the marriage of Andronico and Asteria, and accepts Irene as his bride.

RODELINDA

🎵 Dramma per musica in three acts, 3 hours
🎵 1725
🎵 13 February 1725, King's Theatre, Haymarket,

London, England
📖 Nicola Francesco Haym, after a work based on a 1652 play by Pierre Corneille

Rodelinda is among Handel's masterpieces for the Royal Academy of Music. Dominated by a series of over 30 da capo arias, solo pieces meant to show off one singer at a time, it contains only two duets and one ensemble number. But Handel paced the opera with artistry, using contrasting tempos, keys, and orchestration to build maximum tension. The music for Rodelinda herself is perfectly in tune with her martial devotion to marriage.

✢ Presumably to quell the alto castrato Senesino's envy of the soprano role, Handel added to the singer's role of Bertarido a show-stopping Act III aria, "*Vivi, tiranno*", when he revived the opera later in 1725. ✢

✦ PRINCIPAL ROLES ✦

Rodelinda *soprano*
Queen of Lombardy

Bertarido *alto (castrato)*
Her husband

Grimoaldo *tenor*
Usurper of the throne

Eduige *soprano*
Sister to Bertarido

Unulfo *alto (castrato)*
Adviser to Grimoaldo, loyal to Bertarido

Garibaldo *bass*
Henchman of Grimoaldo

PLOT SYNOPSIS

The Royal Palace in Milan, Italy

ACT ONE Thinking her husband dead, Rodelinda grieves. She is interrupted by the usurper Grimoaldo and declines his offer of marriage. Garibaldo offers him help but secretly intends to occupy the throne himself. Arriving disguised, Bertarido pines for his wife ♣, but Unulfo urges patience. They spy Rodelinda, who agrees to marry Grimoaldo when Garibaldo threatens to murder her son. Distraught, Bertarido considers Rodelinda faithless.

"Dove sei"

ACT TWO Plotting to expose Grimoaldo's villainy, Rodelinda agrees to marriage only if he kills her child before her eyes. He is horrified. When Garibaldo advises him to accept the offer, Unulfo chides Garibaldo for his barbarity. Eduige pledges to aid Bertarido, and Unulfo assures him of Rodelinda's constancy. As husband and wife reunite, Grimoaldo arrives to inform Bertarido that the hour of his death has come. Bertarido and Rodelinda bid a tearful farewell ♣.

"Io t'abbraccio"

ACT THREE Unulfo is mistakenly stabbed as he helps Bertarido escape from prison. Finding Bertarido's cell empty, and his cloak bloodied, Rodelinda and Eduige assume the worst. Garibaldo is about to assassinate Grimoaldo, but Bertarido saves him. Grimoaldo gratefully returns Bertarido to the throne.

Paul Gay as Garibaldo and Jean Rigby as Eduige at the Glyndebourne Festival, 2004. In one of the opera's subplots, Eduige wants to punish Grimoaldo for rejecting her. She and Garibaldo conspire to share the throne.

ORLANDO

🎭 Opera seria in three acts, 3 hours	London, England
📅 1732	📖 After Carlo Sigismondo Capece's libretto based on
🏛 27 January 1733, King's Theatre, Haymarket,	Ludovico Ariosto's epic poem *Orlando furioso* (1516)

With *Orlando*, Handel returned to the enchantment and special effects of his earlier operas, such as the popular *Rinaldo*. Influenced by the English masque, in which spectacle was more important than drama, these operas show little concern for credibility of plots or motivations. But nonetheless, *Orlando* contains some of Handel's finest writing, especially notable in the famous "mad scene" at the end of Act II, in which the music effortlessly captures the wild delusions of the jealous lover Orlando.

> ⚜ The role of Medoro was conceived by Handel's star castrato, Senesino, and that of the magician Zoroastro by his illustrious bass singer Montagnana. Both vocalists joined a rival opera company just after creating *Orlando*. ⚜

> ✦ PRINCIPAL ROLES ✦
>
> Orlando *alto (castrato)*
> A knight errant
>
> Angelica *soprano*
> Queen of Cathay
>
> Medoro *alto (castrato)*
> African prince
>
> Dorinda *soprano*
> A shepherdess
>
> Zoroastro *bass*
> A magician

PLOT SYNOPSIS

A woodland where Zoroastro practises magic

ACT ONE The magician Zoroastro interprets the night sky: Orlando will serve Glory. But Orlando dedicates himself to Love. Orlando's beloved Angelica, Queen of Cathay, offers her heart and her empire to Medoro, an African prince. The shepherdess Dorinda tells Medoro, who once courted her, she still loves him. Protecting Angelica from Orlando's jealousy, Zoroastro magically hides Medoro. Angelica gives a gem to Dorinda, who finds it a poor substitute for Medoro.

ACT TWO Dorinda grieves ♫, and Orlando becomes wildly jealous to learn that Angelica will marry Medoro. Pursuing the lovers, Orlando almost seizes Angelica, but she is borne off in a magic cloud. Orlando loses his senses ♫.

"Se mi rivolgo al prato"

"Ah! perfida, qui sei"

He imagines that Angelica is in Hades; that the Furies pursue him; and that the goddess Proserpina embraces Medoro. Orlando's madness escalates until Zoroastro's chariot lifts him away.

ACT THREE Medoro finds refuge in Dorinda's cottage. But the demented Orlando soon arrives. When Zoroastro turns the scene into a "horrid cavern", Dorinda reports that Orlando has destroyed her cottage and left Medoro for dead under its remains. Crazed, Orlando mistakes Angelica for a sorceress, throws her into the cavern, and sleeps. When Zoroastro's magic releases him from love's grip, Orlando approves of Angelica's marriage to Medoro, and proposes a celebration of Love and Glory.

Alice Coote (*seated*) interprets the role of Orlando in 2003. For this production, the Royal Opera House welcomed the OAE Orchestra, which plays on period instruments.

ALCINA

❧ Dramma per musica in three acts, 3½ hours
♞ 1735
♔ 16 April 1735, Covent Garden, London, England

📖 After *L'isola d'Alcina*, set by Riccardo Broschi (1728), from Cantos VI and VII of the epic poem *Orlando furioso* by Ludovico Ariosto (1516)

Handel created the enchanting *Alcina* to lure audiences away from a new rival company in London, the Opera of the Nobility. With its themes of passionate love and spectacular magic, *Alcina* was the fourth and final time Handel drew on Ariosto's epic poem *Orlando furioso*. The other three were *Rinaldo*, *Orlando*, and *Ariodante*. Following *Alcina*, Handel wrote eight final operas, but *Alcina* was the last of his operatic successes.

◄ Cast as Ruggiero, the castrato Carestini initially rejected "*Verdi prati*", an Act II aria that he found unflattering to his voice. Handel reputedly cursed the vocalist and threatened not to pay him unless he sang the part as scored. ►

> ➹ PRINCIPAL ROLES ➹
>
> Alcina *soprano*
> An enchantress
>
> Ruggiero *soprano (castrato)*
> Captive of Alcina
>
> Morgana *soprano*
> Servant to Alcina
>
> Oronte *tenor*
> Servant to Alcina
>
> Bradamante *alto*
> Beloved of Ruggiero
>
> Melisso *bass*
> Guardian to Bradamante

PLOT SYNOPSIS

Island of the enchantress Alcina

ACT ONE The heartless Alcina transforms men into rocks and beasts on her island. Now, she has fallen in love with Ruggiero, her latest captive. His fiancée Bradamante, disguised as "Ricciardo" to search for Ruggiero, arrives with Melisso, her beloved's old tutor. Alcina's magic has, however, caused Ruggiero to forget Bradamante's existence. Worse, Alcina's servant Oronte becomes jealous when his own beloved, Morgana, falls in love with "Ricciardo". Then, Oronte persuades Ruggiero that Alcina loves "Ricciardo", hoping this will rid him of the rival. When Morgana learns that Alcina is about to transform "Ricciardo" through magic, she reveals her love to the visitor.

Alcina (*right*) uses sex as a form of magic to charm her captives in the Stuttgart Staatsoper production of 2000.

ACT TWO Melisso breaks Alcina's spell over Ruggiero, who finally remembers Bradamante. He strategically feigns continued love for Alcina. When Alcina learns that Ruggiero has betrayed her and plots to escape from her island, she is crushed by grief ♂.

For her part, Morgana is enraged to overhear Ruggiero and Bradamante planning to run off together. Alcina's woe turns to shock when her magic wand appears to have lost its power.

"Ah, mio cor"

ACT THREE With "Ricciardo" unmasked, Morgana turns her affections to Oronte. Alcina threatens revenge on Ruggiero, even as she tries to win him back. While Alcina makes her final appeal, Bradamante warns her lover against Alcina's magic ♿.

Finally, Ruggiero and Bradamante destroy the source of Alcina's power and ruin her palace. It sinks into the sea, Alcina vanishes, and the men she had transformed regain human form.

"Non è amor, ne gelosia"

"It appears that King Louis XVI and Mr
Gluck will be taking us into a new era."

The philosopher Jean-Jacques Rousseau

CHRISTOPH WILLIBALD
GLUCK

Born: 2 July 1714, Erasbach (Germany)
Died: 15 November 1787, Vienna (Austria)

Gluck's name is synonymous with a movement to reform opera that began in the 1750s. Spurred on by Parisian luminary Jean-Jacques Rousseau, reformists advocated putting dramatic action first; eschewing vocal virtuosity for its own sake; and banishing music or dance that failed to serve an opera's dramatic *raison d'être*. Against all odds, Gluck achieved this goal.

Christoph Willibald Gluck, a composer of formidable influence, composed over 40 works of music theatre. Following studies in Prague, Milan, and Venice, he worked in opera capitals across Europe, finally settling in Vienna. His early operas were either in the *opera seria* style, with librettos by Pietro Metastasio, or in the French *opéra comique* vein then fashionable in Vienna's court. But by 1760, change was in the air. Gluck's vision of opera reform called for sharp attention to the libretto and its dramatic fibre, which he saw as opera's heart and soul. Irrelevant dances, diverting music, and the florid da capo arias so cherished by castratos and prima donnas would be sacrificed to opera's chief concern: drama. Indeed, sacrifice was the very theme of Gluck's two masterpieces for the Opéra in Paris, *Iphigénie en Aulide* and *Iphigénie en Tauride*. While their textual sources were drawn from Antiquity, Gluck's key works lit the way to opera's future. A pivotal composer, Gluck closed the Baroque era of Monteverdi, Lully, and Handel, and opened the Classical one that flourished in the masterpieces of Mozart and Cherubini. But his impact did not stop there. Richard Wagner and Richard Strauss were deeply influenced by Gluck, and composers contend with his operas even today.

Soprano Marie Arnet sings Diane (Artemis) and Veronica Cangemi plays Iphigénie (*kneeling*) in the tense final act of *Iphigénie en Aulide* at the Glyndebourne Festival, 2002.

FIRST PERFORMANCES	
1750	**1750** Ezio
	1752 La clemenza di Tito
	1756 Il re pastore
	1758 L'île de Merlin, ou Le monde renversé
1760	
	1762 Orfeo ed Euridice (rev. 1774 Orphée et Eurydice)
	1764 La rencontre imprévue
	1765 Telemaco, o sia L'isola di Circe
	1767 Alceste
1770	**1770** Paride ed Elena
	1774 Iphigénie en Aulide
	1777 Armide
	1778 Iphigénie en Tauride
1780	**1779** Echo et Narcisse

ORFEO ED EURIDICE
(Orpheus and Eurydice)

✍ Azione teatrale per musica in three acts, 1¾ hours
🎭 1762

🏛 5 October 1762, Burgtheater, Vienna (Austria)
📖 Raniero da Calzabigi

Orfeo ed Euridice is, with the exception of Mozart's late masterpieces, the most important 18th-century opera. Its theme recalls opera's roots in Jacopo Peri's 1600 work *Euridice* and in Monteverdi's 1607 *L'Orfeo*. But if Gluck appeared to be looking back, this work took opera on a forward path. Laser-sharp focus on dramatic action, instead of virtuoso distraction, exemplifies Gluck's new approach. In 1774, he revised the score for a French version, *Orphée*, winning him resounding praise in Paris. The opening captures its unique place in music history: a chorus laments Euridice's death in formal, elegiac manner, while Orfeo cries out for her in a thrilling voice heralding the Romantic era's arrival. This hybrid of two distinct sound-worlds is pure Gluck.

> ⚜ When Orfeo encounters Cerberus, guard dog of Hades, at the beginning of Act II, masterful scoring for orchestra and chorus produces a terrifying effect, at once evoking the animal's hellish threats and Orfeo's nervous fear. ⚜

➤ PRINCIPAL ROLES ◄

Orfeo *alto*
Shepherd and musician

Euridice *soprano*
Beloved wife of Orfeo

Amore *soprano*
God of Love

Chorus
Shepherds, Nymphs, Furies, Infernal Spirits, Heroes and Heroines from Elysium

PLOT SYNOPSIS

A grove surrounding the tomb of Euridice; Hades; and places in between, in mythological Antiquity

ACT ONE Mourning shepherds and nymphs gather around Euridice's tomb with flowers and incense. As they sing, Orfeo, reclining on a rock, cries out her name through their orderly lament. Orfeo asks to be left alone with his grief 🎵. He calls to his lost love, Euridice, but in vain, since the only reply he receives is echoes. Suddenly, Orfeo's anger at the gods of the underworld stirs him: with the courage of a hero, he will descend into hell to search for his beloved wife. Amore announces that Jove is moved by Orfeo's grief, and will allow him to make the journey to Hades. If his music calms the dark spirits of the underworld, Orfeo may return Euridice to daylight. But he will lose her forever and live in misery if he beholds her before emerging from the caves of the River Styx. And he is forbidden to speak to her of this decree 🎵. Alone, Orfeo resolves to succeed. When he accepts the challenge that the gods have laid down, thunder sounds and lightning flashes.

"Ah, se intorno a quest'urna funesta"

"Gli sguardi trattieni"

A watercolour set design from 1911 presents the vision of Russian designer Aleksander Jakovlevic Golovin for a naturalistic staging of the opera.

THE GLUCK DREAM TEAM

The first performance of *Orfeo ed Euridice* in Vienna in 1762 assembled talents ideally suited to Gluck's music: the reformist librettist Raniero da Calzabigi; the visionary choreographer Gaspero Angiolini; and the renowned designer Giovanni Maria Quaglio, whose sets mixed formal and natural elements to match the opera's novel sound. Creating the role of Orfeo was castrato Gaetano Guadagni. He had sung oratorios for Handel in London, where he also studied acting with the famous Shakespearean David Garrick. Rare for a castrato, he was noted for avoiding excess.

ACT TWO In a cavern leading to Hades, spirits of the underworld terrify Orfeo, and the barks of Cerberus menace him ♫.

"Chi mai dell'Erebo"

But when Orfeo sings of his grief, they are moved, and open the gates of the infernal region for "the victor". Orfeo enters the sunny Elysian Fields, home to gods and heroes. Orfeo rejoices in its blissful perfection, but cannot find Euridice. Heroes and Heroines present her, noting Orfeo's superhuman loyalty. Without beholding her, Orfeo escorts Euridice away from the Elysian Fields.

ACT THREE Orfeo leads his beloved out through a labyrinth of rocks and wild plants. She asks if he is alive, and if she is. Each question tortures Orfeo, who hurries her along. When he refuses her requests for an embrace or even a glance, she finally calls him a traitor. She asks to remain dead, and he insists he would always come after her ♫.

"Vieni, appaga il tuo consorte!"

As Orfeo nearly turns around, Euridice falls fainting to the ground, asking him to remember her. At last, Orfeo turns around only to see his Euridice die before him. He tries in vain to revive her ♫. Orfeo wants to join her in death, but

"Che farò senza Euridice?"

Amore prevents him. Then, as if rising from sleep, Euridice is renewed to life. The lovers reunited, Amore beckons them to return to earth. In a temple dedicated to Amore, Shepherds join in the dance in joyful celebration of Euridice's return, and sing of the triumph of love and faith.

Czech mezzo-soprano Magdalena Kožená was Orfeo in Robert Wilson's production for the Théâtre du Châtelet in Paris, France, in 1999.

IPHIGÉNIE EN AULIDE

(Iphigenia in Aulis)

🎭 Tragédie-opéra in three acts, 2½ hours
⏱ 1771–1773
🏛 19 April 1774, Paris Opéra, France

📖 Marie François Louis Gand Leblanc du Roullet, after Jean Baptiste Racine's tragedy *Iphigénie* (1674)

Iphigénie en Aulide was Gluck's first opera for a Paris audience. French opera, teeming since Lully with dances and *divertissements*, would never be the same. Gluck's sparer approach prompted mixed reactions, but created a taste for operas of engrossing drama. This work of love and law colliding in Antiquity won acclaim across Europe. Highlights include its magnificent overture, subtle orchestration, and forceful characterizations.

⚜ The opera caused a stir in Paris, not least because the exacting Gluck postponed the dress rehearsal, which Louis XVI had planned to attend. For the first time, the king was forced to adjust his schedule at the last minute. ⚜

⟡ PRINCIPAL ROLES ⟡

Agamemnon *baritone*
Father to Iphigénie

Clitemnestre *soprano*
Mother to Iphigénie

Iphigénie *soprano*
Beloved of Achille

Achille (Achilles) *tenor*
Greek warrior

Calchas *bass*
Priest of Diane

Diane (Artemis) *soprano*
Goddess

PLOT SYNOPSIS

Aulis, Greece, in mythological Antiquity just prior to the Trojan War

ACT ONE Agamemnon despairs that his daughter, Iphigénie, has been named

"Diane impitoyable"

sacrificial victim to appease Diane ♫. Iphigénie travels to Aulis, believing she is to marry Achille. The priest Calchas assures Greek warriors that a victim is arriving, and persuades Agamemnon to approve the sacrifice. Iphigénie appears in prenuptial glory with her mother, Clitemnestre, but is furious to learn that Achille is marrying another. Denying betrayal, Achille regains her love.

ACT TWO Festivities ready Iphigénie for the altar, until she discovers she is to be sacrificed, not married. Inflamed by love, Achille challenges Agamemnon, who only hastens to complete the sacrifice. But "devouring remorse" prevents him from harming his daughter. He pleads with Diane to take his own life instead.

ACT THREE The Greeks thirst for blood, and Iphigénie accepts her lot, even though

Achille wants to fight for her. Clitemnestre laments bitterly ♫. As Iphigénie kneels before an altar on the sea-shore, the High Priest stands with his knife poised high. But the Greeks explode in fury as a wrathful Achille disrupts their ritual, determined to saved Iphigénie. Suddenly, Diane appears. Moved by Iphigénie's obedience and Clitemnestre's tears, she announces that the Greeks may now speed from Aulis without sacrifice. All rejoice, and then depart for Troy, where the heroic deeds they will perform will "astonish posterity".

"Jupiter, lance la foudre!"

Katarina Karnéus plays Clitemnestre at the Glyndebourne Festival in 2002.

IPHIGÉNIE EN TAURIDE

(Iphigenia in Tauris)

🎼 Tragédie lyrique in four acts, 2 hours
🎵 1778
🎭 18 May 1779, Paris Opéra, France

📖 Nicolas François Guillard, after Euripides and the 1757 tragedy by Claude Guimond de la Touche

Iphigénie en Tauride premiered triumphantly at the Paris Opéra, and has since been viewed by many as a masterpiece of 18th-century opera. Its stark and unrelenting examination of tormented souls concludes with a rapid succession of glorious recognition, satisfying revenge, and merciful salvation. The opera abounds in stunning arias, but its uncontested jewel is Iphigénie's *"Ô malheureuse Iphigénie"* from Act II, which has lifted star sopranos to new heights of vocal glory from the first performances to modern productions.

> **→ PRINCIPAL ROLES ←**
>
> **Iphigénie** *soprano*
> Priestess in the temple of Diane
> **Oreste** *baritone* Brother to Iphigénie
> **Pilade** *tenor (haute-contre)* Friend to Oreste
> **Thoas** *bass* Barbaric Sythian
> **Diane (Artemis)** *soprano* Goddess

◄ Gluck had nothing against castratos, but French opera-goers did. They found the castrato disturbing. Thus, the role of Pilade was scored for the haute-contre, France's answer to the Italian castrato. ►

PLOT SYNOPSIS

Tauris, in mythological Antiquity

ACT ONE As a storm fades, Iphigénie laments the storm still raging within her. In Diane's temple, she reveals a nightmare: her mother killed her father, and she herself murdered her dear brother, Oreste. She prays to be reunited with Oreste. Thoas reports that two strangers have come ashore. The Sythians demand that the Greek captives be sacrificed.

French diva Rose Caron astonished audiences in leading tragic roles for 15 years before singing the part of Iphigénie in Paris in 1900.

ACT TWO Oreste and his friend Pilade lament their fates, and object when separated by guards. Alone, Oreste feels curiously serene ♫. But Furies and the ghost of his mother torment him. Iphigénie appears, unrecognized. Extracting news from the Greek prisoner, she learns that her father has been murdered by her mother, in turn slain by her brother

"Le calme rentre dans mon coeur"

Oreste, who "found the death he sought". He leaves, and Iphigénie mourns Oreste's death ♫.

"Ô malheureuse Iphigénie"

ACT THREE Iphigénie explains that one prisoner must return to Mycenae, but the other must die. She orders Oreste to leave for Mycenae, but he persuades her to send Pilade instead.

ACT FOUR Before Diane's altar, Iphigénie musters courage to complete the dreaded sacrifice. As Oreste is ritually presented, they finally recognize one another. Thoas tries to kill them, but Pilade arrives with Greek guards to slay him. Diane sends Oreste and Iphigénie to Mycenae with her temple statues, and all praise the gods.

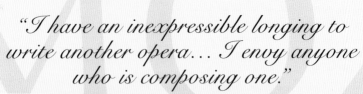

"I have an inexpressible longing to write another opera… I envy anyone who is composing one."

Wolfgang Amadeus Mozart

WOLFGANG AMADEUS
MOZART

Born: 27 January 1756, Salzburg (Austria)
Died: 5 December 1791, Vienna (Austria)

Wolfgang Amadeus Mozart stands alone in the history of opera. Other great opera composers, including Verdi and Wagner, made their mark only in opera, but Mozart's genius embraced every kind of music. Nonetheless, he always had a special passion and a unique gift for opera. During the last decade of his life, he transformed the genre beyond all recognition.

Like no composer before him, Mozart understood that, by exploiting the emotional power of the singing voice, he could give flesh and blood to the *serio* and *buffo* heroes of traditional opera. With his operatic masterpieces, *Le nozze di Figaro*, *Don Giovanni*, *Così fan tutte*, and *Die Zauberflöte*, he went still further. Inspired by challenging librettos, he painted fully-fledged characters through subtle orchestration, harmonically ambitious recitatives, memorable arias, and intricate ensembles. It took Mozart 25 years to reach this pinnacle.

His precocious talent was immediately recognized by his father, Leopold, a respected Salzburg musician, who even helped the boy with his early compositions. But it was as a performer that Mozart first astonished. He was only five when he and his gifted sister, Maria Anna, played the harpsichord at the Bavarian court in Munich. And he was eight when a three-year "prodigy tour" took him to Europe's major cities. With opera flourishing as never before outside Italy, young Mozart was soon drawn to the genre. Returning to Salzburg in 1767, he wrote his first opera, *Apollo et Hyacinthus*, a three-act *intermezzo* in Latin. The next year, he composed *La finta semplice*, an *opera buffa* in Italian, for the archbishop's palace in Salzburg. And a

FIRST
PERFORMANCES

1760

1767
Apollo et
Hyacinthus

1768
Bastien und
Bastienne

1769
La finta semplice

1770
Mitridate,
re di Ponto

1770

1772
Lucio Silla

1775
La finta giardiniera
Il re pastore

1780

1781
Idomeneo,
re di Creta
1782
Die Entführung
aus dem Serail
1786
Le nozze di Figaro
1787
Don Giovanni
1790
Così fan tutte

1790

1791
La clemenza
di Tito
Die Zauberflöte

1800

Matthias Görne as the birdcatcher Papageno displays his caged wares in a vibrant scene from Achim Freyer's production of *Die Zauberflöte* staged at the annual Salzburg Festival in 1999.

few months later, he presented *Bastien und Bastienne*, a German Singspiel, in Vienna. Before he was 13, he had written operas in three distinct styles and languages.

LEARNING IN ITALY

Italy, however, remained the true home of opera, and Mozart felt a need both to complete his education and to make his mark there. From late 1769, he spent 15 months in Italy. He began by learning the art of counterpoint, the harmonious juxtaposition of two or more musical parts. Then, having proved himself in private recitals, he was commissioned to write *Mitridate, re di Ponto*, an *opera seria*, for Milan's royal theatre. Acclaimed as a "little master", he went back there in 1772 to present *Lucio Silla*.

THE SALZBURG YEARS

Yet, for lack of opportunity, over the next nine years he wrote only two operas, *La finta giardiniera* and

Constanze Weber, Mozart's wife, helped to preserve the composer's musical legacy after his premature death.

Il re pastore, both in 1775. In contrast to instrumental music, opera required not only a commission, but also a libretto and singers – and Salzburg had neither a proper theatre nor an opera house. Mozart was also kept busy as court and cathedral organist. Gradually, though, he became desperate to leave the city. "You know how hateful Salzburg is to me," he wrote to a friend. Finally, in 1781, thanks to a commission from Munich, Mozart composed *Idomeneo*, his first mature stage work. By now, he had mastered the musical legacy of the past and was ready to create a new future. Later that year, he left Salzburg forever, breaking his ties with the city's formidable Prince-Archbishop Colloredo at the same time as escaping the loving but controlling embrace of his father.

OPERATIC GREATNESS

The next decade would enshrine him as the Mozart of legend, but it would also prove tumultuous. In 1782, he married the young soprano Constanze Weber, whose sister he had previously wooed. She was often ill and Mozart was frequently swamped in debt. The job he coveted as court composer was also firmly held by Antonio Salieri. But Mozart drove himself hard, composing

Leopold Mozart accompanies the young Wolfgang and his sister, Maria Anna as they perform in Paris in 1763.

prolifically and taking exhausting road trips to other cities. In July 1782, he made his grand entrance into Vienna's opera world with a farcical Singspiel, *Die Entführung aus dem Serail*, which was an immediate success. But the turning-point came in 1784 when he met the Italian poet and librettist Lorenzo da Ponte. Now Mozart could not only pick the subject of his operas, but could also draw strength from da Ponte's daring librettos: *Le nozze di Figaro*, with its rebellious servants, hints at class warfare; *Don Giovanni* celebrates – and eventually punishes – a philandering noble; and *Così fan tutte* suggests women can be as fickle as men. What has put these works at the heart of every opera repertory, however, is their music: beautiful, disturbing, and at times almost painfully intimate.

LORENZO DA PONTE

Starting with *Le nozze di Figaro* in 1785, Lorenzo da Ponte wrote librettos for three of Mozart's late masterpieces. Born into an Italian-Jewish family in 1749, da Ponte became a priest and a poet before legal troubles forced him to flee Venice. In Vienna, where he was befriended by Emperor Joseph II, he worked closely with Mozart between 1784 and 1789. He then resumed his wanderings as a down-at-heel poet, playwright, and librettist, eventually reaching the United States, where he died in 1838.

A LIFE CUT SHORT
In 1791, the last year of his life, Mozart added a fourth jewel to opera's crown, *Die Zauberflöte*. While working on it, he hurriedly wrote *La clemenza di Tito* for the coronation of the

An engraving of the spectacular celestial décor used for the entrance of the Queen of the Night, designed by Karl Friedrich Schinkel for a Berlin production of *Die Zauberflöte* in 1816.

Emperor Leopold II in Prague. Following the premiere of this *opera seria*, Mozart then rushed back to Vienna to complete *Die Zauberflöte*, which opened on 30 September. But only weeks later he was struck down with fever, perhaps brought on by infection. He died on 5 December 1791, just seven weeks short of his 36th birthday. His last great choral work, *Requiem*, was left unfinished.

MITRIDATE, RE DI PONTO
(Mithridates, King of Pontus)

◿ Opera seria in three acts, 3½ hours
🎼 1770
⚕ 26 December 1770, Teatro Regio Ducal, Milan (Italy)

📖 Vittorio Amedeo Cigna-Santi, after Giuseppe Parini's translation of Racine's 1673 tragedy *Mitridate*, first created as an opera in 1767

Mitridate, written when Mozart was only 14, was commissioned by the Austrian governor general of Lombardy. As was common, the composer was given a libretto, one set only three years earlier by Quirino Gasparini. The opera was well received, with Mozart's brilliant coloratura arias bringing cries of "Viva il Maestro, viva il maestrino" and new commissions. But *Mitridate* was then largely forgotten for two centuries.

⊰ This opera taught Mozart that singers were the real stars of opera. Guglielmo Ettore ordered him to rewrite Mitridate's opening aria three times and even used Gasparini's version of the final aria at the premiere. ⊱

> **✦ PRINCIPAL ROLES ✦**
>
> **Mitridate** *tenor*
> King of Pontus
>
> **Aspasia** *soprano*
> His reluctant betrothed
>
> **Sifare** *soprano*
> Mitridate's son, who secretly loves Aspasia
>
> **Farnace** *alto*
> Mitridate's other son, who openly courts Aspasia
>
> **Ismene** *soprano*
> Greek princess

PLOT SYNOPSIS

Nymphaea, the Crimea, around 66–63 BCE

ACT ONE While fighting the Romans, King Mitridate leaves his betrothed, Aspasia, in the care of his sons, Sifare and Farnace. When word of Mitridate's death reaches Nymphaea, Sifare remains loyal to Arbate, the local governor, but Farnace backs the Romans. The siblings also compete for Aspasia, who favours Sifare. Mitridate returns with Ismene, a bride for Farnace. The king, who reported his own death to test the loyalty of his sons, learns that Farnace is wooing Aspasia and orders him to be punished.

ACT TWO Mitridate decides to marry Aspasia at once, but noticing her hesitation, believes she has betrayed him with Farnace. Aspasia and Sifare renew their vows, but decide to separate ♫. Mitridate orders Farnace's arrest for conspiring with the Romans. Farnace discloses that Sifare loves Aspasia. When she in turn confesses her love for Sifare, Mitridate condemns her to die along with his sons.

"Lungi da te mio bene"

ACT THREE Refusing to wed Mitridate, Aspasia readies herself to take poison ♫. The king leaves to fight the Romans, while his freed sons join him in battle. The Romans offer the throne to Farnace but, repenting his treachery, he helps his father defeat them. Fatally wounded, Mitridate pardons his sons and, before dying, blesses the unions of Sifare and Aspasia, Farnace and Ismene.

"Pallid'ombre, che scorgete"

Sally Matthews as Sifare and Aleksandra Kurzak as Aspasia pledge anew their love before separating in Act II of a 2005 production at the Royal Opera House, London.

LUCIO SILLA
(Lucius Sulla)

⚓ Opera seria in three acts, 3½ hours   Milan (Italy)
🎵 1772   📖 Giovanni de Gamerra
🏛 26 December 1772, Teatro Regio Ducal,

Lucio Silla was commissioned for Milan's Teatro Regio Ducal after the success of *Mitridate*. Mozart was given a month to write the opera's 18 arias, but his growing experience shows, notably in how the music reinforces the personalities of the key roles. The score matches the high drama of the story. But *Lucio Silla* was only a moderate success, and Mozart soon left Italy forever.

⊰ *Lucio Silla* was long overshadowed by Mozart's later ventures into *opera seria*, but it has gained popularity in recent years because its political subject is easy to present as a contemporary drama. ⊱

✦ PRINCIPAL ROLES ✦

Lucio Silla *tenor*
A tyrannical Roman dictator

Giunia *soprano*
The object of his lust

Cecilio *soprano*
A dissident Senator and Giunia's betrothed

Lucio Cinna *soprano*
A friend to Cecilio

Celia *soprano*
Silla's sister and Cinna's bride

PLOT SYNOPSIS

Rome around 79 BCE

ACT ONE Cecilio returns to Rome from exile and is informed by his friend Cinna that his bride, Giunia, has been ordered to live in the palace of Lucio Silla, where she is being wooed by the despot. Lucio Silla's sister, Celia, urges him to treat Giunia kindly, but his brutal aide, Aufidio, tells him to take her by force.

Giunia, sung by the Swiss soprano Eva Oltivanyi, prays before her father's tomb in a 1998 production at Garsington Opera, England.

crumbling Roman republic. Cecilio reiterates his love for Giunia ♂. He goes on to threaten Lucio Silla with a sword and is arrested.

"Ah se a morir mi chiama"

Giunia hates Lucio Silla, her father's murderer, and rejects his advances. Learning that she visits her father's tomb daily, Cecilio meets her there and joins with other Romans in praying for Lucio Silla's demise.

ACT TWO Cinna suggests to Giunia that she marry Lucio Silla and then murder him, but she refuses ♂. Meanwhile, Lucio Silla proposes marriage to Giunia, saying that their union will put an end to the civil strife plaguing the

"Ah se il crudel periglio"

ACT THREE In despair, Cinna begs Celia, his betrothed, to pacify her brother, the dictator. Cecilio awaits death in jail and Giunia vows to die alongside him. Then, quite unexpectedly, from the steps of the Capitol, Lucio Silla pardons everyone. He frees Cecilio and reunites him with Giunia. And even though Cinna confesses his hatred of Silla, the ruler forgives him and approves his marriage to Celia. Finally, announcing that in future he will live as any ordinary Roman citizen, Lucio Silla abdicates the throne, bringing joy to the entire city.

IL RE PASTORE
(The Shepherd King)

🎵 Serenata in two acts, 2 hours
📅 1775
🏛 23 April 1775, Archbishop's Palace,

Salzburg (Austria)
📖 Pietro Metastasio

Il re pastore was commissioned by the Prince-Archbishop Colloredo of Salzburg to celebrate a visit by the young archduke, Maximilian Franz. For this event, Mozart was handed Pietro Metastasio's 1751 *opera seria* libretto, which had already been set by a dozen composers. The score contains some beautiful arias and ensembles, but it did not earn Mozart a fresh commission. Five years would pass before he wrote another opera, which would be his first great stage work, *Idomeneo*.

> ✧ **PRINCIPAL ROLES** ✧
>
> **Alessandro** *tenor*
> Alexander the Great
>
> **Aminta** *soprano*
> The future king of Sidon
>
> **Elisa** *soprano*
> Aminta's beloved
>
> **Tamiri** *soprano*
> The usurper Strato's daughter

⊰ Performed before a young archduke, *Il re pastore* could have been interpreted as satirizing Habsburg conquests, but any offence was mitigated by its farcical plot and lively music. ⊱

PLOT SYNOPSIS

Sidon, Lebanon, around 330 BCE

ACT ONE Aminta, a shepherd boy, is joined by his beloved Elisa. She reports that, having ousted the usurper Strato from the throne of Sidon, Alessandro is looking for the rightful heir. Accompanied by Agenore, Alessandro observes Aminta and is impressed. Meanwhile, Agenore recognizes his beloved Tamiri, Strato's fugitive daughter, who is living as a shepherdess with Elisa. He begs Tamiri to follow him, but she distrusts Alessandro. Agenore then hails Aminta as Sidon's new king. Aminta shows no interest in power until Elisa, assuring him that they will soon marry, convinces him to accept the honour ♂.

"Vanne a regnar, ben mio"

Annette Dasch as Aminta (*top*) and Juan José Lopera as Agenore in a semi-staged production at the Théâtre de la Monnaie, Brussels, in 2003.

ACT TWO Agenore prevents Elisa from seeing Aminta, as he is discussing matters of state with Alessandro. Eager to make peace before he leaves for new conquests, Alessandro proposes that Aminta marry Tamiri, his enemy's child. Elisa prefers to die than lose Aminta, while Tamiri is so angry with Agenore for giving her up that she orders him to attend her wedding. Tamiri begs Alessandro to change his mind and Elisa blames him for her distress. Aminta surrenders his royal gowns, saying he cannot be king without Elisa ♂. Finally, recognizing his error, Alessandro appoints Aminta and Elisa as Sidon's rulers and promises that Agenore and Tamiri will also be given a kingdom.

"L'amerò, sarò constante"

IDOMENEO, RE DI CRETA

(Idomeneus, King of Crete)

⚓ Dramma per musica in three acts, 3½ hours

🎵 1780–1781

🏛 29 January 1781, Cuvilliés Theater,

Munich (Germany)

📖 Giambattista Varesco, after Antoine Danchet's 1731 libretto, *Idoménée*, scored by André Campra

Idomeneo, Mozart's third and greatest *opera seria*, anticipates his later masterpieces. Written after a long period in which he concentrated on instrumental music, it stands out for its arias of great beauty and passion, a remarkable quartet, powerful choruses, and rich orchestration. Initially, it was presented only three times, and it only reached Britain and the United States in the mid-20th century. Today, it is considered a major work.

⚔ At 25, Mozart still lacked the power to pick his cast. In the case of *Idomeneo*'s premiere, he described the men who sang Idomeneo and Idamante as "the two worst actors any stage has ever borne". ⚔

✦ PRINCIPAL ROLES ✦

Idomeneo *tenor*
King of Crete

Idamante *mezzo-soprano*
or tenor
Idomeneo's son and heir

Ilia *soprano*
Trojan princess

Elettra *soprano*
Greek princess

Arbace *tenor*
Idomeneo's aide

High Priest *tenor*

PLOT SYNOPSIS

Crete around the 12th century BCE

ACT ONE The Trojan princess Ilia is held captive in Crete where, to prove his love, Prince Idamante releases all Trojan prisoners. Meanwhile, returning home after many years, King Idomeneo is feared drowned. To save himself, he promises Neptune to sacrifice the first person he meets on shore. He is received by a young man whom he at last recognizes as his son, Idamante. The Cretan people celebrate Idomeneo's return, but he is plunged into despair.

ACT TWO Idomeneo orders Idamante to leave for Argos with Elettra, a Greek princess who is in love with the prince. Heartbroken, Ilia tells Idomeneo of her love for Idamante 👤. To punish Idomeneo's betrayal,

"Se il padre perdei"

Neptune sends a monster in a storm to assail the island. The king offers himself as a sacrifice, but Neptune angrily intensifies the storm. The people of Crete flee in terror.

ACT THREE As Idamante prepares to fight the monster, Ilia finally confesses her love for him, but Idomeneo again orders Idamante to flee 👤. With the people growing restive, the king realizes he must sacrifice his son to Neptune. Idamante kills the monster and is ready to die. But when Ilia offers to take his place, Neptune instead orders Idomeneo to abdicate, naming Idamante and Ilia as the new rulers of Crete.

"Andro ramingo e solo"

Norman Shankle as Idomeneo and Karine Babajanian as Elettra, Stuttgart Opera, 2005.

DIE ENTFÜHRUNG AUS DEM SERAIL

(The Abduction from the Seraglio)

🎵 Singspiel in three acts, 2¼ hours
📖 1781–1782
🎭 16 July 1782, Hofburgtheater, Vienna (Austria)

📖 Gottlieb Stephanie, after a 1781 play by
Christoph Friedrich Bretzner

Die Entführung aus dem Serail was Mozart's first opera for Vienna and his first full-length Singspiel, the name given to Germanic opera with spoken dialogue. It is no coincidence that the heroine is called Konstanze: a month after its premiere, Mozart married Constanze Weber. Designed to appeal to the fashion for all things Turkish, the story's frivolity is more than compensated by musical fireworks, with 21 arias, duets, or ensembles.

⌁ Modern audiences may be tested by this opera's lengthy German-language dialogue, but Emperor Joseph II was more impressed by the score. "An awful lot of notes, my dear Mozart," he is said to have remarked. ⌁

> ✦ PRINCIPAL ROLES ✦
>
> **Bassa Selim** *speaking part*
> A Turkish pasha in North Africa
>
> **Konstanze** *soprano*
> A Spanish noblewoman
>
> **Blonde** *soprano*
> Konstanze's English maid
>
> **Belmonte** *tenor*
> Konstanze's betrothed
>
> **Pedrillo** *tenor*
> Belmonte's servant
>
> **Osmin** *baritone*
> Selim's vizier

PLOT SYNOPSIS

Around Bassa Selim's palace in a North African city

ACT ONE Belmonte is looking for his kidnapped love, Konstanze, at Selim's palace. He is chased away by Osmin, Selim's vizier, but he meets Pedrillo, his servant, who is also a hostage. Pedrillo reports that Konstanze is Selim's favourite and that Blonde, her English maid, has been handed to Osmin. Belmonte yearns to be reunited with

"Konstanze, Konstanze" | Konstanze ♂. He then overhears Selim demanding her love. Selim is rebuffed,

and gives Konstanze a day to change her mind. Pedrillo presents Belmonte to the court as an "architect".

ACT TWO Blonde skilfully parries Osmin's advances, while Konstanze laments her

"Martern aller Arten" | plight ♂. Blonde is thrilled to hear of Belmonte's escape

plan, which is set in motion when Pedrillo gives Osmin a

sleeping draught. As Belmonte falls into Konstanze's arms, he and Pedrillo are chastized for doubting their lovers' fidelity.

ACT THREE The women are given the signal to escape, but they are spotted and taken to Osmin, who promises terrible punishment. Selim is all the more furious when he learns that Belmonte's father is his sworn enemy. Then, as Belmonte and Konstanze prepare to die, Selim decides to free the two couples.and all but Osmin celebrate.

Christoph Späth's Selim tries
unsuccessfully to seduce Konstanze,
sung by Desirée Rancatore, in this 2006
production at the Teatro Lirico di Cagliari.

LA CLEMENZA DI TITO

(The Clemency of Titus)

🎵 Opera seria in two acts, 2¼ hours
⏱ 1791
🎭 6 September 1791, Graflich Nostitzsches

Nationaltheater, Prague (Czech Republic)
📖 Caterino Tommaso Mazzolà, after Pietro Metastasio

La clemenza di Tito is Mozart's penultimate opera, but it resembles his earlier works, especially as it is an *opera seria* based on a stock libretto. Commissioned at short notice to write an opera for Leopold II's coronation as King of Bohemia, Mozart completed the score in under three weeks. Rich in lively arias and duets, the work places unusual prominence on female voices, including two written as "trouser roles" of women playing men.

⊰ An opera portraying a magnanimous ruler might have seemed appropriate for an emperor's coronation, but Leopold II's Spanish-born queen, Marie-Louise, dismissed it as "porcheria tedesca" – German rubbish. ⊱

⇌ PRINCIPAL ROLES ⇌

Tito *tenor*
Roman emperor

Vitellia *soprano*
Daughter of former emperor

Sesto *soprano* or *mezzo-soprano*
In love with Vitellia

Servilia *soprano*
In love with Annio

Annio *soprano* or *mezzo-soprano*
In love with Servilia

PLOT SYNOPSIS

Rome, Italy, around 80 CE

ACT ONE Vitellia is furious that Tito is to marry a foreign princess. She tells Sesto to prove his love for her by killing the emperor. When Annio reports that Tito has changed his mind, Vitellia orders Sesto to wait. Instead, Tito decides to marry Sesto's sister, Servilia, but she loves Annio ♫. When

"Ah, perdona al primo affetto"

Servilia reveals this to Tito, he generously withdraws his proposal. Seeing Servilia's joy, Vitellia believes she has again "lost" Tito and dispatches Sesto to murder the emperor. By the time Vitellia learns that she has been chosen as Tito's new bride, Rome is burning. Sesto returns with news that Tito has been killed.

ACT TWO Discovering that Tito is not dead, Sesto confesses his crime to Annio, who urges him to seek the emperor's mercy. Vitellia tells Sesto to flee, but he is arrested for treachery.

Michael Schade as Tito and Dorothea Röschmann as Vitellia in Martin Kušej's modern dress production at the Salzburg Festival in 2003.

Incredulous, Tito wants to hear Sesto admit his guilt. Sesto asks only to be forgiven before he dies. Alone, Tito signs the death warrant, and then destroys it. Unaware of Sesto's reprieve, Annio and Servilia beg Vitellia to intercede. Vitellia, now full of remorse ♫, instead tells Tito of her own role in the plot. Stunned, Tito asks: "How many of you betrayed me?" Yet, out of clemency, he forgives all of them.

"Non più di fiori"

LE NOZZE DI FIGARO

(The Marriage of Figaro)

🎵 Opera buffa in four acts, 3 hours
📅 1785–1786
🎭 1 May 1786, Hofburgtheater, Vienna (Austria)

📖 Lorenzo da Ponte, after Beaumarchais's 1784 play, *La folle journée, ou Le mariage de Figaro*

Le nozze di Figaro is considered by many to be Mozart's greatest opera and, arguably, the most perfect opera ever written. Uniting Mozart and librettist Lorenzo da Ponte for the first time, it combines breathtaking arias and ensembles with a strong, highly entertaining plot. The music also plays a central role in revealing the psychology and temper of the main characters: the count's arrogance, the countess's melancholy, Figaro's fury, and Susanna's mischief. Amidst all the humour and confusion, then, Mozart's score expresses raw emotional truths. Further, he blends arias and recitatives so seamlessly that much of the narrative recitative is as melodic as the set pieces. Today, *Le nozze di Figaro* is a cornerstone of the opera repertoire.

⊲ Beaumarchais's play, *Le mariage de Figaro*, was banned as subversive. But by eliminating political satire and replacing class resentment with sexual rivalry, Mozart and da Ponte won permission for their *opera buffa*. ⊳

✦ PRINCIPAL ROLES ✦

Count Almaviva *baritone*
A rakish Spanish noble

Countess Almaviva *soprano*
His long-suffering wife

Figaro *baritone*
Count Almaviva's valet

Susanna *soprano*
The countess's chambermaid and Figaro's betrothed

Cherubino *soprano* or *mezzo-soprano*
A page boy

Marcellina *soprano* or *mezzo-soprano*
A housekeeper

Bartolo *bass*
A doctor

Basilio *tenor*
A music teacher

PLOT SYNOPSIS

Aguas Frescas, a castle near Seville in Spain

ACT ONE Figaro is to marry Susanna, the countess's maid, but the philandering Count Almaviva wants to exercise his feudal right to the first night with the bride. Susanna reassures Figaro, but he is furious. Marcellina in turn says Figaro promised to marry her in exchange for a loan. Cherubino, a young page who loves the countess above all women, is banished for chasing Barbarina, the gardener's daughter. Cherubino begs Susanna for help ♪. When the count arrives, Cherubino hides. Basilio, the music teacher, then appears and the count also hides. The count then hears of Cherubino's passion for his wife and orders the page to join the army. Figaro cheers him on ♪.

"Non so più cosa son, cosa faccio"

"Non più andrai"

ACT TWO As the countess laments her unloving husband ♪, Figaro unveils a scheme. He will warn the

"Porgi, amor, qualche ristoro"

Giorgio Strehler's classic 1980 production, originally conducted by Sir Georg Solti, was revived scores of times at the Paris National Opera, and is seen here at the Opéra Bastille, Paris, in 2003.

count that his wife has a tryst. Meanwhile, Susanna will arrange to meet the count, but Cherubino will take her place, dressed as a woman. When the count appears, Cherubino hides in a dressing room. The countess pretends Susanna is trying on her wedding dress. Suspicious, the count leaves to get a hammer, letting Cherubino escape. When the count returns, Susanna emerges. Antonio, the gardener, says someone leaped out of the window, but Figaro "confesses" it was he. Marcellina marches in to claim Figaro.

ACT THREE The count has ordered Figaro to marry Marcellina, but Figaro says he needs the consent of his parents, whom he does not know. Marcellina asks if he has a birthmark on his arm. When he so

"Riconosci in questo amplesso" | admits, she swoons. Bartolo the doctor says Marcellina is his mother and he is his father 🎵. Seeing Figaro

hugging Marcellina, Susanna slaps him. Marcellina explains; the count is lost for words. The countess still hopes to win

"Dove sono" | back her husband 🎵. As Figaro's wedding celebrations begin,

Susanna slips the count a note arranging their rendezvous.

ACT FOUR Figaro hides in the garden, as Susanna and the countess arrive

"Deh vieni, non tardar" | in disguise. Susanna is overjoyed to see Figaro 🎵, but he does not recognize

her. Cherubino takes the countess for Susanna and tries to kiss her. The count steps forward and receives the kiss; Figaro rushes out and the count strikes him. As "Susanna" slips away, Figaro spots "the countess", then hears Susanna's voice. With the count now looking for "Susanna", Figaro proclaims his love for "the countess". The count is outraged until "Susanna" unmasks as the real countess. Humbled, the count begs forgiveness. "I am kinder," she says. "I will say yes." Everyone is happy.

BRYN TERFEL

In recent years, no singer has become more identified with Figaro than the charismatic Welsh bass-baritone Bryn Terfel. As his first lead role at the major opera houses of Santa Fe, London, New York, Vienna, and Milan, Figaro not only made his name internationally, but also led him to two other great Mozartian bass-baritone roles, Leporello and Don Giovanni. With a stage presence to match his fine voice, Terfel has since also expanded his repertoire to include such roles as Scarpia in *Tosca*, Falstaff, and Wotan in Wagner's monumental *Ring* cycle.

Carla Dirlikov as Cherubino flirts with Zorana Sadiq's Susanna in Mozart's much-loved *Le nozze di Figaro* at the Banff Summer Festival in Canada, 2004.

DON GIOVANNI

⚐ Dramma giocoso in two acts, 2¾ hours
🎵 1787
♔ 29 October 1787, Graflich Nostitzsches

Nationaltheater, Prague (Czech Republic)
📖 Lorenzo da Ponte, after Giovanni Bertati's
libretto for Giuseppe Gazzaniga's 1787 opera

Don Giovanni was commissioned for Prague after the
city acclaimed *Le nozze di Figaro*. Mozart turned anew
to Lorenzo da Ponte, who took his story from another
Don Giovanni opera recently presented in Venice.
Da Ponte's wit and poetry inspired Mozart's brilliant
score, which brings humour and tragedy – as well
as memorable arias and complex ensembles – to the
essentially grim story of a serial seducer who escapes
all retribution except death. Throughout, the deep
humanity of the music reinforces the drama: it can
even be argued that the music does half the acting.

⚐ Mozart displays mischief during Don Giovanni's final supper scene by
"quoting" from three contemporary operas, including *Le nozze di Figaro*.
Recognizing *Figaro*, Leporello remarks: "I know this piece a little too well". ⚐

> ✦ PRINCIPAL ROLES ✦
>
> **Don Giovanni** *bass* or *baritone*
> A licentious young noble
>
> **Il Commendatore** *bass*
> Killed by Don Giovanni
>
> **Donna Anna** *soprano*
> Il Commendatore's daughter
>
> **Don Ottavio** *tenor*
> A gentleman, Anna's betrothed
>
> **Donna Elvira** *soprano*
> A noble lady abandoned
> by Don Giovanni
>
> **Leporello** *bass*
> Don Giovanni's rascal servant
>
> **Zerlina** *soprano*
> A peasant girl
>
> **Masetto** *bass*
> Zerlina's betrothed

PLOT SYNOPSIS

In and around Don Giovanni's villa

ACT ONE Leporello waits
while his master, Don
Giovanni, seduces yet
another woman. Don
Giovanni runs out
masked, with Anna
in pursuit. Her father,
the Commendatore,
challenges Don
Giovanni. As Anna flees,
the Commendatore is
slain. Anna finds his
body and demands that
Ottavio, her fiancé,
avenge the murder.

English soprano Emma
Albertazzi (1814–1847) as
Zerlina in a contemporary
illustration of the opera.

Elvira laments her love for Don
Giovanni, saying he seduced her with
the promise of marriage. As Don
Giovanni walks off impatiently,
Leporello adds up his master's conquests

"Madamina,
il catalogo è
questo"

🎵. Don Giovanni takes
a fancy to Zerlina and
invites her betrothed,
Masetto, to a party at his

villa. Alone
with Zerlina,
he begins
flirting 🎵.

"Là ci
darem
la mano"

Elvira rushes in to warn
Zerlina against the rake.
Anna is now sure that
Don Giovanni is the
masked killer of her
father, while
Ottavio

"Dalla
sua Pace"

vows to discover the truth 🎵.
Leporello reports that Elvira disrupted
the party, but Don Giovanni wants to
enjoy himself with new
conquests 🎵. As Elvira,
Anna, and Ottavio arrive
wearing masks, Don Giovanni leads
Zerlina away, but she cries for help.
Don Giovanni finds Ottavio waving

"Finch'han
dal vino"

a pistol. The trio take off their masks and threaten him. Don Giovanni is shaken, but defiant.

ACT TWO Don Giovanni exchanges clothes with Leporello so he can seduce Elvira's maid. Elvira hears Don Giovanni begging her forgiveness and wants to believe him. Leporello, now dressed as his master, embraces Elvira, while Don Giovanni, dressed as Leporello, serenades Elvira's maid ♪. Masetto comes looking for Don Giovanni and is promptly punched by "Leporello". As "Don Giovanni" flees Elvira, Anna and Ottavio spot him and he immediately reveals he is Leporello. Ottavio vows to kill Don Giovanni. But Elvira still loves the noble ♪. At the cemetery, Don Giovanni jokes about a woman who took him for Leporello. Suddenly, a voice is heard warning that his laughter will soon end. Seeing the Commendatore's statue, Don Giovanni mocks its threat. Leporello invites the statue to dine with his master, and it nods. Don Giovanni is unperturbed. He

"Deh, vieni alla finestra"

"Mi tradì, quell'alma ingrata"

summons musicians to accompany his dinner. Elvira appears, but is insulted. As she leaves, she screams. The statue of the Commendatore appears. Don Giovanni offers him dinner, but the statue instead invites Don Giovanni to dine with him. Leporello begs his master to refuse, but he agrees. Taking the noble's hand, the statue tells him to repent. "No!" "Repent!" "No!" Then, with a final cry, Don Giovanni is consumed by flames. His enemies arrive and each one decides to start life afresh, now satisfied that Don Giovanni has finally paid for his sins.

Robert Lloyd as the Commendatore and Gerald Finley as Don Giovanni in this opera's dramatic final scene at the Royal Opera House in 2003.

COSÌ FAN TUTTE

(Thus Do All Women)

◭ Dramma giocoso in two acts, 3 hours   Vienna (Austria)
🕮 1789   ⌑ Lorenzo da Ponte
♇ 26 January 1790, Hofurgtheater,

Così fan tutte, ossia La scuola degli amanti, or *Thus Do All Women, or The School of Lovers*, was not recognized as a masterpiece until the 20th century. Although it contains sublime arias and duets as well as two remarkable 19-minute ensembles, its plot was long considered decadent. Somehow, it was acceptable for *Don Giovanni* to depict men as philanderers, but not for *Così fan tutte* to portray women as fickle. Today, the opera stands on its own, rightly celebrated for its lively plot and beguiling score. Yet it is more than simple *divertimento*. Mozart's music gives the story a poignantly realistic dimension by exploring both the universal fear of betrayal and the thrill of unexpected love.

> ✣ **PRINCIPAL ROLES** ✣
>
> Don Alfonso *bass*
> A town philosopher
>
> Fiordiligi *soprano*
> A lady of Ferrara
>
> Dorabella *mezzo-soprano*
> Fiordiligi's sister
>
> Ferrando *tenor*
> Dorabella's betrothed
>
> Guglielmo *baritone*
> Fiordiligi's betrothed
>
> Despina *soprano*
> A scheming chambermaid

⊰ *Così fan tutte* echoes elements in Mozart's own life: he married the sister of a woman he had once loved; and his wife, Constanze, frequently away on health cures, left him to his own devices. ⊱

PLOT SYNOPSIS

Naples, Italy

ACT ONE Don Alfonso warns two young army officers, Ferrando and Guglielmo, that no woman can be trusted. Outraged, they boast of the constancy of their fiancées, the sisters Dorabella and Fiordiligi. Don Alfonso suggests a wager to test the women's fidelity. The officers accept his conditions: to say nothing to their fiancées and, for 24 hours, to obey his orders. Dreaming of their weddings, Fiordiligi and Dorabella admire their lovers' portraits in lockets

A contemporary engraving of Herrn Gunbaum as Ferrando, in Albanian disguise. With the women absent, some tenors remove the customary moustache to sing *"Un'aura amorosa"* in Act I.

♉. Don Alfonso brings word that the men have been mobilized. The women join him in bidding farewell to the soldiers ♉.

"Ah, guarda sorella"

"Soave sia il vento"

Fiordiligi and Dorabella are heartbroken, but the chambermaid Despina assures them that men are easy to find. As part of the test, Don Alfonso bribes Despina to introduce two men to the girls. Disguised as "Albanians", Ferrando and Guglielmo throw themselves at the feet of the astonished sisters. As Fiordiligi proclaims her unwavering

Lillian Watson as Despina (*centre*) looks on as Wendy Dawn Thompson's Dorabella and Sarah-Jane Davies as Fiordiligi nurse the "Albanians", Garsington Opera, 2004.

"Come soglio immoto resta" faithfulness ♂, the men feel confident of winning the wager. But when Don Alfonso orders the men to feign suicide, the sisters at last show concern. A doctor – Despina in disguise – pretends to cure them. To help their recovery, the men ask for a kiss, but are rebuffed.

ACT TWO When Dorabella welcomes the idea of some fun, her sister suggests she pick between the two men. To complicate matters, they swap lovers, Dorabella preferring the "dark-haired" fellow (Guglielmo), and Fiordiligi, the "blonde" (Ferrando). Don Alfonso and Despina lead the women to their "Albanian" suitors. Guglielmo claims to be ill – from love – and

Dorabella surrenders ♂. Fiordiligi rejects Ferrando, but then appears to be wavering ♂. Guglielmo is proud Fiordiligi has remained faithful to him, while Ferrando is upset to learn that Dorabella has even given away his portrait. Finally Fiordiligi admits she loves a second man, but decides to join her lover at the front. Hearing this, Ferrando demands that she plunge a sword into his heart – and she too is won over. Despina announces that the sisters are ready to marry. The officers complain to Don Alfonso, who explains that "thus do all women" – *così fan tutte* ♂. The notary – again Despina – reads out the marriage contract and, as the women sign, Don Alfonso announces their lovers' return. The "Albanians" vanish and reappear in their own guises. When they point to the marriage contracts, the women admit their guilt. When they then show off their "Albanian" disguises, the sisters beg forgiveness. Don Alfonso tells the couples to make up and all conclude that it is better to laugh than to weep.

"Il coro vi dono"

"Per pietà, ben mio, perdona"

"Tutti accusan le donne"

PERHAPS NOT SO FUNNY

Mozart's music is as magical as ever, but opera-lovers have long been disturbed by *Così fan tutte*'s cynical undertone. On one level, it offers an amusing new twist to a familiar story: this time, women, not men, are tempted to be unfaithful. But on another level, it presents a deeply jaded view of romantic love. For all its slapstick and humour, *Così fan tutte*'s temper is melancholic: unusually, an *opera buffa* ends without joy or laughter.

DIE ZAUBERFLÖTE
(The Magic Flute)

♫ Eine Deutsche Oper in two acts, 2½ hours
☙ 1791
♈ 30 September 1791, Freihaustheater auf der

Wieden, Vienna (Austria)
📖 Emanuel Schikaneder

Die Zauberflöte, Mozart's only opera written specifically for a popular audience, is as delightful as it is complex. It can be enjoyed as a fairy-tale, with its magic flute and bells, its animals, clown, and romantic couple. But it is also rife with symbols of Freemasonry and, as such, promotes virtue, love, and wisdom. It is best known for its catchy melodies, the most famous being the Queen of the Night's show-stopping arias, with their furious high F's. Mozart wrote this opera while composing *La clemenza di Tito* and much of his *Requiem*. They exhausted him. He died nine weeks after *Die Zauberflöte*'s premiere.

> ⚔ Wagner viewed *Die Zauberflöte* as the cornerstone of German opera, describing it as "a masterpiece of almost unsurpassable perfection, one which virtually ruled out further expansion of the genre". ⚔

✦ PRINCIPAL ROLES ✦

Sarastro *bass*
A mystic lord

Tamino *tenor*
A prince

Queen of the Night *soprano*
Pamina's fearsome mother

Pamina *soprano*
An imprisoned princess

Papageno *baritone*
A birdcatcher

Papagena *soprano*
His beloved

Monostatos *tenor*
A Moor in the service of Sarastro

Speaker of the Temple *bass*

Three Ladies *sopranos*

PLOT SYNOPSIS

Ancient Egypt, in and around Sarastro's castle

ACT ONE Three Ladies save Tamino from a serpent. Impressed by his beauty, they inform the Queen of the Night. Papageno is dreaming of trapping maidens in his bird net ♦

"Der Vogelfänger bin ich, ja"

FREEMASONRY

Mozart joined the Freemasons in 1784 and wrote several cantatas for their ceremonies. With *Die Zauberflöte*, he created a majestic operatic homage to the movement's ideals of wisdom, friendship, nature, and sacrifice. In the libretto, written by a fellow Mason, Emanuel Schikaneder, Sarastro's mystical sect represents a Masonic lodge and is guided by symbols and rituals of the brotherhood.

when he hears about the serpent. He claims to have strangled it, but the Ladies padlock his lips for lying. Tamino falls for a picture of Pamina, the queen's daughter. The queen tells him he can win Pamina if he rescues her from the monster Sarastro ♦. Tamino is given a magic flute, and Papageno, silver bells. At Sarastro's castle, the Moor Monostatos is enraged to be rebuffed by Pamina. Recognizing Pamina, Papageno reveals Tamino's passion for her. Together, Papageno and Pamina dream of finding love. Meanwhile, entering a temple, Tamino is ready to fight Sarastro. As voices tell him Pamina is alive, his flute-playing attracts friendly animals ♦. Papageno and Pamina are caught by Monostatos, but Papageno's bells set the Moor and slaves dancing. When Sarastro arrives in a chariot drawn by

"O zittre nicht, mein lieber Sohn!"

"Wie stark ist nicht Zauberton"

Stéphane Degout as Papageno and Claire Ormshaw as Papagena in a 2005 production at the Opéra Bastille, Paris, directed by Alex Olle and Carlos Padrissa and designed by the artist Jaume Plensa.

ignoring Tamino's orders to remain silent, an old hag offers him water. She gives her age as 18 years and two minutes, and names Papageno as her sweetheart. She then disappears. Tamino and Papageno are brought food and their magic flute and bells. As Papageno cheerfully digs into the feast, Tamino's flute summons Pamina, but she is heartbroken when he refuses to speak ♪. Papageno's only wish is for some wine and a "little wife". The old hag reappears to offer him marriage or eternal captivity. When he reluctantly accepts her, she turns into Papagena. But he is still unworthy of her. Ready to kill herself, Pamina learns that Tamino still loves her. They have yet to overcome various trials but, together, they triumph over flames and floods. In vain, Papageno plays his pipe to call Papagena, but when he rings his bells, she appears ♪. Monostatos joins forces with the Queen of the Night, but they vanish at sunrise. Finally, with Tamino and Pamina clothed in priestly gowns beside him, Sarastro gives thanks to Iris and Osiris for the reward of beauty and wisdom.

"Ach, ich fühl's"

"Pa, pa, pa... Papagena! Papageno!"

lions, Pamina complains about the brutish Moor, but Sarastro cannot allow her to return to her evil mother. Monostatos drags in Tamino and the lovers recognize each other. Sarastro decides to test Tamino and Pamina for membership of his brotherhood.

ACT TWO Tamino is ready to fight for friendship and love, although he is not allowed to speak to Pamina. The Queen of the Night reappears, telling Pamina to kill Sarastro with a dagger ♪. After the queen vanishes, Monostatos again tries to woo Pamina. With Papageno

"Der Hölle Rache kocht in meinem Herzen"

Italian Opera

H AVING LONG DOMINATED opera, Italian musicians again demonstrated their extraordinary inventiveness in the 19th century. While they faced new competition from Germanic, French, Russian, and Czech opera, they held their own thanks to the gifts of five composers. In quick succession, Rossini, Bellini, Donizetti, Verdi, and Puccini swept the world with their operas.

HOW IT BEGAN

Today, the very term "Italian opera" refers to these and a handful of other 19th-century composers. Yet this burst of creativity did not take place in a vacuum. From the mid-18th century, Italian composers like Niccolò Jommelli, Giovanni Paisiello, and Domenico Cimarosa took up posts in northern Europe, where they also absorbed non-Italian influences. Still more important were the "reforms" taking place in Vienna, where Christoph Willibald Gluck was putting music at the service of dramatic action. Then, soon afterwards, Mozart shattered the lines separating *opera seria* and *opera buffa*, and created stage characters who resembled real people.

Milan's Teatro alla Scala, which was inaugurated by Empress Maria Theresia of Austria in 1778, soon became Italy's leading opera house.

Most crucially, he introduced Germanic harmony and instrumentation to Italian opera and, as such, served as a musical bridge between Mozart and Gioacchino Rossini. But Rossini, who referred admiringly to him as "papa Mayr", is also the reason that he is forgotten. Rossini was only 21 when he burst onto the scene in Venice with *Tancredi* and *L'italiana in Algeri*, the first an *opera seria*, the second an *opera buffa*. Rossini wrote well in both styles throughout his life, although he is best remembered for *opera buffa*, notably

MOZART'S INFLUENCE

These changes were brought to Italy by a Bavarian-born admirer of Mozart and Haydn called Johann Simon Mayr. Unfairly, he is usually mentioned today only as Gaetano Donizetti's teacher yet, in his prime, he was Italy's most influential composer.

An 1834 La Scala poster for *Norma*, which is to this day Bellini's most popular opera.

Il barbiere di Siviglia and *La Cenerentola*. He was, above all, a writer of dazzling vocal parts: their melodies, range, coloratura, and speed, while difficult for singers, excited audiences as never before. This style became known as *bel canto*, or "beautiful singing". And, when Rossini moved to Paris in 1824, it would be his principal legacy.

Still, Rossini demonstrated another crucial talent – that of steering clear of politics in an era of national disarray. From 1796, when Napoleon invaded the Italian peninsula, the old ruling order began to crumble. Then, following Napoleon's defeat in 1815, Italy's traditional kingdoms and duchies reverted to conservative rule: Lombardy and Venetia became Austrian provinces; various duchies were assigned Habsburg princes; Naples and Sicily once again had a Bourbon king; and Rome remained under Papal rule. Political unrest was nonetheless permanent.

An early 19th-century painting by a French artist shows the stage and auditorium of Naples' Teatro di San Carlo, considered by many to be Italy's most elegant opera house.

WATCHED BY THE CENSOR

For the opera world, this meant that every new libretto required approval, with the authorities ever alert to anything minimally critical of the monarchy, the Roman Catholic Church, or foreign occupation. Vincenzo Bellini, who with *Il pirata* in 1827 was proclaimed Rossini's *bel canto* successor, escaped these problems by working with a wily and experienced Milanese librettist, Felice Romani. Bellini's best-known works, *I Capuleti e i Montecchi*, *La sonnambula*, and *Norma*, also avoided political or religious pitfalls. He had written ten operas when he died at 33 in 1835.

In contrast, Donizetti, who also embraced *bel canto*, wrote at least 75 operas. And after Bellini's death, with Rossini now retired in Paris, he was hailed the greatest Italian composer of his day, notably for *L'elisir d'amore* and *Lucia di Lammermoor*. Unlike Rossini and Bellini, however, Donizetti was plagued by censorship. He tried to avert trouble by setting historical operas in Protestant England, as with

Anna Bolena and *Roberto Devereux*. But *Maria Stuarda* was banned by the King of Naples in 1834 because its tragic heroine, Mary Queen of Scots, was Catholic. Then, four years later, his *Poliuto* was also banned in Naples. Tired of squabbling with censors, Donizetti decided to follow Rossini to Paris.

As in the 17th and 18th centuries, Naples and Venice remained important musical cities, while Rome, Florence, Genoa, Bologna, Turin, and Palermo all boasted popular opera houses. But by the 1830s, the Teatro alla Scala in Milan, the most prosperous Italian city, had become the ultimate Italian *palazzo* of opera. And just as Bellini and Donizetti won international recognition only after they triumphed at La Scala,

so it was with their inimitable successor, Giuseppe Verdi. His first opera, *Oberto*, was presented there in 1839; his last opera, *Falstaff*, also premiered at La Scala in 1893.

VERDI THE MAGNIFICENT

Verdi's popularity has been matched by no other Italian composer. He broke free from *bel canto* and took opera into a new orbit of music drama. Like other Italians, he had a natural talent for haunting melodies. But he also had a unique ability to create memorable characters who personified the universal themes of love, honour, power, greed, betrayal, and death. Unsurprisingly, all but two of his operas were tragedies, ranging from the poignancy of *La traviata* to the grandeur of *Don Carlos*.

During Northern Italy's struggle for independence from Austria, the slogan "Viva Verdi!", seen here written on the wall, was also used as a cry for freedom.

ITALIAN OPERA

1814	1829	1835	1853	1867
Napoleon's defeat and Habsburg occupation of much of Italy	Rossini's *Guillaume Tell* at the Paris Opéra	Donizetti's *Lucia di Lammermoor*	Verdi's *La traviata*	Verdi's *Don Carlos* at the Paris Opéra

1825	1850

1816	1831	1849	1861
Rossini's *Il barbiere di Siviglia*	Bellini's *Norma*. Abortive rebellions against foreign rule	Failed Italian uprising against Austrian occupation	Kingdom of Italy proclaimed

Verdi was also loved as a nationalist symbol, a status thrust upon him in 1842 after he wrote *Nabucco*, a story about the Jewish captivity in Babylon that appeared to mirror the plight of Italians under Austrian occupation. And after Nabucco, Verdi reinforced his identity with the "Risorgimento" movement – literally "Rising Again" – with works like *La battaglia di Legnano*, or *The Battle of Legnano*. Lombardy did in fact rise up in 1849, although the rebellion was crushed by Austria. Then, after the Kingdom of Italy was proclaimed in 1861, Verdi served briefly as a member of Parliament.

He still had energy left for several more great works, including the ever-popular *Aida* and his late masterpieces, *Otello* and *Falstaff*, but a new generation of opera composers was also emerging in the 1890s around a more realistic style known as *verismo*. Pietro Mascagni's *Cavalleria rusticana* and Ruggero Leoncavallo's *Pagliacci* are the truest examples of *verismo*, but the fashion was also briefly adopted by Giacomo Puccini, the only composer who could fairly claim to be Verdi's successor. Puccini wrote little, yet his works include some of the most popular operas ever written, notably *La bohème*, but also *Tosca*, *Madama Butterfly*, and *Turandot*.

Indeed, only with the premiere of *Turandot* in 1926, two years after Puccini's death, did Italian opera's great romantic cycle draw to a close and, with it, arguably the richest

period that opera has ever known. Then, from the 1920s, Vienna again transformed opera by introducing atonality. But this time Italian composers and audiences did not follow: to this day, for Italians, an opera that deserves the name is one with good tunes. And by that they inevitably mean a 19th-century opera written by one of their own greats.

BEL CANTO

Bel canto, literally "beautiful singing", was perfected in the early 19th century by Rossini, Bellini, and Donizetti. Characterized by rich melodies, it required performers to sing extended musical phrases and, with sopranos and tenors, to reach very high notes. The result was almost stereotypically operatic: melodrama expressed through stirring tunes and explosions of virtuosity. Then, in the time of Verdi and Wagner, *bel canto* was considered unfashionably simplistic and sentimental. But it had always given singers moments of glory. And from the 1950s, sopranos like Maria Callas, Joan Sutherland, and Montserrat Caballé demonstrated that *bel canto* could still thrill audiences.

The Australian soprano Joan Sutherland, seen here performing in Bellini's Il puritani, *played a key role in the 20th-century revival of* bel canto.

1876 Ponchielli's *La Gioconda*	1892 Leoncavallo's *Pagliacci*	1893 Verdi's *Falstaff*		1924 Death of Puccini	1926 Puccini's *Turandot*
1875		1900			1925
	1890 Mascagni's *Cavalleria rusticana*	1896 Puccini's *La bohème*. Giordano's *Andrea Chenier*	1901 Death of Verdi	1922 Mussolini named Prime Minister	

ROS

"Give me a laundry list and I will set it to music."

Gioacchino Rossini

GIOACCHINO
ROSSINI

Born: 29 February 1792, Pesaro (Italy)
Died: 13 November 1868, Paris, France

Gioacchino Rossini emerged in the early 19th century as the "saviour" of Italian opera. Best remembered for *Il barbiere di Siviglia*, his importance goes far beyond this charming and beloved comedy. He not only rejuvenated *opera buffa* and *opera seria*; with his love for the virtuoso vocal style known as *bel canto*, or "beautiful singing", he also returned the voice to the stage centre of Italian opera.

What most distinguishes Rossini is the sheer exuberance of his music. His deep admiration for Mozart – "my idol and my master", as he once put it – led some early critics to consider him "too German". But such reservations were soon swept away by his strong rhythms, richly coloured orchestration, catchy tunes, and florid arias: he sounded Italian. In all, Rossini wrote 35 operas over two decades, although only a few of his comedies are regularly produced today, notably *Il barbiere di Siviglia*, *L'italiana in Algeri*, *Il turco in Italia*, and *La Cenerentola*. Even so, he bequeathed a sound so recognizable that it is known simply as "Rossinian".

Like many great composers, Rossini was born into a family of musicians. From an early age, he was both a performer – pianist, cellist, and singer – and a composer. By the time he was 21, he had written ten operas, which were, in the main, comedies. Then, with *Tancredi*, he made his entrance into *opera seria*. Hailed as Italy's leading young composer, he was equally at ease with tragedy as with comedy. But he evidently relished *opera buffa*, creating his four most famous comedies in quick succession by the time he was 25. In great demand in Italy, with *bel canto* all the rage, he wrote for opera houses in Venice, Milan, Rome, and Naples. In 1815, Rossini became the artistic

Lucia Cirillo as Cenerentola's jealous stepsister, Tisbe, at the masked ball in Act II of *La Cenerentola*. This 2005 Glyndebourne Festival production was directed by Peter Hall and conducted by Vladimir Jurowski.

FIRST PERFORMANCES

1810
1810
La cambiale di matrimonio

1813
Tancredi
L'italiana in Algeri

1814
Il turco in Italia

1815
Elisabetta, regina d'Inghilterra

1816
Il barbiere di Siviglia
Otello

1817
La Cenerentola
La gazza ladra

1819
La donna del lago
Maometto II

1820

1822
Zelmira

1823
Semiramide

1824
Il viaggio a Reims

1829
Le Comte Ory
Guillaume Tell

1830

director of Naples's Teatro di San Carlo, managed by the talented and famously corrupt impresario, Domenico Barbaia. Although Naples was the cradle of *opera buffa*, its public now expected *opera seria*. And in the years that followed, Rossini created ten musical tragedies, starting with *Elisabetta, regina d'Inghilterra* and ending seven years later with *Zelmira*. Stimulating him were excellent soloists who could handle his coloratura arias, complex ensembles, fast tempos, high notes, and sudden crescendos. Indeed, he often wrote for their voices, not only for Spanish soprano Isabella Colbran, who became his first wife, but also for Giovanni Battista Velluti, the last operatic castrato. However, he did not allow improvised ornamentation: his soloists were expected to sing precisely what he had written.

Isabella Colbran (1785–1845), a Spanish soprano of note, married Rossini in 1822 and went on to sing the lead role in several of the composer's late operas.

his last. Still only 37, and already a legend, Rossini abandoned opera. His reason for doing so, though, is not known. He was certainly wealthy enough to retire. But with opera undergoing radical changes in France, Italy and Germany, he may also have simply concluded that the Rossini era was over.

AN EARLY RETIREMENT

In 1824, now renowned across Europe, Rossini moved to Paris, a city with a rich musical life sustained mainly by foreign composers. He became artistic director of the Théatre-Italien, where in 1825 he presented *Il viaggio a Reims*, his last Italian-language work. From then, he wrote to French-language librettos, climaxing in 1829 with *Guillaume Tell*, a massive four-act opera. It would be

A HAPPY LEGACY

But Rossini's comedies continued to work their charm. As the librettist Felice Romani noted in 1840: "They fill the coffers of all the impresarios in the peninsula, exhilarate the ponderous Germans, inflame the frigid Britons, and make even the pensive Quakers of Pennsylvania dance with joy." Almost two centuries after they were written, more or less the same can still be said of them today. Finally, in 1855, Rossini returned to Paris, where he held court as the music world's elder statesman. He died there at the age of 76 in 1868.

Rossini first made his name in Italy, but Paris became his second home. After his death in Paris on 13 November 1868, thousands of mourners accompanied his funeral cortège.

TANCREDI

❧

🎵 Melodramma eroico in two acts, 2¾ hours
⚎ 1812–1813 (rev. 1813)
🏛 6 February 1813, La Fenice, Venice (Italy)

📖 Gaetano Rossi, with Luigi Lechi, after Voltaire's play *Tancrède*

Written when he was still only 21, *Tancredi* was Rossini's first great opera. While this *opera seria* offers inventive orchestration and remarkable lyricism, its principal innovation is the so-called double aria, an aria which progresses from slow to fast and is repeated. For a new production in Ferrara in March 1813, Rossini replaced his happy ending with a tragic finale closer to Voltaire's original. Today, the Ferrara version is usually preferred.

◁ After this opera's Venice premiere, its best-known aria, *"Di tanti palpiti"*, became an overnight hit and was immediately adopted by the city's gondolieri. Today, it remains a favourite in tenor recitals. ▷

❧ PRINCIPAL ROLES ❧

Argirio *tenor*
Ruler of Syracuse and Amenaide's father

Tancredi *contralto*
An exiled noble

Orbazzano *bass*
Clan leader and Amenaide's suitor

Amenaide *soprano*
Tancredi's lover

Isaura *contralto*
Amenaide's attendant

PLOT SYNOPSIS

Syracuse, Sicily, in the early 11th century

ACT ONE Fearing a Saracen attack, Argirio, Syracuse's ruler, has made peace with his long-time opponent, Orbazzano, and has offered his daughter Amenaide in marriage. But Amenaide loves Tancredi, now in exile, and begs her father to delay her marriage. Argirio rebuffs her and orders the city's enemies, including Tancredi, to "Di tanti palpiti" be put to death. Tancredi appears in disguise ♂, but Amenaide urges him to flee. As crowds gather for the wedding, Orbazzano produces a love letter from Amenaide, purportedly addressed to the Saracen leader, Solamir. Amenaide is arrested and even Tancredi believes her guilty.

ACT TWO As Amenaide prepares to die, "No, che il morir non è" she hopes that Tancredi will one day learn the truth ♂. Suddenly, still in disguise, Tancredi steps forward as her champion and wins her freedom by killing Orbazzano. But he still

Agnieszka Wolska as Amenaide in a 2000 production at the Polish National Opera conducted by the renowned Rossini expert, Alberto Zedda.

thinks she has betrayed him.
VENICE ENDING Tancredi meets Solamir, who promises to spare Syracuse if he can marry Amenaide. Instead, Tancredi defeats the Saracens, and the dying Solamir asserts Amenaide's innocence. Tancredi begs her forgiveness and Argirio names him ruler of Syracuse.
FERRARA ENDING To prove his love for Amenaide, Tancredi leads the Syracusans against the Saracens, but is mortally wounded in battle. Persuaded by Argirio that Amenaide is innocent, Tancredi asks to marry her, then dies.

L'ITALIANA IN ALGERI
(The Italian Girl in Algiers)

✍ Dramma giocoso per musica in two acts, 2¼ hours

🎭 1813

♆ 22 May 1813, Teatro San Benedetto, Venice (Italy)

📖 Angelo Anelli, first set by Luigi Mosca

L'italiana in Algeri is Rossini's most farcical opera. Written in just 27 days, the young composer was forced to use an existing libretto, but he poured his talent into the music. The overture is one of Rossini's most popular, while the sparkling score is rich in testing coloratura arias as well as complex and humorous ensembles. The patriotic aria, *"Pensa alla patria"*, may also have contributed to the opera's success.

⊰ This *opera buffa* shamelessly exploited Europe's fascination with the exotic Orient, but this time with a feminist twist: usually a man is the hero, but here a woman rescues her lover from enslavement. ⊱

PLOT SYNOPSIS

In and around the Bey's palace in Algiers, Algeria

Ildar Abdrazakov as Mustafà appears to trap Daniela Barcellona's Isabella in a 2003 production of the opera at the Teatro dell'Opera in Rome, but in practice the clever and spirited Isabella constantly outsmarts her captor.

ACT ONE Bored with his wife Elvira, Mustafà the Bey decides to marry her off to his Italian slave Lindoro. Lindoro in turn yearns for Isabella, but Mustafà assures him that Elvira will serve him well. Meanwhile, Isabella, who is looking for Lindoro, is captured and sent to Mustafà's harem. The Bey is delighted by her, but she manipulates him with words of love. Seeing Lindoro about to embark for Italy with Elvira, she declares that Mustafà must keep Elvira, while Lindoro will become her slave. Mustafà objects, but Isabella overrules him.

ACT TWO Lindoro is able to persuade Isabella that he was fleeing only to be reunited with her and they agree to escape together. Aware that Mustafà is eavesdropping, Isabella muses aloud on how to please the man she loves ♪. Mustafà believes that she has made herself beautiful for him, but when he meets with Isabella, she annoyingly invites Elvira to join them. Isabella decides to honour Mustafà as her *Pappataci*, slang for a tamed husband. For this, he must eat, drink, and sleep. While she vows to free other Italian slaves and stirs their patriotism ♪, Lindoro plies the Bey with drink. When Mustafà finally realizes that the Italians are escaping, everyone is too drunk to stop them. Recognizing defeat, he turns to Elvira and begs her forgiveness, and bestows his blessing upon the departing lovers.

"Per lui che adoro"

"Pensa alla patria"

IL TURCO IN ITALIA
(The Turk in Italy)

✍ Dramma buffo per musica in two acts, 2¼ hours
🎵 1814
🏛 14 August 1814, La Scala, Milan (Italy)

📖 Felice Romani, after the libretto by Caterino Mazzola for Joseph Seydelman's 1788 opera

Before its premiere, *Il turco in Italia* seemed doomed because Milan's opera-goers suspected Rossini of taking much of the story and music from *L'italiana in Algeri*, the previous year's Oriental *divertimento*. In reality, the story is different and the music all original. The score offers Fiorilla some fine arias and feisty duets, but it relies heavily on ensembles to convey the plotting and misunderstandings that provide much of the comedy.

✦ Echoes of Mozart are not coincidental. Not only was *Così fan tutte* being staged in Milan when Rossini was writing *Il turco in Italia*, but both operas also borrowed from the same libretto. ✦

✦ PRINCIPAL ROLES ✦

Selim *bass*
A Turkish prince

Fiorilla *soprano*
Geronio's flighty wife

Geronio *bass*
Fiorilla's hapless husband

Narciso *tenor*
Fiorilla's former lover

Prosdocimo *bass*
A Poet in search of material

Zaida *soprano*
A Gypsy, Selim's former lover

PLOT SYNOPSIS

Naples, Italy

ACT ONE Preparing a comedy about Geronio's capricious wife, Fiorilla, Prosdocimo the Poet hears the Gypsy Zaida predict Geronio's misfortune. She reveals she was to marry a Turkish noble until he wrongly believed her unfaithful. The Poet says a visiting Turkish prince will intercede on her behalf. Fiorilla falls for the prince, angering her former lover, Narciso. Learning that the prince is called Selim Damelec, the Poet recognizes Zaida's beloved. When Selim and Fiorilla are interrupted by Geronio, they arrange to meet secretly. Instead, Zaida is reunited with Selim. Fiorilla discovers them and a fight erupts between "rivals in love" ♟.

"Ah! Che il cor non m'ingannava"

ACT TWO After Geronio refuses to sell Fiorilla, Selim decides to steal her.

Calling Zaida, Fiorilla tells Selim to pick between them. When he hesitates, Zaida storms out. But after Fiorilla also threatens to leave, Selim chooses her. Selim plans to abduct Fiorilla at a masked ball, but Fiorilla confuses Narciso for Selim, while Selim follows Zaida, thinking she is Fiorilla. Geronio is perplexed to see two Fiorillas and two Selims ♟. The Poet tells Geronio he can win back his wife by filing for divorce. When Fiorilla learns that she has lost Selim and that Geronio wants a divorce, she is remorseful. Finally Geronio forgives her and everyone agrees to forget mistakes born of love.

"Oh! Guardate che accidente"

Inga Kalna attends a masked ball as the flighty Fiorilla in the Hamburg Staatsoper's 2005 staging.

IL BARBIERE DI SIVIGLIA
(The Barber of Seville)

♫ Commedia in two acts, 2¾ hours
⚱ 1816
♇ 20 February 1816, Teatro Argentina, Rome

📖 Cesare Sterbini, after Beaumarchais's 1775 play and Giuseppe Petrosellini's libretto for Giovanni Paisiello's 1782 opera

Il barbiere di Siviglia is one of the greatest comic operas ever written. Composed in barely two weeks, it is a delightful romp packed with wonderful coloratura arias and ensembles, high speed "patter songs", splendid *buffo* characters, and successive laugh-aloud scenes. Like Mozart's great opera, *Le nozze di Figaro*, it was adapted from a Beaumarchais play with a strong and clever plot. Indeed, it demands virtuoso singers who are also exceptional comic actors. Nonetheless, its premiere was a flop because the young composer was thought arrogant for daring to tread the same path as Paisiello's ever-popular opera with the same name. Aware of the problem, Rossini initially called his opera *Almaviva, ossia L'inutile precauzione*. But after a few performances, his version caught on as *Il barbiere di Siviglia*, and its appeal has never faltered.

> **→ PRINCIPAL ROLES ←**
>
> **Count Almaviva** *tenor*
> Rosina's suitor
> **Dr Bartolo** *bass*
> Rosina's guardian and suitor
> **Rosina** *contralto* or *mezzo-soprano*
> Bartolo's ward
> **Figaro** *bass*
> A barber and rascal
> **Basilio** *bass*
> A music teacher

⇥ In his famous Barber's Song, *"Largo al factotum"*, with its "Figaro here, Figaro there, Figaro up, Figaro down," Figaro boasts of his multiple talents. ⇤

PLOT SYNOPSIS

Seville, Spain

ACT ONE Count Almaviva's musicians serenade the beautiful Rosina. Figaro the barber wanders by, singing his own praises ♫,

"Largo al factotum"

and informs the count that Rosina is the ward of Bartolo. Rosina drops a letter from her balcony asking her suitor's name and vowing to escape her guardian who wants to marry her for her money. Eager to be loved for himself, the count gives his name as "Lindoro". Figaro suggests he enter Bartolo's house disguised as a drunken soldier. While Rosina writes to "Lindoro" ♫, Basilio the music teacher warns Bartolo that her secret

"Una voce poco fa"

suitor is Count Almaviva. But Figaro tells Rosina that his cousin "Lindoro" is hopelessly in love with her and awaits a letter. She has one ready. Pretending to be drunk, the count says he has been billetted in Bartolo's house. As Bartolo protests, the "soldier" confides to Rosina

Roberto Frontali as Figaro tries to confuse Ildebrando D'Arcangelo's Bartolo while shaving him in a 1997 production at the Teatro dell'Opera in Rome.

Antonio Siragusa as Count Almaviva in Dario Fo's colourful production, which has toured Europe since 1987, is seen here at the Nederlandse Opera in 2006.

that he is "Lindoro". Summoned by Bartolo, an officer comes to arrest the "soldier", who quietly identifies himself as the count. No one else has much idea of what is going on .

> "Mi par d'esser colla testa"

ACT TWO The count reappears as "Don Alonso", replacing the ailing Basilio, and repeatedly blesses the house . He then reveals that, while visiting the count, he found a letter from Rosina. Bartolo pockets the letter and calls Rosina to her singing lesson. She recognizes "Lindoro" and, when Bartolo falls asleep, they plan to elope. Basilio arrives in good health, but "Alonso" bribes him to leave . As Figaro starts shaving Bartolo, "Lindoro" apologizes for using Rosina's letter, but Bartolo overhears him and sends him packing. Summoned by Bartolo, Basilio says he suspects "Alonso" is really the count. With that, Bartolo decides to marry Rosina immediately. He persuades Rosina that "Alonso" and Figaro intend to kidnap

> "Pace e gioia sia con voi"

> "Buona sera, mio signore"

her for Count Almaviva. Feeling betrayed by "Lindoro", she agrees to marry Bartolo. As "Alonso" and Figaro climb into the house, Rosina accuses them of treachery, saying she loves "Lindoro". But all is forgiven when "Alonso" reveals that he is the count . A notary arrives, believing that Figaro's niece will marry the count. By the time Bartolo returns with soldiers, he discovers the count and Rosina are married. Finally, after more commotion, Bartolo accepts his fate and joins with the company in a celebration of love.

> "Ah! Qual colpo inaspettato"

FIGARO

Figaro was to Beaumarchais what Falstaff was to Shakespeare, a character so mischievously appealing that, after Figaro appeared in *Le barbier de Seville* in 1775, the author revived him in *Le mariage de Figaro* in 1784 and in *La mère coupable* in 1792. Mozart adapted this second play as *Le nozze di Figaro*, leaving Rossini to tackle *Le barbier de Seville* 30 years later. Ironically, these two operas are now better known than the original plays.

LA CENERENTOLA

(Cinderella)

✍ Dramma giocoso in two acts, 2½ hours
⚓ 1816–1817
♇ 25 January 1817, Teatro Valle, Rome (Italy)

📖 Giacomo (Jacopo) Ferretti, after Charles Perrault's *Cendrillon*, and earlier librettos after the same tale

Inspired by the Cinderella fairy-tale, *La Cenerentola* – literally Cinderella – is Rossini's most popular opera after *Il barbiere di Siviglia*. Once again, the composer demands a contralto or mezzo-soprano able to handle extended coloratura passages. The title role also calls for lyricism, not least in the first love duet, while ensembles test other singers with their rapid patter and exquisite ornamentation. The opera includes the *buffo* Don Magnifico, but dark undertones suggest an *opera semi-seria*.

⚺ In Rossini's version of Cinderella, a bracelet replaces the glass slipper of the original tale, probably because it was considered improper for a woman's foot to be shown "naked" on stage. ⚺

> ✦ PRINCIPAL ROLES ✦
>
> Angiolina (La Cenerentola)
> *contralto* or *mezzo-soprano*
> Don Magnifico's step-daughter
>
> Don Ramiro *tenor*
> Prince of Salerno
>
> Dandini *bass*
> The prince's valet
>
> Don Magnifico *bass*
> A baron and La Cenerentola's step-father
>
> Clorinda *soprano* & Tisbe
> *mezzo-soprano*
> Don Magnifico's daughters

PLOT SYNOPSIS

Salerno (Italy)

ACT ONE Angiolina, known as Cenerentola, dreams of a king who chooses a wife for her innocence and goodness, ♪ but her half-sisters, Clorinda and Tisbe, mock her. When Alidoro, a philosopher disguised as a beggar, knocks at their door, the sisters abuse him, but Cenerentola offers him bread and coffee. Learning that Prince Ramiro has decided to pick a bride, the sisters order Cenerentola to prepare their gowns. Awakened from a siesta, Don Magnifico interprets a dream to mean his daughters will become queens. When told Ramiro is

"Una volta c'era un re"

to choose a bride, he believes that his dream will come true. Ramiro arrives disguised as his valet and sees Cenerentola. For both, it is love at first sight ♪. As Cenerentola explains her sad life, Ramiro is touched by her innocence. His valet, Dandini, then arrives disguised as the prince. As the sisters court him, Dandini inspects them with distaste. He then reveals that he risks losing his inheritance if he does not marry. Cenerentola begs

"Un soave non so che"

Jonathan Veira as Don Magnifico harasses Tuva Semmingsen's Cenerentola, at the Royal Danish Theatre in 2005.

Don Magnifico to take her to the palace, but instead he threatens to beat her 🖐. Alidoro invites Cenerentola to the ball and changes her rags for jewels. At the palace, Clorinda and Tisbe fight over Dandini in his role as the prince, but he warns Ramiro that they are vain and bad-tempered. Alidoro then introduces a mysterious veiled lady. When she shows her face, Don Magnifico notices that she resembles Cenerentola.

"Signora, una parola"

ACT TWO Although disturbed by the Cenerentola lookalike, Don Magnifico hopes one of his daughters will become powerful 🎵. Dandini, still disguised as the prince, declares his love for Cenerentola, but she says she loves his valet. When Ramiro "the valet" steps forward, Cenerentola gives him a bracelet and tells him to find the other. Don Magnifico urges Dandini to pick one of his daughters – until Dandini admits that he is only a valet. While Alidoro arranges for Ramiro's carriage to break down outside Cenerentola's home, she is back sweeping floors. She again dreams that a king will pick her, then remembers she prefers the prince's valet. Dandini announces that the

"Sia qualunque delle filglie"

ROSSINI'S CONTRALTOS

Rossini wrote Angiolina in *La Cenerentola* and Rosina in *Il barbiere di Siviglia* for his favourite voice, the contralto. Indeed, the roles are authentic gifts to a voice – now usually the mezzo-soprano – that all too often plays a supporting role to sopranos. Helping sustain the Rossini revival since the 1950s has been a succession of fine coloratura mezzo-sopranos who displayed a great feeling for comic opera, among them Giulietta Simionato, Teresa Berganza (*right*), and Cecilia Bartoli.

---

prince's carriage has overturned in a storm. As Ramiro enters, he sees a bracelet on Cenerentola's arm and declares his love. Don Magnifico and the sisters start insulting Cenerentola 🖐, who begs Ramiro to pardon them. Alidoro warns the sisters that they face misery if they do not seek Cenerentola's mercy. Finally, Don Magnifico kneels before Cenerentola and she also forgives the sisters. As everyone praises her goodness, she recalls her long years of heartache as nothing more than a dream 🎵.

"Siete voi?"

"Non più mesta accanto al fuoco"

LE COMTE ORY
(Count Ory)

🖎 Opéra comique in two acts, 2¼ hours
🕮 1828
⚓ 20 August 1828, Théâtre de l'Académie Royale

de Musique, Paris, France
📖 Eugène Scribe and CG Delestre-Poirson, after their 1816 play inspired by a medieval ballad

Le Comte Ory, Rossini's last comic opera, is distantly inspired by a medieval ballad in which knights end up seducing nuns. In the one-act play offered to Rossini by Eugène Scribe and Charles Gaspard Delestre-Poirson, however, a knight dresses as a nun to seduce a countess. Rossini then asked for a first act to be added. And thanks to its delightful arias, ensembles, and choruses, the opera was soon immensely popular.

⚜ Rossini took half the score of this opera from *Il viaggio a Reims*, written three years earlier. Shocked by the composer's uninhibited self-plagiarism, the embarrassed librettists removed their names from the work. ⚜

✧ PRINCIPAL ROLES ✧

Count Ory *tenor*
A rakish French noble

Adèle *soprano*
Countess of Formoutiers

Isolier *mezzo-soprano*
The count's page

Raimbaud *baritone*
The count's friend

The Tutor *bass*

Ragonde *mezzo-soprano*
A castle official

PLOT SYNOPSIS

Formoutiers, France, in the 12th century

ACT ONE With the lord and men of Formoutiers away on a crusade, Count Ory hopes to win the noble's sister, Adèle. Disguising himself as a hermit, he has his friend Raimbaud spread the word that he is an expert on matters of the heart. Unaware of Ory's ruse, the castle's page, Isolier, consults the "hermit" on his plan to seduce Adèle by entering the castle dressed as a pilgrim. When Adèle reveals her affection for the page, the "hermit" warns her off. The Tutor then unmasks him as Ory. As news arrives of the crusaders' return, Adèle invites Ory to the celebration, but he has other plans.

ACT TWO As the ladies await their knights, cries are heard from female pilgrims fleeing Ory's men. Given refuge in the castle, "Sister Colette" – Ory's new disguise – thanks Adèle for saving them, while other "pilgrims" discover the wine cellar and get drunk 🍷. Isolier recognizes Ory and tips off Adèle. In the darkness of her bedroom, she hides behind Isolier, whom Ory mistakes for the countess and embraces 🍷. Amid the confusion, trumpets sound the Crusaders' arrival and, still dressed as women, Ory and his men escape.

> "Buvons, buvons"

> "À la faveur de cette nuit obscure"

Colin Lee as Count Ory pretends to be a hermit in the guise of a hippie in Rupert Goold's modern production at Garsington Opera in 2005.

GUILLAUME TELL
(William Tell)

❖

⚐ Opera in four acts, 3¾ hours
🎵 1828–1829
♔ 3 August 1829, Théâtre de l'Académie Royale de

Musique, Paris, France
📖 Étienne de Jouy and Hippolyte Louis-Florent Bis, after Schiller's 1804 play *Wilhelm Tell*

Guillaume Tell, Rossini's final opera, was also his only attempt at French *grand opéra*, a style that would soon demand monumental spectacles. Rossini did not forgo lyricism, but he took up the new challenge, introducing declamatory recitatives, stripping arias of excessive "Italian" ornamentation, and emphasizing "patriotic" choruses. Designed to establish his French credentials, *Guillaume Tell* ended Rossini's career on a dramatic note.

⚕ With *Guillaume Tell*, Rossini was eager to demonstrate that he could write a serious political epic but, like its source, Schiller's play *Wilhelm Tell*, it takes many liberties with Switzerland's founding legend. ⚕

➔ PRINCIPAL ROLES ❖

Guillaume Tell *baritone*
A Swiss rebel hero

Arnold *tenor*
Melchthal's son

Mathilde *soprano*
An Austrian princess

Gesler *bass*
Austrian governor
of Switzerland

Melchthal *bass*
Patriarch of
the village

PLOT SYNOPSIS

Canton of Uri, Switzerland, in the early 14th century

ACT ONE During a village feast, Guillaume Tell broods over rebelling against the Austrian occupation. Melchthal, the village patriarch, urges his son Arnold to marry, but the young man loves Mathilde, an Austrian princess. Leuthold has killed an Austrian who tried to rape his daughter. As Tell rows Leuthold to safety, the Austrians seize Melchthal as a hostage.

ACT TWO Arnold and Mathilde are declaring their love for each other ♂ when Tell

"Oui, vous l'arrachez à mon âme"

brings word that the Austrian governor Gesler has murdered Melchthal. As Arnold vows to avenge his father's death, three cantons decide to rise up against the Austrians.

The Italian tenor Giacomo Lauri-Volpi (1892–1979), shown here as Arnold, was a virtuoso of *bel canto* but also mastered heavier dramatic roles of the Italian repertoire.

ACT THREE The Austrians order the Swiss to dance and bow before Gesler's hat. When Tell refuses, he is recognized as the man who helped Leuthold to escape. Gesler says Tell can save himself by shooting an apple off his son's head. But when Tell succeeds ♂, he is taken in chains to a castle in Lake Lucerne.

"Sois immobile"

ACT FOUR Arnold finds weapons hidden for the rebellion. As Tell's wife begs Gesler for mercy, Mathilde offers to take Tell's place. But when the boat carrying Tell is wrecked in a storm, he saves the crew and escapes. Arriving on shore, he kills Gesler with an arrow, while Arnold liberates the town. Everyone then gives thanks for a free Switzerland.

"The music drama must make people weep, shudder, die by means of singing."

Vincenzo Bellini

VINCENZO
BELLINI

Born: 3 November 1801, Catania, Sicily (Italy)
Died: 23 September 1835, Puteaux, near Paris, France

Vincenzo Bellini is the master of *bel canto*, the art of using "beautiful singing" to express high drama. In this, he both followed and improved on Rossini. He stripped arias and ensembles of florid embellishments and turned the voice into something resembling a laser of light cutting through darkness. He wanted to stir the emotions at the same time as pleasing the ear.

To achieve this, he worked slowly, writing only ten operas before his death at 33 – one-third as many as Rossini had composed by the same age. Still, between 1827 and 1835, "Bellini, the divine Bellini", in the words of one fellow composer, was the brightest star of Italian opera, acclaimed above all for his ability to match melody with powerful poetry. "I want something that is at the same time a prayer, an invocation, a threat, a delirium," he told Felice Romani, his principal librettist. His best-known aria, *"Casta diva"* from *Norma*, is all of those things.

Born in Sicily in 1801, Bellini learned music first from his father and grandfather and, by age 10, had already composed church music. At 18, he entered the Real Collegio di Musica in Naples, where Niccolò Zingarelli, an *opera seria* composer of note, shielded him from what he considered to be Rossini's corrupting avant-garde influence. In practice, Bellini looked up to Rossini as he did to Mozart. However, he did heed his old teacher's advice in one important way. "The public want melodies, melodies, always melodies," Zingarelli told him. Legend has it that, years later, while attending *Il pirata*, the opera that made Bellini's name, tears rolled down Zingarelli's face. Bellini's first break, though, came two years earlier in 1825 when he was the student chosen to compose an

<table>
FIRST
PERFORMANCES

1825 — **1825** Adelson e Salvini

1826 Bianca e Fernando

1827 Il pirata

1829 La straniera Zaira

1830 — **1830** I Capuleti e i Montecchi

1831 La sonnambula Norma

1833 Beatrice di Tenda

1835 —
</table>

The Russian soprano Galina Gorchakova takes on the title role of Norma, the most dramatic part in Bellini's repertoire, in a 2003 production at the San Diego Opera.

opera – *Adelson e Salvini* – for the Teatro di San Carlo in Naples. The San Carlo also presented his next, *Bianca e Fernando*, which led La Scala in Milan to commission *Il pirata* in 1827. The acclaim was immediate: Bellini was Rossini's heir! Critics noted that he had purified *bel canto* by simplifying melodies and orchestration to the point that their sole purpose was to convey emotion.

The San Carlo Theatre in Naples, Italy, where *bel canto* was born and where works by Rossini, Bellini, and Donizetti premiered.

GREATNESS BECKONS

Il pirata was especially important for Bellini because it established his relationship with Romani, the admired theatre-poet who also wrote librettos for both Rossini and Donizetti. They followed with *La straniera*, well received at La Scala, and *Zaira*, which flopped when it inaugurated Parma's new opera house. Then, in a burst of creativity, they created Bellini's three most popular operas, *I Capuleti e i Montecchi*, *La sonnambula*, and the monumental *Norma*, which was arguably the high-point of the *bel canto* tradition. In their dramatic intensity, these works pointed the way for Verdi and Puccini.

A PREMATURE DEATH

But in early 1833 Bellini fell out with his librettist over *Beatrice di Tenda*. And with the unravelling of an illicit love affair, Bellini fled to London to oversee the premiere of *Norma*. He then went to Paris, where Rossini arranged for the Théâtre-Italien to present his only Paris opera, *I puritani*. Its January 1835 premiere was a success, but Bellini was unhappy with the libretto and, more than ever, missed working with Romani. Hopes for a reconciliation grew when La Scala asked Bellini for a new opera for Italy's reigning diva, Maria Malibran. He hurriedly adapted *I puritani* to her mezzo-soprano voice, but the score was completed too late for the new season and was not performed until 1985. In the summer of 1835, while planning his return to Italy, Bellini fell ill with acute gastroenteritis and died in Puteaux, outside Paris, on 23 September 1835. A brilliant life had been tragically cut short.

IL PIRATA
(The Pirate)

✍ Melodramma (opera seria) in two acts, 2½ hours
⌛ 1827
⚐ 27 October 1827, La Scala, Milan (Italy)

📖 Felice Romani, inspired by the 1816 play
Bertram, or The Castle of Saint Aldobrand by
Charles Robert Maturin

Il pirata, Bellini's first collaboration with Felice Romani, was also his first international success, performed across Europe within five years of its premiere. Audiences were surprised by the simplicity of its melodic line, immediately distinguishable from Rossini's coloratura-packed scores. While *Il pirata* has dramatic tenor and baritone roles, its tragic tone is set by Imogene's soaring soprano arias and chilling "mad scene" at the end.

⌇ For a little-known composer, still only 26, Bellini was remarkably well paid for *Il pirata*, and he subsequently made a point of always demanding higher fees than his contemporaries for his operas. ⌇

> ✦ **PRINCIPAL ROLES** ✦
>
> **Ernesto** *bass*
> Duke of Caldora
>
> **Imogene** *soprano*
> Ernesto's wife and
> Gualtiero's former
> lover
>
> **Gualtiero** *tenor*
> Former Count of Montalto,
> now a pirate
>
> **Goffredo (Solitario)** *bass*
> A hermit and Gualtiero's
> former tutor

PLOT SYNOPSIS

Sicily in the 13th century

ACT ONE Among shipwreck survivors is Gualtiero, who became a pirate after being banished. When his former tutor welcomes him on shore, he asks for his beloved Imogene. She arrives to help the sailors and learns that the pirates were defeated. She reveals she dreamed that her lover had died ♫. From afar, Gualtiero recognizes her. When they meet outside the castle, she falls into his arms. But he feels betrayed when she confesses that she married his enemy, Ernesto, to save her father's life. She persuades Ernesto to free the sailors. Gualtiero asks her to meet him abroad, but she urges him to leave and faints.

"Quando a un tratto il mio consorte"

ACT TWO Noting Imogene's gloom, Ernesto accuses her of still loving Gualtiero. Imogene says her love for the pirate was no secret when she married Ernesto, but she now loves Gualtiero as someone "dead and buried". Ernesto learns that Gualtiero has landed and orders his capture. Imogene begs Gualtiero to escape, but Ernesto discovers them. The two men fight a duel and Ernesto is killed. After Gualtiero surrenders, saying he is ready to die, Imogene appears, weeping and delirious ♫. As the council condemns Gualtiero, Imogene imagines his scaffold and, totally deranged, expires.

"Oh! s'io potessi dissipar le nubi"

At the 2002 Metropolitan Opera premiere of *Il pirata*, Renée Fleming played Imogene. The production was mounted at her request.

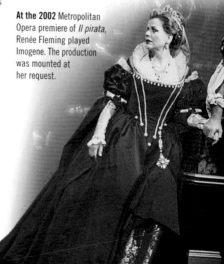

I CAPULETI E I MONTECCHI

(The Capulets and the Montagues)

🎭 Tragedia lirica in two acts, 2¼ hours
🎵 1830
🏛 11 March 1830, La Fenice, Venice

📖 Felice Romani, after a 16th-century novella by Matteo Bandello and an 1818 play by Luigi Scola

I Capuleti e i Montecchi recounts the familiar story of Romeo and Juliet, but uses original Italian Renaissance sources and eliminates many of the characters who appear in Shakespeare's play. As befits a tragic love story, it is a powerfully lyrical work, with Bellini giving the role of Romeo to a mezzo-soprano. Adding drama, the yearning arias by Romeo and Giulietta contrast with the stormy confrontations of the warring clans.

⚐ Bellini was so angered by *Zaira*'s poor reception in Parma one year earlier that he adapted eight movements from that opera to be used in the different story of *I Capuleti e i Montecchi*. ⚐

⟡ PRINCIPAL ROLES ⟡

Capellio *bass*
Head of Capuleti clan

Giulietta *soprano*
Capellio's daughter

Romeo *mezzo-soprano*
Head of the Montecchi clan and Giulietta's lover

Tebaldo *tenor*
Giulietta's husband-to-be

Lorenzo *baritone*
Capellio's adviser and Romeo's friend

PLOT SYNOPSIS

Verona, Italy, in the 13th century

ACT ONE In the Capuleti's palace, Capellio ignores calls for peace from Lorenzo and vows to kill Romeo, the Montecchi leader. Romeo arrives disguised as a Montecchi envoy and proposes reconciliation through Romeo's marriage to Capellio's daughter, Giulietta. When Capellio announces that she will marry Tebaldo, Romeo prepares for combat. Giulietta

Denis Krief's production for the 2005 Festival della valle d'Itria sets the opera in the immediate post-war period to emphasize the group conflict of the title.

is resigned to her fate, but Romeo arrives with Lorenzo and begs her to flee with him 🔊. Unwilling

"Si fuggiere: non noi non resta"

to dishonour her family, she refuses. With Giulietta's marriage about to take place, Romeo comes dressed as a

"Soccorso, sostengo accordagli"

Capulet. As he pleads with his beloved, he is unmasked 🔊 and a fight erupts between the clans.

ACT TWO Assuring Giulietta that Romeo has escaped, Lorenzo proposes she drink a potion that will make her appear dead. Once in the Capuleti's

tomb, he says, Romeo will awaken her. As Capellio arrives, she drinks the potion and begs his forgiveness. When Romeo receives no word from his beloved, he approaches the Capuleti's palace, where he meets Tebaldo. As they duel, they hear a choir lamenting Giulietta's death. Romeo enters the tomb and, seeing Giulietta's inert body, takes poison. Waking, she is horrified to see her dying lover and kills herself. As their bodies are found, the two clans blame one another.

LA SONNAMBULA

(The Sleepwalker)

🎵 Melodramma in two acts, 3 hours
📅 1831
🎭 6 March 1831, Teatro Carcano, Milan (Italy)

📖 Felice Romani, after Eugène Scribe's scenario for the ballet *La somnambule, ou L'arrivée d'un nouveau seigneur*

La sonnambula is a charming pastoral idyll, with a succession of sweet arias and duets compensating for its lack of dramatic punch. The plot is built around unwarranted jealousy: the heroine climbs into the wrong bed while sleepwalking. As the misunderstandings are being cleared up, Bellini offers his most lyrical score to date, so melodic that some critics considered it too lush. Several arias are firm favourites in soprano recitals.

Such was Bellini's perfectionism that he asked his librettist, Felice Romani, to rewrite Amina's final aria, *"Ah! non giunge uman pensiero"*, no fewer than ten times before he was satisfied.

✦ PRINCIPAL ROLES ✦

Amina *soprano*
A peasant girl who sleepwalks

Elvino *tenor*
Amina's betrothed

Count Rodolfo *bass*
A benign feudal lord

Teresa *mezzo-soprano*
Amina's foster mother

Lisa *soprano*
Owner of the inn

Alessio *bass*
Lisa's suitor

PLOT SYNOPSIS

A Swiss village

ACT ONE Amina, an orphan raised by Teresa, is to marry Elvino. She thanks Teresa for her care and dreams of love 🎵. After the marriage contract is signed and rings exchanged, a handsome stranger arrives and, to Elvino's annoyance, flirts with Amina. Teresa sends everyone home, warning them of the village ghost. In the inn, Lisa takes a fancy to the stranger, whom she recognizes as Count Rodolfo. Suddenly, Amina enters his room through a window and Lisa hurries away, leaving a handkerchief. Rodolfo realizes Amina is sleepwalking and leaves her asleep on his bed. Shown the sleeping Amina, Elvino angrily cancels his wedding.

"Come per me sereno"

ACT TWO Convinced that he has been betrayed, Elvino snatches his ring from Amina's finger. Lisa persuades Elvino to marry her, but Rodolfo swears to Amina's innocence. Meanwhile, Teresa asks for silence as Amina is asleep. She displays Lisa's handkerchief, which she found in Rodolfo's room. Elvino now believes Lisa has also betrayed him. Amina appears in her nightdress and, asleep, walks towards a fragile bridge. As the villagers pray for her safety, she crosses the bridge and, kneeling, prays for Elvino. Realizing his error, Elvino places his ring again on her finger. When she awakens, she is surrounded by joy and, forgiving Elvino, is led to the altar 🎵.

"Ah! non giunge uman pensiero"

The Russian soprano Elena Kelessidi as the ever-sleeping Amina at the Royal Opera House in 2002.

NORMA

⚐ Tragedia lirica in two acts, 2¾ hours   📖 Felice Romani, after Alexandre Soumet's 1831
🎭 1831   verse tragedy *Norma*
♇ 26 December 1831, La Scala, Milan (Italy)

In *Norma*, Bellini's finest and most popular opera, the music reinforces the drama to create a deeply moving work. Felice Romani's libretto is stirring, but it is the score that lifts the work to greatness. Surprisingly simple orchestration sustains long and complex ensembles as well as richly melodic arias, notably the spine-tingling *"Casta diva"*, or "Chaste goddess". The role of Norma is particularly testing, requiring a coloratura soprano with a voice of immense power, range, stamina, and virtuosity along with a talent for conveying tragedy on stage. As it happens, the premiere of *Norma* was sabotaged by friends of a rival composer, Giacomo Pacini, prompting Bellini to describe the occasion as "a fiasco, a total fiasco". But within a few years, the opera had conquered Europe and the United States.

> ✦ PRINCIPAL ROLES ✦
>
> **Pollione** *tenor*
> Roman pro-consul and father
> of Norma's children
>
> **Oroveso** *bass*
> Archdruid and
> Norma's father
>
> **Norma** *soprano*
> Druid high priestess
>
> **Adalgisa** *soprano*
> Druid priestess
>
> **Clotilde** *soprano*
> Norma's attendant
>
> **Flavio** *tenor*
> A centurion
>
> **Two children of Norma**
> **and Pollione** *silent*

⚜ Wagner never hid his distaste for most Italian opera, but he made an exception for *Norma*. After hearing Bellini's masterpiece, he said: "We must not be ashamed to shed a tear and express emotion." ⚜

PLOT SYNOPSIS

Roman-occupied Gaul around 50 BCE

ACT ONE In a sacred forest, Archdruid Oroveso and his followers hope the high priestess Norma will lead a revolt against the Roman occupiers. Nearby, the Roman pro-consul Pollione, the father of Norma's two secret children, reveals he loves another priestess, Adalgisa. But he fears Norma's wrath. Expecting an uprising, he hears Norma proclaim that the Gods alone will decide the moment. The Druids obey her as a chaste Goddess 🔊, while she yearns to recover Pollione's love. As

"Casta diva"

the Druids disperse, Adalgisa feels guilty for betraying her vows of chastity. When Pollione reiterates his love for her, she rejects him 🔊. He invites her to Rome and she first refuses, then yields. In her home, Norma is torn between love and hate for her children. Adalgisa arrives to confess she has fallen in love with someone. Norma sympathizes, having herself broken

"Va crudele,
al Dio
spietato"

The Spanish soprano
Montserrat Caballé played a part in the revival of *bel canto*, with Norma one of her preferred roles.

her vow of chastity. But as Adalgisa describes how she was won, Norma recalls Pollione using the same words. Norma asks the name of her lover and, as Pollione approaches, Adalgisa points to him. Turning on Pollione in fury, Norma tells Adalgisa she has been deceived . Adalgisa suddenly realizes that she has taken Norma's lover and decides she must reject him.

"Oh di qual sei tu vittima"

ACT TWO Watching over her sleeping children, Norma imagines they might be better dead, but she draws back from killing them. Summoning Adalgisa, she demands obedience. She then discloses her decision to die and tells Adalgisa to care for her children in Rome. But Adalgisa refuses to leave Gaul and vows to reawaken Pollione's love for Norma. In the sacred forest, Oroveso tells the Druid warriors that a commander worse than Pollione is coming, but that Norma wants her army to disband. Oroveso urges the warriors to hide their hatred until it can explode. Learning Pollione has sworn to abduct Adalgisa, Norma summons her warriors to battle. As they sing to their victory, a Roman is found violating the sacred cloister of the virgins and is captured. When Pollione is brought in, Norma ignores cries to kill him and orders him to leave without Adalgisa and never to return. Pollione prefers to die, but Norma decides Adalgisa will be sacrificed in his stead. Pollione pleads for Adalgisa's life and asks for Norma's dagger to kill himself. Norma then says a different victim will be sacrificed. "Speak then, and name her!" the Druids cry out. As the pyre is prepared, Norma

"Mira, o Norma"

"In mia man"

MARIA CALLAS AS NORMA

Of the many *bel canto* heroines revived by Maria Callas, none matched her powerful voice and fragile personality more perfectly than Norma. As her own life became more tragic, she embraced the role with ever greater passion. "In a lifetime, one can see many great things in the theatre," Mirto Picchi, her first Pollione, recalled, "but to see Maria Callas in *Norma*, what is there to compare to it? As Norma, Maria created the maximum of what opera can be."

Maria Callas as Norma, her most performed role, at the Paris Opéra in 1964.

then reveals that she is the traitress who must die. Suddenly remorseful, Pollione now wants to die with her. The Druids are shocked to learn of Norma's unchaste relationship with a Roman, but Norma begs her father to protect her children. As the Druids call for her sacrifice, Pollione steps forward to die with her. Together, they ascend the pyre.

"Qual cor tradisti"

"I want love, violent love, because without it subjects are cold."

Gaetano Donizetti

GAETANO
DONIZETTI

Born: 29 November 1797, Bergamo (Italy)
Died: 8 April 1848, Bergamo (Italy)

Gaetano Donizetti is in many ways the overlooked master of early Italian Romantic opera. Even today, long after the post-1950s' revival of the florid style known as *bel canto*, or "beautiful singing", only a half-dozen of his 75 or so operas are regularly performed. Yet for more than a decade from 1830, this modest and gregarious melody-maker was the dominant Italian composer of his day.

Although Donizetti stands in the shadow of Rossini and Verdi, he in fact served as a bridge between these two opera giants: like Rossini, he believed in *bel canto*; and like Verdi, he believed that music should reinforce the drama. But he was an innovator too: he eliminated Rossini's excesses – crescendos, double-arias, and the finale aria – and rejected the traditional separation between recitatives and arias, moving towards continuous music. Most of all, he was a hard-working craftsman who wrote splendid tunes.

Born into a poor family, he was given free music tuition by Simon Mayr, a Bavarian-born priest who was music director at Bergamo's main church as well as an accomplished opera composer. Donizetti then gained entry to Bologna's music academy, where he wrote mainly sacred music. But he was drawn to opera, not least because, as a hard-up young composer, he found that 19th-century Italy had an almost insatiable demand for opera. Adept in both *opera seria* and *opera buffa*, over a 12-year period he wrote 31 works, mostly for Naples. Finally, in 1830, he was commissioned to write a *tragedia lirica* for La Scala in Milan. The success of *Anna Bolena* made him a household name, even beyond Italy. Then, 18 months – and four operas – later, he was again acclaimed in Milan, this time for *L'elisir d'amore*, one of his most popular works. Like

FIRST PERFORMANCES

1820

1822
Zoraida di Granata

1825

1830 — **1830**
Anna Bolena

1832
L'elisir d'amore
1833
Lucrezia Borgia
1834
Maria Stuarda
1835 — **1835**
Lucia di Lammermoor

1837
Roberto Devereux

1840 — **1840**
La fille du régiment
La favorite

1843
Don Pasquale
Dom Sébastien
1845 —

Ann Murray plays Mary Queen of Scots in a 1998 English National Opera production of *Maria Stuarda*, one of several operas that Donizetti set in Britain.

Anna Bolena, it benefited from a libretto by Felice Romani, a theatre poet who also wrote for Rossini and Bellini. Working at an extraordinary pace, Donizetti wrote four more operas before La Scala applauded him for *Lucrezia Borgia* in 1833.

STRUGGLES WITH CENSORS

Donizetti often set operas in Protestant Britain in the hope of appeasing Catholic censors. But *Maria Stuarda* was nonetheless banned in Naples in 1834 because of its underlying Protestant-versus-Catholic theme. He re-used some of its score for an opera called *Buondelmonte* and finally presented *Maria Stuarda* at La Scala in 1835. But it was again in Naples, that same year, that he created his most memorable tragedy, *Lucia di Lammermoor*. Donizetti's own life was also marked by tragedy: his wife died in 1837 at the age of 29 after giving birth to their third still-born child. His response to her death was an intense tragedy set in Britain, *Roberto Devereux*,

Virginia Vasselli, Donizetti's wife, died at 29 while giving birth to their third still-born child.

a fictional account of Elizabeth I's love for the Earl of Essex. But the next year, after *Poliuto* was banned in Naples, he moved to Paris where, with Rossini retired and Bellini dead, he had no Italian competitor.

TRIUMPH IN FRANCE

From this period, three operas stand out: *La fille du régiment*, *La favorite*, and *Don Pasquale*, all originally performed in French. But by 1843, when he created his final work, *Dom Sébastien*, a five-act grand opera, the syphilis he had contracted years earlier was rapidly undermining his physical and mental health. A man known for his patience and charm suddenly grew irascible. And worse was to follow. In 1846, he was interned in a private asylum. Finally, his family took him home to Bergamo where, now totally insane, he died in 1848.

The tiny figure of Donizetti emerges from a mental asylum at Ivry, outside Paris, where he spent his final years before being repatriated to Italy to die.

ANNA BOLENA
(Anne Boleyn)

⚄ Tragedia lirica in two acts, 3¼ hours
⌛ 1830
♇ 26 December 1830, Teatro Carcano, Milan (Italy)

📖 Felice Romani, after the plays *Henri VIII* by Marie-Joseph Chénier and *Anna Bolena* by Alessandro Pepoli

Anna Bolena, Donizetti's 30th opera, was his first great triumph and his passport to international fame. While this rendering of Anne Boleyn's execution is historically unreliable, the opera is above all a feast of *bel canto*: it has glorious soprano and tenor arias, a poignant duet between the ill-fated queen and her chosen successor, and masterful finales to both acts. Nonetheless, due to its length, it is usually performed with significant cuts.

⚏ Giuditta Pasta was the diva who made *Anna Bolena* famous. It would take another diva, Maria Callas, to revive this long-forgotten opera in a memorable production at La Scala, Milan, in 1957. ⚏

✧ PRINCIPAL ROLES ✦

Enrico VIII *bass*
King Henry VIII

Anna Bolena *soprano*
The king's second wife

Giovanna Seymour *mezzo-soprano*
The king's third wife

Smeton *mezzo-soprano*
A court musician

Percy *tenor*
Anna's former lover

PLOT SYNOPSIS

Windsor and London, England, in 1536

ACT ONE At Windsor, Giovanna Seymour feels guilty about her love affair with the king. Anna Bolena asks Smeton, her musician, for a song, but it reminds her of her first love, Percy. When Giovanna tells the king she feels shame, he says they will soon be married. He has recalled Percy from exile, intent on proving he is still Anna's lover. Smeton, who adores the queen, overhears her telling Percy the king hates her. When Percy declares his love, she orders him to leave. He tries to stab himself, but Smeton stops him. As Anna faints, the king enters. When Smeton's miniature of Anna falls to the ground, the king has proof of her betrayal and orders her arrest ⚰.

"In quegli sguardi impresso"

ACT TWO In the Tower of London, after urging Anna to admit her guilt, Giovanna confesses she will become the new queen. Horrified, Anna curses her, then pardons her, blaming only the king. To save her life, Smeton "confesses" to adultery with Anna, but the king instead uses it against her. Percy declares that, once married to Anna, he now reclaims her. Stunned, the king dismisses Giovanna's plea for mercy. Awaiting death, Anna recalls her first love ⚰. Then, as a cannon announces the king's marriage, she is led to the scaffold.

"Al dolce guidami"

Darina Takova as Anna Bolena and José Bros as her former lover Percy at the Teatro Regio in Turin, 2005.

L'ELISIR D'AMORE

(The Love Potion)

⚜ Opera comica in two acts, 2 hours
🕮 1832
♛ 12 May 1832, Teatro Canobbiana, Milan

📖 Felice Romani after Eugène Scribe's text for Auber's opera *Le philtre*, itself after Silvio Malaperta's play, *Il filtro*

L'elisir d'amore has long been one of Donizetti's most popular operas, memorable above all for its almost uninterrupted flow of enchanting melodies. Classified as an *opera buffa*, it boasts the required *buffo* character in the quack Dulcamara, who entertains with a typical "patter song", squeezing the greatest number of words into the shortest possible time. But *L'elisir d'amore*'s story also invites lyricism as Nemorino resorts to magic – an elixir of love – in the hope of winning over Adina, the rich and fickle object of his passion. With the score bringing rich colours to the narrative, Nemorino's pining tenor arias and Adina's mischievous coloratura soprano arias pave the way to the couple's happiness. The story had been told just one year earlier, in Paris, in Auber's opera, *Le philtre*. But only Donizetti's version is now remembered.

> ✥ PRINCIPAL ROLES ✥
>
> **Adina** *soprano*
> A rich young landowner
>
> **Nemorino** *tenor*
> A farmer in love with Adina
>
> **Sergeant Belcore** *baritone*
> A visiting soldier
>
> **Dr Dulcamara** *buffo*
> A charlatan doctor
>
> **Giannetta** *soprano*
> A village girl

⚔ In December 1920, Enrico Caruso coughed up blood while singing the role of Nemorino in New York. Despite appeals from the audience, he finished the performance, but he died nine months later. ⚕

PLOT SYNOPSIS

A Basque village in the 19th century

ACT ONE As Adina reads the story of Tristan and Isolde, Nemorino recognizes the impossibility of his love for such a wonderful woman ♣. Suddenly bursting into laughter, Adina reads out to the harvesters on her farm how Isolde conquered Tristan with a love potion. Sgt Belcore arrives with his platoon and, struck by Adina's beauty, promptly proposes to her, suggesting they marry immediately. But Adina is in no hurry and, when Nemorino finally tells her of his love, she declares she is as fickle as the wind and urges him to find another woman ♣.
A trumpet announces the arrival of Dr Dulcamara, a travelling quack, who boasts he can cure every ill. Nemorino discloses that he is love-struck and asks the charlatan about Isolde's love potion.

"Quanto è bella, quanto è cara"

"Chiedi all' aura lusinghiera"

Claiming he has just the trick, Dulcamara gives the naive young man a bottle of cheap red wine, assuring him it will work within 24 hours. Nemorino drains the bottle and is soon tipsy. Meanwhile, when Belcore renews his proposal, Adina agrees to marry him in a week. Belcore then receives orders to leave town. Adina, puzzled by Nemorino's apparent indifference ♣, moves her wedding to the following day. As Belcore and Adina visit the notary, Nemorino sobers up and goes in search of Dulcamara.

"Esulti pur la barbara"

Donizetti observes the antics of the potion-seller Dulcamara at a rehearsal of his opera *L'elisir d'amore*.

died and left him a fortune. When the young farmer returns, his spirits lifted by more wine, the village girls surround him excitedly. And since he knows nothing about his bequest, he believes the potion is at last working. Dulcamara explains Nemorino's odd behaviour to Adina

ACT TWO The wedding party is in full swing, although Adina has not yet signed the marriage contract. She joins Dulcamara in a popular Venetian song about a girl who chooses to marry a poor gondolier rather than a rich senator. As the notary arrives to formalize the marriage, Nemorino needs money to buy more love potion. Seeing no alternative, he enlists, collects a payment from Belcore and goes looking for Dulcamara. A village girl announces that Nemorino's uncle has

and, realizing she loves the young man, he offers her some wine. She responds that she has no need for a magic potion ♘. Seeing a tell-tale tear in Adina's eye, Nemorino now realizes that she loves him ♘. Adina then also confesses her love to him, telling Nemorino that she has purchased his freedom from the army. With Belcore resigned to losing Adina, Dulcamara points to Nemorino's good fortune as proof that his potion brings wealth as well as love. He then sells the remainder of his stock of cheap wine to the crowd and rides away.

"Quanto amore!"

"Una furtiva lagrima"

Bruno Pola as the charlatan Dr Dulcamara hawks his love potion at the Royal Opera House in 1997.

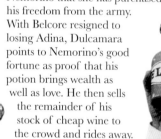

LUCIA DI LAMMERMOOR

(Lucy of Lamermoor)

🖎 Dramma tragico in three acts, 2½ hours
⏳ 1835 (rev. in French 1839)
♇ 26 September 1835, Teatro di San Carlo,

Naples (Italy)
📖 Salvatore Cammarano, after *The Bride of Lammermoor* by Sir Walter Scott

Lucia di Lammermoor has long been Donizetti's most popular work. It represents the climax of Italian Romantic opera and features in two great Romantic novels, Flaubert's *Madame Bovary* and Tolstoy's *Anna Karenina*. A poignant story of family feuds crushing love and life, it also inevitably recalls *Romeo and Juliet*. Best known for Lucia's "mad scene" in Act III, it is packed with other haunting melodies. Lucia and her lover, Edgardo, have stirring arias, as well as a touching duet. The richly woven sextet that ends Act II, with each voice expressing a different emotion, is considered one of the finest ensembles in the opera canon.

✣ PRINCIPAL ROLES ✣

Lucia di Lammermoor *soprano*
Edgardo Ravenswood *tenor*
Lucia's beloved
Enrico Ashton *baritone*
Lucia's brother
Raimondo *bass*
The chaplain
Arturo *tenor*
Lucia's husband
Alisa *mezzo-soprano*
Lucia's confidante

✣ During the Austrian occupation, an 1837 production in Parma was disrupted by police when the female chorus wore white dresses with green and red ribbons, colours representing Italy's independence movement. ✣

PLOT SYNOPSIS

In and around Lammermoor Castle, Scotland, in 1669

ACT ONE Enrico Ashton is lamenting his misfortunes and the delight they must give his mortal enemy, Edgardo Ravenswood. He concludes that the only solution is for his sister, Lucia, to marry into money. Raimondo, the chaplain, says she is too sad over her mother's death to wed, but Normanno, Enrico's friend, says she is already aflame with love. He has witnessed her secret meetings with a man believed to be Edgardo Ravenswood. Enrico is wild with anger. In the castle gardens, Lucia recalls

"Regnava nel silenzio" | "seeing" the stabbing of the lover of an earlier Ravenswood 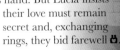. Lucia's

friend, Alisa, begs her to abandon this dangerous love, but she cannot. Edgardo brings word that he must leave for France to seek allies for Scotland and will first ask for Lucia's hand. But Lucia insists

"Ah! Verrano a te sull'aure" | their love must remain secret and, exchanging rings, they bid farewell 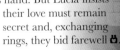.

SIR WALTER SCOTT

Personifying Gothic Romanticism, Sir Walter Scott was enormously popular in 19th-century Europe, with 16 of his novels adapted as operas. Although the best known, Donizetti's *Lucia di Lammermoor* was only one of six operatic versions of *The Bride of Lammermoor*. Bellini's last opera, *I puritani*, was inspired by *Old Mortality*; Rossini turned *The Lady of the Lake* into *La donna del lago*; and Bizet's opera, *La jolie fille de Perth*, is based entirely on *The Fair Maid of Perth*.

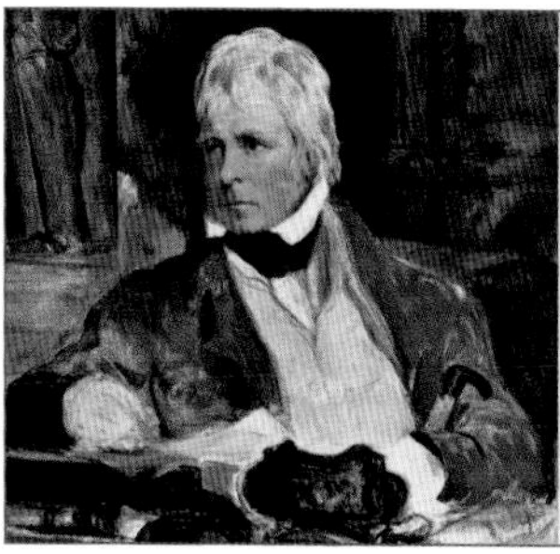

ACT TWO With Enrico nervously awaiting Lucia, Normanno boasts that he has forged a letter from Edgardo to another woman. Lucia arrives looking sad and Enrico tells her he has chosen a husband for her, one whose help he needs. When she says she is already pledged, he gives her the forged love letter. Shattered by Edgardo's betrayal, she awaits the arrival of Arturo, her future husband. Arturo has heard rumours about Lucia's secret love for Edgardo, but Enrico dismisses them and joins him in signing the marriage contract. Lucia too then signs her "death warrant". At that moment, Edgardo bursts in, insisting he still loves her. He and Enrico draw their swords, but he is then shown Lucia's signature on the marriage contract. Stunned, he returns his ring to Lucia.

"Se tradirmi tu potrai"

"Chi me frena in tal momento"

ACT THREE Raimondo interrupts the wedding party to announce that, hearing cries from Lucia's apartment, he entered and found Arturo dead, with Lucia still holding his dagger. As the crowd gasps in horror, Lucia enters, clearly deranged and "hearing" Edgardo's voice. Faced with her mad ravings, Enrico is full of remorse. At the tomb of the Ravenswoods, Edgardo sees lights in Lammermoor Castle and imagines Lucia celebrating her new love. He hears people leaving the castle regretting the "horrendous fate" of a "wretched girl". They tell him that Lucia is dying and with her last breath is calling for him. Raimondo then brings news that she has expired. Devastated, Edgardo stabs himself to be reunited with Lucia.

"Il dolce suono"

"Tu che a Dio spiegasti l'alli"

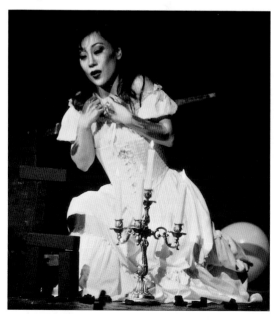

The Korean coloratura soprano Sumi Jo, seen here at the Opéra Bastille, Paris, in 1999, has made Lucia di Lammermoor one of her favourite roles.

MARIA STUARDA
(Mary Stuart)

✍ Opera seria in three acts, 2½ hours
☎ 1834
⚖ 30 December 1835, La Scala, Milan (Italy)

📖 Giuseppe Badari, after Friedrich von Schiller's tragedy

Maria Stuarda, which presents a fictional account of the downfall of Mary Queen of Scots, has a brilliantly lyrical score, one dominated by two great soprano roles, Maria and Elisabetta, but also well supported by the tenor voice of Leicester. Because its plot is rife with conflict, the opera also boasts several stirring duets. No less memorable is the splendid ensemble accompanying Elisabetta's explosive meeting with Maria in Act II.

⊲ Banned first in Naples, then after one performance in Milan, *Maria Stuarda* was not revived until 1958, and its autographed score was only traced in 1989. Today, it is considered one of Donizetti's finest operas. ⊳

> ❖ PRINCIPAL ROLES ❖
>
> Maria Stuarda *soprano*
> Mary Queen of Scots
>
> Elisabetta *soprano*
> Queen of England
>
> Leicester *tenor*
> Elisabetta's favourite
>
> Talbot *baritone*
> Mary's friend
>
> Anna *mezzo-soprano*
> Mary's nurse
>
> Cecil *baritone*
> Lord Chancellor

PLOT SYNOPSIS

England in the 1580s

ACT ONE In the Palace of Westminster, Queen Elisabetta is contemplating a marriage proposal from the French king when courtiers ask her to pardon her imprisoned Catholic cousin, Maria Stuarda. The queen loves Leicester, but worries that he loves Maria.

"Si! Era d'amor l'immagine" Leicester brings a message from Maria, asking to be received ♂. She accuses him of loving Maria, but he denies it.

ACT TWO At Fotheringhay Castle, Maria is in a happy mood ♂ when she hears the sound of the royal hunt. Leicester arrives and promises to free her so they can love each other openly. Elisabetta enters and Maria asks for forgiveness, but the queen curses her as evil. Maria then seals her fate by calling the queen a harlot.

"O nube! che lieve"

ACT THREE At Westminster, the queen initially hesitates to approve Maria's death warrant. When Leicester enters, though, she quickly signs it. Leicester protests, but the queen orders him to witness the execution, telling him to bury his love in Maria's grave. Alone with her friend Talbot in Fotheringhay Castle, Maria worries about her sins. Suddenly, Talbot reveals himself as a secret Catholic priest and receives her final confession. As Maria goes to her death, Leicester arrives, grief-stricken. The Lord Chancellor proclaims that with her death, peace has returned to England.

Susan Parry is an austere Queen Elizabeth dressed for hunting in an English National Opera production of 1998.

LA FILLE DU RÉGIMENT

(The Daughter of the Regiment)

⚐ Opéra comique in two acts, 1½ hours
⚖ 1839 (opera buffa version with recitatives, 1840)
♟ 14 February 1840, Opéra-Comique, Paris, France

📖 JFA Bayard and Jules-Henri Vernoy de Saint-Georges

With *La fille du régiment*, Donizetti's first *opéra comique*, the composer went out of his way to charm Paris audiences with a love story that ends with a rousingly patriotic "Salute to France". The score is rich in lyrical arias and duets but, in keeping with the plot, its choruses also echo military music. Donizetti later adapted it in Italian, replacing spoken dialogue with sung recitative. But today the French version is usually preferred.

⚜ With its nine high C's, the aria *"Pour mon âme"* earned the tenor Luciano Pavarotti the title of "King of the High C's" in 1972, but the same aria also proved his undoing 30 years later when he failed to reach the top notes. ⚜

> **→ PRINCIPAL ROLES ←**
>
> **Marie** *soprano*
> An orphan adopted
> by the regiment
>
> **Tonio** *tenor*
> A Tyrolean peasant
> in love with Marie
>
> **Sergeant Sulpice** *bass*
> Marie's guardian
>
> **Marquise de Birkenfeld**
> *mezzo-soprano*
>
> **Hortensius** *bass*
> The Marquise's steward

PLOT SYNOPSIS

The Swiss Tyrol in 1815

ACT ONE Marie, an orphan raised by soldiers, follows her French regiment to the Tyrol. When her guardian, Sgt Sulpice, sees her with a young man, she recounts how he saved her from a precipice. Soldiers then enter with a Tyrolean suspected of spying, but Marie identifies him as her rescuer. Alone, Marie and Tonio declare their love ⚓. In order to marry the regiment's "daughter", Tonio even enlists. The Marquise of Birkenfeld arrives seeking safe conduct. But when Sulpice recalls that her name was on a letter found with the baby Marie, he discovers that she is Marie's aunt. The Marquise decides that Marie should live in her château.

"Quoi! Vous m'aimez"

ACT TWO The Marquise sets out to turn Marie into a lady with dancing and singing lessons. Marie is briefly cheered when Sulpice joins her in the song of the regiment, but she is not happy about marrying a rich heir. Sulpice urges the Marquise to allow Marie to marry her true love. Marie and Tonio even plan to elope. The Marquise then reveals she is in fact Marie's mother. As Marie prepares to marry the heir, she recounts her happy life with the regiment. The guests are horrified, but the Marquise is touched by her gratitude to the regiment, and decides she can marry Tonio. Led by Marie, all cheer France ⚓.

"Salut à la France"

The American Lily Pons (1898–1976), seen here as Marie, was a coloratura soprano with legions of admirers at the Metropolitan Opera of New York.

LA FAVORITE
(The Favourite)

🎭 Grand opera in four acts, 2½ hours
📅 1840
⚜ 2 December 1840, Paris Opéra, France

📖 Alphonse Royer, Gustave Baez, and Eugène Scribe, after Baculard d'Arnaud's 1764 play *Le Comte de Comminge*

La favorite, Donizetti's second French-language work for the Paris Opéra, recounts the implausible story of a monarch ceding his mistress to a war hero. But, as so often with this composer, the plot is a mere excuse for a glittering score that stands out for its contrasting colours. While a succession of fine arias illustrate the love triangle of Léonor, Fernand, and Alphonse, threats of divorce and excommunication add darker undertones.

⚜ Donizetti wrote *La favorite* in a rush, even borrowing some of the music from *L'ange de Nisida*, his earlier opera about a royal mistress, which was never staged because the theatre went bankrupt. ⚜

PLOT SYNOPSIS

Spain around 1340

ACT ONE Fernand, a novice in the monastery at Santiago de Compostela, confesses to Balthazar, his Superior, that he is haunted by a beautiful woman whom he saw praying in church. When Balthazar sends him away, Fernand traces the woman, Léonor, to an island. She loves him too, but she dare not reveal that she is the king's mistress.

ACT TWO Having defeated the Moors, King Alphonse plans to divorce his wife and marry Léonor. Yearning for Fernand, Léonor begs the king to release her. He refuses, but is upset to read an intercepted love letter to her. Balthazar, also the queen's father, then threatens the king with excommunication if he decides on divorce.

ACT THREE Alphonse receives Fernand as a war hero and offers him any wish. When he asks to marry Léonor, the king agrees ♪. Léonor tries to inform Fernand about her past

"Pour tant d'amour"

Giacomo Prestia as Balthazar chastizes Carlos Alvarez's Alphonse and his mistress Léonor, sung by Violeta Urmana, in the Vienna Staatsoper production in 2003.

before they marry, but the message never reaches him. When he learns the truth from Balthazar, he breaks his sword before the king and returns to the monastery in Santiago.

ACT FOUR The queen has died of sorrow and, at her funeral in Santiago, Fernand remembers his former love ♪. Suddenly Léonor appears in disguise as a novice, weak and ill. Fernand tells her to leave, but his passion is rekindled. He prepares to flee with her, but she dies in his arms.

"Ange si pur"

DON PASQUALE

⚐ Opera buffa in three acts, 2 hours
🕮 1842
♜ 3 January 1843, Théâtre-Italien, Paris, France

📖 Giovanni Ruffini and Gaetano Donizetti, after Angelo Anelli's libretto for Pavesi's opera *Ser Marc'Antonio*

Don Pasquale is Donizetti's comic masterpiece. In the opera, a love story somehow triumphs over absurd characters, unlikely disguises and much confusion. With a dazzling score keeping the plot moving apace, farcical scenes lead to sweet soprano and tenor arias and love duets. At the heart of the opera, though, is the great *buffo* character of Don Pasquale. His Act III duet with Malatesta is acknowledged to be one of the highpoints of the entire work.

> ✦ PRINCIPAL ROLES ✦
>
> **Don Pasquale** *bass*
> A foolish old bachelor
>
> **Ernesto** *tenor*
> Don Pasquale's nephew
>
> **Norina** *soprano*
> A young widow
>
> **Dr Malatesta** *baritone*
> Don Pasquale's friend

⚐ *Don Pasquale*'s plot is an old stand-by borrowed from Ben Jonson's 1609 play, *Epicene or The Silent Woman*. This play has also inspired other operas, including *Die schweigsame Frau* by Richard Strauss. ⚐

PLOT SYNOPSIS

An Italian region

ACT ONE Old Don Pasquale wants a bride. Thinking him foolish, his friend Malatesta offers his "sister" who, he says, has just left a convent. Delighted, Don Pasquale prohibits his nephew, Ernesto, from marrying the beautiful widow, Norina. Ernesto is heartbroken ♪. Meanwhile, Malatesta persuades Norina to marry Don Pasquale in the guise of "Sofronia" as a way of winning Ernesto.

"Sogno soave e casto"

ACT TWO Once the marriage contract is signed, Don Pasquale's shy bride becomes a noisy, bossy wife. Informed of Malatesta's scheme, Ernesto is again confident of Norina's love. Don Pasquale realizes he has made a terrible mistake.

ACT THREE Don Pasquale is shocked to see "Sofronia" leaving for the theatre without him. They argue and she strikes him, persuading him it is time to flee his marriage. Norina drops a note purportedly from Ernesto. Don Pasquale summons Malatesta for help. Ernesto is serenading Norina when Don Pasquale rushes in to eject "Sofronia". Malatesta announces that a new wife will soon arrive – Norina. When "Sofronia" protests, even Don Pasquale agrees to his nephew's marriage. Finally, realizing he has been tricked, Don Pasquale forgives everyone.

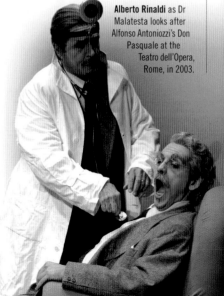

Alberto Rinaldi as Dr Malatesta looks after Alfonso Antoniozzi's Don Pasquale at the Teatro dell'Opera, Rome, in 2003.

PIETRO
MASCAGNI

Born: 7 December 1863, Livorno (Italy)
Died: 2 August 1945, Rome, Italy

Mascagni won instant fame almost accidentally: unbeknownst to him, his wife sent the score of *Cavalleria rusticana* to a competition for one-act operas – and it won. The work's immediate worldwide popularity prompted others to write operas in the same *verismo* style, but Mascagni himself never matched its success.

CAVALLERIA RUSTICANA
(Rustic Chivalry)

🎭 Melodramma in one act, 1¼ hours
🕮 1889
♈ 17 May 1890, Teatro Constanzi, Rome, Italy

📖 Giovanni Targione-Tozzetti and Guido Menasci, after Giovanni Verga's play

Cavalleria rusticana vividly depicts life in a Sicilian village where love, betrayal, and honour become the ingredients of a tragedy foretold. The score sets the mood with a chorus and an Easter hymn, but soon arias and duets come to drive the drama. The best-known solo is Santuzza's *"Voi lo sapete, o mamma"*.

PLOT SYNOPSIS

A Sicilian village on Easter Sunday in the late 19th century

Turridu returns from military service to discover that his fiancée, Lola, has married a local cart-driver, Alfio. When Turridu seduces another girl, Santuzza, leaving her pregnant, Lola decides to win him back. On Easter Sunday, Santuzza hopes to see Turridu in church. Lucia, his mother, says he has left on an errand.

American mezzo-soprano Tatiana Troyanos as Santuzza begs Plácido Domingo's Turridu not to abandon her in a 1976 production at the San Francisco Opera.

Santuzza tells Lucia that she fears Lola has again conquered Turridu 🔔. Turridu tries to reassure Santuzza, then pushes her away when he sees Lola. Burning with jealousy, Santuzza tells Alfio of Lola's betrayal. Alfio challenges Turridu to a duel. Turridu seeks his mother's blessing 🔔 and begs her to care for Santuzza should he not return. A terrible scream announces Turridu's death. Lucia and Santuzza collapse in grief.

"Voi lo sapete, o mamma"

"Mamma, quel vino è generoso"

MASCAGNI AND LEONCAVALLO

The names of Pietro Mascagni and Ruggero Leoncavallo are invariably linked. They carried the late 19th-century Italian literary movement called *verismo*, or "realism", into opera, each with a single memorable work, *Cavalleria rusticana* for Mascagni and *Pagliacci* for Leoncavallo. These short operas are often presented together.

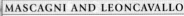

RUGGERO
LEONCAVALLO

Born: 23 April 1857, Naples (Italy)
Died: 9 August 1919, Montecatini, Italy

Leoncavallo was a struggling composer when Mascagni's *Cavalleria rusticana* inspired him to try *verismo* in opera. The result, *Pagliacci*, was a triumph. But, like Mascagni, Leoncavallo left little mark with his later works. He wrote a version of *La bohème*, but it was overshadowed by Puccini's opera, which premiered 18 months earlier.

PAGLIACCI
(The Clowns)

✍ Dramma in a prologue and two acts, 1¼ hours   📖 Ruggero Leoncavallo
☎ 1891–1892
♇ 21 May 1892, Teatro dal Verme, Milan, Italy

Pagliacci shows a *commedia dell'arte* play repeating itself tragically in real life. Its setting among villagers and strolling players placed it squarely in the *verismo* movement, contributing to its success. The best-known aria, *"Vesti la giubba"*, with its plaintive cries of *"Pagliaccio"*, is also a favourite for tenor recitals.

PLOT SYNOPSIS

Montalto in Calabria, Italy, in the late 19th century

PROLOGUE Tonio, the clown, announces to the audience that the perils of love will be presented on stage.

ACT ONE As strolling players prepare their show, Canio, their leader, says he expects the crowd to laugh at his wife's infidelity in the play. But in real life, he warns, he would avenge such treachery. His wife, Nedda, is alarmed. When Tonio tries to kiss her, she strikes him. But she is in love with Silvio, a villager, and agrees to run away with him. Overhearing them, Tonio summons Canio, but Nedda urges Silvio to flee. When she refuses to identify her lover, Canio realizes he has become *"Vesti la giubba"* the jealous husband he will enact in the play ☐.

ACT TWO On stage, "Colombina" (Nedda) awaits her lover, "Arlecchino" (Beppe). When "Taddeo" (Tonio) arrives first, she throws him out. She then welcomes "Arlecchino", and they prepare to elope. Returning unexpectedly, "Pagliaccio" (Canio) hears "Colombina" telling her lover to flee – in the same words used earlier by Nedda. "Pagliaccio" shouts that he is no longer a clown ☐, *"No, Pagliaccio non son"* and stabs her. As she lies dying, she calls for her lover. Canio then kills Silvio. With that, Tonio announces, "The play is over".

The great Italian tenor Beniamino Gigli, seen here in 1946 when he was 56, sang the role of Canio, the "Pagliaccio", throughout his long career.

UMBERTO
GIORDANO

Born: 27 August 1867, Fóggia, Italy
Died: 12 November 1948, Milan, Italy

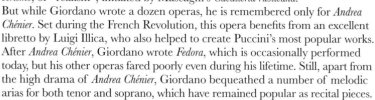

Umberto Giordano was swept up by the operatic fashion for *verismo*, or "realism", initiated by Mascagni's *Cavalleria rusticana*. But while Giordano wrote a dozen operas, he is remembered only for *Andrea Chénier*. Set during the French Revolution, this opera benefits from an excellent libretto by Luigi Illica, who also helped to create Puccini's most popular works. After *Andrea Chénier*, Giordano wrote *Fedora*, which is occasionally performed today, but his other operas fared poorly even during his lifetime. Still, apart from the high drama of *Andrea Chénier*, Giordano bequeathed a number of melodic arias for both tenor and soprano, which have remained popular as recital pieces.

ANDREA CHÉNIER

🕮 Dramma di ambiente storico in four acts, 2¼ hours
🗓 1894–1896

🎭 28 March 1896, La Scala, Milan, Italy
📖 Luigi Illica

Andrea Chénier is inspired by the French Romantic poet André Chénier, whose courageous stand against the excesses of the French Revolution cost him his life. Built around Illica's strong libretto, the opera evokes revolutionary Paris through songs like *"Ça Ira"* and *"La Carmagnole"*. While allowing Chénier to defend his ill-fated idealism, Giordano and Illica add romance to the political mix: Chénier competes with a servant-turned-revolutionary for the love of an aristocratic woman. Through these three roles, Giordano displays his talent for lyrical intensity. The best-known melody is Maddalena's aria mourning her mother, *"La mamma morta"*, slain by a mob. No less poignant is the final duet, *"Vicino a te"*, when Maddalena chooses to die with Chénier.

> **PRINCIPAL ROLES**
>
> **Andrea Chénier** *tenor* A poet
> **Maddalena di Coigny** *soprano* An aristocrat and Chénier's beloved
> **Contessa di Coigny** *mezzo-soprano* Maddalena's mother
> **Carlo Gérard** *baritone* A servant in the Coigny family
> **Roucher** *bass* Chénier's friend
> **Incredibile** *tenor* A dandy spying for the revolutionaries

⚜ During his final weeks, André Chénier's muse was an aristocrat called Anne de Coigny, but his infatuation was not reciprocated: de Coigny neither died at his side nor even mentioned him in her memoirs. ⚜

A costume design for Maddalena di Coigny in a 19th-century production of Giordano's opera staged at the Paris Opéra, France.

PLOT SYNOPSIS

Before and after the 1789 French Revolution

ACT ONE Before a party at the Coigny's château, one servant, Gérard, curses the "gilded house". But when he sees the countess's daughter, Maddalena, his anger melts. Guests ignore news of unrest in Paris. The poet Chénier dedicates an ode to love to Maddalena, but guests are scandalized when he denounces poverty ♫. Gérard returns with a crowd of beggars and, tearing off his uniform, announces he is resigning. The countess calls for dancing to resume.

"Un dì all'azzurro spazio"

ACT TWO Five years later, in a Paris café, Chénier is watched by a spy, Incredibile. His friend, Roucher, urges the poet to flee. But he refuses, saying he awaits a mysterious woman who says she is in danger and signs her letters as "Hope". Gérard, now a revolutionary, is looking for the same woman. A maid leads Chénier to her mistress, Maddalena. Recognizing Maddalena, Chénier is overwhelmed by love and vows to protect her with his life. Summoned by the spy, Gérard arrives and is wounded in a fight with Chénier. Nonetheless, he warns Chénier that he is being sought as a counter-revolutionary.

ACT THREE At a Revolutionary Tribunal, Gérard calls for donations to help France against its enemies. As the crowd sings *"La Carmagnole"*, Incredibile reports Chénier's capture, urging Gérard to sign the poet's indictment. Gérard hesitates, ashamed that he is now ruled only by hate and love ♫. But he signs the paper. Maddalena begs Gérard to save Chénier. When Gérard recalls his love for her, she offers her body in exchange for Chénier's life. Gérard is moved by her account of her mother's death in a fire set by revolutionaries ♫. At his trial, Chénier defends his fight against hypocrisy and even Gérard speaks up for him, but the judge orders his death.

"Nemico della patria?!"

"La mamma morta"

ACT FOUR While Chénier writes a final poem, Gérard arrives with Maddalena, who takes the place of a condemned woman. Alone, Chénier and Maddalena fall into each other's arms, vowing eternal love. Summoned to their execution, they cry out, "We welcome death together!"

Katarzyna Suska as the Countess (*centre*) urges her guests to ignore the approaching revolution and continue dancing in a 2005 staging at the Polish National Opera.

"When I am alone with my notes, my heart pounds and the tears stream from my eyes."

Giuseppe Verdi

GIUSEPPE
VERDI

Born: 9/10 October 1813, Le Roncole, near Busseto, Italy
Died: 27 January 1901, Milan, Italy

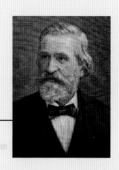

Giuseppe Verdi is the most successful and widely performed composer in opera history. He was not a musical pioneer in the manner of Mozart or Wagner. Yet, more than any other composer, through the sheer number of immortal works he created, he made opera what it is today. No opera season in the world is complete without the inclusion of at least two of his major pieces.

The intense melodrama of his works has become synonymous with the word "operatic". And even when the plots of his operas seem implausible, they still address universal themes of love, betrayal, violence, power, and death. Verdi was also a man of his times and, with several of his works interpreted as allegories for Italy's struggle for freedom and unification, he was credited with helping to forge a national identity. But it was above all his talent for matching unforgettable melodies to moments of high drama that carried his name across the world. Indeed, for half a century, Verdi dominated Italian opera and shared the limelight with only one other composer, Richard Wagner. While Wagner's work is often admired for its German intensity, however, it is the very universality of Verdi's operas that sustains their enduring popularity.

Born in the village of Le Roncole near Busseto in northern Italy, Verdi had church organists as his first teachers, and he was gifted enough for a local merchant, Antonio Barezzi, to finance his studies. But, at 18, Verdi was too old to enter the Milan Conservatory, and instead learned the art of counterpoint and fugue from a private teacher. In April 1836, he was named Busseto's music master and, weeks later, married his teenage sweetheart,

The Belgian soprano Isabelle Kabatu captures the exoticism of the title role of *Aïda* on the open-air stage of Rome's Baths of Caracalla in Paolo Miccichè's 2005 production, conducted by Plácido Domingo.

FIRST PERFORMANCES
1830
1839 Oberto
1842 Nabucco
1844 Ernani
1846 Attila
1840
1847 Macbeth
1849 Luisa Miller
1851 Rigoletto
1850
1853 Il trovatore
La traviata
1857 Simon Boccanegra I
1859 Un ballo in maschera
1860
1862 La forza del destino
1867 Don Carlos
1870
1871 Aïda
1881 Simon Boccanegra II
1880
1887 Otello
1890
1893 Falstaff
1900

Barezzi's daughter, Margherita. By then, he was working on his first opera, *Oberto*, which was presented at La Scala in Milan in November 1839. Then tragedy struck.

After his two children had died in infancy, Verdi's wife died in June 1840. Not surprisingly, his next work, *Un giorno di regno*, was a flop; he would not write another *opera buffa* until *Falstaff*, over 50 years later.

RECOGNITION

In 1842, with *Nabucco*, his fortune changed. It was the moment, Verdi later remarked, when his career truly began. With its chilling soprano arias and the melancholic – and catchy – chorus, *"Va, pensiero"*, *Nabucco*'s portrayal of the Jews' captivity in Babylon rang true to northern Italians living under Austria's stern rule. The opera's success placed Verdi on the throne of Italian opera, one previously occupied by Rossini (now retired), Bellini (now dead), and Donizetti (settled in Paris). Suddenly, everyone wanted him and, in what he would later describe as the life of "a galley slave", Verdi responded: over the next 17 years, he wrote 20 operas for

The piano score for the opera *Nabucco*, Verdi's first popular hit, was issued by the composer's music publisher, Edizioni Ricordi.

theatres in Italy, London, and Paris. It was also in Paris in 1847 that he again met the soprano Giuseppina Strepponi, who had sung in *Nabucco* five years earlier and whom he finally married in 1859.

THE POPULAR TOUCH

While not all his works after *Nabucco* were equally successful, *Macbeth* and *Luisa Miller* were well received. But then a trio of operas, which premiered between March 1851 and March 1853, placed Verdi in a class of his own. *Rigoletto*, with its ever-popular tenor aria *"La donna è mobile"*, was soon staged around the world. *Il trovatore*, an intense melodrama with some of Verdi's greatest melodies, was a still bigger hit.

Verdi's death at the age of 87 prompted national mourning, with thousands, of people accompanying his funeral cortège through Milan on 30 January 1901.

La traviata, his most popular opera today, had an unhappy premiere in Venice in March 1853, but a revised version a year later was acclaimed. Even so, through the 1850s, Verdi did not slow down, presenting *Les vêpres siciliennes* in Paris, *Simon Boccanegra* in Venice, and *Un ballo in maschera* in Rome.

By now, Verdi was considered a national treasure. Having supported Italy's fight for liberation, he agreed to serve as a deputy in the Turin parliament after Italy's unification in 1861. He also devoted more time to a large farm he had bought years earlier outside Busseto. Immensely wealthy and already contemplating retirement, he nonetheless accepted three foreign commissions: for the Imperial Theatre in St Petersburg in 1862, he wrote *La forza del destino*; for the Paris Opéra in 1867, he created the five-act grand opera *Don Carlos*, later to become *Don Carlo* in a four-act Italian version; and for the Cairo Opera in 1871, he wrote his incomparable Pharaonic epic, *Aïda*. And, with that, Verdi returned to life as a country gentleman. But few years passed before his music publisher, Giulio Ricordi, persuaded the composer

RISORGIMENTO

Although Verdi was hardly a political activist, the patriotic tone of several of his operas, starting with *Nabucco*, turned him into a symbol of the *Risorgimento*, or "Rising Again" (*below*), the 19th-century movement that climaxed in Italy's unification as a kingdom in 1861. Famously, cries of "Viva Verdi" were understood to be an acronym for "Viva Vittorio Emmanuele Re D'Italia" – "Long Live Vittorio Emmanuele, King of Italy". But for decades after unification, Verdi himself continued to be viewed as the personification of Italian nationhood. His death marked the end of an era.

to rework *Simon Boccanegra* and hired a young composer and librettist, Arrigo Boito, to revise the original libretto. The partnership flourished and *Simon Boccanegra II*, the version performed today, had its premiere in 1881. Ricordi then guided the duo towards Verdi's final masterpieces, *Otello* in 1887 and *Falstaff* in 1893, adaptations, respectively, of Shakespeare's *Othello* and *The Merry Wives of Windsor*. They provided a fitting climax to Verdi's career because he had always loved Shakespeare and, after *Macbeth*, had hoped to adapt *King Lear*. They also drew from him powerfully expressive scores of almost continuous music.

Nearly 80 years old when *Falstaff* was presented, Verdi spent his final years revered like a secular deity. After his death on 27 January 1901, the 20,000 mourners at his funeral spontaneously burst out singing *"Va, pensiero"* from *Nabucco* as his cortège passed through the streets of Milan.

NABUCCO

✂ Dramma lirico in four parts, 2¼ hours
⚓ 1841 (rev. 1842)
⚲ 9 March 1842, La Scala, Milan (Italy)

📖 Temistocle Solera, after the 1836 play
Nabucodonosor by Anicet Bourgeois and
Francis Cornue

Nabucco, Verdi's first major success, won him immediate acclaim. Daringly, he takes on the Biblical story of the Jews captive in Babylon with a large cast of soloists and chorus. And unusually, its most memorable song, *"Va, pensiero"*, is a chorus sung almost entirely in unison. But the opera also includes fine soprano, tenor, and bass arias as well as a remarkable duet in which Abigaille and Nabucco wrestle for power.

⚊ *Nabucco* is best known for the lilting melody of *"Va, pensiero"*, but Italians also embraced the Hebrew slave chorus as an allegory for their own struggle for freedom against Austrian occupation. ⚊

> ### → PRINCIPAL ROLES ←
>
> **Nabucco** *baritone*
> King of Babylon
>
> **Abigaille** *soprano*
> A former slave thought to
> be Nabucco's daughter
>
> **Fenena** *soprano*
> Nabucco's daughter
>
> **Ismaele** *tenor*
> King of Jerusalem's nephew
>
> **Zaccaria** *bass*
> High Priest of Jerusalem
>
> **High Priest of Babylon** *bass*

PLOT SYNOPSIS

Jerusalem and Babylon in the 6th century BCE

PART ONE JERUSALEM Babylon's King Nabucco advances on Jerusalem, where his daughter, Fenena, is held hostage. Zaccaria, the High Priest, leaves her with Ismaele, her secret Jewish lover. Abigaille, Nabucco's other daughter, offers to spare the Jews if Ismaele returns her love, but he rejects her. When Nabucco appears, Ismaele saves Fenena from Zaccaria's dagger, but the Temple is destroyed.

PART TWO THE UNBELIEVER In Babylon, Abigaille discovers she was born a slave ♭. Believing Nabucco dead, the Babylonians beg Abigaille to seize power. As Zaccaria announces Fenena's conversion to Judaism, Nabucco returns, proclaiming he is a god, but he is struck by lightning.

"Anch'io dischiuso un giorno"

Matteo Manuguerra cuts an impressive regal figure as Nabucco, King of Babylon, in a San Francisco Opera production staged in 1982.

a lament of yearning for their homeland ♬, while Zaccaria prophesies the fall of Babylon.

"Va, pensiero"

PART THREE THE PROPHECY Nabucco denounces Abigaille as a slave, but she tears up the incriminating document. She also refuses the throne in exchange for Fenena's life. On the banks of the Euphrates, the captive Hebrews sing

PART FOUR THE BROKEN IDOL As Fenena prepares to die, Nabucco begs the God of the Hebrews for forgiveness. Fenena and other Hebrews are standing before the sacrificial altar when cries of "Viva Nabucco" are heard. Nabucco destroys the false idol and frees the Hebrews. Full of remorse, Abigaille poisons herself as Nabucco is proclaimed king of kings.

MACBETH

✍ Opera in four acts, 2¾ hours
⏰ 1846–1847 (rev. 1864–1865)
♜ 14 March 1847, Teatro della Pergola,

Florence (Italy)
📖 Francesco Maria Piave, after Shakespeare's *Macbeth* (1605–1606)

Verdi took immense care in recreating *Macbeth* as opera, determining the shape of the libretto, and capturing the tormented psychology of the protagonists with his music. The result was his most inventive and idealistic opera so far. Even more than in Shakespeare, the drama centres on Macbeth and Lady Macbeth: their Act I duet and her Act IV "sleepwalking scene" are highlights.

⚜ The misadventures often associated with Shakespeare's *Macbeth* reached into opera in 1988 when a man jumped to his death from the balcony of the Metropolitan Opera in New York during a performance of Verdi's *Macbeth*. ⚜

→ PRINCIPAL ROLES ←

Macbeth *baritone*
A general and future king

Lady Macbeth *soprano*

Duncan *silent*
King of Scotland

Banquo *bass*
A general

Macduff *tenor*
A Scottish noble

Malcolm *tenor*
Duncan's son

PLOT SYNOPSIS

In and around Macbeth's castle in 11th-century Scotland

ACT ONE Witches predict that Macbeth will become Thane of Cawdor and King of Scotland and that Banquo will father future kings. When Macbeth becomes Thane of Cawdor, Lady Macbeth sets in motion the prophecy of kingship ♪. With King Duncan asleep in Macbeth's castle, she forces her reluctant husband to kill him. Macduff comes to wake Duncan and finds him murdered.

"Vieni! T'affretta!"

ACT TWO Now king, Macbeth decides that Banquo and his children must die. But although Banquo is killed, his son escapes. When Banquo's ghost appears during a banquet, Macbeth panics, crying out at the spectre, which he alone can see. His wife tries to distract the guests, but Macduff decides to flee Scotland for England.

ACT THREE The witches assure Macbeth that "no man of woman born" will harm him, while another apparition tells him he is safe until Birnam Wood moves towards him. Alarmed to see a vision of eight kings passing before him, the last of whom is in the form of Banquo, Macbeth decides to kill Banquo's son as well as Macduff's wife and children.

ACT FOUR As Macduff plans revenge, Lady Macbeth imagines blood on her hands while sleepwalking ♪. Macbeth sees Birnam Wood approaching, but boasts that "no man of woman born" can hurt him. Macduff replies that he was "ripped" from his mother's womb and slays Macbeth.

"Una macchia è qui tuttora"

Kathleen Broderick in the disturbing role of Lady Macbeth at the Theater an der Wien, Austria, in 2000.

RIGOLETTO

🎵 Melodramma in three acts, 2 hours
📆 1850–1851
🏛 11 March 1851, La Fenice, Venice (Italy)

📖 Francesco Maria Piave, after Victor Hugo's tragedy *Le roi s'amuse* (1832)

Rigoletto was the opera that founded Verdi's international reputation: within ten years it had been staged in some 250 opera houses around the world. The catchy tenor aria, *"La donna è mobile"*, certainly helped spread its fame, but it is also sustained by a daring plot, one that Venetian censors only accepted after two revisions. Musically, *Rigoletto* represented a clear break with the past: Verdi eliminated entrance arias and finale ensembles and added pace through Rigoletto's *recitativo cantando*, or melodic sung recitative. Unusually for Verdi, this is also an opera dominated by a baritone voice.

⚜ Verdi was so certain that he had written a hit song in *"La donna è mobile"* that he instructed orchestra members not to whistle or sing it outside rehearsals in the theatre before the premiere. ⚜

✦ PRINCIPAL ROLES ✦

Duke of Mantua *tenor*
A rakish noble

Rigoletto *baritone*
The duke's hunchback jester

Gilda *soprano*
Rigoletto's daughter

Sparafucile *bass*
A hired assassin

Maddalena *contralto*
Sparafucile's sister

Giovanna *mezzo-soprano*
Gilda's chaperon

Count Monterone *baritone*
The duke's enemy

Countess Ceprano
mezzo-soprano

PLOT SYNOPSIS

In and around Mantua in 16th-century Italy

ACT ONE At a palace ball, the Duke of Mantua is musing on a young woman he plans to win. But first he decides to conquer Countess Ceprano ♪. His hunchbacked jester, Rigoletto, ridicules her husband. But when he mocks Count Monterone, whose daughter has been seduced by the duke, he is shocked when Monterone curses him. Rigoletto is stopped by Sparafucile, who offers his services as a killer. Sending him away, he embraces his daughter Gilda. He pledges his love for her and, telling her to let no-one into the house, he leaves ♪. Now realizing that Gilda is Rigoletto's daughter, the duke enters and, posing

"Questa o quella per me pari sono"

"Figlia"

The cover of the Italian magazine *Musica e Musicisti* ("Music and Musicians") shows Rigoletto being comforted by a conductor.

as a student, declares his love for her. She is swept off her feet ♪. A group of men plan to kidnap Gilda, believing she is Rigoletto's mistress, but they tell the jester that they have come to capture Ceprano's wife. They blindfold Rigoletto and have him hold up a ladder against his own house. When he hears Gilda's cries, he remembers Monterone's curse.

"Caro nome"

ACT TWO Upset that Gilda has been stolen from him, the duke is delighted to learn she is in the palace. Rigoletto arrives, feigning nonchalance until he realizes that Gilda is with the duke.

As the courtiers scoff at him, he shouts that she is his daughter. Gilda appears and, alone with her father, she confesses she fell for a young student, but was then seized and brought to the palace ♘. On his way to jail, seeing the duke's portrait, Monterone admits defeat. Rigoletto also dwells on his own ill fate and vows revenge.

"Tutte le feste al tempio"

ACT THREE While Gilda still loves the duke, Rigoletto wants her to know he is worthless. Peeping into Sparafucile's house, she recognizes the duke in disguise and hears him call for wine, proclaiming that no woman can be trusted ♘. As the duke woos Maddalena,

"La donna è mobile"

The Duke of Mantua's courtiers abandon the noble's most recent conquest in David Pountney's production at the New Israel Opera in 2000.

Sparafucile's sister, Rigoletto points him out to Sparafucile as the man to be killed ♘. He then pays the assassin, saying he will return to collect the body. When Maddalena understands her new lover is to die, she pleads for his life. Finally Sparafucile agrees to kill the next visitor to arrive. Overhearing the plan, Gilda decides to save the duke. She knocks on the door and is stabbed. Rigoletto takes the body in a sack, but then suddenly hears the duke's voice. In panic, he cuts open the sack and finds Gilda. She begs his forgiveness and, as she dies, Rigoletto realizes the curse has come true.

"Bella figlia d'amore"

TITO GOBBI

Tito Gobbi, one of the finest baritones of the mid-20th century, is perhaps best known for singing Scarpia opposite Maria Callas in Puccini's *Tosca*, but the role that he made his own was Rigoletto (*right*). It not only suited his mid-range voice, but it also enabled him to display his great acting talent, one that required him to be an odious and sadistic jester to the cynical duke as well as a protective and loving father to the ill-fated Gilda. During a long career, Gobbi also sang other major Verdi characters, including Iago in *Otello*, and the title role in *Simon Boccanegra*.

IL TROVATORE
(The Troubadour)

- 🎵 Dramma in four parts, 2¼ hours
- ⏳ 1851–1853 (rev. 1856)
- 🏛 19 January 1853, Teatro Apollo, Rome (Italy)
- 📖 Salvatore Cammarano and Leone Emanuele Bardare, after the 1836 play *El trovador* by Antonio García Gutiérrez

Il trovatore is an immensely popular opera in which an implausible plot is transformed by a dizzying succession of magnificent melodies. Along with *Rigoletto* and *La traviata*, it forms the great trilogy of Verdi's middle years, but it is the most traditional of the three: a melodrama about chivalry, honour, valour, and tragic love powered by unremittingly high voltage music. Leonora, Manrico, and the count are all given passionate arias. But Verdi was most drawn to Azucena, the Gypsy "outsider" whose burning desire for revenge is finally rewarded by the opera's tragic dénouement.

⚜ Lovers of Italian opera never miss a chance to relive *Il trovatore*'s soul-drenching story and music, but music critics have long expressed doubts about its music as too "easy" to enjoy. ⚜

✣ PRINCIPAL ROLES ✣

Count di Luna *baritone*
Commander in the army of Aragon

Leonora *soprano*
Lady-in-waiting to the Princess of Aragon

Manrico *tenor*
A Gypsy and rebel

Azucena *mezzo-soprano*
A Gypsy

Ferrando *bass*
A captain in di Luna's guard

Ines *soprano*
Leonora's confidante

Ruiz *tenor*
A soldier in Manrico's band

PLOT SYNOPSIS

Zaragoza and Castellor in northeast Spain in the early 15th century.

PART ONE Captain Ferrando recounts the tragic story of Count di Luna's brother: the baby's nurse awoke to find a Gypsy peering at him with an evil eye. When the boy fell ill, the witch was burned at the stake. But her daughter killed the

"Tacea la notte placida" | baby. Now the count has sworn revenge. Leonora eagerly awaits her troubadour lover 🎵, but the

count, who also loves her, lurks nearby. Hearing singing, she recognizes her lover but in the dark embraces the count in error. The troubadour steps out and identifies himself as Manrico, a rebel. The two men leave to duel.

PART TWO At a Gypsy camp, Azucena describes a woman's horrible death at

"Stride la vampa" | the stake 🎵. She tells her son Manrico how his grandmother was killed by the old count.

Hearing her cries, Azucena seized the count's son and threw him into the

flames, only to discover she had murdered her own baby. When Manrico is shocked, she insists

The Italian tenor
Salvatore Licitra as Manrico protects Barbara Frittoli's Leonora at La Scala in 2000.

AZUCENA

Divas are invariably sopranos, the voice favoured by opera lovers and composers for its ability to provide drama through high notes. But the "darker" sound of mezzo-sopranos is in many ways more emotional. This is certainly true with Azucena, one of the finest mezzo-soprano roles in opera. It is an immensely challenging part and the most difficult to cast in *Il trovatore*. Even the role's great arias are introspective.

Irina Mishura as Azucena at the Royal Opera House in 2004.

PART THREE The count is besieging Castellor castle, where Manrico has taken Leonora. When a Gypsy is captured near the count's camp, he interrogates her about the child stolen years earlier. She denies all knowledge, but Ferrando recognizes her. As she is tied up, she cries out for Manrico, revealing she is the mother of the count's rival. He orders her burned at the stake. Manrico comforts Leonora ♪, but, as they prepare to marry, Manrico sees that a pyre has been prepared for Azucena. He rushes to rescue his mother.

"Ah sì, ben mio, coll'essere"

PART FOUR Outside a prison, Leonora pines for Manrico ♪. As monks sing a *Miserere*, she offers herself to the count in exchange for Manrico's life, then sucks poison from her ring. Leonora comes to free Manrico, but he accuses her of selling her love ♪. Begging him to flee, she reveals she is dying. When the count realizes he has been deceived, he orders Manrico's execution. Almost gleefully, Azucena tells him that he has killed his brother.

"D'amor sull'ali rosee"

"Ha quest' infame l'amor venduto"

he is her son, but is angry he did not kill the count in their duel. He says he heard a cry from heaven. Believing Manrico dead, Leonora has entered a convent. The count, also sure of Manrico's death, plans to abduct her ♪. At first, hearing the nuns praying, he loses his nerve. But as he comes forward to claim her, Manrico also appears and his men disarm the count.

"Il balen del suo sorriso"

LA TRAVIATA
(The Fallen Woman)

🎵 Melodramma in three acts, 2 hours
⏳ 1853 (rev. 1854)
🏛 6 March 1853, La Fenice, Venice (Italy)

📖 Francesco Maria Piave, after the 1852 play
La dame aux camélias by Alexandre Dumas *fils*

La traviata is among the world's favourite operas, yet it flopped at its Venice premiere. The music cannot be faulted: lyrical and dramatic arias of great beauty; opera's most famous "drinking song" or brindisi; the extended duet between Violetta and Giorgio Germont; the richly scored ensemble that ends Act II; and Violetta's poignant last testament. *La traviata* was evidently beyond the talents of the first cast. But soon afterwards its qualities were widely acclaimed.

⚜ Although the courtesan was a fixture of European society, until the 1890s, it was thought proper to set *La traviata* in an earlier era. ⚜

⟶ PRINCIPAL ROLES ⟵

Violetta Valéry *soprano*
A courtesan

Alfredo Germont *tenor*
Violetta's lover

Giorgio Germont *baritone*
Alfredo's father

Baron Douphol *baritone*
Violetta's suitor

Flora *mezzo-soprano*
Violetta's friend

Annina *soprano*
Violetta's maid

PLOT SYNOPSIS

In and near Paris, France, in 1850

ACT ONE Violetta Valéry, a Paris courtesan, is receiving guests when Alfredo Germont is introduced as an admirer. Violetta invites him to make a toast and Alfredo leads the crowd in a drinking song 🍷. "Libiamo ne' lieti calici" Alfredo tells Violetta he has loved her for a year, but she says she has only friendship to offer him. As the party breaks up, Violetta feels disturbed, realizing she has never truly loved or been loved, yet concluding it is her destiny to "flutter from pleasure to pleasure" 🍷. "Sempre libera" Suddenly, hearing Alfredo serenading her, she again contemplates love before dismissing it as madness.

ACT TWO Now living happily with Violetta outside Paris, Alfredo learns from a maid that Violetta has sold her horses and carriages to pay for their upkeep. Embarrassed to be living off her, Alfredo leaves for Paris 🍷. "O mio remorso!" Violetta, puzzled by his absence, is

Rolando Villazón as Alfredo admires Anna Netrebko's Violetta at the Salzburg Festival, 2005.

At a party, Violetta's guests turn eagerly as Marcelo Álvarez's Alfredo raises a toast to his beautiful hostess at La Scala in 2002.

distracted by an invitation to a party at Flora's that night. Giorgio Germont, Alfredo's father, arrives to accuse Violetta of ruining his son. When she shows that she has been keeping them, Germont remarks nastily about exploiting the fruits of her past. He then explains that if his daughter is to marry, Alfredo must end his shameful affair with Violetta ♻. Violetta at first objects, but finally agrees to his demand. Germont suggests she leave unannounced, but she begs him to tell his daughter of her sacrifice. In tears, Violetta is writing to Alfredo when he returns. She entreats him to love her forever and runs out. Moments later, a messenger brings her letter. When Alfredo sees Flora's invitation, he vows revenge. At Flora's party, Alfredo is winning at cards when Violetta arrives with Baron Douphol. After Alfredo angers Douphol by winning money from him gambling, Violetta begs him to leave for his own safety, but refuses to follow him. Shocked and angered, Alfredo calls the guests together and throws his winnings at her. As she swoons, Germont rebukes his son, who is now full of remorse. Slowly coming round, Violetta tells him that one day he will understand.

"Pura siccome un angelo"

ACT THREE Terminally ill, Violetta re-reads a letter from Germont recounting that, after wounding the baron in a duel, Alfredo left the country, but will soon return. She knows it is too late ♻. Then, as carnival music streams through the window, Annina announces Alfredo's arrival. Falling into each other's arms, they vow never again to be apart. Excitedly, Violetta promises to get well, but she knows she is dying ♻. As Germont and the doctor arrive, she gives a miniature portrait to Alfredo. Suddenly, crying out that she feels better, she dies.

"Addio del passato"

"Ah! Gran Dio!"

THE REAL TRAVIATA

Marie Duplessis was a famous Paris courtesan long before Alexandre Dumas *fils* relived their affair in his 1848 novel and play *La dame aux camélias*. Born into poverty but with ample wit and beauty, she rose quickly to host salons attended by *le tout Paris*. In 1847, only 23, she died of tuberculosis. Dumas never forgot her, writing years later of "her cherry red lips". In *La traviata*, Verdi shows he too was charmed by this "fallen woman".

UN BALLO IN MASCHERA
(A Masked Ball)

✍ Melodramma in three acts, 2¼ hours
☙ 1857–1858
♆ 17 February 1859, Teatro Apollo, Rome (Italy)

📖 Antonio Somma, after Eugène Scribe's libretto
Gustave III, set by Daniel Auber in 1833

Un ballo in maschera is often called Verdi's love poem, his *Tristan und Isolde*. While not among his most performed operas, it is a work of great sophistication. It not only combines dramatic and lyrical music but, with almost Shakespearean panache, it also switches seamlessly between the humorous and the tragic. In all, it is a profoundly romantic opera, with Riccardo's clandestine meeting with Amelia in Act II offering what is arguably Verdi's finest love duet.

⚹ *Un ballo in maschera* originally portrayed the murder of Sweden's Gustave III. But since no king could be killed on an Italian stage, the victim became the governor of an English colony in the Americas. ⚹

➤ PRINCIPAL ROLES ◄

Riccardo, Earl of Warwick *tenor*
English colonial governor

Renato *baritone*
Riccardo's secretary

Amelia *soprano*
Renato's wife

Ulrica *contralto*
A fortune-teller

Oscar *soprano*
A page

Samuel and Tom *bass*
Conspirators

PLOT SYNOPSIS

Boston, New England, in the 17th century

ACT ONE Riccardo, the governor, loves Amelia, the wife of Renato, his secretary. When Renato warns him of a plot to kill him, he decides to consult Ulrica, the fortune-teller. Meanwhile, Amelia asks Ulrica for help in fighting her love for Riccardo and is told to pick a herb at midnight. Ulrica then warns Riccardo he will die by the next hand he shakes. As two conspirators, Samuel and Tom, turn away from him, Riccardo seizes Renato's hand.

ACT TWO Riccardo and Amelia finally confess their love ♪.

"Non sai tu che se l'anima mia"

Renato appears and warns Riccardo that a gang awaits him. The governor tells Renato to escort Amelia without seeing her face. Tom and Samuel arrive, and Amelia's face is bared in the confusion. Renato vows revenge.

ACT THREE Renato joins Samuel and Tom in their plot. Riccardo decides to send Renato and Amelia to England, but yearns to see Amelia one last time ♪ and ignores a warning not to attend the masked ball. Amelia recognizes Riccardo and begs him to flee, but Renato appears and stabs him. Telling Renato that his love for Amelia was chaste, Riccardo pardons the conspirators and dies.

"Ma se m'è forza perderti"

Alberto Cupido as Riccardo
interrogates Oscar, a page sung by Ofelia Sala, in a 2002 production at the Deutsche Oper in Berlin.

LA FORZA DEL DESTINO

(The Force of Destiny)

❧

⌖ Opera in four acts, 3¼ hours
⧗ 1861 (rev. 1867–1869)
♆ 10 November 1862, Imperial Theatre,

St Petersburg, Russia
⌨ Francesco Maria Piave, after the 1835 play *Don Álvaro, o La fuerza del sino*, by Ángel de Saavedra.

Commissioned by the Imperial Theatre in St Petersburg, *La forza del destino* is a powerful and passionate work that helped to inspire Mussorgsky's monumental *Boris Godunov*. Rich in choruses designed to appeal to the Russian sense of spectacle, it also boasts extraordinary set pieces, among them the opening love duet of Alvaro and Leonora; Leonora's penitence arias in Acts II and IV; and the pre-duel duet between Alvaro and Carlo.

⇥ Verdi always insisted on approving the singers for his premieres. In this case, when he arrived in St Petersburg, he vetoed the unfortunate soprano cast as Leonora and refused to rehearse until she was replaced. ⇤

→ **PRINCIPAL ROLES** ←

Marchese di Calatrava *bass*

Leonora *soprano*
Calatrava's daughter

Don Carlo *baritone*
Calatrava's son

Don Alvaro *tenor*
Leonora's lover, a
half-caste Inca prince

Preziosilla *mezzo-soprano*
A Gypsy

Father Superior *bass*

PLOT SYNOPSIS

Spain and Italy in the 18th century

ACT ONE Leonora is torn between eloping with Alvaro, her South American lover, and staying loyal to her father, the Marchese di Calatrava. When she agrees to leave, the Marchese appears and challenges Alvaro, who throws down his pistol, accidentally killing him.

ACT TWO The Marchese's son, Carlo, tells guests at an inn that he is pursuing a foreigner who murdered a close friend's father and abducted his sister. A Gypsy predicts a terrible future for him. Meanwhile, Leonora, disguised as a man, is given refuge in a monastery ♂, where no one will know her identity.

"La Vergine degli angeli"

The legendary tenor Enrico Caruso as Alvaro holds the dying Leonora, sung by Rosa Ponselle, in this opera's final scene in a 1918 production in New York.

ACT THREE Having joined the Spanish army in Italy, Alvaro rescues Carlo in battle, but they do not recognize each other and pledge friendship. When Alvaro is wounded, Carlo finds a picture of Leonora in his belongings. Challenged to a duel, Alvaro insists he never seduced Leonora, but Carlo says she must also die. Their duel is interrupted and Alvaro decides to enter a monastery.

ACT FOUR Carlo tracks down Alvaro and demands a fresh duel ♂. Wounded, Carlo cries out for a priest and Alvaro runs to Leonora's cave. They recognize each other, but Leonora hurries to help Carlo. Moments later, she reappears bleeding, mortally wounded by Carlo in a final act of revenge. Dying, she pardons Alvaro.

"Invano Alvaro"

DON CARLOS/DON CARLO

⚓ Grand opera in five acts, 3½ hours (four-act version, 3 hours)
☷ 1866–1867 (rev. 1872); Italian version 1882–1883

♔ 11 March 1867, Paris Opéra, France
📖 Joseph Méry and Camille du Locle, after Schiller's 1787 dramatic poem *Don Carlos, Infant von Spanien*

Don Carlos, Verdi's most ambitious opera, has long been burdened by its very size. Verdi dropped Act I for the Italian version, *Don Carlo*, but he later restored it to create the now preferred "Modena version". Both in its paean to freedom and its musical grandeur, *Don Carlos* is a *tour de force*. Among its many highlights are the duets between Carlos and Elisabeth and the confrontation between Philip and the Grand Inquisitor.

⚐ Although Paris demanded lengthy five-act operas, the first version of *Don Carlos* still had to be cut by half an hour because the last train left Paris for the suburbs at 12.25 AM. ⚐

→ PRINCIPAL ROLES ←

Philip II *bass*
King of Spain

Don Carlos *tenor*
The Spanish heir

Elisabeth de Valois *soprano*
Philip's bride

Rodrigo, Marquis de Posa *baritone*
Don Carlos's friend

Eboli *mezzo-soprano*
Lady-in-waiting

Grand Inquisitor *bass*

PLOT SYNOPSIS

France and Spain, around 1560

ACT ONE Don Carlos travels incognito to France to meet Elisabeth and gives her a casket with his likeness. When

"De quels transports poignants"

she recognizes him, they celebrate their union ♫. But they learn she must wed his father, King Philip.

ACT TWO Upset by Spain's occupation of Flanders, Carlos urges Elisabeth to have the king send him there. She admits that she loves him, while King Philip harbours suspicions about her loyalty.

ACT THREE Carlos mistakes Eboli for the queen. When Eboli realizes his love is not for her, she vows revenge. As the king watches heretics burning in an *auto-da-fé*, Carlos demands to be made regent of Flanders. Rebuffed, he draws his sword, but his friend Rodrigo disarms him.

ACT FOUR The Grand Inquisitor approves Philip's plan to kill his son and declares Rodrigo a heretic. Philip finds Carlos's portrait in Elisabeth's casket and accuses her of adultery. When Rodrigo visits Carlos in prison, he is murdered. Eboli helps Carlos to escape.

ACT FIVE Elisabeth urges Carlos to forget her and to save Flanders. As they bid each other a tender farewell ♫, King Philip arrives to arrest

"Au revoir dans un monde"

them. Carlos retreats towards the tomb of his grandfather, and the spectre of Charles V pulls him to safety.

Productions of *Don Carlos*, like this one at the Opéra Bastille, Paris, in 1999, are frequently rich in royal pomp and religious ritual.

SIMON BOCCANEGRA

🎵 Melodramma in a prologue and three acts, 2¼ hours

🎼 1880–1881 (a radical revision of the 1857 score)

🏛 24 March 1881, La Scala, Milan, Italy

📖 Francesco Maria Piave and Arrigo Boito, after Antonio García Gutiérrez's 1843 play, *Simón Boccanegra*

Simon Boccanegra is a father–daughter love story enclosed within a weighty political drama. Although rarely performed, even in its final 1881 form, it is a stirring opera, dominated by low male voices: two baritones and two basses. It has few arias, but instead evokes the mood of conspiracy through a wealth of rich duets and ensembles. The great novelty of the 1881 revised version is the chamber council scene in Act I, one of Verdi's finest finales.

⊰ Even Verdi considered his 1857 version of *Simon Boccanegra* to be depressing, cold, and monotonous. He was therefore all too happy to rework it with the librettist Arrigo Boito over 20 years later. ⊱

> → PRINCIPAL ROLES ←
>
> **Simon Boccanegra** *baritone*
> A corsair and later Doge
>
> **Amelia Boccanegra (Grimaldi)** *soprano*
> Boccanegra's "lost" daughter
>
> **Gabriele Adorno** *tenor*
> Amelia's lover
>
> **Jacopo Fiesco** *bass*
> A former Doge
>
> **Paolo Albiani** *bass*
> A plebeian
>
> **Pietro** *baritone*
> A plebeian

PLOT SYNOPSIS

Genoa, Italy, in the mid-14th century

PROLOGUE Nominated to succeed Fiesco, a hated patrician, as Doge, the corsair Simon Boccanegra hopes to be reunited with Fiesco's daughter, Maria. Fiesco, knowing that Maria has died, says he will forgive Simon only when he gives up Amelia, Maria's missing daughter with Simon. As Simon discovers Maria's body, cheers announce his election as Doge.

ACT ONE Twenty-five years later, Amelia's lover Gabriele and her guardian Andrea (Fiesco) are conspiring against Simon. Suspecting the Doge wants her to marry Paolo, she says she loves another. When she also reveals she is an orphan, Simon recognizes his lost daughter ♻. Gabriele tries to kill Simon, but Amelia stops him.

'Figlia!... a tal nome'

ACT TWO Paolo has poisoned Simon's water and convinced Gabriele that Amelia is Simon's mistress. Amelia denies betrayal. When Simon drinks the poisoned water and falls asleep, Gabriele prepares to kill him. Learning that Simon is Amelia's father, he pledges loyalty to the Doge.

ACT THREE As bells from the wedding of Amelia and Gabriele ring out, Simon recognizes Andrea as Fiesco. Reconciled with his enemy at last ♻, Simon dies in the arms of Fiesco, proclaiming Gabriele his successor with his last breath.

"Piango, perchè mi parla"

Gabriele (Plácido Domingo, *left*) is reunited with Amelia (Kallen Esperian), Royal Opera, 1997.

AÏDA

⚐ Opera in four acts, 2¼ hours
☒ 1870 (rev. 1871)
♇ 24 December 1871, Opera House, Cairo, Egypt

▢ Antonio Ghislanzoni, after Camille du Locle's French version of Auguste Mariette's proposed storyline

Aïda, Verdi's most spectacular work, is an exotic Italian opera with authentic Egyptian roots. Cairo's Opera House opened in November 1869 with *Rigoletto*, but the archeologist Auguste Mariette persuaded the Turkish governor of Egypt to commission an "Egyptian opera" from Verdi. Mariette then invented the story which became *Aïda*. In creating the triumphal march of Act II, Verdi took his inspiration from French grand opera. Hugely dramatic and musically exciting, *Aïda* was an immediate success and, within ten years, had been performed in 155 opera houses around the world.

> ✦ PRINCIPAL ROLES ✦
>
> The King of Egypt *bass*
> Amneris *mezzo-soprano* The Egyptian king's daughter
> Aïda *soprano* An enslaved Ethiopian princess
> Radamès *tenor* An Egyptian captain
> Ramfis *bass* High Priest of Isis
> Amonasro *baritone* Aïda's father, King of Ethiopia

⚏ Having had its premiere in Cairo's opera house in 1871, *Aïda* returned to Egypt in 1987 with a dramatic outdoor production before the 3,000-year-old Temple of Amenhotep III beside the Nile in today's Luxor. ⚏

PLOT SYNOPSIS

Egypt, at the time of the Pharaohs

ACT ONE At the royal palace in Memphis, Radamès hopes to lead the Egyptian army against the invading Ethiopians, inspired by his love for Aïda, a captured Ethiopian princess ♟. But Radamès is also loved by Amneris, the Egyptian princess. When the king enters, Ramfis, the High Priest, names Radamès as Egyptian commander. As Radamès is led away to be blessed, Aïda worries he will fight her father, Amonasro, the Ethiopian king ♟.

"Celeste Aïda, forma divina"

"Ritorna vincitor"

LUCIANO PAVAROTTI

Luciano Pavarotti was the leading tenor divo of the late 20th century, albeit hailed more for the remarkable timbre of his voice than for his stage performances. He covered the entire 19th-century Italian repertoire, from the *bel canto* of Rossini and Donizetti to the dramatic operas of Verdi and Puccini, with Radamès in *Aïda* one of his best-known roles. By singing before vast crowds in stadiums around the world, he helped carry opera to new audiences.

ACT TWO As Moorish slaves dance, Aïda enters looking forlorn. Amneris feigns sympathy and tests her by announcing that Radamès has been killed. Seeing Aïda's distress, Amneris accuses her of loving Radamès. She then reveals that Radamès lives and, as Aïda thanks the gods, announces that she is Aïda's rival. Aïda begs for mercy, but Amneris vows revenge. Radamès returns to Thebes victorious, leading a triumphal march. Suddenly, Aïda recognizes

Fiorenza Cedolins as Aïda deceives Walter Fraccaro's Radamès into betraying his country in a pivotal scene from Act IV of this exotic production of Verdi's well-loved opera, staged at the Teatro Regio in Torino, Italy, in 2005.

her father among the prisoners. Disguised as a soldier, he tells the Egyptian king of Amonasro's death and asks him to free the Ethiopian prisoners. When Radamès supports the appeal, the king concurs and offers Amneris to Radamès. Aïda is heartbroken.

ACT THREE Awaiting Radamès on the banks of the Nile, Aïda laments she will never again see Ethiopia ♫. Her father appears, again ready to attack Egypt. He says he knows Radamès loves her and demands that she discover Egypt's military secrets. Seeing Aïda, Radamès

"O patria mia"

promises to tell the king of his love for her. Warning of Amneris's wrath, she insists they flee now ♫ and asks how they can avoid the Egyptian legions. He then reveals the army's route. As Amonasro steps forward, Radamès realizes with horror that he has betrayed Egypt and waits to be arrested. In the confusion, the Ethiopians escape.

"Fuggiam gli ardori inospiti"

ACT FOUR Amneris begs Radamès to justify his action so she can plead for his life ♫, but he refuses, saying he will not exchange his life for Aïda's death. Amneris responds that Aïda has not died, but he must promise never to see her again. He again refuses. As Ramfis orders Radamès buried in a sealed tomb, Amneris collapses in despair. Inside the dark tomb, Radamès is awaiting his death when Aïda suddenly appears, saying she has come to die with him. Seeing there is no escape, they fall into each other's arms and bid the world farewell ♫. As Aïda dies, Amneris can be heard imploring peace.

"Giò I Sacerdoti adunansi"

"O terra, addio; addio, valle di pianti"

Cairo Opera celebrated the tenth anniversary of its new theatre and the silver jubilee of the 1973 October War by presenting *Aïda* at the Giza Pyramids in October 1998.

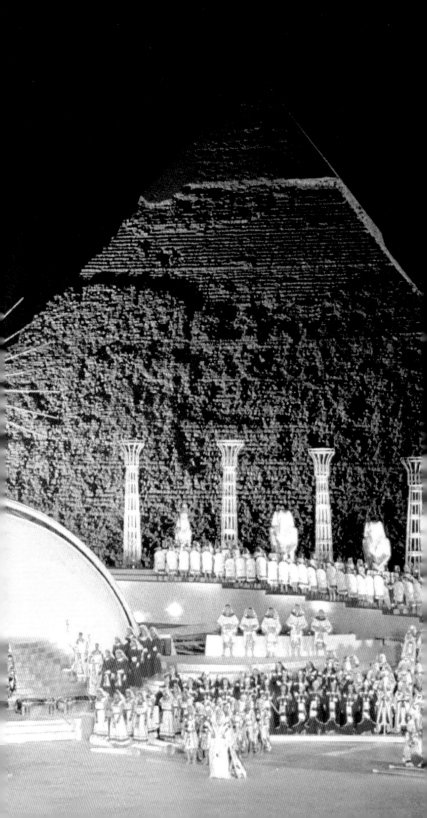

OTELLO
(Othello)

🎭 Dramma lirico in four acts, 2¼ hours
📖 Arrigo Boito, after Shakespeare's *Othello*
🗓 1884–1886 (rev. 1887)
🎦 5 February 1887, La Scala, Milan, Italy

Otello is considered to be the finest of the more than 200 operas based on Shakespeare's plays. For operatic purposes, Arrigo Boito's fast-paced libretto may even have improved on *Othello* by eliminating Act I and focusing immediately on Iago's evil machinations. Verdi in turn devoted enormous energy to writing, revising, and polishing what some experts consider his greatest opera. It includes one of the most demanding tenor parts in the entire opera repertoire, although few arias. Instead, Verdi uses deeply expressive orchestral writing to create near-continuous music. As a musical drama, it evokes Richard Wagner; melodically, though, it remains thoroughly Italian.

⊲ At the premiere of *Otello*, Verdi was called to take a bow 15 times during the performance and, at the final curtain, the entire audience rose to its feet, shouting, "Viva Verdi!". ⊳

➤ PRINCIPAL ROLES ←

Otello *tenor*
A Venetian general of Moorish extraction, now governor of Cyprus

Desdemona *soprano*
Otello's wife

Iago *baritone*
Otello's ensign

Emilia *mezzo-soprano*
Iago's wife and Desdemona's companion

Cassio *tenor*
A Venetian officer

Roderigo *tenor*
A Venetian gentleman

Ludovico *bass*
A Venetian ambassador

Montano *bass*
The former governor of Cyprus

PLOT SYNOPSIS

Cyprus in the late 15th century

ACT ONE Surviving a fierce storm, Otello arrives in Cyprus as the island's new governor. His perfidious ensign, Iago, pretends to help Roderigo win Otello's wife, Desdemona, but his real intent is to avenge Cassio's promotion over him. He persuades Cassio to drink, and then warns Roderigo that Cassio is his rival for Desdemona's love. Roderigo provokes a fight in the course of which Cassio wounds the island's retiring governor. Otello is furious at the disturbance and demotes Cassio. Eventually Otello is left alone with Desdemona and together they reminisce over how they fell in love ♻.

"Già nella notte densa"

An elegant poster for a new production of *Otello* staged at the Teatro Sociale in Como, Switzerland, in 1899.

ACT TWO Iago assures Cassio that Desdemona will persuade Otello to reinstate him. Iago then celebrates his own evil in a blasphemous Credo ♻. Observing Cassio with Desdemona, Iago asks Otello if he trusts Cassio. Otello's reaction is immediate, but Iago warns him against jealousy. Desdemona seeks pardon for Cassio. Otello complains of a burning head and, when Desdemona wipes his brow with a handkerchief, he throws it to the ground. Emilia picks it

"Credo in un Dio crudel"

up, but Iago, her husband, grabs it. He pretends to calm Otello, who angrily demands proof of his wife's impurity. Iago recounts hearing Cassio talk in his sleep of making love to Desdemona and seeing Cassio carrying Desdemona's handkerchief. As Otello falls to his knees, they swear vengeance ♏.

"Si, pel ciel marmoreo giuro"

ACT THREE Otello says his head hurts again and he asks Desdemona for her handkerchief. She offers one, but he demands the one he gave her. He then accuses her of being false, but she swears that she is faithful. Pushing her from the room, he plunges into despair ♏. With Otello observing them, Iago asks Cassio in a soft voice about his mistress. Otello sees Cassio laugh and display to Iago an

"Dio! Mi potevi scagliar"

PLÁCIDO DOMINGO

Admired as much for his beautiful and expressive voice as for his prowess as an actor, Plácido Domingo has sung and recorded more roles than any tenor in operatic history. Born in Spain, raised in Mexico, Domingo was perhaps most famous for his dramatic portrayal of the ill-fated Moor in Verdi's *Otello*. More recently, he has taken on Wagner, with Parsifal a favourite role. An all-round musician, Domingo is also general director of the Washington National Opera and the Los Angeles Opera.

embroidered handkerchief left in his lodgings. With Otello now convinced of Desdemona's betrayal, Iago suggests strangling her in her bed of sin. Venetian ambassadors bring word that Otello has been recalled to Venice and Cassio will succeed him. Forcing Desdemona to her knees, Otello tells her to weep. Everyone is shocked by Otello's inexplicable behaviour, except Iago, who urges him to complete the task. Iago then tells Roderigo that it is time to murder Cassio.

ACT FOUR Sitting with Emilia, Desdemona sings the "Willow Song" taught to her as a child ♏. After a heartfelt farewell, Emilia then leaves her alone to pray ♏. Otello bursts in, enraged. Desdemona begs for her life, protesting her innocence, but he strangles her. Emilia brings word that Cassio has killed Roderigo, and then sees Desdemona. She calls for help and, as others arrive, she reveals Iago's treachery. Destroyed by what he has done, Otello stabs himself and, giving Desdemona a final kiss, he dies.

"Mi madre aveva"

"Ave Maria"

After murdering his wife Desdemona, David Rendall's Otello discovers her innocence and is racked by remorse in Peter Hall's production at the Glyndebourne Festival in 2005.

FALSTAFF

🎵 Commedia lirica in three acts, 2¼ hours
📅 1889–1892 (rev. 1893–1894)
🏛 9 February 1893, La Scala, Milan, Italy

📖 Arrigo Boito, after Shakespeare's *The Merry Wives of Windsor*

Falstaff, Verdi's final opera, was also his first comic opera since the disaster of *Un giorno di regno* 53 years earlier. Written almost secretly because Verdi was not sure he would live to finish it, it showed that, at 79, he was still full of surprises. As in *Otello*, *Falstaff* abandons set-piece arias for the Wagnerian model of continuous music. But unlike *Otello*'s familiar territory of tragedy, *Falstaff* reveals Verdi's humour through its almost talkative orchestration, "comic fugues", and riotous ensembles, one with 12 voice parts. He parodies not only Rossini's comic operas, but also some of his own dramatic works. La Scala's audiences were puzzled at first, but its overwhelming charm soon won them over.

→ Rossini thought Verdi "too melancholy and serious" to write *opera buffa*, while Verdi feared appearing "frivolous". But *Falstaff* rejuvenated him. At the end of the score, he scribbled: "On your way, old John!". ⊱

→ PRINCIPAL ROLES ←

Sir John Falstaff *baritone*
A paunchy dissolute knight

Ford *baritone*
A wealthy local

Fenton *tenor*
A young gentleman

Dr Caius *tenor*
The local physician

Bardolph *tenor* &
Pistol *baritone*
Falstaff's henchmen

Alice Ford *soprano*
Ford's wife

Nannetta *soprano*
Ford's daughter

Mistress Quickly *contralto*
The inn-keeper

Meg Page *mezzo-soprano*
Alice Ford's friend

PLOT SYNOPSIS

Windsor, England, in the early 15th century

ACT ONE Dr Caius storms into the Garter Inn protesting that Falstaff's men, Bardolph and Pistol, stole his money. Falstaff also wants money – for wine. He has a solution: he has fallen for two Windsor wives, Alice Ford and Meg Page, and has love letters for each. His sidekicks refuse to deliver them out of honour, but Falstaff has his own idea of honour: "Can honour fill your belly?" ♪

"L'Onore! Ladri!"

Alice and Meg receive identical letters from Falstaff and, with Mistress Quickly, the inn-keeper, they decide to teach him a lesson. Meanwhile, Ford hatches his own plan after learning of Falstaff's plan to seduce his wife. As the women resume their plotting, Nannetta, Alice's daughter, and Fenton steal hidden kisses ♪.

"Torno all'assalto'

ACT TWO Mistress Quickly tells Falstaff that Alice can receive him that afternoon. As Falstaff beams, Ford arrives disguised as "Fontana", complaining that his love for Alice Ford is not returned. He offers Falstaff money to seduce her, so he can follow. Falstaff agrees, boasting that he will

An ornate Italian edition of *Falstaff* depicts the fat knight in contemplation of a jug of ale.

"E sogno? O realta" soon be cuckolding Alice's husband. Alone, Ford gives way to jealousy ♫. At Ford's house, Falstaff declares his love for Alice, but she notes that he already loves Meg Page. When Meg is announced, Falstaff hides behind a screen. Ford and others rush in, empty a laundry basket and search the house. Alice moves Falstaff to the laundry basket, but sounds of kissing behind the screen convince Ford that Falstaff has been found. Instead he discovers Fenton and Nannetta. Amid the confusion, Alice has her servants tip the laundry basket – and Falstaff – into the Thames.

ACT THREE Falstaff is consoling himself with wine ♫ when Mistress Quickly tells him to meet Alice at midnight in Windsor Park, where he must dress as the "Black Huntsman". The others take note that the huntsman's ghost sometimes appears, wearing long horns and accompanied by fairies. While Alice tells Nannetta to come as a bride, Ford orders Dr Caius to don a friar's hood and be ready to marry Nannetta. Fenton is dreaming of love ♫ when Alice gives him a friar's hood. At midnight, Falstaff arrives and tries to embrace Alice but, hearing witches approach, he throws himself on

"Mondo ladro"

"Dal labbro il canto"

At the English National Opera in 1997, Alan Opie as Falstaff wears the horns of the "Black Huntsman" and is mocked by "fairies".

the ground. Dressed as fairies, satyrs, and witches, everyone pinches and insults the prostrate knight until he repents. It is then time for Dr Caius to marry Nannetta, but another masked couple joins them. When the ceremony is over, Dr Caius has wed Bardolph by mistake. With Falstaff happy not to be the only fool, everyone leaves for a feast.

FALSTAFF

From the moment Falstaff appeared in Shakespeare's *Henry IV Part I*, he became one of theatre's most beloved rascals. Even Elizabeth I was charmed and reportedly asked for a play about Falstaff in love. Shakespeare swiftly penned *The Merry Wives of Windsor* (the inspiration for Verdi's opera), then brought Falstaff back for *Henry IV Part II* and killed him off in *Henry V*. Yet somehow the fat knight lived on, inspiring at least four operas, although only Verdi's *Falstaff* is now still performed.

Tito Gobbi, the Italian baritone, as Falstaff in Budapest, 1968.

"If only I could find my subject,
a subject full of passion and pain."
Giacomo Puccini

GIACOMO
PUCCINI

Born: 22 December 1858, Lucca (Italy)
Died: 11 November 1924, Brussels, Belgium

Giacomo Puccini enjoys a unique place in the history of opera thanks to *La bohème*: for over a century, this tragic love story set among down-at-heel Parisians has been the most performed work in the entire canon. It was not, however, an isolated triumph. Although Puccini created only ten operas in a 40-year career, *Tosca*, *Madama Butterfly*, and *Turandot* are beloved for their beauty and passion.

Puccini was born into a family of Tuscan musicians, taking his first lessons from his father and uncle. But it was a performance of Verdi's *Aïda* in Pisa in 1876 that won him over to opera. Years later, he explained: "God touched me with His little finger and said, 'Write for the theatre, only for the theatre.'" When he entered the Milan Conservatory in 1880, he then had the good fortune to have an opera composer, Amilcare Ponchielli (*La Gioconda*), among his teachers. In 1884, his first opera, *Le villi*, was a huge success, but his second, *Edgar*, flopped, prompting the music publisher Giulio Ricordi to send him to Bayreuth to learn from Wagner's *Die Meistersinger von Nürnberg*. Upon his return, he wrote *Manon Lescaut*, the first work to bring him international recognition. Then, over the next 12 years, with *La bohème*, *Tosca*, and *Madama Butterfly*, he was unchallenged as Verdi's heir.

What these operas have in common is the power of their melodies and melodrama to move audiences, even to tears: in each, a beautiful heroine – Manon, Mimì, Tosca, and Cio-Cio-San – dies tragically. The shocking and violent reality they portrayed also placed them inside a turn-of-the-century Italian movement called *verismo*. As it happens, Puccini's off-stage life was also not short of drama. In his twenties, he provoked a scandal by running

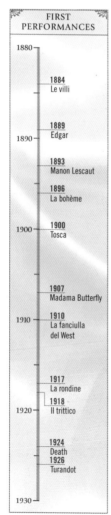

FIRST PERFORMANCES

1880 —

1884
Le villi

1889
Edgar
1890 —

1893
Manon Lescaut

1896
La bohème

1900 —
1900
Tosca

1907
Madama Butterfly

1910 —
1910
La fanciulla del West

1917
La rondine
1918
Il trittico
1920 —

1924
Death
1926
Turandot

1930 —

Tosca, **an opera in which the heroine** is herself a diva, is Puccini's most dramatic. Act II (*left*) climaxes with Tosca's daring murder of the evil police chief Scarpia.

away with a married woman, Elvira Gemignani, with whom he had a son long before they finally married in 1904. Even then, his eye would wander, and another scandal erupted in 1908 when a young maid in his household committed suicide: ever-jealous, Elvira had wrongly accused her of carrying Puccini's child.

DISTRACTIONS

Still, other reasons account for his slow pace of writing. Wealthy at an early age, he enjoyed travelling and had a passion for cars. Indeed, a serious car accident stopped him from working for eight months in 1903. But he also wavered before choosing a subject, combing plays and books for exotic tales. He would then become fully engaged with his writers in shaping the libretto, often adding his own characters and scenes. After *Madama Butterfly*, he was distracted when a group of (now forgotten) young composers accused him of writing "petit bourgeois" operas. This criticism may

well have led the ever-sensitive Puccini to write his next opera, *La fanciulla del West*, around an American theme for an American audience. But it also signalled a change in Puccini's music, with greater emphasis on narrative composition and less on catchy tunes. In this opera, non-Italian influence was evident: of Wagner, and also Debussy, Richard Strauss, and Stravinsky. All came together in the marvellous inventiveness of Puccini's final – unfinished – opera, *Turandot*, first performed in 1926, two years after his death. Yet even with the unquestioned virtuosity of *Turandot*, Puccini's music has continued to divide opera lovers, some

An Italian poster evokes the scene in Act II of *Tosca* where Tosca murders Scarpia.

happy to be embraced by its melodic warmth, others put off by its unabashed sentimentality. Still, Puccini's place in operatic history is secure. Although he wrote more than half his operas in the 20th century, he was in spirit a 19th-century composer and, as such, brought three centuries of Italian-dominated opera to a brilliant close.

Puccini, who loved fast cars, is seen here with an Isotta Fraschini. In the back seat on the left is his wife, Elvira Gemignani.

MANON LESCAUT

🎵 Lyric drama in four acts, 2 hours
📆 1889–1892 (rev. 1893 & 1922)
🏛 1 February 1893, Teatro Regio, Turin, Italy

📖 Ruggero Leoncavallo and others, based on the Abbé Prévost's 1731 novel, *L'histoire du Chevalier des Grieux et de Manon Lescaut*

Manon Lescaut, Puccini's first international success, established his reputation for life. He took a risk by returning to a story that had already been set by Auber and Massenet, but he plagued no fewer than seven librettists until he was happy. The result is a deeply lyrical opera, with memorable arias and duets tracking Manon's ill-fated passage through love, frivolity, and finally exile to her miserable death in a distant desert.

⇥ Puccini was unworried that Massenet had written *Manon* nine years earlier. "He feels it as a Frenchman, with powder and minuets," he said. "I shall feel it as an Italian, with a desperate passion". ⇤

⇸ PRINCIPAL ROLES ⇷

Manon Lescaut *soprano*
Il Cavaliere Renato des Grieux *tenor*
Manon's lover
Lescaut *baritone*
Manon's brother
Geronte di Ravoir *bass*
Manon's wealthy suitor
Edmondo *tenor*
Des Grieux's friend

PLOT SYNOPSIS

France and Louisiana, US, in the 18th century

ACT ONE Outside an inn in Amiens, Des Grieux is flirting with girls when a coach arrives with an elderly official, Geronte, accompanied by Manon and her brother Lescaut, a soldier. Des Grieux promptly falls for Manon ♂, but she is bound for a convent. Learning that Geronte plans to abduct Manon, he persuades her to come with him to Paris.

"Donna non vidi mai"

ACT TWO In Paris, Geronte's wealth has won over Manon, but she still yearns for Des Grieux ♂. When he appears, her love is reawakened. They prepare to escape, but she is reluctant to leave her jewels. Her brother warns that Geronte has denounced her as immoral and, when she delays once more, police arrest her.

"In quelle trine morbide"

ACT THREE Des Grieux and Lescaut hope to free Manon before she is deported from Le Havre to America. Through a cell window, Des Grieux tries to reassure her,

but soon the jailed women are led towards the prison ship. As Manon is pushed aboard, Des Grieux persuades the captain to hire him as a deckhand.

ACT FOUR Lost in a Louisiana desert, Manon faints. Des Grieux revives her, then sets off to look for water. Manon remembers her "horrible past". When Des Grieux returns empty-handed, she expires, vowing her love will never die.

The Italian soprano Daniela Dessì as a briefly-wealthy Manon Lescaut in Act II of a 2003 production of Puccini's opera in Seville, Spain.

LA BOHÈME

🎵 Opera in four acts, 1¾ hours
⏳ 1893–1895 (rev. 1896)
🏛 1 February 1896, Teatro Regio, Turin, Italy

📖 Giuseppe Giocosa and Luigi Illica, based on episodes from Henry Murger's 1845 play *Scènes de la vie de bohème*

La bohème, arguably the world's favourite opera, had a stormy birth: another composer, Ruggero Leoncavallo, was already working on the story and accused Puccini of theft. Both versions were staged, but only Puccini's is remembered. Its strength lies in the perfect marriage of an intensely poignant story and a richly melodic score. The best-known arias show Rodolfo and Mimì falling in love in Act I, but the Act III quartet is also a *tour de force*. The story reminded Puccini of his days as a destitute student. After composing the final scene, he recalled, "I began to weep like a child".

⇥ After the premiere of *La bohème*, a Turin newspaper wrote: "Even as it leaves little impression in the minds of the audience, *La bohème* will leave no great trace on the history of opera". ⇤

PLOT SYNOPSIS

Paris, France, in 1830

ACT ONE Spending Christmas Eve in a Paris garret, Rodolfo, a poet, and Marcello, a painter, fight the cold by burning Rodolfo's manuscript in a stove. As Colline, a philosopher, joins them, two boys bring food, drink, and cigars. Ready for a feast, Schaunard, a musician, enters waving money and announces they must eat out. The landlord Benoît wants his rent, but the men distract him with wine and talk of women. When he admits philandering, the men feign shock and chase him away. As they head for Café Momus, Rodolfo says he must finish an article. Hearing a knock, Rodolfo finds a young woman needing a light for her candle. Coughing violently, she faints and Rodolfo revives her with some wine. She loses her key, and he helps look for it on the floor. Suddenly her cold hand touches his and, moved, he introduces himself 🔊. Hesitatingly, Mimì gives her name and says she lives alone. As his friends call, urging him to make haste, Rodolfo and Mimì realize that they have fallen in love.

The title page of the first edition of *La bohème*, published by Giulio Ricordi, emphasizes the carefree lifestyle enjoyed by the bohemians.

"Che gelida manina"

ACT TWO In a crowded Left Bank street, Rodolfo buys Mimì a red bonnet before joining his friends at Café Momus. Everyone seems happy until Marcello sees his former mistress, Musetta, arriving with her aged suitor, Alcindoro. She treats Alcindoro with disdain and plays up to Marcello ♫. Pretending her feet hurt, she sends Alcindoro to buy her new shoes and falls into Marcello's arms. The waiter brings the bill to the revellers, who slip away and leave Alcindoro to pay for their fun.

"Quando me'n vo"

ACT THREE Two months later, Mimì tells Marcello that, because of Rodolfo's constant jealousy, she must leave him. When Marcello promises to intercede, Rodolfo confesses that he still loves her. Mimì's coughs and sobs reveal her presence. Full of remorse, Rodolfo leads her into the tavern, where she sadly bids farewell to him ♫. Then, as a fight erupts between Marcello and Musetta, Rodolfo and Mimì decide to stay together until the spring.

"Addio. Donde lieta uscì"

ACT FOUR Months later in the garret, as Rodolfo and Marcello try to forget their lost loves ♫, Musetta arrives with an ailing Mimì. To pay for a doctor, Musetta decides to sell her earrings,

"O Mimì, tu più non torni"

CARUSO AND MELBA

Enrico Caruso, the most admired tenor of the early 20th century and the first to become a recording star, made his débuts at both La Scala and Covent Garden in *La bohème*. When Puccini first heard him, he exclaimed: "Who has sent you to me? God?" Caruso was also famous for his practical jokes. One victim was the Australian soprano Nellie Melba. During a London performance of *La bohème*, as he grasped Melba's "frozen hands" in Act I, Caruso slipped her a warm sausage. She was furious, but recalled the story with humour years later.

and Colline says goodbye to his overcoat ♫. Between coughs, Mimì tells Rodolfo that she always loved him and falls asleep. As the others return, they notice she has died. Finally Rodolfo too understands and collapses in tears.

"Vecchia zimarra"

Luciano Pavarotti sings Rodolfo opposite Mirella Freni's Mimì in a production at the Exhibition Hall Theatre, Beijing, in 1986.

TOSCA

⚏ Opera in three acts, 2 hours
🎬 1896–1899
♇ 14 January 1900, Teatro Costanzi, Rome, Italy

📖 Giuseppe Giacosa and Luigi Illica, after Victorien Sardou's 1887 play, *La Tosca*

Tosca, Puccini's most plot-driven opera, is a feverish drama of love, jealousy, courage, and death. After the composer saw Sarah Bernhardt in Sardou's *Tosca*, he quickly recognized the play's operatic potential. Driven by Tosca's fiery temperament, the score is packed with stirring arias and duets. At its heart is the powerful Act II confrontation between Tosca and Scarpia, where each uses sex as a weapon until Scarpia lies dead at Tosca's feet. To keep pace with the action, Puccini's orchestration is stormier than anything he had written before. For poetry, he noted, he substituted passion.

> ✦ PRINCIPAL ROLES ✦
>
> **Floria Tosca** *soprano*
> A prima donna
> **Mario Cavaradossi** *tenor*
> Her lover
> **Baron Scarpia** *baritone*
> Police chief of Rome
> **Cesare Angelotti** *bass*
> A fugitive rebel
> **Sacristan** *baritone*
> **Spoletta** *tenor*
> Scarpia's henchman

⚔ *Tosca* is famous for its production mishaps. Once, poorly briefed extras in the firing squad shot Tosca instead of Cavaradossi; another time, Tosca leaped to her death, landed on a trampoline and reappeared. ⚔

PLOT SYNOPSIS

Rome, Italy, 17 and 18 June 1800

ACT ONE Angelotti, a fugitive republican, is hiding in the church of Sant'Andrea della Valle, where Mario Cavaradossi is completing a painting of Mary Magdalene. The sacristan says the portrait resembles a woman who prays in the church, but Cavaradossi muses that, while painting the "unknown beauty", he thinks only of Tosca, his mistress ♪.

"Recondita armonia"

When Angelotti emerges from hiding, Cavaradossi offers his help. When Tosca arrives, Angelotti again hides. Dreaming of love, she tells Cavaradossi to meet her after her evening concert. But then she recognizes the portrait

Emilio de Marchi (1851–1901), one of the greatest tenors of Puccini's time, created the role of Cavaradossi in Rome in 1900.

of the Marchesa Attavanti, Angelotti's sister, and explodes with jealousy. Cavaradossi reassures her of his love ♪ and finally persuades her to leave.

"Mia gelosa"

Angelotti reappears and, as a cannon shot announces his escape, Cavaradossi offers his villa as a hideout.

Hunting for the fugitive, Scarpia the police chief finds only a fan forgotten in the church by Angelotti's sister. When Tosca returns, Scarpia provokes her by saying the portrait is of a loose woman and by displaying the fan as evidence. Furious, Tosca heads for Cavaradossi's villa, followed by Scarpia's agents. As a Te Deum celebrates a royalist victory over Napoleon, Scarpia dreams of winning Tosca.

Catherine Malfitano, playing Tosca, appears to leap off the Castel Sant'Angelo in a 1992 production televised live from the opera's original settings.

ACT TWO In the Palazzo Farnese, the police chief

"Ha più forte sapore" | Scarpia yearns for Tosca ♪. The escaped prisoner has not been found, but Cavaradossi is dragged in. Interrogated about Angelotti, he says he knows nothing. As Tosca arrives, he is taken away. She hears his groans and Scarpia says she can end the torture. She refuses to cooperate but, as the torture intensifies, she finally reveals Angelotti's hiding place. Cavaradossi feels betrayed by Tosca, but is elated by news of a royalist defeat and cries "Victory!" Scarpia angrily orders his execution. But he then tells Tosca that, if she gives herself to him, she can still save her lover's life. Distraught,

Tosca asks if she deserves this fate ♪. As word arrives | "Vissi d'arte" of Angelotti's suicide, she finally accepts Scarpia's terms, but insists that her lover also be freed. Scarpia says that, after a mock execution, they can flee. As he signs a safe-conduct, Tosca stabs him in the heart, crying "Die, you fiend! Die! Die!"

ACT THREE A few hours later, awaiting execution in the Castel Sant'Angelo, Cavaradossi | "E lucevan le stelle" is dreaming of Tosca ♪. Suddenly, she arrives with the safe-conduct. Explaining how she killed Scarpia, she tells her lover that a carriage awaits them | "O dolci mani" ♪. But first he must undergo a mock execution. Cavaradossi is led to the roof of the castle and shots ring out. As he falls, Tosca tells him to lie still until the soldiers have left. Then, in horror, she realizes he is dead. As officers return to arrest her for murdering Scarpia, she leaps to her death.

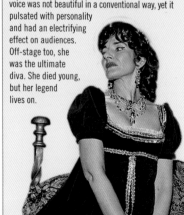

MARIA CALLAS (1923–1977)

The most charismatic soprano of the 20th century, Maria Callas (*below*) was best known for high voltage roles like Tosca, appropriately herself a temperamental opera singer. Callas's formidable voice was not beautiful in a conventional way, yet it pulsated with personality and had an electrifying effect on audiences. Off-stage too, she was the ultimate diva. She died young, but her legend lives on.

MADAMA BUTTERFLY

🖉 A Japanese tragedy in three acts, 2 hours
☙ 1902–1903 (rev. 1904–1906)
♇ 17 February 1904, La Scala, Milan, Italy

📖 Giuseppe Giacosa and Luigi Illica, after
David Belasco's 1900 play *Madame Butterfly*,
from a short story by John Luther Long

Madama Butterfly is a hauntingly lyrical opera which, in its day, mirrored the West's new interest in Japan. Puccini himself studied Japanese folk songs and manners in a bid for authenticity. But while he borrows some Japanese motifs and imitates some Japanese melodies, the music remains Italian. Unusually, though, this is a tragedy laced with cruelty. Only 15 and already a geisha when she meets Pinkerton, the purity of her love contrasts fiercely with the American's predatory cynicism. This innocence is conveyed in the sumptuous duet closing Act I, the ever-hopeful "One Fine Day", and even in the farewell to her child. Puccini described it as his most "deeply-felt and imaginative" opera.

> ➜ PRINCIPAL ROLES ◆
>
> Cio-Cio-San (Madama
> Butterfly) *soprano*
> A geisha
>
> Suzuki *mezzo-soprano*
> Cio-Cio-San's maid
>
> BF Pinkerton *tenor*
> An American naval lieutenant
>
> Sharpless *baritone*
> The American consul
>
> Kate Pinkerton *mezzo-
> soprano*
> Pinkerton's American wife
>
> Goro *tenor*
> A marriage broker

⚔ Conducted by Arturo Toscanini, the premiere of *Madama Butterfly* was "a real lynching", in Puccini's words. Paid hecklers even revealed to Milan that the lead soprano, Rosina Storchio, had borne Toscanini's child. ⚔

PLOT SYNOPSIS

A hillside house overlooking Nagasaki harbour, Japan, around 1900

ACT ONE Goro, the marriage broker, shows Lt Pinkerton his new home and introduces his future wife's maid, Suzuki. But the American consul Sharpless warns the American against the marriage.

"Dovunque al mondo" Boasting of a different love on every shore ♂, Pinkerton says he is delighted by his pretty Japanese bride, who flutters "like a butterfly", but adds that one day he will marry "a real American bride". Butterfly (Cio-Cio-San) arrives, beaming with happiness. Butterfly says she is 15 and

An Italian poster for the 1904 premiere of Puccini's opera *Madama Butterfly*.

became a geisha after her family fell on hard times. As her relatives gather for the wedding, she shows Pinkerton the dagger used by her father to commit *hara-kiri*. After they are married, her uncle, a Buddhist priest, chastizes her for becoming a Christian. Butterfly's shocked family leaves and the newly-wedded couple at last celebrate their love ♂. | "Viene la sera"

ACT TWO Butterfly has heard nothing from Pinkerton in three years, but she is convinced he will return, even imagining his first words to his "dear little wife" ♂. Sharpless brings a letter from Pinkerton, but Butterfly gives him no chance to read it. She tells a wealthy suitor, Prince Yamadori, that she is still married. Finally Sharpless begins the letter, but Butterfly keeps interrupting him. When he asks what she would do

HISTORY REPEATED

The cultural misunderstanding that shapes *Madama Butterfly* has its roots in the American decision to force an end to Japan's isolation in 1854. This resulted not only in the gradual Westernization of Japanese public life, but also in the frequent visits of US Navy warships to Japanese ports, including Nagasaki. By the turn of the century, a love affair between an American officer and a geisha was not only plausible, but also common.

Matthew Perry, the American naval commander of the fleet that "opened" Japan, is depicted at Yokohama in this print.

when his father returns. The harbour gun heralds a ship and, peering through a telescope, Butterfly cries out that it is Pinkerton's. She mocks Suzuki's lack of faith, telling her to scatter the house with flower petals. She dons her bridal gown.

ACT THREE After waiting all night, Butterfly falls asleep just as Pinkerton arrives with Sharpless. Suzuki sees a woman with them and realizes it is Pinkerton's wife. Suzuki is devastated, but Sharpless and Pinkerton ask her to persuade Butterfly to give up her child. Seeing the flowers, Pinkerton is upset and, feeling forever haunted by Butterfly's "sweet face", he flees ♫. As Butterfly looks for Pinkerton, she instead finds the American | "Addio, fiorito asil!" woman who is now his wife. Reluctantly, she agrees to give up her son, but only if Pinkerton comes for him. Alone, Butterfly gives their son an American flag and bids | "Tu? tu?tu? tu? Piccolo Iddio!" him farewell ♫, then stabs herself with her father's dagger. As Pinkerton returns, she collapses and dies.

if Pinkerton never returned, she replies she would again become a geisha or, better, die. He urges her to accept Yamadori's proposal, but she surprises him by bringing out a blue-eyed child "Che tua madre" | ♫. As he leaves, Sharpless asks the boy's name; she says he is Sorrow but will become Joy

Yoko Watanabe as Cio-Cio-San and Giacomo Aragall as Lt Pinkerton in the Act I wedding scene at the Théâtre du Capitole in Toulouse, France, in 1996.

LA FANCIULLA DEL WEST
The Girl of the Golden West

- ✍ Opera in three acts, 2 hours
- 🕮 1908–1910
- ♇ 10 December 1910, Metropolitan Opera,

New York, US
- 📖 Guelfo Civinini and Carlo Zangarini, after David Belasco's 1908 play *The Girl of the Golden West*

La fanciulla del West has long been considered an oddity in Puccini's work, a lyrical opera set among roughneck gold miners in the American West. But he wrote it only partly to please his American fans. As *Madama Butterfly* and *Turandot* testify, he liked stories about faraway places. Musically, it also represented a change of direction, with the fast-paced narrative accompanied by continuous music, which is only rarely interrupted for arias. Its New York premiere, conducted by Arturo Toscanini, was a triumph.

✣ PRINCIPAL ROLES ✣

Minnie *soprano*
Owner of the Polka Saloon

Dick Johnson (Ramerrez) *tenor*
A bandit

Jack Rance *baritone*
A sheriff

Ashby *bass*
Wells Fargo agent

⛧ The Royal Opera House described *La fanciulla del West* as "opera's very own spaghetti western", not only because it boasts a gun-toting outlaw, but also because it includes nods to American folk music and ragtime. ⛧

PLOT SYNOPSIS

Cloudy Mountains, US, during the California Gold Rush, around 1849–1850

ACT ONE After breaking up a fight among miners, Sheriff Rance reminds Minnie, the saloon's straitlaced owner, that he loves her. As talk turns to the bandit Ramerrez, a man enters, giving his name as Johnson. He and Minnie have met and their warmth angers Rance. A captured bandit whispers to Johnson that the gang is ready to rob the saloon, but he has fallen for Minnie, who invites him to visit her.

ACT TWO Minnie receives Johnson in her mountain home and, after describing her happy life alone there ♪, she allows herself to be kissed, her first kiss. As a snow storm rages, Rance arrives, forcing Johnson to hide. Warning Minnie that Johnson is really Ramerrez, Rance leaves. Furious, Minnie expels Johnson, but he is shot on her doorstep. She hides him in the loft, but Rance returns to find fresh blood. Minnie challenges him to poker: Johnson's life against her love. She cheats and Rance accepts defeat, leaving Johnson unconscious in Minnie's arms.

> "Oh, se sapeste"

ACT THREE Miners catch Johnson, and Rance authorizes summary justice. Accepting death, Johnson's sole request is that Minnie believe him to be free ♪. Suddenly Minnie arrives, draws a pistol and reminds the miners of everything she had done for them. Finally they decide they cannot refuse her, and Minnie and Johnson ride away.

> "Ch'ella mi creda libero"

The Argentine tenor José Cura as the fugitive outlaw Dick Johnson wooes Minnie, the prim saloon-keeper sung by the American soprano Andrea Gruber, in a production at the Royal Opera House in 2005.

IL TRITTICO
The Triptych

⚄ Triptych of one-act operas
⚄ 1915–1918

♁ 14 December 1918, Metropolitan Opera, New York, US

These three operas are now rarely performed together because they make for a very long evening. More often, theatres present just two, or twin one with another short opera. *Gianni Schicchi*, Puccini's only comic opera, is especially entertaining, with its mischievous depiction of cunning outmanoeuvring greed.

IL TABARRO

⚄ One-act opera, 1 hour   📖 Giuseppe Adami
⚄ 1915–1916

Paris, France, in the late 19th century

Living on a barge on the Seine in Paris, Michele is tormented by the conviction that his wife Giorgetta is having an affair with Luigi, a stevedore ♂. When she plans a secret tryst with him, Luigi sees a light in the barge and mistakes it for the signal to visit her. Instead, he encounters Michele, who strangles him, and then conceals the body under a cloak – *un tabarro* – until Giorgetta comes home.

"Nulla, silenzio"

SUOR ANGELICA

⚄ One-act opera, 1 hour   📖 Giovacchino Forzano
⚄ 1917

Italy in the 17th century

Angelica, a nun, has long been ostracized by her family. Her aunt, a princess, arrives unexpectedly to announce that Angelica's illegitimate child, the reason for her reclusion, has died. In despair ♂, Angelica takes poison, then remembers that suicide is a mortal sin. She prays fervently for salvation to the Madonna who appears with Angelica's lost child to lead the dying nun towards heaven.

"Senza Mamma"

GIANNI SCHICCHI

⚄ One-act opera 1 hour   📖 Giovacchino Forzano
⚄ 1917–1918

Florence, Italy, in the 13th century

The family of the recently deceased Buoso Donati is horrified to learn that he has left his fortune to a monastery. The wily Gianni Schicchi is quickly summoned and, at the insistence of his daughter Laurette ♂, pretends to be Donati. A notary is summoned and, imitating the ailing Donati, Schicchi writes a fresh will, bequeathing most of Donati's property to himself.

"O mio babbino caro"

Geraldine Farrar as Suor Angelica is guided towards heaven in the closing moments of this opera's premiere at the Metropolitan Opera, New York, in 1918.

TURANDOT

✍ Opera in three acts, 1¾ hours
🎞 1920–1924 (completed by Franco Alfano 1925–1926)

♔ 25 April 1926, La Scala, Milan, Italy
📖 Giuseppe Adami and Renato Simoni, after Carlo Gozzi's 1762 play *Turandotte*

Turandot has never enjoyed the popularity of *La bohème* or *Tosca*, but in many ways it represents the zenith of Puccini's career, an extraordinary spectacle of high drama and musical invention. It has several fine arias, including *"Nessun dorma"*, popularized by Luciano Pavarotti during the 1990 World Cup. Further, while dominated by Calàf's high-risk love for Turandot, the opera gives a pivotal role to the loyal slave girl, Liù, a tragic heroine in the mould of Mimì. Many of *Turandot's* melodies, woven seamlessly into the flowing narrative of the score, suggest the influence of Wagner and Debussy. But Puccini adds a distinctly Oriental colour.

⬑ A 1998 staging of *Turandot* in its original setting of Beijing's Forbidden City signalled China's growing interest in Western opera. Acted before a 14th-century Ming Dynasty temple, hundreds of Chinese soldiers were used as extras. ⬏

⇾ PRINCIPAL ROLES ⇽

Princess Turandot *soprano*

Emperor Altoum *tenor*
Turandot's father

The Unknown Prince, Calàf *tenor*
Turandot's suitor

Timur *bass*
Exiled King of Tartary and Calàf's father

Liù *soprano*
A slave

Ping *baritone*
Grand Chancellor of China

Pang *tenor*
Lord of provisions

Pong *tenor*
Lord of the Imperial Kitchen

A Mandarin *baritone*

PLOT SYNOPSIS

Ancient Beijing, China

ACT ONE A crowd awaits the execution of the Prince of Persia, the latest suitor to fail Princess Turandot's test of love: those who cannot answer three riddles must die. Amid the jostling, a young woman cries out as an old man stumbles. Rushing to help, Calàf recognizes his father, Timur, deposed King of Tartary. He asks the woman why she also risks her life. Because, Liù says, one day Prince Calàf smiled at her. Finally, amid great pomp, Turandot confirms the execution. Calàf is overwhelmed by her beauty and resolves to win her. The emperor's ministers, Ping, Pang, and Pong, discourage him, telling him Turandot is just like any other woman.

UNFINISHED WORK

When Puccini died in 1924, he left *Turandot's* final love duet unfinished. It was completed by Franco Alfano, a minor Italian composer, but the mystery remains how Puccini intended it to sound. The conductor Arturo Toscanini interrupted the premiere to announce: "Here the opera ends, because at this point the Maestro died." After that, Alfano's finale was included.

Gwyneth Jones as Turandot opposite Plácido Domingo's Calàf at the Royal Opera House, 1984.

When Calàf shouts that only he loves her, Liù begs him to give up 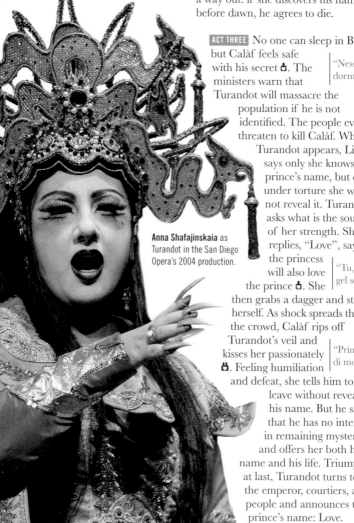. He urges Liù to look after his father , then strikes the ceremonial gong.

"Signore ascolta!"

"Non piangere, Liù"

ACT TWO Ping, Pang, and Pong recall executions they have witnessed: ten in the Year of the Dog, 13 already in this Year of the Tiger. They hear trumpets announce Turandot's grand entrance. She explains that her cruelty and chastity are to avenge the suffering of an ancient Chinese princess. She then warns her unnamed suitor that there are three riddles but one death. Calàf answers the first two riddles. Turandot then poses the last: "Ice that burns, and with your flame, it freezes you still more; bright and dark, in wanting you free, it further enslaves you; in accepting you as a slave, it makes you king." Calàf answers, "Turandot". The devastated princess begs to be released from her pledge. Wanting her love, the "unknown" prince offers a way out: if she discovers his name before dawn, he agrees to die.

"In questa reggia"

ACT THREE No one can sleep in Beijing, but Calàf feels safe with his secret. The ministers warn that Turandot will massacre the population if he is not identified. The people even threaten to kill Calàf. When Turandot appears, Liù says only she knows the prince's name, but even under torture she will not reveal it. Turandot asks what is the source of her strength. She replies, "Love", saying the princess will also love the prince. She then grabs a dagger and stabs herself. As shock spreads through the crowd, Calàf rips off Turandot's veil and kisses her passionately. Feeling humiliation and defeat, she tells him to leave without revealing his name. But he says that he has no interest in remaining mysterious and offers her both his name and his life. Triumphant at last, Turandot turns to the emperor, courtiers, and people and announces the prince's name: Love.

"Nessun dorma"

"Tu, che di gel sei cinta"

"Principessa di morte"

Anna Shafajinskaia as Turandot in the San Diego Opera's 2004 production.

Germanic
Opera

ROMANTIC OPERA FOUND ITS GERMAN VOICE at the start of the 19th century, and reached its apex in Richard Wagner's mammoth *Ring* cycle of 1876. In the interim, new theatres in dozens of German-speaking cities staged popular Romantic operas. Germanic lore provided stories, and large symphonic orchestras wed densely textured music to powerful singing.

OPERAS IN GERMAN BEFORE BEETHOVEN

Operas in German had been written since the 17th century as Singspiels, which included speaking as well as singing. The earliest were based on sacred subjects, as with Johann Thiele's *Adam und Eva* of 1678, which inaugurated Hamburg's Oper am Gänsemarkt, the first public opera house beyond Venice. In the early 18th century, the secular Singspiel gained momentum in this theatre, which premiered works – often in German, French, and Italian – by the composers Reinhard Keiser and Georg Philipp Telemann. George Frideric Handel's early operas, including his 1705 *Almira*, in German and Italian, were also first given in the Oper am Gänsemarkt. Yet, while Hamburg became the Singspiel capital, courts in Baden-

A diabolical midnight forest scene from Weber's *Der Freischütz* decorated French tins of meat extract as the opera gained popularity outside Germany.

Baden, Dresden, Hanover, Mannheim, Munich, Vienna, and other regions welcomed Italian composers and librettists to elevate and entertain them – in Italian. Even the German-speaking Gluck and Mozart were influenced chiefly by Italian music. Indeed, most of Mozart's operas were in Italian, but his last, *Die Zauberflöte*, energized the German Singspiel in 1791, and inspired hilarious operas

Richard Strauss (*front centre, holding baton*) is pictured conducting the sizeable Berlin Philharmonic Orchestra in 1908.

from the Berlin-born Albert Lortzing. An accomplished actor and tenor, Lortzing even sang a lead role for the 1837 Leipzig premiere of his operetta-like *Zar und Zimmermann*.

STURM UND DRANG: GERMAN ROMANTICISM

After the French Revolution of 1789, Europe was engulfed by Romanticism. In literature and painting as well as drama, passionate Romantic heroes quested for individuality, freedom, and love. They also sought to unlock higher truths encased in collective lore, or trumpeted by Nature, usually at its most forbidding. Indeed, thriving as it did on turbulent intensity, German Romanticism was known as *Sturm und Drang*, "Storm and Stress". This ambience permeated the works of writers including Schiller and Goethe. Romantic idealization of folk culture also inspired the brothers Jacob and Wilhelm Grimm to collect traditional German fairy-tales and myths. With a new body of literature available to librettists, the ground was fertile for a new kind of German opera. Premiering in

Soprano Wilhelmine Schroeder-Devrient (1804–1860) stirred strong passions, and inspired Wagner to compose three lead roles for her.

1805, Beethoven's *Fidelio* was the first Singspiel to embrace Romantic humanism in subjects of equality, liberty and justice. It called for a large chorus to express its social and political themes; a symphonic orchestra; and soloists who could be heard over it. Yet Beethoven's German opera was based on a French play.

NATIVE LORE FOR GERMAN OPERAS

In 1816, Carl Maria von Weber conducted the Prague premiere of a Romantic opera based on German story material: *Faust*, by Louis Spohr. But it was Weber himself who wrote the first major Romantic German opera, *Der Freischütz*, in which a man enters into a pact with the devil to win the woman he adores. This Singspiel's action is set in a forest that initial audiences of 1821 recognized from German lore: it was replete with hunting, folkloric dancing and singing, supernatural figures, and a satanic nocturnal thunderstorm. A huge success, *Der Freischütz* triggered an upsurge of operas based on native sources. Among

them was *Hans Heiling* of 1833, by the Leipzig-based Heinrich Marschner. Like Weber's, his Singspiel intertwined folk music with thrilling symphonic music to tell a traditional story of love and supernatural forces. Based on Bohemian folk literature, *Hans Heiling* called for an orchestra augmented by a thunder-machine, and three menacing trombones playing from below the stage. Richard Wagner also fell under Weber's spell. Just nine when he attended *Der Freischütz*, he was quick to pick out the notes of its spine-tingling overture on his family's piano.

WAGNERIAN OPERA

German Romantic opera reached its pinnacle with Wagner. Once Wagner found his stride, Singspiels and Italianate number-operas would be side-tracked in German-speaking opera houses. After the Prussian revolutionary period of 1848 to 1850, he melded mythical stories to seamless, powerful symphonic music in masterpieces including the *Ring* cycle. New voice types, brilliant and forceful, emerged in the Heldentenor, or "heroic tenor", and Germanic soprano. Wagner also joined naturalistic stage action and scenery to intense music and heartfelt words with the aim of serving the dramatic essence of the opera or, as he would redefine it, the "total art form", or *Gesamtkunstwerk*. Layered harmonic textures, at times even pushing tonality to its limit, gave new musical expression to the drama's action and emotional world. In constructing a theatre near Munich, the Bayreuth Festspielhaus, Wagner also introduced new ways to stage and attend opera. In an era increasingly bereft of sacred experience, he believed that music dramas should fully absorb audiences in mystical truths.

Such was Wagner's sway that no major composer in his wake remained untouched. His assistant

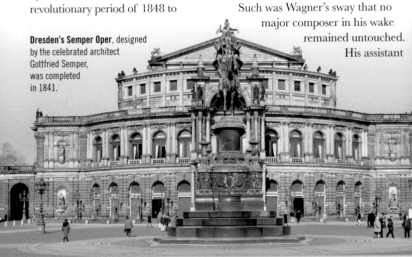

Dresden's Semper Oper, designed by the celebrated architect Gottfried Semper, was completed in 1841.

GERMANIC OPERA

1805 Beethoven's *Fidelio*	1806 End of the Holy Roman Empire (Napoleonic Occupation)	1821 Weber's *Der Freischütz*	1850 Wagner's *Lohengrin*
1800		**1825**	**1850**
1816 Spohr's *Faust*		1833 Marschner's *Hans Heiling*	1848-50 Prussian revolutionary period	1865 Wagner's *Tristan und Isolde*

Richard Wagner, in his signature beret, is pictured in Bayreuth, Germany, amid family members and artists who created his *Ring* cycle of 1876, which premiered in the opera house Wagner had built, the Festspielhaus.

for *Parsifal* in Bayreuth, Engelbert Humperdinck, wrote the 1893 *Hänsel und Gretel* under the sign of Wagner. Even in post-World War I Vienna, where experiments in modern music flourished, the city's child prodigy Erich Wolfgang Korngold mesmerized audiences as much with his mastery of Wagnerian techniques as with his own Romantic voice in *Die tote Stadt*.

Wagner's rightful heir was arguably the Bavarian Richard Strauss. Strauss's father, a famous musician, detested Wagner's music, but his son's first opera, the 1894 *Guntram*, was nonetheless thoroughly Wagnerian. Then, with the startling *Salome* in 1905 and *Elektra* in 1909, Strauss stretched tonality far beyond the frontiers Wagner had charted in *Tristan und Isolde* so that, with his modern approach, he effectively deserted Romantic opera territory. Strauss's operas thereafter continued to range in style, but each explored the rhythms, spoken and poetic, of

the German language. Viennese waltzes and Mozartian sound enveloped *Der Rosenkavalier* and *Arabella*, composed in 1911 and 1933 respectively, while his final work, the 1942 *Capriccio*, recalled even earlier music by Rameau and Gluck. After World War II, German opera would take cues less from Wagner and Mozart than from the 20th century's avant-garde: composers Arnold Schoenberg and Alban Berg of the Second Viennese School, or Kurt Weill and librettist Bertolt Brecht, whose collaboration flourished prior to Hitler's seizure of power in Weimar Germany.

VIENNESE OPERETTA

Operetta, from the Italian for "little opera", was a riotously comical form of catchy tunes and festive dancing. Jacques Offenbach, the German expatriate composer, gave the form new life in Paris with works like *La belle Hélène*. His operettas toured widely, from London to Vienna. There, Johann Strauss Jr defined the charming, bubbly sound of Golden Age Viennese operetta for international audiences in his vigorously popular *Die Fledermaus*. Enlivened by waltzes, champagne galas, and mischievous match-making, the operetta then adopted nostalgic and bittersweet tones in its Viennese Silver Age, notably in Franz Lehár's much-loved work *Die lustige Witwe*.

LUDWIG VAN
BEETHOVEN

Born: 16 December 1770, Bonn (Germany)
Died: 26 March 1827, Vienna (Austria)

No name in music history evokes greater drama or more sublime lyricism than that of Ludwig van Beethoven. Nor has any composer left opera fans so mystified by his limited operatic output. While his nearly 400 works include symphonies, concertos, ballets, and songs, they boast only one opera: *Fidelio*.

The young Beethoven studied under his father, and at age eight was performing publicly. With his first work published at age 12, Beethoven's talents landed him in Vienna, first in 1787 to meet Mozart, and again in 1792 to study with Franz Joseph Haydn and Antonio Salieri. Stirred by the lively Viennese opera scene, he turned to his own opera in 1804, *Fidelio*, which tells a story of marital love's triumph over injustice. By this time, Beethoven was complaining of hearing problems that would leave him deaf. But even as he struggled with *Fidelio*, he pursued other opera projects, including a *Macbeth* based on Shakespeare's tragedy. At the end of his life, he was at work on an opera based on *Faust*, the lyrical narrative fiction by Johann Wolfgang von Goethe. Beethoven believed it would be his masterpiece.

THE RESCUE OPERA

As a young violist in his native Bonn, Beethoven performed in operas by Mozart and Gluck. But inspiration to compose his own opera came from Luigi Cherubini's *Lodoïska*, a "rescue opera" that riveted Paris before it triumphed in 1802 Vienna. Rescue operas, about an innocent person heroically freed from wrongful captivity, were popular in Paris after the French Revolution. Dialogue advanced these action-packed *opéras comiques*. Like these, *Fidelio* is spoken as well as sung, and thus is called a Singspiel.

The piano Beethoven used when working at Brunswick Mansion in Martonvásár (Hungary) remains on display.

FIDELIO

⚉ Opera in two acts, 2¼ hours
⚋ 1804–1805, rev. 1806 and 1814
⚘ 20 November 1805, Theater an der Wien, Vienna

📖 Joseph Von Sonnleithner and Georg Friedrich Treitschke, after the French play *Léonore, ou L'amour conjugal* (1789) by Pierre Gaveaux

First performed in 1805, *Fidelio* was twice revised before the opera was successfully given in 1814. The opera offers a dual challenge to its performers: lead roles require powerful vocalists able to sing over the large German orchestra, but important spoken exchanges favour singers who also shine as actors. *Fidelio* bears Beethoven's unmistakable musical signature, and offers glorious music, particularly for the Prisoners' chorus at the end of Act I, and Florestan's exquisite aria opening Act II.

> ↦ **PRINCIPAL ROLES** ↤
>
> **Don Pizarro** *baritone*
> Governor
>
> **Florestan** *tenor*
> A prisoner
>
> **Leonore (Fidelio)** *soprano*
> Florestan's wife
>
> **Rocco** *bass*
> Jailer
>
> **Marzelline** *soprano*
> Rocco's daughter

⚏ *Fidelio*'s premiere took place on one of the most disastrous dates in opera history: 20 November 1805, a matter of days after Napoleon Bonaparte occupied Vienna. Theatre patrons had evacuated the city, leaving an audience that consisted mainly of rowdy French officers. ⚏

PLOT SYNOPSIS

A state prison in Spain, in springtime

ACT ONE In the courtyard of the state prison, Marzelline dreams of marrying the new employee, Fidelio. Marzelline's father, Rocco, approves of the match. But "Fidelio" is in fact Leonore, a loving wife disguised as a man to free her wrongfully jailed husband, Florestan. The governor Don Pizarro plots to murder Florestan, and instructs Rocco to dig a grave for him in the prison's dungeon. Leonore is horrified, but affirms her "faith in wedded love". She persuades Rocco to defy Pizarro's orders and release the prisoners into the courtyard. All the prisoners save Florestan emerge to discover light, air, and a taste of liberty 🎧.
Furious, Pizarro orders them back to their cells.

"O welche Lust"

Set design by Stéphane Braunschweig and Giorgio Barberio Corsetti suggests freedom beyond imprisonment at Berlin's Staatsoper Unter den Linden in 1995.

ACT TWO Florestan suffers in his dungeon cell, but imagines an angel liberating him 🎧. Rocco and "Fidelio" arrive to dig Florestan's grave.

"Gott! Welch Dunkel hier!"

But when Pizarro prepares to slay Florestan, "Fidelio" reveals her true identity. The minister Don Fernando, Florestan's old friend, arrives just in time to save the day. All the prisoners are released, and Don Fernando is amazed to see his old friend Florestan, whom he believed long dead. Marzelline is no less surprised to discover that her beloved "Fidelio" is Florestan's wife. Once Pizarro is arrested and led off to be executed, Leonore celebrates the courage love gave her to free her husband.

CARL MARIA VON
WEBER

Born: c.18 November 1786, Eutin (Germany)
Died: 5 June 1826, London, England

Carl Maria von Weber catapulted Germanic opera into the new aesthetic idiom of the day: Romanticism. Mozart and Beethoven had scored operas in German, but Weber also employed German stories. Fusing the folkloric to the classical, his greatest work, *Der Freischütz*, sent German opera on a path towards Wagner.

Dramatic, intense, colourful – words capturing Weberian opera also describe Weber. He grew up in an itinerant theatre troupe led by his father. Musical studies were interrupted in each town as the family decamped for another. Still, Weber scored his first opera (now lost) in Munich at age 13. In Freiburg, he composed a second, of which fragments survive. *Peter Schmoll und seine Nachbarn* was scored in Salzburg and staged in Augsburg in 1803. Pursuit of training led him to Vienna, where he was posted to Breslau as the theatre's Kappellmeister. Still only 17, Weber began a two-year struggle to reform the theatre's repertoire. Then, in a bizarre turn of events, he accidentally drank acid used for engraving scores. Following his recovery, he accepted posts first in Prague, and later in Dresden, where he scored the ground-breaking *Der Freischütz*. A commission from Vienna yielded *Euryanthe*, and another from London, *Oberon*. For this last opera, Weber ignored doctor's orders and travelled to London, where he died at age 40.

From 1818 to 1824, the composer summered in Dresden. Weber's former home (*right*) is now the Carl Maria von Weber Museum, dedicated to his life and work.

FIRST PERFORMANCES

1800

1803
Peter Schmoll und seine Nachbarn

1810

1810
Silvana

1811
Abu Hassan

1820

1821
Der Freischütz

1823
Euryanthe

1826
Oberon, or The Elf King's Oath

1830

OBERON, OR THE ELF KING'S OATH

✍ Romantic opera in three acts, 2 hours
⏳ 1825–1826
♜ April 12, 1826, Covent Garden, London, England

📖 James Robinson Planché, after the poem
by Christoph Martin Wieland (1780)

Weber wrote this opera while dying of tuberculosis. His libretto was in English, and based on a poem that drew certain characters from Shakespeare's *A Midsummer Night's Dream*. But the opera's story is different. It is framed by a popular overture – with its inaugural horn call, impish woodwinds, and expressive strings – and a "Turkish" finale. Despite its uneven score, the music won plaudits from the likes of Richard Wagner.

❧ Planché blamed criticism of the libretto on the public, which he said could handle only "Ballads, duets, choruses, and glees, provided they occupy no more than the fewest number of minutes possible". ❧

> ✦ PRINCIPAL ROLES ✦
>
> Oberon *tenor*
> King of the Elves
>
> Puck *contralto*
> His servant
>
> Huon *tenor*
> Duke of Guienne
>
> Sherasmin *baritone*
> His squire
>
> Reiza *soprano*
> The Caliph's daughter
>
> Fatima *mezzo-soprano*
> Reiza's attendant

PLOT SYNOPSIS

Oberon's fairy palace, Baghdad, Tunis, and France, in medieval times

ACT ONE Oberon, the Elf King, and his wife argue over which is the more loyal gender, and refuse to agree until they meet equally loyal human lovers. Puck, Oberon's servant, has found a potential couple: Sir Huon has been charged by King Charlemagne to travel to Baghdad and seize the Caliph's daughter, Reiza, for his bride. To inspire the pair, Oberon presents a vision of Reiza to Huon and vice versa. Huon lauds love and the glory of combat ♫. Reiza awaits her knight.

"From boyhood trained in battlefield"

ACT TWO Under the protection of Oberon's magic horn, Huon storms the Caliph's banquet hall, claiming Reiza and killing her betrothed. As Huon, Reiza, and their two servants escape, Puck conjures elemental spirits to shipwreck their boat. Reiza curses the ocean ♫ but, spotting a boat,

"Ocean! Thou mighty monster!"

hopes for rescue. Pirates disembark and move to kill Huon, but Reiza throws herself upon him. Both are carried off.

ACT THREE In Tunis, the two servants, Sherasmin and Fatima, comfort one another. Huon finds them and discovers Reiza is in the Emir's harem. He steals into the harem, and resists the temptation of the women. The Emir condemns the intruder. When Reiza begs for Huon's life, she is also condemned to death. Oberon appears to save them and praise their mutual fidelity.

In a painting of a scene from Act II, Huon claims Reiza and slays her betrothed. Weber complained that too much of the libretto's action is spoken rather than sung.

DER FREISCHÜTZ
The Freeshooter

✍ Romantic opera in three acts, 2½ hours
⚐ 1817–1821
♆ 18 June 1821, Schauspielhaus, Berlin

📖 Johann Friedrich Kind, after the German folk story retold by Johann August Apel and Friedrich Laun in *Gespensterbuch* (1811)

Der Freischütz, from a folk story about a man who sells his soul to win a marksmanship contest, premiered to immediate success in 1821. It was soon translated into a host of languages, including English, Dutch, French, Hungarian, Polish, and Russian. Weber's intrepid masterpiece captured the diabolical force of human passions and fears. Composers, notably Wagner, were deeply influenced by its German themes and brilliant orchestration. Cosmic struggles – between good and evil, providence and hazard, dreams and reality, love and death – provide the dramatic core of *Der Freischütz*. The work also delivers charming solos, traditional songs, and rousing choruses. But some of its most astounding music, including the overture, is instrumental.

⚐ Satanic storm music for the Wolf's Glen scene concluding Act II unsettled early audience members. German doctors treating these patients referred to the unique medical condition as *Freischützfieber* ("Freischütz Fever"). ⚐

→ PRINCIPAL ROLES ←

Ottokar *baritone*
Prince of Bohemia

Kuno *bass*
Head forester

Kaspar *bass*
First huntsman

Max *tenor*
Second huntsman

Kilian *baritone*
Rich villager

Agathe *soprano*
Daughter to Kuno

Ännchen *soprano*
Cousin to Agathe

Eremit (Hermit) *bass*
A religious man
of the forest

Samiel *speaking part*
The Black Huntsman

PLOT SYNOPSIS

A Bohemian forest in the 17th century

ACT ONE In the forest, Kilian celebrates victory in a shooting match. Kuno, head forester, arrives just in time to prevent violence between Kilian and the jealous huntsman Max. Kuno warns Max that, if he aims to win the hand of his daughter, Agathe, he must succeed in an ancient shooting contest at dawn. Alone, Max bemoans his bad luck ♫. But, feigning friendship, the huntsman Kaspar distracts Max with wine-drinking ♫. Kaspar demonstrates magic bullets. They guarantee success in the contest, but must be fetched at midnight in the haunted Wolf's Glen. Out of love for Agathe, Max agrees to meet there. Kaspar is thrilled to have ensnared Max ♫.

"Durch die Wälder"

"Hier im ird'schen Jammerthal"

"Schweig', schweig'!"

ACT TWO At home, the lovesick Agathe tells her cousin, Ännchen, that she was warned of danger by the religious hermit living in the forest. Alone, sleepless Agathe admires the night sky and seeks God's protection, until Max's

"Leise, leise, fromme Weise"

arrival brings joy ♪. When Max reports that he must venture into the Wolf's Glen, Agathe is terrified. At midnight in Wolf's Glen, Kaspar seals a bargain with the demonic Samiel: six bullets will hit their marks; the seventh will hit a target of Samiel's choosing. Max discovers Kaspar alone, practising his dark arts. When a hellish storm erupts, Max calls out for Samiel. The Black Huntsman appears, riveting Kaspar and Max with fear.

ACT THREE The next morning, Max and Kaspar have spent six bullets. Max still has the seventh bullet, fated to kill his beloved Agathe. At home in her bridal

"Und ob die Wolke"

gown, Agathe believes that God watches over her ♪. She tells Ännchen of her bad dream: that she was a white dove, shot down by Max. All gather in the forest for the wedding feast. At a distance, Kaspar climbs a tree to spy on the party. Max prepares to take his final shot: Ottokar selects a white dove, and Max follows it to a tree with his rifle. He fires just as Agathe rushes towards him, begging him not to shoot. The dove escapes as Agathe and Kaspar fall. Agathe has fainted, but Kaspar, hit by his own bullet, dies in agony. Upon confessing his deeds to

A ROMANTIC GERMAN OPERA

Der Freischütz marked the arrival of Romantic German opera. Throughout the 19th century, operas by Heinrich Marschner, Richard Wagner, and Engelbert Humperdinck would recall elements that Weber was the first to integrate in his operatic masterpiece. Chief among them were supernatural powers; the dark forest setting; powerful forces of nature such as the thunderstorm; rural life in the form of hunting or festivities and folkloric elements.

A watercolour from the late 1930s by Nuremberg-based set designer Heinz Grete depicts the hellish world of the Wolf's Glen in the opera's second act.

Ottokar, Max is exiled. But the venerable hermit intervenes: Max's weakness was human, and should be forgiven. Ottokar decrees that Max may marry Agathe after a year of virtuous conduct. All join the hermit in prayer, vowing faith in divine providence.

Carola Höhn sings the role of Agathe at the Staatsoper Unter den Linden in Berlin in 2006.

ALBERT
LORTZING

Born: 23 October 1801, Berlin, Prussia (Germany)
Died: 21 January 1851, Berlin, Prussia (Germany)

Albert Lortzing viewed himself as a humble entertainer, but he is recognized today as the master of 19th-century comic opera in German. Born to a family of itinerant actor–musicians, he took to the stage in his boyhood. Music lessons followed, but he was largely self-taught. An early opera was about his favourite composer: *Szenen aus Mozarts Leben*, or *Scenes from Mozart's Life*. But his first success, *Zar und Zimmermann*, would prove to be a light comic masterpiece. Of Lortzing's 14 operas spanning 30 years, his 1845 *Undine*, based on a fairy-tale, has also touched audiences worldwide. Lortzing died of a stroke the day after his final opera premiered.

ZAR UND ZIMMERMANN
(Tsar and Carpenter, or The Two Peters)

🎵 Comic opera in three acts, 2¾ hours
📅 1837
🎭 22 December 1837, Theater der Stadt,
Liepzig (Germany)
📖 Albert Lortzing, after Georg Christian Römer's translation of a French play of 1818

Zar und Zimmermann, packed with infectious songs and a beloved "clog dance", premiered in Leipzig to no fanfare but soon became a favourite opera in German-speaking Europe. It was then presented to audiences in their own languages from London to Lisbon, and as far as St Petersburg, reaching the American stage in 1852.

→	PRINCIPAL ROLES	←

Peter Michaelov *baritone* Russia's Tsar Peter in disguise
Peter Ivanov *tenor* Carpenter in love with Marie
Van Bett *bass* Mayor of Saardam
Marie *soprano* Van Bett's niece
Marquis de Châteauneuf *tenor* French ambassador
Widow Browe *contralto* Shipyard employer

This Singspiel playfully transfers a historical Peter the Great – the Russian tsar did work incognito in Dutch shipyards – into a tightly woven fictional world of mistaken identities, military secrets, and sweet romantic love.

⚓ From 1833 to 1844, Lortzing worked as an actor and *buffo* tenor at the Stadttheater in Leipzig. There, he sang the role of Peter Ivanov for the 1837 premiere of *Zar und Zimmermann*. His mother, Charlotte Sophie Lortzing, created the opera's shipyard employer, Widow Browe. ⚓

Peter Ivanov the carpenter (Erich Zimmermann) reads Peter the Great's letter in the final scene for a 1954 production at the Städtischen Oper in West Berlin.

PLOT SYNOPSIS

Shipyards and interiors in Saardam, Holland, in 1698

ACT ONE Russia's Tsar Peter, passing as "Peter Michaelov", labours cheerfully in a Saardam shipyard alongside Peter Ivanov and other carpenters. Ivanov loves Marie, the niece of Van Bett, Saardam's mayor. But, as a Russian army deserter, he fears that marriage will be impossible. Marie urges him

"Die Eifersucht ist eine Plage" | not to be jealous of other men . Tsar Peter hears troubling news

from Moscow just as Van Bett arrives, swelling with governmental self-

"O sancta justicia! Ich möchte rasen" | importance ♪. When Lord Syndham, an English envoy, offers him 2,000 pounds if

he can find the foreign "Peter", Van Bett suspects Ivanov of elaborate crimes. Meanwhile, a French Marquis, also an envoy, recognizes Tsar Peter and assures him of France's loyalty.

ACT TWO In a tavern, shipbuilders celebrate a wedding. Driving Ivanov wild with jealousy, the Marquis flirts

"Lebe wohl, mein flandrisch Mädchen" | with Marie ♪. Just as Tsar Peter learns of a Moscow uprising and prepares

to return home, a Dutch officer arrives to arrest all foreigners lacking legitimate business. Both Peters are identified as the tsar, and a confused Van Bett threatens to jail everyone.

ACT THREE In the city hall, Van Bett rehearses a cantata to honour Ivanov,

"Sonst spielt' ich mit Szepter, mit Krone und Stern" | whom he believes is Russia's tsar. Alone, Tsar Peter recalls his childhood ♪. Ivanov arranges

for Michaelov to depart. In return, Michaelov offers him a letter, to

be opened later. Ivanov is enthroned and fêted with a "national dance", in fact a ballet performed in clogs. When news arrives of Michaelov's escape, Ivanov unseals and reads the letter: Michaelov announces himself as the missing Russian tsar, and approves the marriage of Ivanov and Marie. French windows are thrust open to reveal Tsar Peter bidding farewell from aboard a ship bound for Moscow. Finally, all praise the beloved Tsar Peter.

A ballet danced in clogs is a much-loved highlight of the opera's final act, performed here at the Theater Erfurt in Erfurt, Germany in 2003.

> "*I write music with an*
> *exclamation point!*"
>
> *Richard Wagner*

RICHARD
WAGNER

Born: 22 May 1813, Leipzig (Germany)
Died: 13 February 1883, Venice, Italy

Richard Wagner pushed opera to unsurpassed heights of musical intensity and revolutionized the entire opera-going experience. Unlike Mozart and Verdi, Wagner took charge of every aspect of his operas. He wrote the librettos, scouted for singers, conducted, and even created a unique opera house. His monumental *Ring* cycle, comprising four operas, holds a place of its own in Western culture.

Wagner was a man of extremes in every aspect of his life, from opera to politics and from theoretical writings to intimate affairs, but above all in his music and its wide-ranging influence. Wagner's strident positions on virtually every subject have also made it difficult to separate personal failings from creative achievements. His biological father was reputedly Ludwig Geyer, his mother's lover and her second husband after Friedrich Wagner. A prominent actor, Geyer sparked the boy's passion for theatre and even put him on stage in children's roles. Growing up in Dresden, and harbouring ambitions to be a playwright, Richard, who then went by the possibly Jewish name Geyer, devoured works by Shakespeare and Goethe. Tellingly, he was at first interested in music for its dramatic uses. Although he had not completed high school, Wagner studied at the University of Leipzig, where he immersed himself in Beethoven. His first opera, *Die Feen*, or *The Fairies*, came at age 20 under the influence of Weber's *Der Freischütz*. He was soon invited to direct regional opera houses, including that of Magdeburg, which premiered his second opera, *Das Liebesverbot*, or *The Ban on Love*, based on Shakespeare's *Measure for Measure*. But it closed on its opening night, when a backstage love triangle resulted in violence.

Rhinemaidens in the opening moments of *Das Rheingold*, staged and lit by Robert Wilson at the Théâtre du Châtelet in Paris, 2005.

FIRST PERFORMANCES	
1835	**1836** Das Liebesverbot, oder Die Novize von Palermo
	1842 Rienzi, der Letzte der Tribunen
1845	**1843** Der fliegende Holländer
	1845 Tannhäuser
	1850 Lohengrin
1855	
	1865 Tristan und Isolde
1865	**1868** Die Meistersinger von Nürnberg
	1869 Das Rheingold
1870	**1870** Die Walküre
1875	**1876** Siegfried Götterdämmerung Der Ring des Nibelungen
1880	
	1882 Parsifal

EXILE AND MATHILDE

While in political exile, Wagner was unable to stage his operas in German theatres. Residing in Zurich, he devoted himself instead to conducting, composing, reading the philosopher Arthur Schopenhauer, and writing. Key

DRESDEN AND MINNA

Following trying times in Riga and Paris, Wagner welcomed returning to Dresden for the successful 1842 premiere of *Rienzi*. He soon settled there with his actress wife Christine Wilhelmine Planer, known as Minna. *Der fliegende Holländer* premiered in Dresden the following year and, while the opera initially confused audiences expecting an Italianate work like *Rienzi*, it has since been recognized as the first to convey Wagner's peerless musical signature. A gifted conductor, Wagner was then employed to lead the court opera in Dresden, where his *Tannhäuser* fared better in 1845. *Lohengrin* followed, but by then Wagner's radical politics prevented a production in the court's opera house. In 1848, the French Revolution kindled rebellion in most German territories and, embracing the new ideas, Wagner joined the Dresden uprising of 1849. When the uprising was crushed, Wagner was forced to flee; some of his comrades were jailed.

essays included "The Artwork of the Future", which articulated Wagner's famous idea of opera as a subsuming *Gesamtkunstwerk* or "total artwork". It pictured music drama as a kind of art able to fuse distinct forms of expression, from poetry, music, and movement, to stagecraft and scenery. Under the pseudonym Freigedank, or "Free Thought", he also wrote "Judaism in Music", his infamous attack on Jewish composers; the tract would later endear him to Hitler and Nazi Germany. At the same time, Wagner mined medieval German and Nordic poetry for opera material to capture his mystical ideas about the power of love and German identity. By 1852, he had completed the libretto for his four-opera cycle *Der Ring des Nibelungen*, and by 1857 he had composed its first two operas – *Das Rheingold* and *Die Walküre* – as well as part of the third, *Siegfried*. But 1857 also brought a wild passion for the married Mathilde Wesendonk, Wagner's adoring muse for the sizzling eroticism coursing through *Tristan und Isolde*. After

KING LUDWIG II OF BAVARIA

Soon after he was crowned King of Bavaria in 1864 at age 18, Ludwig II (1845–1886) became Wagner's patron. Known as the Mad King, Ludwig was, like Wagner, devoted to realizing extravagant dreams. One building project was the fairy-tale-like castle, Neuschwanstein (*right*), which he had decorated with Wagnerian opera scenes. In 1886, Ludwig was declared insane and relieved of his kingly duties. On 13 June, he drowned himself. Trying to save him, his doctor drowned as well.

Minna intercepted a love letter to Mathilde, Wagner left Zurich. But in 1861, with the German ban on him repealed, he moved from Paris, where he was then based, to Prussia, where he began to score his only comic opera: *Die Meistersinger von Nürnberg*.

BAVARIA AND COSIMA

The sudden patronage of Bavaria's King Ludwig II brought Wagner to Munich in 1864. Royal support brought relief from debt, and returned Wagnerian opera to the stage after a break of 15 years. In 1865, *Tristan und Isolde* premiered victoriously under the baton of Wagner's friend Hans von Bülow. However, that same year also brought the birth of another Isolde: Wagner's daughter by von Bülow's wife, Cosima. Ensuing scandal caused Ludwig to move Wagner to Switzerland,

where the composer inspired and befriended – but later fell out with – the philosopher Friedrich Nietzsche. Although he now lived outside Bavaria, Wagner still fathered two more children with Cosima. When she finally divorced von Bülow, another name was added for a time to Wagner's list of estranged friends: Cosima's father, the composer and conductor Franz Liszt. Wagner married Cosima in 1870, and settled on Bayreuth as the location for the theatre he had long envisaged. Residing in Wahnfried, a Bayreuth villa, and touring widely to raise funds to realize his gigantic plan, Wagner oversaw the construction of the Festspielhaus and completed the final operas of his *Ring* cycle: *Siegfried* and *Götterdämmerung*. Finally, in 1876, 28 years after he had dreamed it up, the *Ring* premiered. His last opera, *Parsifal*, was written especially for the Festspielhaus. Following its summer premiere in 1882, Wagner wintered in Venice, where a heart attack ended his life in February 1883. He was buried in the garden at Wahnfried.

Richard Wagner (*centre*) presents his work to his wife Cosima, her father Franz Liszt, and the German writer Hans von Wolzogen at his Bayreuth home, Wahnfried House, 1882.

DER FLIEGENDE HOLLÄNDER
(The Flying Dutchman)

🎭 Romantische Oper in three acts, 2¼ hours   Saxony (Germany)
📖 1840–1842; (rev. 1846; 1852; 1860)   📖 Richard Wagner
🏛 2 January 1843, Hoftheater, Dresden,

Der fliegende Holländer is arguably the opera in which Wagner found his voice. Inspired by the story of a man condemned to sail the seas forever, the opera's Romantic elements include a nocturnal storm, supernatural forces, and tragic love. Act II offers the heroine Senta's ballad and her love duet with the Flying Dutchman. The Norwegian sailors' rousing song, *"Stauermann! Lass die Wacht"*, cheerfully opens Act III. Even greater music comes when the Dutchman's crew delivers a terrifying song in response.

⚓ In 1839, Wagner fled debtors' prison in Riga. He escaped across the Russian border at night to board a boat for London. A violent storm held the vessel on Norway's coast. Its sounds later served him in this opera. ⚓

✦ PRINCIPAL ROLES ✦

Der Holländer
(The Dutchman) *baritone*
He is doomed to wander

Daland *bass*
A Norwegian sea captain

Senta *soprano*
His daughter, devoted
to the Dutchman

Mary *mezzo-soprano*
Her nurse

Erik *tenor*
A poor huntsman
in love with Senta

Der Steuermann (The
Steersman) *tenor*

PLOT SYNOPSIS

On the coast of Norway

ACT ONE The Norwegian captain Daland and his sailors pause in a violent storm. As they sleep, the Dutchman anchors his own ship and yearns to end his cursed existence: every seven years, he is cast ashore to seek a beloved; when she proves unfaithful, he returns to sea ♫. Daland agrees to give his daughter's hand to the Dutchman in exchange for riches.

"Die Frist ist um"

ACT TWO Girls at spinning wheels sing of love in Daland's home. His daughter Senta counters with a ballad about the legendary Flying Dutchman, whom she longs to save. Erik, a man who loves her, warns her that he dreamed she was ensnared by the satanic Dutchman. Her father returns with her betrothed. The Dutchman is smitten by the angelic Senta, and she vows fidelity.

ACT THREE Aboard the Norwegian ship, sailors and girls celebrate. But they are terrified by ghostly sailors singing of their unlucky captain aboard the Flying Dutchman's ship ♫. On land, Erik reminds Senta of her former vow to love him. Hearing them, the Dutchman reveals his identity and returns to sea, where his boat sinks. Senta leaps from a cliff to join her beloved, and the lovers' spirits soar into the heavens.

"Johohoe! Johohoe!"

At Berlin Staatsoper Unter den Linden in 2001, the opera unfolds as Senta's fantasy of a demon saved by her love.

TANNHÄUSER

🎼 Grosse romantische Oper in three acts, 3 hours
🎵 1843–1845 (rev. 1847–1852; 1861; 1875)
🎭 Dresden version: 19 October 1845, Hoftheater,

Dresden, Saxony (Germany); Paris version: 13 March 1861, Théâtre Impérial de l'Opéra, Paris, France
📖 Richard Wagner

The opera centres around the singers' contest at Wartburg castle and Tannhäuser's behaviour there. Featuring arias, ensembles, and recitatives, it is in the "number opera" form. But the opera also shows Wagner beginning to move toward the through-composed approach that would characterize his subsequent operas. The evocative Act III prelude presents a musical narrative of Tannhäuser's pilgrimage, and hints at Wagner's growing interest in continuous music to portray dramatic action.

⚜ Wagner described Wolfram as "a poet and artist", making Dietrich Fischer-Dieskau, the renowned interpreter of German art songs, a perfect fit for the role and Act III's "Ode to the Evening Star" in 1954 for his Bayreuth début. ⚜

→ PRINCIPAL ROLES ←

Tannhäuser *tenor*
A former minstrel knight

Elisabeth *soprano*
A chaste princess,
his beloved

Hermann *bass*
Landgrave of Thuringia,
her uncle

Wolfram *baritone*
A minstrel knight

Walther *tenor*
A minstrel knight

Venus *soprano*
Goddess of love

PLOT SYNOPSIS

Venus's grotto, the Wartburg (Germany), and its surroundings

ACT ONE Having spent months in Venus's embrace, Tannhäuser begs his leave. She tries to retain him, but shrinks away when he invokes the Virgin Mary. Minstrel knights discover Tannhäuser, but he is reluctant to join them. He only relents when they mention his beloved Elisabeth.

ACT TWO Elisabeth jubilantly greets the Hall of Song ♦. She and Tannhäuser reunite, while Hermann announces that Love is the theme of the singers' contest. Wolfram offers an air about the virtue of chastity, and Tannhäuser counters by praising sensual desire. To the

"Dich, teure Halle"

At Bayreuth in the 1970s, Gwyneth Jones famously sang as both Venus (*right*) and Elisabeth.

audience's horror, he responds similarly to the others' songs. Elisabeth protects him from the mob, and Tannhäuser vows to seek pardon in Rome.

ACT THREE Wolfram observes Elisabeth as she awaits Tannhäuser. Failing to see him among returning pilgrims, she beseeches the Virgin Mary to take her life, and leaves to die at the Wartburg. Wolfram discovers Tannhäuser, who bitterly recounts his travels and the pope's verdict: his staff would sooner flower than he can be absolved ♦.

In despair, the former knight calls Venus to receive him. Wolfram frantically advises him to repent and tells him Elisabeth prays for him as an angel in heaven. Tannhäuser, redeemed, falls dead. The pilgrims express awe that the papal staff has bloomed.

"Hör an Wolfram, hör an!"

LOHENGRIN

⚼ Romantische Oper in three acts, 3½ hours
☳ 1845–1848
♇ 28 August 1850, Grand Ducal Court Theatre,

Weimar (Germany)
📖 Richard Wagner

Lohengrin places supernatural Arthurian romance elements in the historical reign of King Heinrich I of Saxony (876–936) to form a hybrid opera. Characters are sharply etched – the Lady Macbeth-like Ortrud, for example – while the chorus, responding to action as the plot unfolds, often resembles one from Ancient Greek drama. The most frequently played excerpt was always the beloved "Bridal Chorus", *"Treulich geführt"*, which opens Act III, although Wagner complained that it lost its dramatic sense when amputated from the opera. *Lohengrin*, shaped throughout by symphonic music, has been interpreted both as an early masterpiece and as a major stepping stone towards Wagner's *Ring* cycle.

> ➔   **PRINCIPAL ROLES**   ➔
>
> Lohengrin *tenor*
> Knight of the Grail, son of Parsifal
>
> Elsa von Brabant *soprano*
> She rejects Friedrich's marriage bid
>
> Count Friedrich von Telramund *baritone*
> He accuses Elsa of fratricide
>
> Ortrud *soprano* His wife, a sorceress
>
> König Heinrich der Vogler (King Heinrich)
> *bass* He prepares for war
>
> Der Heerrufer des Königs
> (the king's Herald) *baritone*

⚐ Wagner was in political exile in Switzerland when *Lohengrin* premiered in Weimar. He had hoped to be present and at one point even planned to sneak across the border to attend the opera in disguise. Instead, he passed the night in a pub in Lucerne called The Swan. ⚐

PLOT SYNOPSIS

In and near Antwerp, under King Heinrich I of Saxony

ACT ONE On a river bank, König Heinrich unifies his people to defend Germany. But discord surrounds Count Friedrich, who accuses Elsa von Brabant of murdering her brother. He adds that when she also rejected his marriage bid, he married Ortrud instead. Summoned, Elsa says that a certain knight will be her champion ♣. The king calls for combat before God to settle the murder accusation. All marvel when a glorious knight arrives on a boat led by a swan. Elsa agrees to the knight's terms: if he wins, she must marry him, but never enquire about his identity. The knight vanquishes Friedrich, and spares his life. All but Friedrich and Ortrud rejoice.

"Einsam in trüben Tagen"

ACT TWO In Antwerp's fortress, the court celebrates. Outside, the resentful Ortrud persuades Friedrich to seek revenge ♣. When Elsa steps onto a balcony to confess her joy to the evening breezes, Ortrud cunningly elicits her pity. In a moment of privacy, Ortrud relishes her scheme ♣. Ortrud warns Elsa not to trust the knight. But Elsa feels sorry for Ortrud, who lacks faith in trust. In the morning, the king's Herald proclaims the knight "Protector of Brabant". Elsa arrives in her wedding procession, but Ortrud interferes, accusing the knight of sorcery. When the king and knight parade by, Friedrich

"Der Rache Werk sei nun beschworen"

"Entweihte Götter!"

calls out for the knight to reveal his name. The knight refuses to tell him, and notes Elsa's trembling. Ortrud and Friedrich savour her distress. The couple enters the Minster to be married.

ACT THREE The wedding party blesses the couple in the bridal chamber. Alone,

"Das süsse Lied verhallt"

they celebrate their love 🍷. But Elsa, troubled by doubt, asks the knight to reveal his name. Friedrich suddenly attacks, but falls to the knight. The knight instructs Elsa to go to join the king. On the river bank, Heinrich greets warriors preparing to be led by the knight in shining armour, and is surprised to see Elsa. The knight arrives. He presents Friedrich's body, and accuses his wife of breaking her vow. He reveals that he is Lohengrin, son of Parsifal. As a knight of the Grail, he may serve the world, but must return to the Grail's seat at Montsalvat if his

"In fernem Land"

identity is discovered 🍷. As all bitterly despair at the loss of their hero, the

"Mein lieber Schwan!"

swan and boat reappear 🍷. Ortrud boasts that her magic transformed Elsa's brother into the swan. Lohengrin prays, then rejoices when a dove arrives in response. Removing a chain from the

Ben Heppner as Lohengrin and Karita Mattila as Elsa in Robert Wilson's production for the Metropolitan Opera in New York, 2006. The singers charged each pose and gesture of Wilson's staging with rich emotion.

swan, he transforms the bird back into Elsa's brother, Gottfried. Lohengrin's boat, led now by the dove, departs. Calling out to her husband, Elsa dies in her brother Gottfried's arms.

PREMIERE OF 1850

Wagner was composing *Lohengrin* when Europe was rocked by France's 1848 Revolution. He had hoped to premiere the opera in Dresden. But following his participation in the Dresden uprising of 1849, his works were banned in German principalities. From Zurich, where he was living in exile, Wagner petitioned his friend and fellow composer–conductor Franz Liszt (*right*), who finally succeeded in arranging a premiere in Weimar. *Lohengrin* was given there in 1850, with Liszt relying on Wagner's notes to lead the orchestra.

TRISTAN UND ISOLDE
(Tristan and Isolde)

⚄ Handlung in three acts, 3¾ hours
☙ 1856–1859
♇ 10 June 1865, Königliches Hof-und National

Theater, Munich, Bavaria (Germany)
📖 Richard Wagner

Tristan und Isolde is about romantic love so transcendent that it may only achieve perfection in the eternity of death. This tragic tale had been told in the 13th century by Gottfried von Strassburg, whose *Tristan* inspired the composer to set aside the *Ring* cycle. Wagner had been engrossed in Arthur Schopenhauer's writings about sexual desire and death, the opera's key subjects. But, like Tristan, he was also in love with a forbidden woman. Mathilde Wesendonck was the married muse for Wagner's expression of erotic love too great for the physical world to contain. Striking harmonic textures seem to make the lovers' suffering ache with beauty. And by testing the absolute limits of tonality, the opera was a crucial step towards atonal modern operas.

⚌ In 1857–1858, Wagner set five poems by Mathilde Wesendonck for female voice and piano. One of the *Wesendonck Songs*, *Träume* or *Dreams*, spawned music that Wagner used for Act II of *Tristan und Isolde*. ⚌

PLOT SYNOPSIS

At sea near Cornwall, and in castle grounds in Cornwall and Brittany

ACT ONE Aboard Tristan's ship, Isolde rages. They love each other, but Tristan is obliged to ignore her as he escorts her to Cornwall to marry his uncle, King Marke. Isolde's attendant, Brangäne, appeals to Tristan, whose companion, Kurwenal, insists that Lord Tristan is not in Isolde's thrall. And yet, Isolde's fury mounts as she recalls Tristan's debt to her: he first came to

The storyline of Wagner's *Tristan und Isolde* is based on a popular romance of medieval Celtic origin.

Ireland on the verge of death, wounded by the Irish Lord Morold. Isolde was duty-bound to slay Tristan, who had killed Morold, but instead she saved him ☙. Suicidal, Isolde asks Brangäne to fetch a death potion. Her gaze then meets Tristan's. When she seeks vengeance for the death of Morold, to whom she was betrothed, Tristan offers her his sword and invites her to slay him. In response to his request, Isolde gives Tristan a drink of "reconciliation". Both quaff the potion. Then, expecting to die, they instead embrace in passionate love ☙.

> "Wie lachend sie mir Lieder singen"

> "Wie sich die Herzen wogend erheben!"

As the boat moors, Brangäne reveals to Isolde that she replaced the death potion with an elixir of love. In despair, Isolde falls unconscious.

"IMPOSSIBLE" ROLES

Tristan und Isolde was to premiere in Vienna in 1861, but was cancelled after 77 rehearsals left Wagner defeated. Indeed, the title roles are among the most physically taxing of the repertoire, and were musically unlike anything heard at the time. Finally, in 1865, the husband and wife singers Ludwig and Malwine Schnorr von Carolsfeld created Tristan and Isolde (*left*). Ludwig gave four legendary performances, only to die a month later. Some accused the monstrous opera role of killing its Heldentenor.

ACT TWO As night descends in the garden of Cornwall's castle, Brängane warns Isolde against Tristan's "friend" Melot, who is off hunting with King Marke. But Isolde asks Brängane to beckon Tristan by putting out the torchlight. Reunited, Tristan and Isolde wish for an oblivion in which they may love forever, released from the world ♫. Brangäne warns that daylight approaches. But Tristan assures Isolde that their love is unconquerable, even by Death. When Brangäne again warns them, the lovers hope for an eternal night ♫. Returning from the hunt to discover the lovers, Marke is devastated, and Melot is exposed as a traitor. Tristan challenges Melot, then lowers his sword as Melot strikes him.

"O sink hernieder, Nacht der Liebe"

"O ew'ge Nacht, süsse Nacht!"

ACT THREE Tristan lies near death at his family castle in Brittany. He is awakened by the music of a shepherd's reed-pipe. Kurwenal assures Tristan that he will heal in his old home. But Tristan corrects his friend to insist that he awakens in a mysterious place and longs for Death. Kurwenal explains that Isolde has been summoned to heal him. Tristan senses her ship approaching. The boat indeed arrives, sending Tristan into a blissful delirium ♫. Isolde appears. Tristan rises and goes to her, only to die in her arms. A second ship brings Marke, Melot, and Brangäne, who has told Marke of the love potion. Kurwenal slays Melot. Marke laments; he had intended for Tristan and Isolde to marry. But Isolde cannot hear him; she is enraptured by the love she shared with Tristan ♫. Isolde, as if exalted, sinks onto Tristan's corpse. Finally, Marke blesses the lovers' bodies.

"O diese Sonne!"

"Mild und leise wie er lächelt"

At the Opéra Bastille in 2005, Peter Sellars staged characters before immense videos by Bill Viola to engulf audiences in Wagner's majestic music.

DIE MEISTERSINGER VON NÜRNBERG

(The Mastersingers of Nuremberg)

   ♫ Music drama in three acts, 4¼ hours
   ■ 1862–1864; 1866–1867
   ♔ 21 June 1868, Königliches Hof-und National

Theater, Munich, Bavaria (Germany)
📖 Richard Wagner

Die Meistersinger von Nürnberg, Wagner's only comical opera, was written during a pause in the composition of the *Ring* cycle. It is unique among Wagner's mature operas for including a string of stand-alone numbers. These are built into Wagner's libretto, the only one for which the composer invented an original storyline. A goldsmith's daughter and a knight fall in love, but may not marry until they have navigated their way through the zany world of Nuremberg's Mastersingers. The opera belongs to Hans Sachs, a lovable cobbler, inspired poet, and wise Mastersinger. Folksy and funny, the opera offers great entertainment, then shifts gear to conclude with a paean to German culture.

> ✄ *Die Meistersinger von Nürnberg*, Hitler's favourite opera, was used to enliven Nazi Party congresses in Nuremberg. In 1995 Berlin, director Götz Friedrich succeeded with a risky production set in post-war Nuremberg. ✄

❖ PRINCIPAL ROLES ❖

MASTERSINGERS

Hans Sachs *bass*
A cobbler

Veit Pogner *bass*
A goldsmith

Sixtus Beckmesser *baritone*
Town clerk

Fritz Kothner *bass*
A baker

Walther von Stolzing *tenor*
A young Franconian knight

Eva *soprano*
Daughter of Veit Pogner

Magdalene *mezzo-soprano*
Her nurse

David *tenor*
Apprentice to Hans Sachs

PLOT SYNOPSIS

Nuremberg, Bavaria, in the mid-16th century

ACT ONE Walther von Stolzing, a knight newly arrived in Nuremberg, has fallen for the goldsmith's daughter, Eva, who returns his love. In church, Walther learns that Eva's hand in marriage will be the prize of a Mastersinger contest the next day, and he suddenly wishes to become a Master in order to compete. David, apprentice to the Mastersinger and cobbler Hans Sachs, outlines for Walther the bewildering basics of the art form ♫. As their Song School commences in the church, fellow Masters are introduced to Walther by Pogner, Eva's father. Sachs is welcoming; but Beckmesser frowns on Walther's inclusion, and Kothner eagerly consults the guild's rulebook. Walther sings rapturously of spring's arrival while Beckmesser interrupts and, as the Marker of errors, notes many faults.

"Der Meister Tön' und Weisen"

Robert Dean Smith (*left*) played Walther to Jan-Hendrik Rootering's Hans Sachs in Graham Vick's production at the Royal Opera House, London, in 2002.

Sachs tries to defend Walther's song whilst others attack it ♫. Amidst the rude commotion, Walther completes his song and departs angrily.

"Halt, Meister! Nicht so geeilt!"

ACT TWO On the eve of the contest, Eva learns that her beloved Walther failed to impress the Masters. In his workshop,

Allied bombs destroyed the Berlin Staatsoper, which reopened with *Meistersinger* in 1955. Harry Kupfer's 2005 staging (*above*) marked the theatre's 50th year.

"Was duftet doch der Flieder"

Sachs ponders Walther's sweet singing 🔊. When Eva discovers that Beckmesser intends to serenade her that night, she proposes that her nurse Magdalene appear in her place. Walther persuades Eva to elope with him. As they run down an alley, they are forced to hide. Beckmesser comes up the alley with his lute to serenade "Eva", in fact Magdalene. Walther and Eva observe as Sachs disrupts Beckmesser's music by hammering loudly over it. Neighbours are awakened, while David, who loves Magdalene, explodes in jealousy only to knock the lute from Beckmesser's grip. A fight breaks out. A Night Watchman finally returns quiet to the streets.

ACT THREE On the day of the competition, Walther reports a dream and Sachs notes it down as poetry. Beckmesser, delighted by prospects of winning Eva with poetry by the great Sachs, pockets the lyrics and limps off, still sore from the previous night's events. Walther praises Eva in a song. When Sachs calls it a Master melody, Eva rejoices 🔊. Guilds parade into a meadow for the festival. Sachs greets the townspeople and praises art, while Beckmesser sweats over the lyrics he has yet to memorize. A strange performance is given by Beckmesser, the first to compete 🔊. But Walther's singing dazzles everyone 🔊. Eva then crowns Walther the winner, and Sachs welcomes him among the Mastersingers, the keepers of "a holy German art".

"Selig, wie du Sonne meines Glückes lacht"

"Morgen ich leuchte in rosigem Schein"

"Morgenlich leuchtend im rosigen Schein"

HANS SACHS

In about 1520, the Lutheran cobbler Hans Sachs became a Mastersinger in Nuremberg, home to one of the region's famously strict Song Schools that traced their origins to refined medieval courts. Creating thousands of Master Songs, Sachs gained popularity in his lifetime. The writer JW von Goethe rediscovered Sachs's works, and in 1776 paid tribute to the cobbler–poet in a poem that inspired Albert Lortzing's opera of 1840, *Hans Sachs*, and Wagner's *Die Meistersinger von Nürnberg*.

DER RING DES NIBELUNGEN

(The Nibelung's Ring)

R ICHARD WAGNER'S *Der Ring des Nibelungen* encompasses four operas: *Das Rheingold*, *Die Walküre*, *Siegfried*, and *Götterdämmerung*. The cycle was intended for presentation over four consecutive evenings. Requiring over 15 hours to perform, Wagner laboured for 28 years to complete the *Ring*, arguably the greatest single operatic work of all time. In 1876, it premiered in Bayreuth at the Festspielhaus, and has since been given around the world.

THE RING: FROM IDEA TO OPERA

The *Ring* cycle was sparked by France's Revolution of 1848. Following events in France, Wagner began to picture a "theatre of Revolution" portraying the dramatic upheaval of established orders. He was also absorbed in the traditional literature favoured by Romantic thinkers and artists of his day. His mystical political visions and fecund imagination galvanized one another as he read: the Norse myths recounted in the *Eddas*, other Scandinavian narratives such as the *Völsunga Saga*, the German folklore and mythical tales collected and published by the brothers Grimm, and *Das Nibelungenlied*, a major medieval German epic. By 1848, Wagner had already written "Siegfried's Death", the text for a heroic opera to express his new-found passions. Captivated by the hero, he wove Siegfried's story into a web of themes and threads suggestive of a cosmos unto itself. He then set out to create that world. He peopled it with his own mix of Germanic heroes and gods who would, in the end, be

"The Death of Siegfried", a theme from Germanic lore, inspired countless works of art. It was Wagner's starting point for what was to become the *Ring* cycle.

engulfed in sacrificial, revolutionary flames. Wagner began composing the preliminary opera in 1853, and finished the final one only in 1874. King Ludwig II of Bavaria, Wagner's patron, provided financial and political backing for the *Ring* premiere of 1876. Wagner also raised funds for the project, but the first Festival at Bayreuth proved a financial disaster.

Siegfried slays the dragon Fafner in this mural in Ludwig II's famous Neuschwanstein Castle in Germany.

to characters, objects, and ideas which evolve as the operas unfold. For example, the motif for the sword called Nothung takes the sharp and gleaming shape of the weapon, while that of the character Hunding rumbles with crude foreboding to announce his disposition and his place in the cycle's story. Even used for less tangible matters, such as the curse placed on the Ring, motifs are subtly deployed to look forward or backward to the moments when they are most strikingly expressed. They are introduced, altered, expanded, and interwoven to shape storied layers of evocative musical textures.

MOTIFS IN THE RING

The *Ring* forms its own musical and dramatic world. Among its innovations is the use of some 200 musical themes known as "motifs". Wagner tied these

---

⇥ THE ROLES IN THE RING CYCLE ⇤

The *Ring* evokes mythic proportions, but is built around surprisingly few soloists who appear in clear groupings. Its story pits love against power and greed, with love ultimately proving to be the greatest force of all. Major roles include Wotan, Brünnhilde, Siegfried, and the Nibelung Alberich.

RHINEMAIDENS Seductive nymphs of the river Rhine
Woglinde, Wellgunde, Flosshilde

NIBELUNGS Gnomes of Nibelheim, a subterranean realm
Alberich, Mime, Hagen

GIANTS Builders of Valhalla, the fortress of the gods
Fasolt, Fafner (In *Siegfried*, Fafner appears as a dragon)

GODS Residents of Valhalla, they are doomed to perish
Wotan (disguised as "the Wanderer" in *Siegfried*), Fricka,
Loge, Freia, Donner, Froh, Erda

WÄLSUNGS Descendants of Wälse, a pseudonym for Wotan
Siegmund, Sieglinde, Siegfried

VALKYRIES Chaste warriors, daughters of Wotan
Brünnhilde, Gerhilde, Ortlinde, Waltraute, Schwertleite,
Helmwige, Siegrune, Grimgerde, Rossweisse

NORNS Daughters of Erda who spin fates on golden rope
First Norn, Second Norn, Third Norn

GIBICHUNGS Royals residing in a palace near the Rhine
Gunther, Gutrune

OTHERS Hunding, Woodbird

POSSESSORS OF THE MAGIC RING

The Nibelung Alberich forswears love to win the Ring from the Rhinemaidens. The Ring, which is called the Nibelung's even though Alberich stole it, brings its owner limitless riches and power. But in the opening opera, Alberich puts a curse on the Ring: anyone other than himself who touches it, and is aware of its magic, is doomed. In the final opera, Brünnhilde sacrifices herself to remove the curse, and the Ring ends up where it began: in the river Rhine, to be guarded by the seductive Rhinemaidens.

DAS RHEINGOLD			DIE WALKÜRE	SIEGFRIED	GÖTTERDÄMMERUNG	
1. The Rhinemaidens				6. Fafner, now a dragon	9. Siegfried	
	3. Wotan, lord of the gods					10. Brünnhilde
2. Alberich, a Nibelung	4. Fasolt, a Giant	5. Fafner, his brother	Remains with Fafner	7. Siegfried, a Wälsung	8. Brünnhilde, Siegfried's wife	11. The Rhinemaidens

DAS RHEINGOLD
(The Rhinegold)

🎵 In one act, 2½ hours
🖊 1853–1854
♬ 22 September 1869, Königliches Hof- und

Nationaltheater, Munich, Bavaria (Germany)
📖 Richard Wagner

Das Rheingold, the first of four operas forming Wagner's *Ring* cycle, is subtitled *A Preliminary Evening*. This opera was written to set the stage for the trilogy of operas to follow on subsequent evenings: *Die Walküre*, *Siegfried*, and *Götterdämmerung*. Even before the curtain rises, the music pulls the audience into a mystical realm populated by gods and otherworldly creatures. Scene Three is set below the earth, in Nibelheim, the domain of the Nibelungs, or gnomes. The opera is about one of them, Alberich, who upsets the cosmic balance of the world by stealing the magic gold of the river Rhine. Highlights abound in the opera's fourth and final scene, which includes the fantastic solo of the god Donner as he unleashes thunderbolts.

> ✦ **PRINCIPAL ROLES** ✦
>
> Wotan (Odin) *high bass* Lord of the gods
> Loge *tenor* The wily god of Fire
> Freia *high soprano* The goddess of Love
> Erda *contralto* The primeval mother
> Donner *high bass* God of Strength
> Alberich *high bass* Lord of the Nibelungs
> Mime *tenor* His brother,
> a smith who forges a magic helmet
> Fasolt *high bass*; Fafner *low bass*
> Giants, they built Valhalla for Wotan
> Woglinde *high soprano*; Wellgunde
> *high soprano*; Flosshilde *low soprano*
> Rhinemaidens

> ◃ The opera begins with a chord in E flat which continues for 136 bars. Wagner noted that the pitch and drone-like effect, meant to capture the unceasing flow of the river Rhine, came to him as he was half asleep. ▹

PLOT SYNOPSIS

A mythical valley of the river Rhine

SCENE ONE Three sensuous nymphs frolic in the Rhine as they guard the river's precious gold. Alberich, a Nibelung, emerges from a chasm, and lusts after them. The nymphs reject him, but explain that whoever wears a ring made from the Rhine's gold possesses absolute wealth and power; to take the gold, one must forswear love. Alberich curses love, seizes the gold, and escapes.

SCENE TWO Below a mountain-top fortress, the goddess Fricka complains to her husband, Wotan: he has promised her sister Freia, goddess of Beauty, to the Giants in exchange for their building his fortress. Wotan insists that he will not give them Freia. The Giants Fasolt and Fafner arrive, seeking Freia. The god Loge reports that Alberich has stolen the Rhinegold. Fasolt seizes Freia, and refuses to return her unless the Rhinegold is handed to the Giants by evening. The Giants depart with Freia, whose absence spells death for the gods. Wotan and Loge resolve to recover the Rhinegold from the Nibelung.

For the 1876 premiere of the *Ring* in Bayreuth, a special contraption with hand-manoeuvred dollies and poles was constructed to provide the illusion that the Rhinemaidens were swimming in the river.

✦ AN OPERA HOUSE AHEAD OF ITS TIME ✦

The Bayreuth Festspielhaus, which was inaugurated in 1876 with the first *Ring* cycle, was a theatre unlike any built before it. The orchestra pit (*right*) was sunken and concealed from the audience so that music seemed to emerge organically from the staged drama. Breaking further with tradition, Wagner eliminated hierarchical loges and boxes in which the wealthy had long enjoyed privileged sightlines and acoustics in theatres. In the democratic Festspielhaus, all could view and hear the opera equally. But perhaps Wagner's most radical step was the least architectural: he was the first to darken the house in order to direct audience attention to the only source of light: the stage. And with no aisles between seats, audiences were prevented from circulating during performances. Through these simple yet striking innovations, those attending the opera were to be absorbed not in mere entertainment, but in a mystical, even sacred event.

SCENE THREE In a subterranean cavern, Alberich tests the Tarnhelm, a magic helmet forged by his brother, Mime; it renders him invisible. Alberich departs. Mime tells Wotan and Loge that Alberich terrorizes the Nibelungs with a ring made of the Rhinegold. Loge promises freedom. Alberich forces the Nibelungs to pile up gold, and boasts that he will rule the world. Loge tricks Alberich into transforming himself into a toad. Loge and Wotan capture Alberich and climb up from the depths of the earth.

SCENE FOUR Wotan receives the Nibelung treasure in exchange for Alberich's release. Alberich whispers a spell into the Ring. When Wotan takes the Ring, Alberich warns that it will bring death, then disappears. The Giants arrive with Freia. Wotan gives them the treasure and helmet, but not the Ring. Erda, mother of the gods, rises from below to command the Ring's surrender ♣. Freia is returned. Fasolt grabs the Ring, but is clubbed by Fafner, who takes the Ring. Wotan notes the power of the Ring's curse. Donner climbs a peak to make a thunderstorm ♣. During the storm, Fafner hauls off his treasure. When a rainbow bridge appears, Wotan invites Fricka to step along it to the hall, Valhalla ♣. The gods follow, save Loge. In the valley, the Rhinemaidens lament the lost Rhinegold ♟.

"Wie alles war, weiss ich"

"Heda! Heda! Hedo!"

"Abendlich strahlt der Sonne Auge"

"Rheingold! Rheingold!"

In the *Ring* production of 1976 in Bayreuth, directed by Patrice Chéreau and designed by Richard Peduzzi, the Rhine "river" took the form of a hydroelectric dam.

DIE WALKÜRE

(The Valkyrie)

In three acts, 3¾ hours
1856–1857; 1864–1865; 1869–1871
26 June 1870, Königliches Hof- und

Nationaltheater, Munich, Bavaria (Germany)
Richard Wagner (written 1851–1852)

Die Walküre, the second opera of Wagner's *Ring* cycle, follows *Das Rheingold* and precedes *Siegfried* and *Götterdämmerung*. In productions of the *Ring*, audiences often prefer *Die Walküre* to other operas in the cycle. It introduces many of Wagner's most memorable motifs, or musical themes. The most famous is for the extraordinary Valkyries, immortal female warriors. But as with all Wagner operas, love is the main subject. Act I is about the passionate yet forbidden romance between a brother and sister. Their offspring, Siegfried, is the subject of the next opera in the *Ring* cycle. Act III deals with Wotan's tragic love for his disobedient Valkyrie daughter, Brünnhilde.

≈ "The Ride of the Valkyries", which opens Act III, can produce strong responses, even outside opera houses. It tops Britain's Royal Automobile Club Foundation list of the most dangerous music to play while driving. ≈

↟ PRINCIPAL ROLES ↟

Brünnhilde *soprano*
A Valkyrie, Wotan's
favourite daughter

Gerhilde, Ortlinde,
Waltraute, Schwertleite,
Helmwige, Siegrune,
Grimgerde, Rossweisse
sopranos and contraltos
Valkyrie daughters of Wotan

Wotan (Odin) *high bass*
Lord of the gods

Fricka *mezzo-soprano*
His wife

Siegmund *tenor*
A Wälsung separated from
his twin in infancy

Sieglinde *soprano*
His twin sister

Hunding *bass*
Husband to Sieglinde

PLOT SYNOPSIS

In mythic realms of the Germanic past

ACT ONE Fleeing attackers in a storm, a man takes refuge in a hut. Sieglinde discovers him in her hut, and they fall in love. Her husband, Hunding, arrives. The guest explains that, as a baby, he was separated from his twin. Recognizing the visitor as his kin's enemy, Hunding warns that they must fight to the death come daylight. Alone with the man, Sieglinde informs him of a sword hidden there.

They embrace, and Siegmund celebrates their union ♪. Realizing that he is her twin, Sieglinde tells him his name: Siegmund. He retrieves the sword and names it "Nothung". Sieglinde throws herself into his arms as he calls her sister and wife.

"Winterstürme wichen dem Wonnemond"

ACT TWO In the mountains, Wotan orders his Valkyrie daughter Brünnhilde to protect his mortal son Siegmund, who must retrieve the Ring from the Giant Fafner. Wotan's wife, Fricka, argues that Siegmund will fail because the magic sword prevents him from acting freely. Wotan finally agrees. He tells Brünnhilde the story of the Ring

The one-eyed Wotan (Bryn Terfel) holds back Brünnhilde (Lisa Gasteen) in a production at London's Royal Opera House in 2005.

and how, having touched it, he is cursed to forswear love. Wotan orders her to ensure that Siegmund falls to Hunding in their battle. Sieglinde urges Siegmund

"Siegmund! Sieh auf mich!"

to flee without her. When he refuses, she sleeps in his arms. Brünnhilde warns Siegmund of his death ♂, but then, moved by his devotion to Sieglinde, vows to protect him. Yet, during the battle, Wotan uses his divine spear to shatter Siegmund's sword, Nothung. Hunding slays Siegmund; Brünnhilde sweeps Sieglinde away on horseback; and Wotan kills Hunding.

ACT THREE In the mountains, Valkyries collect slain battle heroes who will gain new life serving the gods in their

"Hojotoho! Hojotoho!"

fortress, Valhalla ♨. Fleeing Wotan's rage, Brünnhilde arrives with Sieglinde. To save Sieglinde, Brünnhilde directs her to the East, where Fafner hoards the Ring, and where Wotan will not follow. She gives the pregnant Sieglinde fragments of Nothung, for her future son. Wotan delivers his punishment to Brünnhilde: banishment, and a sleep that will last until a man claims her. Brünnhilde pleads fruitlessly that she acted for love, and to express Wotan's deepest wishes. She asks for her body to be ringed in fire so that only

a courageous man may win her. Wotan tenderly bids her farewell ♂. He

"Leb' wohl, du kühnes, herrliches Kind!"

encircles his daughter in a wall of magic fire, and decrees that no one who fears his spear will ever penetrate its flames.

Hildegard Behrens, a Brünnhilde legend, played the role at the Metropolitan Opera in 1990.

HEROIC VOCALISTS

The singers who created principal roles in the 1876 premiere of the *Ring* were nearly as heroic as the characters they depicted. The remarkable German soprano Amalie Materna (*right*) sang Brünnhilde in each of the operas in which the favourite Valkyrie appears: *Die Walküre*, *Siegfried*, and *Götterdämmerung*. Today, lead singers are given rest days between performances, but Materna took on the notoriously demanding role in three different operas over three consecutive evenings.

Albert Niemann was the celebrated Heldentenor who interpreted Siegmund in *Die Walküre*. He hoped to create the character of Siegfried in the *Ring* cycle's final two operas. But Wagner felt that Niemann's voice and bearing were too mature to portray the younger, friskier hero. Instead, the part went to tenor Georg Unger, who had also sung Froh in *Das Rheingold* for the Bayreuth premiere. The entire cycle was conducted by the Austrian Hans Richter.

SIEGFRIED

🔊 In three acts, 4¼ hours
📅 1856–1857; 1864–1865; 1869–1871
🎭 16 August 1876, Festspielhaus, Bayreuth,

Bavaria (Germany)
📖 Richard Wagner (written 1851–1852)

Siegfried, the third opera in Wagner's *Ring* cycle, is preceded by *Das Rheingold* and *Die Walküre*, and followed by *Götterdämmerung*. *Die Walküre* ended with the pregnant heroine Sieglinde fleeing into the woods, and with the Valkyrie Brünnhilde condemned to sleep in a ring of fire until rescued. This opera skips ahead: Sieglinde's child is now a young man, Siegfried. Since Sieglinde died in childbirth, Siegfried was raised by a Nibelung, Mime. Siegfried is defiant, boastful, and even arrogant. But these are not negative traits. Instead, they reflect his unconquerable nature and innate heroism. Act III features exceptional music, when Wotan as "the Wanderer" bares his soul to the goddess Erda, and when Siegfried and Brünnhilde fall in love.

> **PRINCIPAL ROLES**
>
> Wotan (Odin) *bass* Lord of the gods, he travels as "the Wanderer"
> Erda *contralto* Primeval goddess of Wisdom
> Brünnhilde *soprano* Daughter of Wotan and Erda
> Siegfried *tenor* Grandson of Wotan, he wins the Ring
> Mime *tenor* A Nibelung, he raised Siegfried and hopes to seize the Ring
> Alberich *bass* His brother, who aims to regain the Ring
> Fafner *bass* In the form of a dragon, he hoards the Ring
> Woodbird *soprano* A bird who guides Siegfried

⚄ After composing Act II in 1857, Wagner dropped the opera in order to devote himself to *Tristan und Isolde*. When he returned to *Siegfried* years later, his style had evolved. Act III therefore sounds unlike the earlier acts. ⚄

PLOT SYNOPSIS

Mythic realms of the Germanic past

ACT ONE   Before his cave in the woods, Mime, a Nibelung blacksmith, schemes: if his foster child Siegfried could wield the sword Nothung to slay the dragon Fafner, Mime could take the Ring from the dragon's cave. Mime informs Siegfried that his mother was Sieglinde, and that Nothung was his father's sword. Alone, Mime fails to repair the shattered sword. Wotan, disguised as "the Wanderer", informs him that it must be forged by a man who has never known fear. When Siegfried hopes to learn about fear, Mime explains that Fafner can teach him. Siegfried joyously forges his father's sword on an anvil ♂. The task completed, he celebrates by using Nothung to sever the anvil.

"Nothung! Nothung! Neidliches Schwert!"

Walther Kirchhoff

ACT TWO   At night near Fafner's cave, the Nibelung Alberich awaits a chance to grab the Ring. Wotan also observes. By daylight, Mime deposits Siegfried there. Lonely and hoping to communicate with a bird, Siegfried blows his

Walther Kirchhoff was one of many pre-war Heldentenors who incarnated the character of Siegfried in realistic stagings.

✢ THE 1876 RING PREMIERE IN BAYREUTH ✦

The *Ring* premiere of 1876 was a momentous occasion. It inaugurated Wagner's singular opera house in Bayreuth, the Festspielhaus, and offered music theatre of unprecedented scope and depth: a sequence of four operas whose interlinked musical and mythical elements formed an independent aesthetic sphere. The cycle was given three times over the course of a festival initiated in high pomp on 13 August. For the opening ceremony, Emperor Kaiser Wilhelm led a full royal cortège. Notable festival guests included the composer Tchaikovsky and the philosopher Friedrich Nietzsche. On stage, audiences beheld naturalistic stage décor realized from artwork by the Viennese landscape painter Joseph Hoffmann. Special effects included flying Valkyries in full medieval battle garb. Deemed a major work of art, the *Ring* was also a major expense. So much so, that the cycle was not staged again in Bayreuth's Festspielhaus until 1896.

Wagner and Liszt meet Kaiser Wilhelm I at the opening of the Festspielhaus in Bayreuth.

horn. This awakens Fafner, whom Siegfried first mocks, then slays with his sword. An accidental taste of dragon blood allows Siegfried to understand the bird, who instructs him to fetch the Ring and a helmet, the magic Tarnhelm, from Fafner's treasures. Since Siegfried can also hear Mime's unspoken plans to decapitate him, he slays the Nibelung. The bird informs Siegfried of a sleeping maid: if he walks through a ring of fire, he can make her his bride. The bird leads him to Brünnhilde, Wotan's daughter.

ACT THREE By a cave at the base of a mountain, "the Wanderer" awakens the earth goddess Erda, Brünnhilde's mother 🔊. When she has no wisdom to offer, he urges her to

"Wache, Wala! Wala! Erwach'!"

envision his downfall: he will now yield power to his mortal son, the redeeming Siegfried. He encounters Siegfried, armed with Nothung, and warns that his spear has broken the sword before. Happy to meet his father's enemy, Siegfried destroys Wotan's spear with his sword. Lightning strikes, and Siegfried is plunged into a sea of fire. Brünnhilde is asleep under a tree, where Siegfried discovers her. He kisses her, and she awakens joyfully 🔊. She instantly falls in love, but hesitates upon recalling her vows of chastity for the purity of Valhalla, fortress of the gods. Siegfried urges her to wake up her spirit, too, and accept his love. Finally, Brünnhilde blissfully accepts love, and bids Valhalla goodbye 🔊.

"Heil dir, Sonne!"

"Fahr' hin, Walhalls, leuchtende Welt!"

Wieland Wagner, the composer's grandson, revolutionized Bayreuth's *Ring* stagings in the 1950s, as with this 1951 production of *Siegfried*.

GÖTTERDÄMMERUNG

(The Twilight of the Gods)

✍ Prologue and three acts, 4¼ hours   Bavaria (Germany)

🎙 1869–1874   📖 Richard Wagner (written 1848–1852)

🏛 17 August 1876, Festspielhaus, Bayreuth,

Götterdämmerung completes Wagner's *Ring* cycle. It follows *Das Rheingold*, *Die Walküre*, and *Siegfried*, which ended with Siegfried and Brünnhilde falling in love. In *Götterdämmerung*, they live in a forest cavern, until Siegfried leaves to seek heroic adventures. The opera introduces Hagen, whose fanatical desire to win the Ring sets in motion the cycle's tragic conclusion. Also new are Hagen's half-brother, King Gunther, and Gunther's sister Gutrune, both pawns in Hagen's plot. Unlike the other *Ring* operas, this one employs a chorus, for which Wagner scored mainly rousing but also solemn passages. Highlights include Act III's "Funeral March" and Brünnhilde's final solo.

> ⚶ In the final scene, Brünnhilde rides her horse, Grane, into the flames of Siegfried's funeral pyre. For the Bayreuth premiere of 1876, Grane was played by King Ludwig II of Bavaria's black stallion, Cocotte. ⚶

PLOT SYNOPSIS

Mythic realms of the Germanic past

PROLOGUE The three Norns, who spin gold into fate, foresee the twilight of the gods. But when their rope of destiny is severed, they vanish forever. Brünnhilde

"Zu neuen Taten teurer Helde" | bids her beloved Siegfried farewell before their cave dwelling ♩. Before he departs to gain glory, they exchange love tokens: he gives her the Ring he won upon slaying the dragon Fafner, and she gives him her horse, Grane.

ACT ONE In a palace on the Rhine, Hagen advises his half-brother, King Gunther, to marry the wondrous Brünnhilde, who is guarded by a wall of fire. Hagen believes that Siegfried can win her, and a love potion could then secure Siegfried for Gunther's sister, Gutrune. Siegfried arrives and drinks the potion. He falls in love with

Gutrune and forgets Brünnhilde. In a ritual pact, Siegfried vows to seize Brünnhilde for Gunther. Hagen watches Siegfried depart on his mission ♩. At home, Brünnhilde receives | *"Hier sitz' ich zur Wacht"* her request to save the gods by surrendering the Ring Siegfried gave her. Using his magic helmet to resemble Gunther, Siegfried arrives at dusk. He grabs the Ring from Brünnhilde and forces her into the cave, where they sleep chastely on either side of his sword.

ACT TWO Asleep by the Rhine, Hagen hears his Nibelung father, Alberich, urging him to own the Ring. At dawn, Siegfried returns to Gutrune. When Gunther arrives with Brünnhilde, she goes unrecognized by Siegfried. Noticing her Ring on Siegfried's finger,

Brünnhilde accuses him of betrayal. But Siegfried vows loyalty to Gunther, and denies being Brünnhilde's husband. Apart, Hagen persuades Brünnhilde and Gunther that Siegfried must die. Brünnhilde reluctantly joins the dual marriage procession with Gunther.

ACT THREE Out hunting, Siegfried meets the Rhinemaidens, who warn of his imminent death. Found by Gunther and Hagen, Siegfried recounts his youth to them. After Hagen's latest potion reminds Siegfried of Brünnhilde ♫, Hagen slays Siegfried.

"Brünnhilde! Heilige Braut!"

Robert Wilson used colour to weave visual motifs in his staging of *Götterdämmerung* at the Théâtre du Châtelet, Paris, in January 2006.

Aggrieved, Gunther and his men return Siegfried's body to the palace. There, hoping to take the Ring from Siegfried's finger, Hagen slays Gunther. However, Brünnhilde captures the Ring and, to cleanse it of the curse, she wears it as she sacrifices herself in Siegfried's funeral pyre ♫. The Rhinemaidens recover the Ring and drown Hagen. As foretold, flames consume the gods and their celestial fortress, Valhalla.

"Starke Scheite schichtet mir dort"

➤ THE RING CYCLE AFTER WAGNER ←

The *Ring* premiere in 1876 was so costly that it was not given again until 1896, when Bayreuth was headed by the composer's widow, Cosima Wagner. After World War II, their grandsons Wieland and Wolfgang Wagner (*right*) changed the course of the cycle's production history by supplanting realism with abstraction. But the most legendary production since Wagner's day was arguably the 1976 centennial *Ring* directed by Patrice Chéreau. Costuming gods in business suits, he imbued the cycle with modern resonances.

While some directors have preserved traditional Wagnerian staging, others have brought fresh visions of the work. A notable 21st-century example is Robert Wilson, whose minimalist *Ring* for Zurich and Paris, employed radical lighting effects to explore darkness as a form of illumination. Wagner's *Ring* is considered difficult, even intimidating, to stage, yet it is being produced with increasing frequency on opera stages around the world.

PARSIFAL

🎭 Bühnenweihfestspiel in three acts,
4–4½ hours
🎬 1877–1882

🎭 26 July 1882, Festspielhaus, Bayreuth,
Bavaria (Germany)
📖 Richard Wagner

Parsifal, Wagner's final opera, has troubled some scholars with its depiction of religious fervour, purity of caste, and women as sexually depraved heathens. More frequently, audiences and conductors rank it as Wagner's most exquisite opera. It creates a mysterious effect in which, as one Grail knight puts it, "time becomes space". Medieval romance, Buddhism, Christianity, and philosophy inform a sacred operatic idiom built of ceremonial tableaux. Indeed, the opera's structure resembles a ladder into divine rapture. Compassion translates states of agony or sin into sources of redemption and salvation, and the final scene is lifted by glorious harp music.

> ✦ PRINCIPAL ROLES ✦
>
> **Titurel** *bass*
> Founder of the
> Knights of the Grail
>
> **Amfortas** *baritone*
> His son, tainted
> guardian of the Grail
>
> **Gurnemanz** *bass*
> An elderly knight of the Grail
>
> **Parsifal** *tenor*
> An "innocent fool!"
>
> **Klingsor** *bass*
> A vengeful magician
>
> **Kundry** *soprano*
> A heathen healer,
> cursed to be a seductress

⚔ *Parsifal* has produced vehement reactions. In his 1887 *On the Genealogy of Morals*, Wagner's former friend Friedrich Nietzsche attacked its Christianity and moralizing, qualities that invited Nazi praise in the 1930s. ⚓

PLOT SYNOPSIS

Castle and domain of the guardians of the Grail at Montsalvat, in the fictional Middle Ages

ACT ONE The knight Gurnemanz awakens at Montsalvat to prepare a bath for the suffering Amfortas. The angry magician Klingsor has stolen Montsalvat's Holy Spear and used it to pierce Amfortas's side. Gurnemanz recalls a prophecy: "an innocent fool enlightened through compassion" will save Amfortas. When a "sacred swan"

falls dead, its killer, a young man (Parsifal), is presented to Gurnemanz. The man, unaware of his own identity, is shocked when Kundry, a pagan woman, knows his past. Gurnemanz escorts him into the hall, where Grail knights parade ceremonially. In torment, Amfortas laments serving as the Grail's sinful guardian ♂. The knights take communion, while the visitor marvels at the power of pity and love. Amfortas's wound reopens. The guest is moved but, when he fails to articulate what he feels, Gurnemanz ejects him.

"Nein! Lass ihn unhenthüllt!"

ACT TWO Klingsor conjures Kundry. She is enraged to be cursed to seduce knights, even though the one who

Plácido Domingo's Parsifal, seen here at the Metropolitan Opera in New York in 1992, is among the great tenor's noted Wagner roles.

spurns her will remove the curse. A man marvels at Flower Maidens in the castle's magic garden , but he rejects their tantalizing advances. Kundry surprises him by calling him Parsifal, as his mother did; she claims that his mother died of sorrow over him. Compassion for Amfortas floods the aggrieved Parsifal ♿. Resisting Kundry's sexual advances, he encourages her to receive Grace. Her erotic energy rises as she tries anew to lure him ♿. Finally, she curses him and releases him to Klingsor. The magician hurls the Holy Spear at Parsifal. When it hovers over him, Parsifal grasps it from the air to form the sign of the Cross. The castle sinks into quaking earth, and Kundry collapses screaming as Parsifal departs.

"Hier war das Tosen!"

"Amfortas! Die Wunde! Die Wunde!"

"So war es mein Kuss"

ACT THREE Gurnemanz, more aged than before, emerges from a hut at Montsalvat. He discovers Kundry lifeless, but soon

WOLFRAM VON ESCHENBACH

Wolfram von Eschenbach was a major poet of the German Middle Ages. Dating from around 1200, his *Parzival* was an lively epic narrative recounting the adventures of a foolish man whose sufferings bring wisdom and the honour of guarding the Holy Grail. In playful and rhythmic poetry, Wolfram was the first to bring the Grail theme from French into German literature. Wagner portrayed the poet in his opera *Tannhäuser*.

Medieval illumination of Wolfram's Parzival.

revives her. He then notes a knight in black armour, improperly outfitted for a Good Friday. Questioned, the man thrusts the Holy Spear into the ground; he disarms and removes his helmet. Gurnemanz is astonished to behold Parsifal, who says he brings salvation for Amfortas ♿. Gurnemanz anoints Parsifal with holy water, while Kundry washes his feet. Parsifal baptizes a weeping Kundry. Hailed the King of Knights by Gurnemanz, Parsifal gazes serenely at blossoming Nature. In the hall, knights bear Amfortas on his litter, and the body of his father, Titurel, in a coffin. They also carry the Grail shrine. Displaying his wound, Amfortas begs the knights to take his life. Parsifal presents the Holy Spear. Miraculously healed, Amfortas staggers in ecstasy. A white dove hovers over Parsifal's head as Kundry and others kneel before him.

"Nur eine Waffe taugt"

The German mezzo-soprano Waltraud Meier is famous for her fierce yet sympathetic Kundry. Others celebrated in the role include Martha Mödl, Christa Ludwig, and Olive Fremstad.

JOHANN STRAUSS THE YOUNGER

Born: 25 October 1825, Vienna (Austria)
Died: 3 June 1899, Vienna (Austria)

The Waltz King of Vienna was meant to become a banker. But he defied the wishes of his father, composer Johann Strauss the Elder, and took up musical studies in 1845. In 1863, he was appointed Court Ball Music Director under Emperor Franz Joseph I. French operettas by Jacques Offenbach were then all the rage in Vienna, and Strauss found that the light form, combining speech and self-contained songs, was ideally suited to his effervescent music. He scored over a dozen operettas, beginning with *Indigo*, for which he created the immortal "Blue Danube" waltz. But none would rival *Die Fledermaus* for enchanting music and indestructible popularity.

DIE FLEDERMAUS
(The Bat)

✍ Comic operetta in three acts, 2¼ hours
☗ 1873–1874
♇ 5 April 1874, Theater an der Wien, Vienna (Austria)

📖 Carl Haffner and Richard Genée, after the French play *Le réveillon* (1872), by Henri Meilhac and Ludovic Halévy

Die Fledermaus, now held to be the quintessential Viennese operetta, premiered in 1874 to no special enthusiasm. Yet, within a few years, it gained enormous popularity in German-speaking opera houses, and by the end of the century achieved the international success it has enjoyed since. Its plot was taken from a satirical French comedy by Jacques Offenbach's librettists, but Strauss's work treats the story with a lighter and sweeter touch that would come to define Vienna's "Golden Age" operetta. Endearing pranks drive the action forward, and the cast of lovable schemers delights audiences. Throughout, richly-orchestrated

A masked guest graces Prince Orlofsky's champagne party in Act II of *Die Fledermaus* at the Holland Park Opera in London in 1994.

❖ PRINCIPAL ROLES ❖

Gabriel von Eisenstein *tenor*
Husband to Rosalinde

Rosalinde von Eisenstein *soprano*
Wife to Gabriel

Alfred *tenor*
A singing teacher in love with Rosalinde

Dr Falke *baritone*
Gabriel's doctor

Frank *baritone*
Prison warden

Prince Orlofsky *mezzo-soprano*
Bored, wealthy Russian prince

Adele *soprano*
Rosalinde's maid

music sounds weightless and free from artifice. There are memorable solo vocal parts, but the consistent show-stoppers are ensembles, where Strauss's vocal music is just as refined and sparkling as the champagne that flows so copiously in Act II.

⚜ For the 2001 festival in Salzburg, Austria, director Hans Neuenfels turned waltzing revellers into orgiastic cocaine fiends. Many Strauss fans were offended, and one audience member even sued the Salzburg Festival. ⚜

Bass-baritone Angelo Gobbato parties as Frank, the prison warden, in the Cape Town Opera's 2004 production in South Africa.

PLOT SYNOPSIS

Vienna, Austria, in the mid-19th century

ACT ONE An irresistible tenor named Alfred serenades Rosalinde in the street below her home. Inside, her maid Adele, eager to attend Prince Orlofsky's masked ball, requests the night off, but her timing is bad: Rosalinde's husband is about to serve a jail sentence. Alfred urges Rosalinde to receive him that evening while her husband, Gabriel von Eisenstein, is in prison. Eisenstein returns home in a fury with his inept lawyer, Dr Blind. His doctor, Falke, proposes a "healthful" plan: delay jail until 6 AM, and instead attend Orlofsky's party disguised as "Marquis Renard". Rosalinde grants Adele the night off, while Eisenstein (heading to the party) and Rosalinde (awaiting Alfred) feign separation anxiety 🎵. Alfred is drinking copiously at Rosalinde's when Warden Frank arrives to fetch his prisoner. Rosalinde persuades him that Alfred is Eisenstein and, pleased to be taken for "Rosalinde's husband", Alfred is carted off to jail.

"So muss allein ich blieben"

ACT TWO Prince Orlofsky receives his disguised guests 🎵. Falke confides in the prince that amusement is in store: the "Marquis" (Eisenstein) flirts with a "Hungarian countess" (Rosalinde), who pockets his fancy watch as a love-token before delivering

"Ich lade gern mir Gäste ein"

a Hungarian song "from her country" 🎵. Falke explains his nickname, Dr Bat: after a night of masked partying, the "Marquis" left him to pass out in his bat costume. Falke was ridiculed the next day as he made his way home, and now hopes to avenge himself with a practical joke on the Marquis. Orlofsky proposes a champagne toast, and the revellers waltz 🎵. As the clock strikes six, Eisenstein rushes off to the jailhouse.

"Klänge der Heimat!"

"In Feuerstrom der Reben"

ACT THREE Frosch, a drunk jailer, copes with the hyperactive tenor mistaken for Eisenstein, and Frank, the warden, wakes with a hangover in his prison office. The "Marquis" arrives to learn "Eisenstein" was arrested dining with his wife. Posing as their lawyer, Eisenstein counsels Alfred and Rosalinde and, appalled by details of their tryst, finally unmasks. Yet, when Rosalinde produces his watch, he is suitably humiliated. Falke reveals his prank – "the Bat's revenge" – to all who have gathered at the prison 🎵. Eisenstein learns that everyone was in on the joke from the outset, although in an aside Alfred leaves some doubt about just how much of his seduction was merely staged. Blame for any misconduct is placed on King Champagne.

"O Fledermaus, o Fledermaus"

ENGELBERT
HUMPERDINCK

Born: 1 September 1854, Siegburg (Germany)
Died: 27 September 1921, Neustrelitz, Germany

Engelbert Humperdinck, among the last of the Romantic German composers, left his mark on music history with the opera *Hänsel und Gretel*. This and a later opera, *Königskinder* or *Royal Children*, were based on fairy-tales that injected new literary sources and sound-worlds into opera. Humperdinck began his career as a student of architecture in Cologne, but switched his studies to music when his talents were noticed. Recognition for early scores led him to Naples in 1880, where he impressed Richard Wagner enough to be appointed his assistant in Bayreuth in 1881–1882. Wagner's influence was strong, but Humperdinck developed an approach and sound all his own.

HÄNSEL UND GRETEL
(Hansel and Gretel)

⚎ Märchenoper in three acts, 2 hours
⚑ 1890–1893
⚏ 23 December 1893, Court Theater,

Weimar (Germany)
📖 Adelheid Wette, from the folk-tale recorded by Jacob and Wilhelm Grimm (1812)

Premiering under the baton of Richard Strauss, *Hänsel und Gretel* was an instant success in Germany and has since become one of the world's best-loved operas. The libretto splices regional realism into the more abstract fairy-tale. Humperdinck's score responds brilliantly. Throughout, the orchestra weaves symphonic threads, thick or delicate, yet also delivers isolated tunes derived from traditional songs or sacred hymns. Wagner's influence can be heard in the prelude to Act II, "The Witches' Ride", and Italian *verismo* peppers the score, as shown when Gertrud screeches in frustration, or the

✧	PRINCIPAL ROLES	✧

Hänsel *mezzo-soprano* Younger brother to Gretel
Gretel *soprano* Sister to Hänsel
Gertrud *mezzo-soprano* Mother to the children
Peter *baritone* Father to the children, a broom-maker
Sandman *soprano* Sprinkler of magic sand
Witch *mezzo-soprano* Wicked resident of the Gingerbread House

Witch cackles unnervingly. The Witch only appears in the last act, but music that is tied to her role menaces from the outset, and even swoops into the opera's final bars, well after the children have destroyed her.

Two young singers take on the roles of Gretel and Hänsel in a realistic production given at the Opéra-Comique in Paris in 1900.

⚎ On Christmas day, 1931, *Hänsel und Gretel* became the first opera to be broadcast live from the stage of the Metropolitan Opera House, New York, initiating a beloved radio tradition in the United States. ⚎

PLOT SYNOPSIS

Below Mount Ilsenstein, a woodland inhabited by a Witch and fairies

ACT ONE Hänsel and Gretel stave off hunger at home by dancing and singing

"Brüderchen, komm" | 🔔. When Gertrud discovers her children neglecting their chores,

she sends them into the forest to gather strawberries. Alone, she laments their poverty, but her husband, Peter, returns laden with food after a successful day's

"Ral la la la" | work 🔔. Joy turns to fear when Peter tells

his wife of the forest witch who eats children. Gertrud rushes out to look for Hänsel and Gretel in the forest, and Peter follows her.

ACT TWO In the forest, Hänsel's basket brims with strawberries and a birdcall announces day's end. Imitating birds, the children gobble up the berries. They consider picking more but, as night falls, they are lost, afraid, and tired. The kindly Sandman sprinkles their eyes with magic sand to assure sweet dreams. Alone,

"Abends, will ich schlafen gehn" | the children say their prayers 🔔.

Just as they have prayed, angels descend from heaven to offer the children protection.

ACT THREE Awakened by a Fairy sprinkling dewdrops, Gretel describes to her brother the dream she has had

"Mir träumte" | of angels 🔔. Hänsel also dreamed of the

angels, and points in the direction they departed. There, they behold a heavenly Gingerbread House. As they nibble at it, its fabled Witch discovers them and casts spells: Hänsel is caged, and Gretel made motionless, until the Witch releases her from the spell so that she can help to fatten up Hänsel. Gretel carefully observes the method used to release the spell. Ecstatic over her plot

to turn the children into gingerbread, the Witch mounts her broomstick and takes to the air 🔔. Gretel

"Hurr hopp hopp" | secretly removes the spell cast on Hänsel. When the

returning Witch orders her to check the oven for hotness, Gretel cleverly persuades her to demonstrate the technique. Hänsel and Gretel then shove the Witch into the oven and slam its door on her. Hänsel and Gretel soon discover that their triumph has released other children from the Witch's spells, as the gingerbread children come alive. Peter and Gertrud arrive just as the children remove a large gingerbread witch from the oven. The reunited family joins forces with the freed children to assure all that God answers the prayers of the needy.

Ute Walther incarnates the wicked Witch and Andion Fernandez plays the caged Hänsel at the Deutsche Oper in Berlin in 2003.

FRANZ
LEHÁR

Born: 30 April 1870, Komorn (Hungary)
Died: 24 October 1948, Bad Ischl, Austria

Franz Lehár, master of the 20th-century operetta, composed 38 operatic works that premiered in an era of European turbulence, from 1893 to 1938. The most enduring of these, the 1905 work *Die lustige Witwe*, was also the first to win Lehár international renown. Later works, including *Das Land des Lächelns*, enjoy periodic revivals.

Franz Lehár learned violin and piano from his father, a military bandmaster. Franz Sr's frequent postings exposed young Franz to a wide variety of music all over Central Europe. His first composition, a song, came at age 11, and a year later he studied music in Prague. By age 20, Lehár proudly served as the youngest-ever military bandmaster of the Austro-Hungarian Empire; German Emperor Wilhelm II decorated him for his conducting in 1894. Operetta scores soon followed, as did new postings. In Vienna, the empire's capital, the 29-year-old Lehár composed for grand ceremonial parades and concerts, and by 1902 was known Europe-wide as creator of the much-loved "Gold and Silver Waltz". After his masterpiece, *Die lustige Witwe*, Lehár had little success until the charismatic star tenor Richard Tauber attracted attention to Lehár's operettas of the 1920s. Later, *Die lustige Witwe* was touted as Hitler's favourite operetta but, with a Jewish wife, Lehár's years in Austria under Nazi rule were not untroubled.

FIRST PERFORMANCES

1890

1893
Rodrigo

1896
Kukuška

1900

1905
Die lustige Witwe

1909
Der Graf von Luxemburg

1910

1910
Zigeunerliebe

1920

1925
Paganini

1927
Der Zarewitsch

1928
Friederike

1930

1929
Das Land des Lächelns

1938
Giuditta

1940

Bandmaster Lehár leading the 26th Hungarian Infantry Regiment Band in Vienna in 1900, at the time of the so-called Boxer Rebellion.

DIE LUSTIGE WITWE
(The Merry Widow)

🖋 Operetta in two acts, 2½ hours

📅 1905

🏛 30 December 1905, Theater an der Wien,

Vienna, Austria

📖 Viktor Léon and Leo Stein, from Henri Meilhac's 1861 play *L'attaché d'ambassade*

Die lustige Witwe premiered triumphantly in 1905, and soon shattered attendance records well beyond Europe. Lehár had concocted just the musical cocktail for the day: one part shimmering imperial festivity in the old Viennese style, to one part warm nostalgia. With the new century, audiences craved the idea of a sweeter, less troubled era. Little could compete with such heart-grabbers as the *"Lippen schweigen"* waltz in Act III of *Die lustige Witwe*.

↭ Mania for *Die lustige Witwe* swept the New World in 1907: over 5,000 performances were given in the United States; in Buenos Aires, Argentina, the operetta was staged in five theatres at the same time. ↭

→ PRINCIPAL ROLES

Baron Zeta *tenor*
Ambassador to France from Pontevedro*

Count Danilo Danilowitsch *tenor*
Lazy playboy from Pontevedro*

Camille de Roussillon *tenor*
In love with Valencienne

Hanna Glawari *soprano*
Rich young widow from Pontevedro*

* A fictional Balkan country

PLOT SYNOPSIS

Paris, France

ACT ONE Baron Zeta, Ambassador from Pontevedro, honours his sovereign's birthday with a gala. The arrival of newly widowed, hugely wealthy compatriot, Hanna Glawari, stirs eligible bachelors. For the benefit of "the Fatherland", Zeta wants Hanna's wealth to remain in Pontevedro, and urges countryman Danilo to woo her. By chance, Danilo was Hanna's first love, but his aristocratic family had rejected her, a mere commoner. Danilo, fond of Cancan dancers and dinners at Maxim's, shows no interest in Hanna. The ambassador's wife, Valencienne, quietly nudges Camille de Roussillon in the widow's direction, even though he has fallen for Valencienne.

ACT TWO The following day, Hanna entertains in high Pontevedrian style in her garden, recounting the story of Vilja, a forest sprite, and flirting with Danilo ☙. As they dance, Danilo's old feelings for Hanna return. Meanwhile, Camille insists on a kiss, which Valencienne will

"Vilja, o Vilja"

only give him in the garden pavilion. Baron Zeta is alerted. By the time he and Danilo check the pavilion, Hanna has replaced his wife. Zeta is relieved. And when Danilo departs for Maxim's in a jealous rage, Hanna knows he loves her. At Hanna's home, Cancan girls celebrate flirting on the boulevards of Paris. Hanna explains her pavilion trick to Danilo, and differences are mended by a romantic waltz. The Baron is reassured of his wife's fidelity. In a finale, all agree that women are difficult to understand.

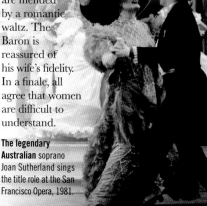

The legendary Australian soprano Joan Sutherland sings the title role at the San Francisco Opera, 1981.

ERICH WOLFGANG
KORNGOLD

Born: 29 May 1897, Brünn (Brno, Czech Republic)
Died: 29 November 1957, Hollywood, California, US

Erich Wolfgang Korngold emerged as a major Romantic composer in World War I Vienna, just as the city discovered Modernism. He was 18 when his first operas, *Der Ring des Polykrates* and *Violanta*, premiered on the same night. His masterpiece was *Die tote Stadt* of 1920. Korngold fled Vienna in 1934 when, as a Jew, he was threatened by the rise and spread of anti-Semitism.

Korngold was 10 when the composer Gustav Mahler recognized his talent and recommended that he study with Alexander Zemlinsky. At 11, the boy wrote a ballet, *Der Schneemann*, or *The Snowman*, which premiered at the Hofoper in Vienna when he was 13. Not since Mozart had a child prodigy so riveted Vienna. Two operas of marked Wagnerian influence followed, and won praise from the likes of Richard Strauss. Then came *Die tote Stadt*, the opera that earned the 23-year-old Korngold lasting renown. The opera was strongly rooted in the German Romantic tradition yet, with its refined structure and haunting story, offered an otherworldly portrayal of lost love. Korngold believed that his next opera, *Das Wunder der Heliane*, or *The Miracle of Heliane*, was a better opera but, despite its daring music, it never fared as well. With the Nazi influence mounting in Austria, Korngold emigrated to the United States, where he became an acclaimed Hollywood film composer. In 1949, he returned to Vienna. But when his last opera, *Die Katrin* or *Catherine*, and other works were ridiculed, he left Austria to settle once again in Hollywood.

HOLLYWOOD FILMS

In Hollywood, Korngold joined other Jewish composers fleeing Fascism in Europe. Hungarian Karl Hajos, Ukrainian Dmitri Tiomkin, German Franz Waxman, and fellow Viennese Max Steiner were among them. Korngold's exceptional and influential film scores earned him four Academy Award nominations and two Oscars, for *Anthony Adverse* (1936) and *The Adventures of Robin Hood* (1938) (*below*).

This photograph shows Erich Wolfgang Korngold and his family arriving in New York City. Having been driven from Austria as Nazi control tightened there, the Jewish Korngolds settled in Los Angeles.

DIE TOTE STADT
(The Dead City)

🎵 Opera in three scenes, 2 hours
📼 1917–1919
🎭 4 December 1920, Stadttheater, Hamburg,
Germany; and Opernhaus, Cologne, Germany
📖 Paul Schott, after the novel *Bruges-la-Morte* (1892) by Georges Rodenbach

Die tote Stadt was based on a Symbolist novel of hallucinatory connections between sexual desire and mourning. Bold for its time, the opera was also a success. It was given at the Metropolitan Opera in New York in 1921, and, with much-loved numbers including the *"Pierrotlied"*, remains popular worldwide today.

⋈ The libretto is by Paul Schott, in fact a pseudonym for Erich Korngold and his father, Julius Korngold, then Vienna's leading music critic. It was through Julius that Erich, age 10, met the composer Gustav Mahler. ⋈

> ✦ **PRINCIPAL ROLES** ✦
>
> **Paul** *tenor*
> A resident of Bruges obsessed with his dead wife
>
> **Marie/Marietta** *soprano*
> Paul's late wife/A dancer in the opera
>
> **Frank** *baritone*
> Paul's friend
>
> **Brigitta** *contralto*
> Paul's servant

PLOT SYNOPSIS

Bruges, Belgium, at the end of the 19th century

SCENE ONE Paul's home is a lugubrious shrine to his dead wife, Marie. He alarms his friend Frank with news that Marie is alive. Paul receives Marietta, an opera dancer resembling Marie. Marietta's singing mesmerizes him ♪ *("Glück, das mir verblieb")*. But her erotic dance movements unveil Marie's portrait, which Paul venerates. Alone, Paul envisions Marie becoming Marietta.

SCENE TWO In a nocturnal dreamscape before Marietta's house, Paul ponders the "Dead City" of Bruges ♪ *("Was ward aus mir?")*. Frank upsets Paul because he, like Paul, now makes love to Marietta. Paul sees Marietta dance a "resurrection scene" for her friends. Alone with Marietta, Paul is hostile. But when she exudes seduction, he vows love. To cure him, she insists they make love in Marie's room. They rush to Paul's house.

SCENE THREE In the morning, Marietta addresses Marie's portrait, asking for peace. When a religious procession absorbs Paul's attention, Marietta dances wildly with a braid of Marie's "sacred" hair. Incensed, Paul uses it to strangle her. To his horror, she dies. Waking, Paul puzzles over his dream. Marietta retrieves her umbrella and departs. Finally, Paul locks the door to Marie's room.

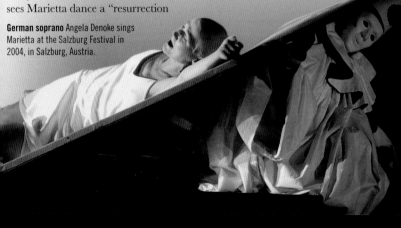

German soprano Angela Denoke sings Marietta at the Salzburg Festival in 2004, in Salzburg, Austria.

"I have always paid the greatest possible attention to natural diction."

Richard Strauss

RICHARD
STRAUSS

Born: 11 June 1864, Munich, Bavaria (Germany)
Died: 8 September 1949, Garmisch-Partenkirchen, Bavaria (Germany)

Richard Strauss is often described as the last German Romantic composer. But his operatic influences cannot be relegated to any one style. Strauss composed 15 operas, and they range from the astonishing and dissonant *Salome*, arguably the first modern opera, to his waltz-studded homage to Mozart, *Der Rosenkavalier*.

Richard Strauss has earned a peerless place in opera history. In 1905, his intensely modern *Salome* broke all rules dear to Romantic opera. But, beginning with *Der Rosenkavalier* in 1911, many Strauss operas were profoundly Romantic. And by the time of his final opera, *Capriccio*, in 1942, Strauss was drawn to the earlier music of Rameau and Gluck. Many have tried to explain why Strauss would abandon the avant-garde for less innovative, even nostalgic approaches to opera. Interestingly, though, no matter how his music is classified, Strauss is now viewed as perhaps the most important opera composer of the 20th century, with the only other viable contender being Benjamin Britten.

Like many innovators, Strauss was sharply criticized, but he never doubted his own talent. Some of his success can be attributed to the remarkable synergies he found working with poet-playwright Hugo von Hofmannsthal. The young librettist's approach was dense, symbolic, and reflective. He preferred storylines of primordial drama and philosophical depth, even as Strauss pressed him for lighter material. They could easily have been incompatible; instead they created opera magic.

Like his revered Mozart, Strauss was a child prodigy. His father played horn for the Bavarian Court Orchestra in Munich, where Strauss first composed at age four. At

American soprano Renée Fleming appears at London's Royal Opera House in 2000 as the incomparable Marschallin in *Der Rosenkavalier*, the most popular opera Richard Strauss created with librettist Hugo von Hofmannsthal.

FIRST PERFORMANCES

1890	
	1894 Guntram
1900	**1901** Feuersnot
	1905 Salome
	1909 Elektra
1910	**1911** Der Rosenkavalier
	1916 Ariadne auf Naxos
	1919 Die Frau ohne Schatten
1920	
	1924 Intermezzo
	1928 Die ägyptische Helena
1930	**1933** Arabella
	1935 Die schweigsame Frau
1940	**1938** Daphne
	1942 Capriccio
	1949 Death
1950	**1952** Die Liebe der Danae
1960	

five, he was scoring songs. Orchestral works and chamber pieces were soon to follow, and his first symphony was performed when he was 16. Strauss lived for music; he composed his *Violin Concerto* during a mathematics class that bored him, and left school with nearly 150 completed works. At age 20, he led an orchestra in the premiere of his first major commission, sparking a meteoric career that would take him to top conducting posts in Munich, Berlin, and Vienna. He also conducted his first opera, the Wagnerian *Guntram*, in 1894. Although his father had disliked Wagner, Strauss eventually embraced him as a major influence alongside Mozart. Still, while *Guntram* was a critical failure, it brought Strauss personal success: its principal soprano, Pauline de Ahna, became his devoted, life-long wife. A turn in his career came in 1905 with the shocking *Salome*. Based on the play by

Richard Strauss, seated at the piano, is joined by cast and crew members of a silent film adaptation of *Der Rosenkavalier*, released in 1926. It was accompanied by recorded music scored by Strauss for the project.

Oscar Wilde, it was variously censored and cancelled. But, with its daring story, new symphonic sound, and dazzling vocal parts, it galvanized opera houses wherever staged.

A WRITING PORTRAIT

A second atonal opera followed in 1909: *Elektra*, the first fruit of Strauss's legendary collaboration with Hofmannsthal. No pair had been so perfectly matched in opera history since Lorenzo da Ponte fired Mozart's imagination in 1780s' Vienna. Indeed, they inspired pioneering works: *Der Rosenkavalier* was the first and *Arabella* was the last Mozartian Strauss opera. Between these came *Ariadne auf Naxos*, in which Mozartian and Wagnerian spirits are said to vie for Strauss's musical soul, and *Die Frau ohne Schatten*, again echoing Mozart. Strauss then penned his own conversational libretto for *Intermezzo*, based on everyday exchanges in his home. *Die ägyptische Helena* followed, its Homeric libretto by Hofmannsthal. Strauss described the opera as "Greek Wagner". July of

STRAUSS SOPRANOS

Strauss's distinctive scoring for soprano voices has produced specialized "Strauss sopranos". In operas and other works, the voices of Strauss sopranos seem to soar on divine ribbons of breath lifted further by the orchestra. In the composer's day, these rare vocalists included his wife, Pauline de Ahna, and Lotte Lehmann, who sang nine lead Strauss roles. Later specialists include Lisa della Casa, Renée Fleming, Jessye Norman, Maria Reining, Elisabeth Schwarzkopf, Cheryl Studer, and Deborah Voigt.

Lotte Lehmann, one of Strauss's favorite sopranos as the Marschallin in his opera Der Rosenkavalier.

1929 brought double tragedy: minutes before the funeral for Hofmannsthal's son Franz, who had committed suicide, the librettist suffered a stroke and died. In 1932, Strauss began working with Austrian librettist Stefan Zweig on *Die schwiegsame Frau*. Books by "the Jew Zweig" were soon publicly burned in Munich. Nazi Germany's annexation of Austria in 1934 occurred while Zweig was visiting London; he never returned home. When *Die schwiegsame Frau* premiered in Dresden in 1935, Zweig's name was omitted from the programme until Strauss, then head of the music department in the Nazi Ministry of Propaganda, intervened. But a letter from Strauss to Zweig was intercepted and presented to Hitler. Its anti-Nazi tone forced Strauss to resign from his post. In 1941, he moved

The title page of a score from 1905 Berlin offering piano and vocal parts for a scene from Strauss's opera *Salome*, created in that year.

his family from Bavaria to Vienna. Once there, Strauss used his sway and influence as a cultural icon in order to shield his Jewish daughter-in-law and grandchildren from persecution, or worse.

THE WAR YEARS

Zweig meanwhile worked behind the scenes revising Josef Gregor's librettos for Strauss's *Friedenstag*, an anti-war opera, and *Daphne*, based on Greek myth. Then, in 1942, Zweig and his wife, now émigrés in Brazil, used poison to commit double suicide. *Capriccio*, whose story had been Zweig's idea, premiered that year. This, Strauss's last opera, held audience attention in Munich until the opera house was bombed by Allied forces in 1943. Following Germany's defeat in 1945, Strauss took shelter in Switzerland, fearing punishment for his earlier associations with the Nazis. After the Allied DeNazification Board cleared his name in 1948, he returned to his home in Bavaria a few months before his death in 1949. In 1952, at the Salzburg Festival that Strauss had helped to create, *Die Liebe der Danae* premiered posthumously. A "cheerful mythology in three acts", its libretto had been sketched by Hofmannsthal in 1920. Allied air raids, and then post-war politics, prevented an earlier premiere, although Strauss had attended a wartime reading of the work in Salzburg in 1944, on his 80th birthday. Always vying with the dominant musical trends during his lifetime, Strauss came to be seen as the greatest opera composer of the first half of the 20th century.

SALOME

✍ Drama in one act, 1¾ hours
⏱ 1904–1905
♔ 9 December 1905, Königliches Opernhaus,

Dresden, Saxony (Germany)
📖 Richard Strauss, from Oscar Wilde's play
Salomé (1893)

The opening night of *Salome* in Dresden brought 38 curtain calls, but mixed reactions from the critics. Today *Salome* stands as a masterpiece, and is arguably the first modern opera. It delves into linked obsessions – Herod's with Salome; Salome's with Jokanaan; and Jokanaan's with God. By turns illustrating and probing the libretto, the orchestra produces exquisite effects, notably in the string section, where Strauss called for new bowing and fingering techniques. Cruelty, perversion, and fixation pervade this work, much as moonlight bathes the palace terrace where its action is set. But however troubling its themes, the opera's velvety, high-tension music grips audiences. And interpretations of Salome and Herod are rarely forgotten.

> ✦ **PRINCIPAL ROLES** ✦
>
> **Herod** *tenor*
> King of Judea
>
> **Herodias** *mezzo-soprano*
> Lover to Herod
>
> **Salome** *soprano*
> Herodias's daughter
>
> **Jokanaan (John the Baptist)** *baritone*
> Prophet and prisoner
>
> **Narraboth** *tenor*
> Young Syrian captain
> of the guard
>
> **Others:** Nazarenes view Jokanaan as a prophet of the Messiah, but Jews bitterly disagree

⊰ The opera was to be given in Vienna under the baton of Gustav Mahler, but the Catholic Archbishop deemed it immoral. He was not alone. In London, the opera was barred until 1910. And in New York in 1907, *Salome* was cancelled after only one performance at the Met due to pressure from its patron JP Morgan. ⊱

PLOT SYNOPSIS

A terrace off the banquet hall of Herod's palace in Israel, c.30 CE

Herod arranged his brother's murder because he was in love with his brother's wife, Herodias. Now Herod craves her young daughter, Salome. But the popular prophet Jokanaan (John the Baptist) predicts the ruin of Herod's court. Herod has imprisoned him, forbidding Narraboth, captain of the prison guard, to release him. As the opera begins, Herod celebrates his birthday within his palace. From a moonlit terrace, Narraboth is captivated by Salome's beauty. As she escapes Herod's lustful staring, a voice holds her spellbound. It is the imprisoned Jokanaan, who invokes the Messiah and curses Herodias. Salome persuades Narraboth to defy orders and

Salome (Karita Matilla) lusts to kiss the mouth of the decapitated Jokanaan in a production directed by Lev Dodin at the Opéra Bastille, Paris, in 2003.

"Wo ist sie, die den Hauptleuten Assyriens sich gab?"

"Jokanaan! Ich bin verliebt in deinen Leib"

fetch the prisoner. Jokanaan appears ♪. Salome is first repulsed, then magnetized ♪. As she lusts for the prophet, Narraboth, in despair, stabs himself and dies. The prophet rejects Salome's advances, urging her to seek the Lord's forgiveness. But she fixates on his mouth, pleading for a kiss. Jokanaan is returned to his cell in the cistern, swearing Salome is cursed. Salome also swears: that she will kiss his mouth. Herod bursts onto the terrace and attempts to lure Salome. Herodias begs Herod to hand over the prisoner to the Jews, but Herod refuses to endanger the "holy man". A group of Jews argues

"In Wahrheit weiss niemand"

that Jokanaan is no prophet ♪, but the Nazarenes disagree, reminding all of the Messiah's miracles. Herod frets to learn that this man is able to raise the dead, and asks where he is. A Nazarene offers unsettling news: He is everywhere. With new force, the voice from below terrifies Herodias with warnings. Herod begs Salome to dance for him. In exchange, he promises her anything she wishes. Ignoring her mother's objections, Salome dances the Dance of the Seven Veils. Delighted, Herod asks what Salome desires. She wants Jokanaan's head, on a silver platter. Herod offers her anything else

"Ah! Du willst nicht auf mich hören"

"Es ist kein Laut zu vernehmen"

he has ♪. But Salome insists. "Let her have what she asks for," Herod finally consents. Salome listens for Jokanaan's cries ♪, and is tortured to hear no suffering. When the head is delivered, Herod recoils; Herodias is pleased; and the Nazarenes kneel to pray. Triumphantly, Salome kisses Jokanaan's mouth ♪.

"Ah! Du wolltest mich nicht deinen Mund küssen lassen"

As Herod departs, a black cloud hides the moon. In darkness, Salome notes the bitter taste of Jokanaan's mouth, "perhaps the taste of love". Suddenly, with Salome flooded in light, Herod commands her death. Soldiers rush forward and crush her with their shields.

DANCE OF THE SEVEN VEILS

"But when Herod's birthday was kept, the daughter of Herodias danced before them, and pleased Herod" *Gospel of St Matthew* (14.6). The first Salome, Marie Wittich, refused to perform the Dance of the Seven Veils. "I won't do it. I'm a decent woman," Strauss recalled her objecting. A ballerina served as the stout soprano's improbable body double. Many Salomes have since yielded the scene to a dancer, but intrepid vocalists, such as Ljuba Welitsch (*below*), show off their seduction skills in the famous dance.

ELEKTRA
(Electra)

✍ Tragedy in one act, 1¾ hours
☙ 1906–1908
♱ 25 January 1909, Semper Opernhaus, Dresden,

Saxony (Germany)
📖 Hugo von Hofmannsthal, based on his play (1903),
after the tragedy by Sophocles, 5th century BCE

Elektra is an opera of raw and startling emotions. Strauss was reluctant to compose it so soon after the disturbing *Salome*. But Hugo von Hofmannsthal, initiating their legendary collaboration, encouraged him to set the libretto. Primeval desires for wrongs to be righted propel the unforgiving action of this dissonant opera, as shocking today as it was in 1909. Elektra, a gigantic and riveting role, attracts dramatic sopranos of huge stamina.

⊰ Strauss found an ingenious way to conjure the spirit of Agamemnon, slain by his wife and avenged by his daughter, Elektra: in the opening bars, the orchestra alone heaves up the sound of the name "Ag-a-mem-non". ⊱

✦ PRINCIPAL ROLES ✦

Elektra *soprano*
Daughter to Klytämnestra
and slain Agamemnon

Klytämnestra *mezzo-soprano*
Mother to Elektra

Chrysothemis *soprano*
Younger sister
to Elektra

Orest *baritone*
Brother to Elektra

Aegisth *tenor*
Lover to Klytämnestra

PLOT SYNOPSIS

Ancient Mycenae, courtyard of the royal palace

"Agamemnon! Agamemnon! Wo bist du, Vater?"

Alone, Elektra invokes her father, slain by her mother ♂. Asking for his help, she promises to dance before his tomb when his murder has been avenged. Elektra seeks allies in her quest for revenge, but her sister Chrysothemis would rather live normally, and not be entwined in vengeance. Their mother Klytämnestra, burdened by horrid nightmares, asks Elektra what ritual sacrifice will purge her of them. She is terrified when Elektra names Klytämnestra herself as the sacrificial victim. Elektra wonders why her mother's shock turns to frenzied laughter upon receiving a message, then refuses to believe the news: that her brother, Orest, is dead. Elektra proceeds with her plan. Like a beast, she digs the ground, searching for the buried hatchet used to slay her father. A man arrives, and tension mounts until

"Was willst du fremder Mensch?"

Elektra recognizes Orest ♂. She hears her mother's screams within the palace, and rejoices that Orest

Deborah Polaski (seen here at the Royal Opera in 1997) has sung Elektra more than 300 times, filling the gap left by Birgit Nilsson and Astrid Varnay.

has begun to avenge their father. Orest then kills his mother's lover, Aegisth. The palace erupts: some celebrate vengeance; others grieve for the victims. As she promised her father, Elektra dances "a dance without name". When her dance reaches its apex, she dies.

DER ROSENKAVALIER

(The Knight of the Rose)

❧

♫ Comedy for music in three acts, 3¼ hours
⏳ 1909–1910
♆ 26 January 1911, Hofoper, Dresden, Saxony

(Germany)
📖 Hugo von Hofmannsthal

Der Rosenkavalier has enthralled audiences since its 1911 premiere. Sensuous symphonic music manages to exude fizzier Viennese pleasures, from prank-playing to waltzing. Strauss's librettist Hugo von Hofmannsthal concocted a Mozartian story of modern yet timeless sensibilities. The poetry of his libretto inspired extraordinary music. Indeed, the vocal trio towards the end of Act III is held by many to be among the most exquisite vocal ensembles in opera.

⚲ *Der Rosenkavalier* caused such a sensation that, following its premiere in 1911, rail operators ran additional trains from German-speaking Europe to take unprecedented throngs of opera-goers to Dresden. ⚲

> ❧ **PRINCIPAL ROLES** ❧
>
> **Feldmarschallin, Princess Werdenberg** *soprano*
> Lover to young Octavian
>
> **Octavian, Count Rofrano** *mezzo-soprano*
> Selected as rose-bearer
>
> **Baron Ochs auf Lerchenau** *bass*
> Betrothed to Sophie for her dowry
>
> **Herr von Faninal** *baritone*
> Rich father to Sophie
>
> **Sophie** *soprano*
> Falls in love with Octavian

PLOT SYNOPSIS

Vienna, Austria, in the era of Mozart

ACT ONE The Feldmarschallin breakfasts with Count Octavian, her lover. When Baron Ochs surprises them, Octavian is rapidly disguised as a maid, "Mariandel". Ochs seeks someone to present the traditional silver rose to his fiancée, Sophie. Distracted by "Mariandel's" charms, he accepts the Marschallin's proposal that Octavian should be his *Rosenkavalier*. The Marschallin

"Da geht er hin" | laments the passing of her youth ♪. She enjoys a bittersweet moment with her lover, sensing their affair will soon end.

Adrianne Pieczonka as the Marschallin enjoys a last morning with the Octavian of Angelika Kirchschlager, Salzburg 2004.

ACT TWO Octavian delivers the silver rose to Sophie ♪, and they fall in love. Sophie's love deepens when Octavian defends her honour in a swordfight with Ochs. But her father ejects Octavian from their home. Ochs's mood lifts when a letter from "Mariandel" proposes meeting "tomorrow night".

"Mir ist die Ehre widerfahren"

ACT THREE In an inn, Ochs is tormented by Octavian's co-conspirators as he tries to seduce "Mariandel". When Ochs tells police he dines with his fiancée, Sophie's father erupts. Octavian is unmasked and Ochs humbled. Finally, the Marschallin endorses Octavian's love for Sophie ♪.

"Marie Theres'!"

ARIADNE AUF NAXOS

Ariadne on Naxos

✍ Opera in a prologue and one act, 2 hours
⌛ 1911–1912 (rev. 1916)
♆ 4 October 1916, Hofoper, Vienna (Austria)

(2nd version)
📖 Hugo von Hofmannsthal

In 1912, *Ariadne auf Naxos* was given as an opera attached to a play that librettist Hofmannsthal had based on Molière's *Le bourgeois gentilhomme*. But it was the revised version of 1916, an opera-within-an-opera, that would enter the repertory. Intertwining threads from *opera seria* and *commedia dell'arte*, the work is a striking exploration of the divine power of music. Among the little miracles is Ariadne's brief solo *"Gibt es kein Hinüber?"*

> ❖ **PRINCIPAL ROLES** ❖
>
> Prima Donna & Ariadne *soprano*
> Tenor & Bacchus *tenor*
> Composer *mezzo-soprano*
> Zerbinetta a comedienne
> Harlequin a member of her troupe

⇥ Legendary soprano Lotte Lehmann rose to instant fame singing the Composer in the 1916 premiere. Strauss turned the part over to her at the first rehearsal, when the originally-cast soprano was unwell. ⇤

PLOT SYNOPSIS

Vienna, Austria, and a grotto on the isle of Naxos

PROLOGUE In the home of Vienna's richest man, post-supper festivities are in preparation. The Music Master complains about the programme. A new opera by his student, the Composer, is to be followed by fireworks and then an *opera buffa* presented by Italians. The situation becomes worse when the Major-Domo announces minutes before the performance that his master has changed the programme: the tragic opera and the Italian piece will be performed at the same time, followed by fireworks at precisely 9 PM. The furious Composer is pressed to revise his *Ariadne auf Naxos* so that it integrates the alien Italian

Natalie Dessay as Zerbinetta in Laurent Pelly's production for the Paris Opéra, 2003.

opera. His mood softens when he starts a conversation with Zerbinetta, the Italian soprano. She understands his work.

THE OPERA Ariadne, abandoned on the isle of Naxos, awaits eternal peace in death ♪. Italians sing and dance to cheer her. Ariadne retreats further into the grotto, even as Zerbinetta attempts to lift her spirits, drawing on her own experiences ♪.

"Es gibt ein Reich"

"Grossmächtige Prinzessin"

Nymphs announce the arrival of the youthful god Bacchus, whose voice draws Ariadne from her cave. As she emerges, Ariadne falls breathless, and Bacchus's love gives her new life. As a canopy is gently lowered, the passionate lovers are magically transformed.

DIE FRAU OHNE SCHATTEN

(The Woman without a Shadow)

⚐ Opera in three acts, 3¼ hours   📖 Hugo von Hofmannsthal
⌛ 1914–1917
♇ 10 October, 1919, Staatsoper, Vienna (Austria)

Strauss's underperformed masterpiece, *Die Frau ohne Schatten*, follows two pairs of lovers to emotional and spiritual salvation. As a daughter of the King of Spirits, the Empress lacks that crucial symbol of humanity, a shadow, and spends the opera considering whether or not to steal one from a human woman. Strauss's music, driven, opulent, and cataclysmic, matches Hofmannsthal's searching, abstract libretto.

⚐ Lotte Lehmann, who created the Dyer's Wife, claimed not to mind the Empress's musical pre-eminence: "I was perfectly content to sing myself into a state of near prostration and then gradually fade towards the end". ⚐

> ✦PRINCIPAL ROLES ✦
>
> **Empress** *soprano*
> Daughter of Keikobad, King of Spirits
>
> **Emperor** *tenor*
> Her husband
>
> **Nurse** *mezzo-soprano*
> Her protector in the world of spirits
>
> **Barak** *baritone*
> A dyer and good-hearted man
>
> **Dyer's Wife** *soprano*
> His unhappy wife

PLOT SYNOPSIS

A mythical time and place

ACT ONE The Empress has no shadow, and learns that the Emperor will turn to stone if she does not obtain one. She and the Nurse resolve to find a shadow among humans. In their home, Barak the dyer is mocked by his Wife. The Empress and Nurse offer themselves as servants to the Wife, and promise her luxury if she casts off her shadow and renounces her marriage bed. She does so, but is disturbed to hear the voices of her unborn children beckoning her.

ACT TWO The Nurse conjures a Young Man to tempt the Wife. The Wife anxiously awakens her husband, whom the nurse drugged, only to gloat over her near infidelity. When she vows to forfeit her shadow and fertility, he is enraged. Suddenly finding him manly and worthy of respect, she pleads for his mercy before they are both swallowed into the earth.

ACT THREE Barak and his Wife, now penitent and separated into two cells in "Mir anvertraut" | the bowels of the earth, long for one another ⚰.

Beloved Strauss soprano Inge Borkh (*right*) is Barak's wife and Wagnerian powerhouse Martha Mödl is the Nurse at the Bayerische Staatsoper in 1963.

The Nurse is condemned to wander the mortal realm. Refusing to accept a shadow that comes at the cost of Barak's happiness with his Wife, the Empress is rewarded with a shadow of her own. Her action frees the Emperor, and both couples are reunited ⚰.

"Nun will ich jubeln"

ARABELLA

🖋 Lyric comedy in three acts, 2½ hours
🏛 1930–1932
♜ 1 July 1933, Staatsoper, Dresden (Germany)

📖 Hugo von Hofmannsthal, based in part on his own novel, *Lucidor* (1910)

Strauss saw Arabella as "a second *Rosenkavalier*", a light romantic opera set in early Vienna, and marked by the uplifting tempos of the waltz. The premiere of *Arabella* was not so successful, but over time the opera has gained popularity. It is now often called Strauss's most romantic work. Vocal parts offer strong and gratifying roles for virtuoso singers, and the theme of love at first sight triggers gorgeous music.

⊣ Strauss found the text for Arabella's solo *"Mein Elemer!"* inspiring, and sent a telegraph of thanks to Hugo von Hofmannsthal. Delivered on 15 July 1929, the day of the librettist's death, it was never read. ⊢

➤ PRINCIPAL ROLES ◆

Count Waldner *bass*
Retired Cavalry Officer

Adelaide *mezzo-soprano*
Wife of Waldner

Arabella *soprano*
Daughter to the Waldners

Zdenka *soprano*
Sister to Arabella

Mandryka *baritone*
A mysterious, rich foreigner

Matteo *tenor*
An officer in love with Arabella

PLOT SYNOPSIS

Vienna (Austria) in 1860 on Shrove Tuesday – the last night of Carnival

ACT ONE In their hotel residence, Adelaide Waldner hopes that her daughter, Arabella, will marry a wealthy suitor. Arabella's sister, Zdenka, who passes for a boy to save the family from financial ruin, plots to help Matteo, an officer, win Arabella. But Arabella has other ideas. She has fallen for a mysterious foreigner she saw in the street ♂.

"Aber der Richtige wenn's einen gibt für mich auf dieser Welt"

Count Waldner explains to his wife that, to attract a suitor, he sent a picture of Arabella to a rich old friend. Mandryka, the friend's nephew, suddenly appears. He explains: his uncle died, so he opened the letter, and came to woo Arabella himself. Arabella has no interest in Count Elemer, a Viennese suitor, but he whisks her off to a grand Carnival ball.

Karita Mattila delivers Arabella, a role once embodied by diva Lisa Della Casa, at a Théâtre du Châtelet production in Paris, 2005.

ACT TWO In a magnificent public ballroom, Arabella's parents introduce her to Mandryka, her mysterious foreigner. She promises to love him forever ♂, after the Carnival dance. As Arabella waltzes with her former suitors, Zdenka passes Matteo a room key supposedly "from Arabella". Mandryka, overhearing, is outraged.

"Und du wirst mein Gebieter sein"

ACT THREE Arabella returns to the hotel alone, puzzling Matteo as she is unaware of any key. Discovering them, Mandryka threatens to leave Vienna. Zdenka reveals the plot and her true identity as a girl, and is then betrothed to Matteo. All are humbled and forgiven, and Arabella and Mandryka fall into each other's arms.

CAPRICCIO

Conversation piece for music in one act, 2¼ hours
1940–1941
28 October 1942, Nationaltheater, Munich (Germany)
Clemens Krauss and Richard Strauss

Capriccio was inspired by *Prima la musica e poi le parole* (1786), a comical work by Antonio Salieri and librettist Giambattista Casta about tensions among opera artists. Before Nazi annexation drove him from Austria, Jewish librettist Stefan Zweig had proposed the subject to Strauss. While strikingly modern, *Capriccio* revisits Classical forms. It was popular in Munich, until Allied bombs destroyed the opera house in October 1943.

The opera's opening string sextet premiered in the Viennese home of Nazi controller Baldur von Schirach in recognition of the tranquillity he assured the part-Jewish Strauss family. They had moved from Bavaria to Vienna in 1941.

PRINCIPAL ROLES

Countess *soprano*
A young widow

Count *baritone*
Her brother

Flamand *tenor*
A composer

Olivier *baritone*
A poet

La Roche *bass*
A theatre director

Clairon *contralto*
A famous Parisian actress

PLOT SYNOPSIS

A château near Paris, France, in the late 18th century

A poet, composer, theatre director, and performers gather in the château of a Countess and her brother. A string sextet composed by Flamand prompts poet Olivier to ask which the Countess will prefer: words or music; poet or composer. Olivier reminds that words come first, then music. Flamand sees things the other way around. The director, La Roche, says they are both wrong: people go to operas for the scenery. The actress Clairon reads a scene with the enamoured Count, and Olivier presents a love sonnet to the Countess. When Flamand puts the poem to music, the Countess praises the marriage of words and music. La Roche is invited to describe his theatre project. But quarrelling breaks out as Flamand and Olivier suggest the title Flying Machines and Trapdoors. The director defends his art, and pleads for the stage to be peopled "with beings like us, who speak our language!". The Countess, moved, commissions an opera on the spot, and her brother finds the perfect story: "Today's events!" He escorts Clairon back to Paris as other guests depart. Composer and poet leave reconciled, already at work on the new opera. The Countess ponders how the opera will end. Who is the victor: poet or composer? Called to supper, she hums Flamand's melody, inspired by Olivier's sonnet.

"Holà! Ihr Streiter in Apoll!"

"Morgen mittag um elf!"

Kiri Te Kanawa, famous for her Countess in Mozart's *Figaro,* lavishes her creamy voice on Strauss's lady at the Glyndebourne Festival in 1998.

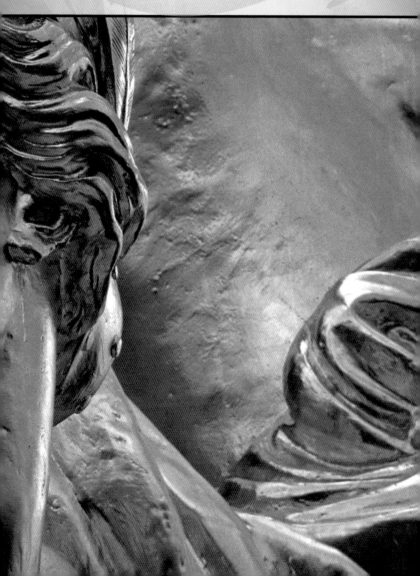

French Opera

THE PARIS OPÉRA DATES BACK to the court at Versailles in 1669, evidence enough that opera has long played a prominent role in French society. Yet opera only assumed a distinct French personality in the 19th century with the arrival of *grand opéra*, a five-act spectacle more lavish than anything ever staged before. In reaction, *opéra comique* and operetta also flourished.

A ROYAL BEGINNING

Until the 1789 Revolution, opera in France was dominated successively by three great musicians: Jean-Baptiste Lully, the Italian-born court composer to Louis XIV; Jean-Philippe Rameau, court composer to Louis XV; and Christoph Willibald Gluck, the German-born reformer of *opera seria*. The fact that only Rameau was French-born was not accidental. France had always welcomed foreign composers, and continued to do so even after the Revolution demanded patriotic librettos and scores.

Indeed, the dominant musicians of the Napoleonic era were two Italian expatriates, Luigi Cherubini and Gaspar Spontini, both skilled at satisfying the public's thirst for high drama. Cherubini's "rescue opera", *Lodoïska*, was performed to great acclaim throughout the 1790s, although he is best remembered today for *Médée*. Spontini, whose most popular work was *La vestale*, in turn prepared the way for *grand opéra* through his extravagant productions.

One early requirement for *grand opéra* was a stirring historical subject. Fitting this criterion, Daniel-François-

Esprit Auber's *Masaniello, ou La Muette de Portici*, which premiered at the Paris Opéra in 1828, recounted a 17th-century Neapolitan uprising against foreign occupation. Then, in an extraordinary example of life imitating art, the opera's premiere in Brussels in August 1830 provoked a rebellion which five weeks later led to Belgium's independence from the Netherlands.

A 1900 poster by Émile Bertrand promotes an early Paris production of *Cendrillon*, Jules Massenet's popular retelling of the Cinderella fairy-tale.

THE RISE OF GRAND OPÉRA

While Auber persuaded the Paris Opéra that *grand opéra* was its destiny, the composer most identified with operatic extravaganza was Giacomo Meyerbeer. A German-Jewish immigrant, he dominated French opera more than any composer since Rameau. Starting in 1831 with *Robert le diable*, he followed up with such crowd-pleasers as *Les Huguenots*, *Le prophète*, and *L'africaine*. In the process, he also established the model for *grand opéra*: five-act works with ballet and recitatives (that is, no spoken dialogue), accompanied by large casts, massive choruses, rich costumes, elaborate décor, even pyrotechnics. Italian composers, who considered acclaim in Paris to be the ultimate form of glory, were quick to take note. Already in 1829, Rossini, by then settled in Paris, presented *Guillaume Tell*, his only *grand opéra*. In 1843, Donizetti, then also an expatriate in Paris and eager for attention, tried his hand at *grand opéra* with *Dom Sébastien*. Years later, Verdi too made his entry to Paris through *grand opéra* with *Les vêpres siciliennes* in 1855 and, again, with *Don Carlos* in 1867.

In contrast, the failure in 1838 of *Benvenuto Cellini*, Hector Berlioz's first *grand opéra*, led the composer to be ostracized by the Paris Opéra. And when he returned to *grand opéra* with *Les Troyens* 25 years later, by then widely acclaimed for his orchestral music, Berlioz was again rebuffed by the Paris Opéra. Yet, within a decade or so, *grand opéra* began to lose popularity. And despite Meyerbeer's prominence in mid-19th-century Paris, his operas had vanished from the stage by 1900. The same fate awaited Spontini and Auber, while even once-popular works by Fromental Halévy – *La Juive* – and Ambroise Thomas – *Mignon* and *Hamlet* – are only occasionally performed today.

The Opéra itself, albeit tradition-bound, was hardly grand: after the Salle du Palais-Royal went up in flames in 1763, it had seven homes before it occupied the Salle de la rue Le Peletier in 1821. Only when Emperor Napoleon III narrowly

The new Paris Opéra at the Palais Garnier, opened in 1875, underlined the important role opera played in the city's social life.

escaped assassination as he left this theatre in 1858 did he order a large stand-alone opera house to be built in the heart of Paris. But by the time Charles Garnier's giant structure opened in 1875, Napoleon had been overthrown. Nonetheless, the new Opéra soon became the gathering place of *le tout Paris*.

Fortunately, other theatres had always welcomed composers who resisted the Paris Opéra's rules. Rossini, Bellini, and Donizetti had preferred the Théâtre-Italien, while the Théâtre-Lyrique first presented Charles-François Gounod's popular mid-century operas, *Faust* and *Roméo et Juliette*, as well as Georges Bizet's first major opera, *Les pêcheurs de perles*. In contrast, Bizet's timeless triumph, *Carmen*, opened at the Opéra-Comique, as did Jules Massenet's *Manon*. However, the Opéra-Comique refused Massenet's masterpiece, *Werther*, as too gloomy; it premiered in Vienna.

A LIGHTER TOUCH

These three composers – Gounod, Bizet and Massenet – effectively accelerated the demise of *grand opéra* by turning away from spectacular historical tableaux towards more intimate drama. They also embraced melodies with an Italianate lyricism, which was not coincidental since all three spent lengthy periods in Italy as winners of the prestigious French prize, the Prix de Rome. During the last decades of the century, three other French composers also made their mark, albeit each with only one opera that is still performed: Camille Saint-Saëns with *Samson et Delila*; André Messager with *Véronique*; and Gustave Charpentier with *Louise*.

FRENCH OPERA

1789 French Revolution	**1807** Spontini's *La vestale*	**1829** Rossini's *Guillaume Tell* **1835** Halévy's *La Juive*
1775	1800	1825
1797 Cherubini's *Médée*	**1828** Auber's *Masaniello, ou La Muette de Portici*	**1831** Meyerbeer's *Robert le diable*

At the same time, just as *opera buffa* had parodied *opera seria* in the 18th century, the operetta appeared in reaction to *grand opéra*. This form of musical entertainment soon caught on across Europe and would later spawn the no-less-popular Viennese operetta. In Paris, the fashion was born with Jacques Offenbach, a German-Jewish immigrant, who became operetta's reigning composer, with a series of hilarious and tuneful shows, starting in 1858 with *Orphée aux enfers*. Then, 23 years later, with *Les contes d'Hoffmann*, Offenbach demonstrated that he too could write opera.

Finally, under the belated influence of Wagner, French opera began to shed its neo-Italian guise. In fact, the two leading French composers of the new century, Claude Debussy and Maurice Ravel, paid little attention to the stage. However, while Ravel's two operas, *L'heure espagnole* and *L'enfant et les sortilèges*, were merely light amusement, Debussy's *Pelléas et Mélisande* made a major contribution to opera's development. With its through-composed score flowing around a mysteriously poetic libretto, the work is

The Opéra Bastille, built to mark the bicentenary of the French Revolution in 1989, is evidence of opera's popularity.

OPERA WITH BALLET

By requiring *grand opéra* to include lengthy interludes of ballet, the Paris Opéra was continuing a tradition begun by Lully in the court of Louis XIV. But there was another, less lofty, reason for dancing – the ballerinas. In the 19th century, many wealthy men attended the opera to hear the music and to see the girls. Then, during the intervals or after the show, they would head to the Foyer de la Danse to meet their favourite dancer. Today, the ballet interludes are usually omitted from performances, and the Foyer de la Danse is no longer in use.

now viewed as Romantic opera's bridge to modernity. Still, a past age is strangely recorded for posterity on the façade of the Palais Garnier, as the Paris Opéra became known after the opening of the modern Opéra Bastille in 1989. In gold lettering, it proclaims the names of the seven opera composers considered eternal in 1875. Mozart is placed in the centre, accompanied by Beethoven and Rossini. But many people entering the theatre today might not recognize the other names: Spontini, Meyerbeer, Auber, and Halévy. They represent the glory of *grand opéra* that was.

1848 Paris insurrection	1858 Offenbach's *Orphée aux enfers*	1866 Thomas's *Mignon*	1875 Bizet's *Carmen*	1875 Opening of the Paris Opéra in the Palais Garnier		1900 Charpentier's *Louise*
1850				1875		1900
	1859 Gounod's *Faust*	1863 Berlioz's *Les Troyens* (acts III-V)	1871 French defeat in the Franco–Prussian war	1881 Offenbach's *Les contes d'Hoffmann*	1884 Massenet's *Manon*	1902 Debussy's *Pelléas et Mélisande*

LUIGI
CHERUBINI

Born: 14 September 1760, Florence, Italy
Died: 15 March 1842, Paris, France

Luigi Cherubini, an Italian-born composer who made his
name in Paris, set the stage for the rise of 19th-century French
opera. A prolific composer of sacred music and operas, renowned for his
innovative orchestration and choral writing, he is best known today for his
Requiem in C minor. Arriving in Paris two years before the French Revolution,
Cherubini responded skilfully to the political convulsions of the 1790s in four
popular operas, *Lodoïska*, *Eliza*, *Médée*, and *Les deux journées*. From 1822 until his
death, he was director of the Paris Conservatoire of Music, where the opera
composers Daniel Auber and Fromental Halévy were among his students.

MÉDÉE
(Medea)

✍ Opera in three acts, 2¼ hours
🕮 1796–1797
♆ 13 March 1797, Théâtre Feydeau, Paris, France

📖 François Benoît Hoffmann, after Corneille's 1635
tragedy, itself after Euripides

Médée is Cherubini's operatic masterpiece,
a work of daunting intensity which uses
the power of music to transform a Greek
myth into a very human drama. Inspired
by Euripides's 431 BCE tragedy, it tells of
the Colchis princess who commits murder
to help her lover Jason steal the Golden
Fleece, and then kills their children to
punish his betrayal. Musically, *Médée*
bridges Gluck's Classicism and 19th-
century dramatic opera. It is dominated
by the large demands on its lead soprano,
who drives the narrative with forceful

> **→   PRINCIPAL ROLES   ←**
>
> Médée *soprano* A sorceress princess
> Jason *tenor* Father of Médée's children
> Créon *bass* King of Corinth
> Dircé *soprano* Créon's daughter
> Néris *mezzo-soprano* Dircé's maid
> Captain of the Guard *baritone*

⊲ Maria Callas, who frequently performed
Médée, once warned students at a masterclass
of the perils of high-powered soprano roles:
"In opera, passion without intellect is no good.
You will be a wild animal, not an artist". ⊳

arias and duets. But it also skilfully explores Médée's vacillation between love and hate, life and death. The only one of Cherubini's operas still to be performed today, often in its Italian version, *Médée*'s importance also lies in its influence on both Beethoven and Weber.

PLOT SYNOPSIS

Corinth, Greece, in mythological Antiquity

ACT ONE Dircé, King Créon's daughter, is preparing to marry Jason, who has abandoned Médée, the mother of his two children. Sailors bring in the Golden Fleece, stolen by Jason from the Colchis, as a gift for Dircé. As Jason promises to protect Dircé from Médée's wrath ♪, Médée herself arrives to reclaim him. Warning that she will kill Dircé if Jason's marriage goes ahead, she begs him to return to her, reminding him of their love and children ♪. Rebuffed, Médée vows revenge. Briefly united, they recognize the terrible suffering unleashed by the Fleece.

"Eloigné pour jamais"

"C'est la mère de tes enfants"

ACT TWO As a crowd calls for Médée's death, she worries about losing her children. Créon orders her to leave Corinth, but she begs for one day's grace so she can see them again. When Créon reluctantly agrees, Médée decides to use the day to kill Dircé. Jason tells her that the children can stay with her until she leaves. Néris, Médée's maid, anticipating doom, promises her undying loyalty ♪. With mounting fury, Médée instructs Néris to take as wedding gifts for

"Ah, nos peines"

Dircé a robe and diadem given to her by Apollo. As she watches Créon and his followers enter the Temple of Hera for Jason's wedding to Dircé, Médée seizes a blazing torch from the altar and awaits her moment of revenge.

ACT THREE Imagining herself being strangled by serpents, Médée takes a dagger to kill her children, but Néris intercedes. Néris has delivered the gifts to Dircé, who is preparing to wear them to please Jason. But Médée believes the children must die because Jason, their father, is a traitor ♪. Suddenly Jason is heard mourning Dircé, who has been poisoned by Médée's gifts. As a crowd calls for her death, Médée grabs her two children and locks herself in the temple. Néris rushes out, screaming that Médée is about to slay the children. The sorceress appears, accompanied by three Furies, waving a bloodied dagger. "Their blood has avenged me," she cries. As the temple bursts into flames, Médée and the Furies disappear into the fire.

"Qu'est-ce donc? Je suis Médée!"

Anna Caterina Antonacci as Médée confronts Giuseppe Gipali as her errant husband Jason in Yannis Kokkos's production at the Théâtre du Châtelet, Paris, in 2005.

GIACOMO
MEYERBEER

Born: 5 September 1791, Berlin, Germany
Died: 2 May 1864, Paris, France

Giacomo Meyerbeer stands out for the popularity that he enjoyed in his lifetime and the neglect that he suffers today. But he merits a place in the history of opera as the originator of French *grand opéra*, a five-act extravaganza of ballet, elaborate décor, rich costumes, and heroic stories and music. The colossal sound and scale of Meyerbeer's operatic works inspired both Verdi and Wagner.

Born in Berlin into a wealthy German Jewish family, Jakob Liebmann Meyer Beer was a child prodigy as a pianist. He changed his name when he moved to Italy in his twenties to study opera. There, he won plaudits in 1824 for *Il crociato in Eggito*. He moved to Paris where, with *Robert le diable* in 1831, he established *grand opéra* as the dominant operatic form of much of the 19th century. Fours years later, again working with the librettist Eugène Scribe, he triumphed with *Les Huguenots*. In 1842, he became music director to the Prussian court in Berlin, but he was never fully embraced by Germanic composers. Despite having helped the young Wagner, he was maliciously targeted in Wagner's vitriolic essay, *Judaism and Music*. In 1849, Meyerbeer returned to Paris to present *Le prophète*. His final opera, *L'africaine*, was in rehearsal when he died unexpectedly in Paris in 1864. It premiered at the Paris Opéra the following year.

FIRST PERFORMANCES

1820

1824
Il crociato in Egitto

1830
1831
Robert le diable

1836
Les Huguenots

1840

1849
Le prophète

1850

1854
L'étoile du nord

1859
Dinorah

1860

1864
Death

1865
L'africaine

1870

Set design for the premiere of Meyerbeer's final opera, *L'africaine*, at the Paris Opéra, France, in 1865.

ROBERT LE DIABLE

(Robert the Devil)

◿ Grand opéra in five acts, 4 hours   ▭ Eugène Scribe
⌛ 1828–1831
⚜ 21 November 1831, Paris Opéra, France

Robert le diable, Meyerbeer's first *grand opéra*, won him overnight recognition as a major composer and, within a decade, the opera had been performed across Europe. The wrenching struggle between good and evil is accompanied by daring orchestration and dramatic solo roles, with the score pitting two "good" sopranos against an "evil" bass who fight for the soul of the tenor. The opera's final trio announces the happy outcome.

⚜ Meyerbeer and his librettist, Eugène Scribe, risked Roman Catholic wrath when, in Act III, they had "fallen" nuns resuscitated from their tombs and recruited to do the Devil's work. ⚜

> **⬦ PRINCIPAL ROLES ⬦**
>
> **Robert** *tenor*
> Duke of Normandy
>
> **Bertram** *bass*
> His father, the Devil
>
> **Isabelle** *soprano*
> A Sicilian princess and
> Robert's beloved
>
> **Alice** *soprano*
> Robert's half-sister
>
> **Raimbault** *tenor*
> A minstrel

PLOT SYNOPSIS

Sicily in the 13th century

ACT ONE Robert, the Duke of Normandy, is in Sicily to court Princess Isabelle. He is enraged when a minstrel recounts that he was born of the Devil. Alice, Robert's half-sister, brings their mother's last testament, but says he is unworthy to receive it. When Robert's father, Bertram, arrives, Alice recognizes him as the Devil. Encouraged by Bertram to gamble, Robert loses everything, including armour needed to joust for Isabelle.

A 19th-century costume design gives a dapper air to the evil Robert le diable.

ACT TWO Isabelle gives Robert fresh armour for his duel against the Prince of Grenada. Bertram lures Robert away by sending him on a fruitless mission and, as a result, he misses the tournament and loses Isabelle.

ACT THREE Alice overhears Bertram summoning evil spirits and flees, protecting herself with a cross. Bertram tells Robert he can win Isabelle if he collects a magic branch from a tomb. "Nonnes qui reposez" | Then Bertram awakens dead nuns ♫ to guide Robert to the branch.

ACT FOUR Robert decides to kidnap Isabelle, but when she pledges her love for him ♫, he takes the decision to break the magic branch, destroying its power to create sleep. "Robert, toi que j'aime"

ACT FIVE Outside Palermo Cathedral, Bertram tells Robert that he can recover his power if he signs an irrevocable pact with the Devil before midnight. Robert is willing, but Alice distracts him. When church bells ring out midnight, Bertram vanishes and Isabelle appears before Robert in a bridal gown.

LES HUGUENOTS
(The Huguenots)

◿ Grand opéra in five acts, 4 hours   📖 Eugène Scribe and Émile Deschamps
🎼 1832–1836
♆ 29 February 1836, Paris Opéra, France

Les Huguenots, Meyerbeer's finest work, was also the most successful *grand opéra* of its age, with more than 1,000 performances at the Paris Opéra by 1900. It was bold for a Jewish composer to address the St Bartholomew's Day Massacre of 24 August 1572, when thousands of Protestants, or Huguenots, were slain by Catholics. But, rather than offending his audiences, Meyerbeer thrilled them with a vast spectacle involving seven major roles as well as huge choruses representing soldiers, students, and church congregations. The demands of this opera – both the cost of staging it and the complexity of the score – explain why it is rarely performed today.

✠ To evoke Huguenot worshippers, Meyerbeer quotes from Bach's famous setting of the hymn *A Mighty Fortress is our God*, written by Martin Luther in 1529 after a friend was burned at the stake by Catholics. ✠

✦ PRINCIPAL ROLES ✦

Marguerite de Valois *soprano*
Sister of Charles IX

Raoul de Nangis *tenor*
A Protestant noble

Valentine *soprano*
Raoul's Catholic beloved

Le Comte de Nevers *baritone*
Valentine's Catholic
betrothed

Le Comte de Saint-Bris *bass*
Valentine's Catholic father

Marcel *bass*
A devout Huguenot henchman

Urbain *soprano*
Page to Marguerite

Maurevert *bass*
A Catholic noble

PLOT SYNOPSIS

France in 1572

ACT ONE With Charles IX trying to end France's religious wars, the Count of Nevers receives a Protestant, Raoul de Nangis, in his castle. Raoul tells of falling for a lady whom he saved from rascals ♿. Marcel, Raoul's follower, provokes Catholic guests with a Huguenot ditty. A woman arrives and Raoul recognizes her as the lady he rescued. Nevers reports that she was his fiancée, who came to call off their wedding. A page, Urbain, passes Raoul an invitation to go blindfolded to a mysterious destination ♿. Nevers recognizes Queen Marguerite's crest on the envelope.

"Plus blanche que la hermine"

"Une dame noble et sage"

ACT TWO Frolicking with her ladies by a river ♿, Marguerite is pleased that Valentine can now marry Raoul. But Valentine says her father, the Count of Saint-Bris,

"O beau pays"

LA REINE MARGOT

Although she is only sketchily portrayed in *Les Huguenots*, Marguerite de Valois, or more familiarly La Reine Margot, was a woman equally skilled in love affairs as politics. Her brother, Charles IX, chose her to wed the Protestant Henri de Navarre in the hope of ending France's Wars of Religion. But their marriage in August 1572 was immediately followed by the massacre of Huguenots in Paris. In 1589, Margot's husband became Henri IV and, by converting to Catholicism, finally brought peace to France.

but Marguerite says that Valentine wanted to avoid an unhappy marriage. Saint-Bris announces that Valentine is already married to Nevers.

ACT FOUR Valentine is lamenting her unhappy fate and continuing love for Raoul ♂ when Raoul bursts in, determined to see her one last time. When the sound of footsteps forces him into hiding, he hears Saint-Bris tell Catholic nobles of the plan to massacre Protestants, although Nevers refuses to join the plot. Raoul must warn his co-religionists, but Valentine begs him to stay, confessing her love for him. Raoul now imagines escaping with Valentine. But when church bells signal that the massacre has begun, Raoul rushes away.

"Je suis seule chez moi"

ACT FIVE Huguenot nobles are receiving Marguerite when Raoul brings word of the massacre. Finding him, Valentine promises him royal protection if he will convert, but he refuses. She accepts Raoul's Protestant faith instead ♂. Marcel then pronounces them married. Catholics open fire on fleeing Protestants. Spotting a woman with two wounded men, Saint-Bris demands their identity. When they say they are Huguenots, he orders them shot. As Valentine falls, Saint-Bris recognizes his daughter. Marguerite appeals for calm, but the killing goes on.

"Ainsi je te verrai périr?"

objects. Raoul arrives and, while enchanted by the queen's beauty, learns he is to marry Saint-Bris's daughter. But on recognizing the woman as Nevers's former fiancée, he refuses, insulting the Catholic nobles.

ACT THREE Nevers and Valentine enter a church for their wedding, but only Nevers emerges, saying Valentine wants to pray alone until dusk. Marcel delivers a challenge from Raoul to Saint-Bris, who then orders Count Maurevert to ambush Raoul. Overhearing this, a veiled Valentine warns Marcel ♂, who does not recognize her. As Raoul prepares for the duel, Maurevert appears with armed men. Arriving unexpectedly, Marguerite demands an explanation for the commotion. Marcel points to Valentine as his informant and tears off her veil. Even Raoul is shocked,

"O terreur!"

Amanda Thane, in the role of Valentine, prepares to give her life for her lover's religious faith at the Royal Opera House in 1997.

> *"I gave myself over entirely to the study and cult of great dramatic music."*
>
> *Hector Berlioz*

HECTOR
BERLIOZ

Born: 11 December 1803, La Côte-Saint-André, France
Died: 8 March 1869, Paris, France

Hector Berlioz was an enormously influential composer, considered by many to be the creator of the modern orchestra, yet his work has always been better appreciated in Britain and Germany than in France. Berlioz's career in opera proved particularly frustrating, with the Paris Opéra refusing to receive him after the failure of *Benvenuto Cellini* in 1838.

Although Berlioz played and wrote music in his teens, his parents sent him to Paris to study medicine. He was 21 before he finally devoted himself entirely to composition, writing a *Messe solennelle* that same year. He followed with symphonies, cantatas, and songs, and, in 1830, at his fourth attempt, won the Prix de Rome. Upon his return, by using literary works as the inspiration for choral symphonies, he established himself as a leader of musical Romanticism.

However, with the hostile reception given to *Benvenuto Cellini*, Berlioz's opera career began badly and he soon felt excluded from the social heart of Paris musical life. His next theatre piece, *La damnation de Faust*, was presented in concert in 1846 and was not staged until 1893. Even his greatest opera, *Les Troyens*, had a troubled birth, with only Acts III to V performed in his lifetime. *Béatrice et Bénédict*, which premiered in Baden-Baden in 1862, was well received, but it reached Paris only in 1890.

Berlioz struggled to win recognition as an opera composer, but he could not be ignored as a music critic. He was often scathing of fellow composers, although he evidently listened carefully to their work. Thus, while disliking much of Meyerbeer's music, he singled out elements for praise. Only the long-forgotten Spontini could do no wrong: Berlioz ranked him alongside Beethoven and Weber as the modern masters who most influenced him.

A blood-spattered Brindley Sherratt as the Ghost of Hector in Richard Jones's 2004 production of *Les Troyens* at the English National Opera.

FIRST PERFORMANCES

1820

1823
Estelle et Némorin (lost)

1830

1838
Benvenuto Cellini

1840

1846
La damnation de Faust

1850

1862
Béatrice et Bénédict

1860

1863
Les Troyens (Acts III-V)

1869
Death

1870

1880

1890
Les Troyens (Acts I-II)

1890

BENVENUTO CELLINI

⚅ Opera semi-seria in two acts, 2¾ hours
⚄ 1836–1838 (rev. 1851–1853)
⚇ 10 September 1838, Paris Opéra, France

📖 Léon de Wailly and Auguste Barbier, after Benvenuto Cellini's late 16th-century autobiography, *Vita*

Benvenuto Cellini flopped at its premiere and never recovered. Its story, loosely adapted from Cellini's life as a sculptor and adventurer, is absurd, but the public objected mainly to the score's innovative rhythms and orchestration. Even in rehearsals, Berlioz faced what he later called "the indifference and obvious distaste" of most singers. Still rarely performed, the opera's daring inventiveness is now recognized and applauded.

⚐ Berlioz brought a revised version of *Benvenuto Cellini* to Covent Garden in 1853 in the hope of rescuing it from oblivion, but even Queen Victoria's presence at the opening did not shield him from boos. ⚑

✦ PRINCIPAL ROLES ✦

Benvenuto Cellini *tenor*
A sculptor and adventurer

Giacomo Balducci *bass*
Pope Clement's treasurer

Teresa *soprano*
Balducci's daughter

Ascanio *mezzo-soprano*
Cellini's apprentice

Fieramosca *baritone*
Cellini's rival

Pompeo *baritone*
Fieramosca's friend

PLOT SYNOPSIS

Rome, Italy, during Carnival week in 1532

ACT ONE The Pope has commissioned a statue from Benvenuto Cellini. But Balducci, the Pope's treasurer, favours a rival sculptor, Fieramosca, because Cellini is courting his daughter, Teresa. With Carnival in full swing, Cellini proposes eloping with Teresa ♫, but Fieramosca overhears Cellini's plan to dress as a monk. Balducci appears and, as Cellini slips away, Fieramosca hides. When Teresa speaks of seeing a strange man, Balducci discovers Fieramosca in her room. Ascanio, Cellini's apprentice, brings money from the Pope to finish the statue. Fieramosca and his friend Pompeo, in monks' habit, join the festive crowd. A fight erupts and Cellini kills Pompeo. As cannon shots announce the end of Carnival, Cellini escapes.

"O mon bonheur"

ACT TWO Cellini is preparing to flee with Teresa ♫ when Balducci announces that she will marry Fieramosca. The Pope then threatens to withdraw Cellini's commission if the statue is not completed by nightfall. While workers hurry to finish the statue, Fieramosca challenges Cellini to a duel. Teresa is shocked when Fieramosca reappears, but he has come to disrupt work on the statue. Finally the Pope arrives to witness the casting. A shortage of metal forces Cellini to use every object he can find and, with an explosion, the statue finally appears. The Pope is satisfied with the result and Balducci cedes Teresa to Cellini.

"Ah! Le ciel, cher époux"

Paul Charles Clarke as Cellini embraces Anne-Sophie Duprels's Teresa in Renaud Doucet's 2005 production at the Opéra National du Rhin in France.

LA DAMNATION DE FAUST
(The Damnation of Faust)

❧ Légende dramatique in four parts, 2¼ hours
⌛ 1829 and 1845–1846
♔ 6 December 1846, Opéra-Comique, Paris, France

📖 Hector Berlioz and Almire Gandonnière, after Goethe's *Faust Part I*

La damnation de Faust, while first performed in concert and never intended as an opera, is now frequently staged with success. In his twenties, already intrigued by the Faust legend, Berlioz set eight scenes from Goethe's *Faust Part I*, which he later incorporated into *La damnation de Faust*. This *légende dramatique* is more a succession of tableaux than a flowing narrative, but it is distinguished by powerfully romantic songs and expressive orchestration.

✦ PRINCIPAL ROLES ✦

Faust *tenor*
An elderly philosopher
Méphistophélès *bass*
A Satanic man
Marguerite *mezzo-soprano*
An innocent victim of Méphistophélès
Brander *bass*
A drinker

✍ A talented writer, Berlioz took the liberty of inventing an opening scene and locating it in Hungary so that he could make use of *Rákóczy's March*, an orchestral piece written years earlier. ◃

PLOT SYNOPSIS

Hungary and Germany in the early 16th century

PART ONE Faust wanders the Hungarian plains and, while happy over the coming of spring, is disturbed by the sound of dancing peasants and army bugles. He cannot share the pleasure of others.

PART TWO At home in Leipzig, Faust prepares to drink poison, but is cheered to hear Easter hymns. Méphistophélès appears and, promising him pleasure, leads him to a tavern. But Faust is put off by the drunken scene ♫. Beside the River Elbe, Méphistophélès has him "Une puce gentille" dream of the beautiful Marguerite. When he awakens, he yearns for her.

PART THREE Through Méphistophélès's magic, Faust enters Marguerite's chamber as she dreams of a lover "Autrefois un roi de Thule" ♫. As she sleeps, Méphistophélès further enchants her. Awakening to find Faust beside her, she surrenders to his advances.

PART FOUR Learning that Marguerite is to die for murdering her mother, Faust wants to save her and begs Méphistophélès for help. Méphistophélès demands Faust's soul in exchange and, once Faust agrees, they mount black horses and charge into a flaming abyss. Faust is forever damned, while Marguerite is welcomed to heaven by angels.

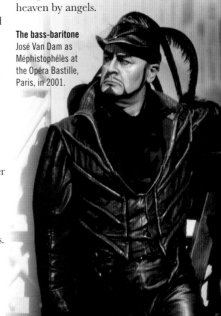

The bass-baritone
José Van Dam as Méphistophélès at the Opéra Bastille, Paris, in 2001.

LES TROYENS
(The Trojans)

♫ Grand opéra in five acts, 3¾ hours
🗓 1856–1858 (rev. 1859–1860)
♑ Acts III–V: 4 November 1863, Théâtre-Lyrique,

Paris, France; Acts I–II concert performance:
7 December 1879, Théâtre du Châtelet, Paris, France
📖 Hector Berlioz, after Virgil's *Aeneid* (19 BCE)

Long fascinated by Virgil's *Aeneid*, Berlioz finally adapted the epic for *Les Troyens*, a spectacular five-act opera, with 22 roles, huge choruses, and ballet. Today, the two-part work is often presented on successive evenings: Acts I and II, which were never staged in Berlioz's lifetime, as *The Fall of Troy*; and Acts III to V, which recount the tragic love story of Dido and Aeneas, as *The Trojans in Carthage*.

⚏ Fearing new rejection by Paris opera-goers, Berlioz was only convinced to write *Les Troyens* by the insistent encouragement of Liszt's mistress, Princess Carolyne Sayn-Wittgenstein, who, like Liszt, admired Berlioz's work. ⚏

⟶ PRINCIPAL ROLES ⟵

Cassandre (Cassandra) *mezzo-soprano*
A Trojan prophetess

Chorèbe (Corebus) *baritone*
An Asian prince

Priam *bass*
King of Troy

Énée (Aeneas) *tenor*
Trojan hero

Didon (Dido) *mezzo-soprano*
Widowed Queen of Carthage

PLOT SYNOPSIS

Troy and Carthage, Tunisia, in legendary Antiquity

ACT ONE THE FALL OF TROY The Greeks withdraw from Troy after a long siege, but leave behind a large wooden horse. Cassandre, the prophetess, warns that Troy is doomed, but her beloved, Chorèbe, ignores her. Énée reports the death of a priest who called for the destruction of the horse. In a procession ♫, the horse, carrying Greek soldiers, enters the city.

"Du roi des dieux, o fille aimée"

ACT TWO The ghost of Hector, a Trojan leader, urges Énée to flee and found a new Troy in Italy. At the fall of Troy, Chorèbe dies and Cassandre stabs herself. As Énée escapes, his palace is consumed by flames.

ACT THREE THE TROJANS IN CARTHAGE Didon's subjects vow to protect her from Iarbas, the Numidian king. The Trojans arrive. When Iarbas attacks Carthage, Énée comes to the city's defence.

ACT FOUR Didon and Énée are in love, but satyrs call out "Italy!" to Énée. As dancers celebrate Carthage's victory over Iarbas, Didon and Énée rejoice in their happiness ♫.

"Nuit d'ivresse et d'extase infinie"

ACT FIVE Didon begs Énée to stay, but the ghosts of Trojan heroes tell him to go. As Énée's fleet sails, Didon ascends a funeral pyre and stabs herself with his sword.

Plácido Domingo as Énée (*right*) leads a chorus of Trojans in a 1983 production of *Les Troyens* at the Metropolitan Opera in New York.

BÉATRICE ET BÉNÉDICT

(Beatrice and Benedict)

⚜ Opéra comique in two acts, 1½ hours
🎭 1860–1862 (rev. 1863)
♇ 9 August 1862, Neues Theater, Baden-Baden,

Germany
📖 Hector Berlioz, after Shakespeare's *Much Ado About Nothing* (1598 or 1599)

A great admirer of Shakespeare, Berlioz followed many earlier stage adaptations of *Much Ado About Nothing* in eliminating peripheral characters and focusing attention on the famously argumentative love between Beatrice and Benedick. His delightful score captures the story's many moods, with the conspiracy to seal the couple's love evoked in lovely duets and trios. After *Les Troyens*, Berlioz found relief in this opera's charm.

✣ Tired of French sniping at his work, Berlioz was even annoyed when Paris critics hailed a "new" cheerful and funny Berlioz in *Béatrice et Bénédict*, as if his earlier music had been entirely unappealing. ✣

> ✣ **PRINCIPAL ROLES** ✣
>
> **Léonato** *spoken role*
> Governor of Messina
>
> **Héro** *soprano*
> Léonato's daughter
>
> **Claudio** *baritone*
> A soldier and Héro's betrothed
>
> **Béatrice** *soprano*
> Léonato's niece
>
> **Bénédict** *tenor*
> A soldier
>
> **Don Pedro** *bass*
> A victorious general

PLOT SYNOPSIS

In and around Léonato's palace in Messina, Italy

ACT ONE Léonato, governor of Messina, welcomes Don Pedro and his army after their victory over the Moors. While Léonato's daughter, Héro, excitedly awaits her betrothed, "Je vais le voir" | Claudio ♂, Béatrice, the governor's niece, pokes fun at another soldier, Bénédict. He responds by calling her "Lady Disdain". After Béatrice leaves, Don Pedro suggests that Bénédict marry her, but he would rather die a bachelor. As the court musician Somarone rehearses his choir, Don Pedro and Claudio decide to become matchmakers. They ensure that Bénédict hears them discuss Béatrice's deep love for him. They then arrange for Béatrice to discover how much Bénédict loves her.

ACT TWO As the choir amuses a banquet, Béatrice admits to herself that she has fallen for Bénédict ♂. But, in public, she still scoffs at the idea of marriage. After Héro leaves to don her bridal dress, Béatrice bumps into Bénédict and, while they again spar, both are in a flutter. A wedding march leads the party to Don Pedro, who presides as Héro and Claudio sign their marriage contract. He then asks, "Who else is marrying?" Finally Bénédict says he will marry Béatrice out of pity; and she agrees only to save his life. As they make peace, everyone celebrates. "Il m'en souvient"

Ann Murray as Béatrice and Philip Langridge as Bénédict at the English National Opera in 1990.

CHARLES-FRANÇOIS
GOUNOD

Born: 17 June 1818, Paris, France
Died: 18 October 1893, Saint-Cloud, Paris, France

Charles-François Gounod was famous in his lifetime for both his choral music and his operas. Among his sacred works, *La Rédemption* and *Ave Maria*, derived from a Bach Prelude, are still popular. But he is best remembered for his two most successful operas, *Faust* and *Roméo et Juliette*, which are regularly performed around the world.

In his life as in his music, Gounod was divided between religion and more worldly interests. After studying church music in Rome, he spent two years in the seminary of Saint-Sulpice in Paris. But he was later renowned for his admiring circle of beautiful women. When he tried his hand at opera, he won critical praise for *Sapho*. His career then took off after he met the librettists Jules Barbier and Michel Carré, with whom he adapted works by Molière (*Le médecin malgré lui*), Goethe (*Faust*), and Shakespeare (*Roméo et Juliette*). All three operas stand out for their melodic arias and innovative orchestration. Gounod's opera about Provence, *Mireille*, also created a fashion for regional themes. When the 1870–1871 Franco–Prussian war interrupted his career, he moved to London and, for some years, "Gounod's Chorus" became the official choir at the Royal Albert Hall. In the late 1870s, he returned to Paris and wrote three more operas. But by then, younger composers were making their mark.

FIRST PERFORMANCES

1850

1851
Sapho

1858
Le médecin malgré lui

1859
Faust

1860   **1860**
Philémon et Baucis

1862
La reine de Saba

1864
Mireille

1867
Roméo et Juliette

1870

The mansion at Saint-Cloud outside Paris, where Gounod spent his retirement after his return from London in the mid-1870s and where he died.

FAUST

✍ Opera in five acts, 3½ hours
☎ 1856–1859
⚓ 19 March 1859, Théâtre-Lyrique, Paris, France

📖 Jules Barbier and Michel Carré, after Carré's 1850 play *Faust et Marguerite* and Goethe's *Faust Part I*

Faust secured Gounod's reputation as a major composer and soon became enormously popular worldwide, even being chosen to inaugurate the Metropolitan Opera in New York in 1883. While the plot is disturbingly cynical, a richly expressive score transforms the opera into a romantic tragedy. Orchestration and choruses highlight the battle that is taking place between good and evil. The composer then reserves his sweetest melodies for love duets between Marguerite and Faust.

⌐ *Faust*'s depiction of the destructive power of love moved Charles Dickens, who wrote: "It has affected me and sounded in my ears like a mournful echo of things that lie in my own heart." ⌐

✥ PRINCIPAL ROLES ✥

Faust *tenor*
An elderly philosopher

Méphistophélès *bass*
A satanic man

Marguerite *soprano*
An innocent victim of Méphistophélès

Wagner *baritone*
A student

Valentin *baritone*
A soldier and Marguerite's brother

PLOT SYNOPSIS

Germany in the early 16th century

ACT ONE Contemplating suicide, Faust summons Satan. Méphistophélès answers, promising him wealth, power, and youth in exchange for his soul. After Méphistophélès conjures up a vision of Marguerite, Faust accepts the pact.

ACT TWO Valentin asks friends to protect his sister, Marguerite, while he is away at war. When Méphistophélès mocks Marguerite, Valentin draws his sword, but Méphistophélès snaps it. Faust offers Marguerite his arm, but she turns away.

ACT THREE While Faust dreams of love ♂, Méphistophélès leaves Marguerite a jewel box. Her delight encourages Faust to declare his love for her. She begs him to leave, then calls him back.

"Oui, c'est toi! Je t'aime"

Australian soprano Nellie Melba (1861–1931) included Marguerite among her favourite roles.

As he returns to her, Méphistophélès laughs with sadistic glee.

ACT FOUR Now the abandoned mother of Faust's child, Marguerite prays to God, but Méphistophélès replies. Back from the front, Valentin rushes to Marguerite's cottage. Méphistophélès urges Faust to follow. Valentin tries to avenge his sister, but Faust wounds him. Before dying, Valentin curses Marguerite.

ACT FIVE Surrounded by dancing witches, Faust has a vision of Marguerite in jail for killing their child. He enters her cell and again they dream of love. But Marguerite refuses to leave with him. As she expires, her soul rises to heaven.

ROMÉO ET JULIETTE

(Romeo and Juliet)

✍ Opera in a prologue and five acts, 3¼ hours
☛ 1865–1867
♱ 27 April 1867, Théâtre-Lyrique, Paris, France

📖 Jules Barbier and Michel Carré, after Shakespeare's 1599 tragedy, *Romeo and Juliet*

Roméo et Juliette is a lushly romantic opera which, while remarkably faithful to Shakespeare's tragedy, dwells even more closely on the ill-fated couple. In Act V, set in the Capulets' vault, Gounod and his librettists also bow to operatic tradition: they keep Roméo alive long enough so that he and Juliette can die in each other's arms. While the libretto borrows freely from Shakespeare's language, it also prolongs the lovers' reunions to allow ample time for four long touching duets. Roméo and Juliette also have stirring arias, while Stéphano the page, a soprano "trouser role", invariably wins applause for "his" single aria. The generational dimension to this tragedy is underlined by the strong bass roles of Lord Capulet and Frère Laurent, who contribute to the fatal dénouement.

⚘ Thanks to *Roméo et Juliette*, Gounod became known as the "musician of love", a title he happily embraced when, at 70, he said that love was at the heart of his life and his art. ⚘

✦ PRINCIPAL ROLES ✦

Roméo *tenor*
The heir to the Montaigu family

Juliette *soprano*
Lord Capulet's daughter

Capulet *bass*
The head of the Capulet family

Mercutio *baritone*
Roméo's closest friend

Tybalt *tenor*
Capulet's nephew

Pâris *baritone*
Juliette's designated husband

Frère Laurent *bass*
A local monk

Gertrude *mezzo-soprano*
Juliette's nurse

Stéphano *soprano*
Roméo's page

PLOT SYNOPSIS

In and around the Capulets' mansion and in the Capulet vault in Verona (Italy)

PROLOGUE The Chorus announces that only the death of two young lovers ended the centuries-old feud between the Montaigus and the Capulets.

ACT ONE Hosting a masked ball, Lord Capulet introduces his young daughter, Juliette, to the guests, who include his nephew, Tybalt. Roméo, a hated young Montaigu, enters the party with Mercutio.

Eidé Norena (1884–1968), one of the finest sopranos of the inter-war years, played Juliette to great acclaim.

Roméo is upset by a dream, but Mercutio teases him. Suddenly Roméo sees Juliette and falls madly in love with her. Juliette's nurse, Gertrude, suggests Count Pâris as an ideal husband, but Juliette says she will follow only her heart ♪. Taking her aside, Roméo begins wooing her. But they are interrupted by Tybalt, who threatens Roméo. Capulet prevents a fight.

"Ah! Je veux vivre"

ACT TWO Hiding from Capulet guards, Roméo stands below Juliette's bedroom waiting for dawn ♪. Appearing on the balcony, Juliette laments that Roméo's Montaigu name could separate them. Roméo then appears and they declare their love for

"Ah! Lève-toi, soleil"

ALAGNA AND GHEORGHIU

The French tenor Roberto Alagna and the Romanian soprano Angela Gheorghiu (*below*) are among the opera stars of the new century, but they also happen to be married. This has added a true-life dimension to their frequent appearances as both happy and tragic operatic lovers. They first sang together in London productions of *La bohème* and *Roméo et Juliette*, but they have since expanded their repertoire to *L'elisir d'amore*, *Tosca*, *Il trovatore*, and *Carmen*.

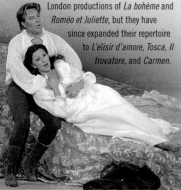

each other. Capulet servants search for a Montaigu, but they find no one. Alone again, Juliette asks Roméo to send word of when and where they will marry.

ACT THREE Frère Laurent, seeing a chance for peace between the families, agrees to marry the couple secretly. Still waiting in the Capulet's garden, Roméo's page,

"Que fais-tu, blanche tourterelle"

Stéphano, imagines turtle-doves kissing ♂. But he is caught by the Capulet servants. Mercutio defends the boy, then Tybalt arrives and fights Mercutio. Roméo tries to separate them, saying the time for hatred is over. But the fighting resumes and Tybalt kills Mercutio. Furious, Roméo slays Tybalt. The Duke of Verona denounces both families for feuding, then sends Roméo into exile.

ACT FOUR Together on their wedding night, Juliette forgives

"Nuit d'hyménée"

Roméo for killing her cousin ♂. As dawn breaks, Roméo leaves Verona. Capulet informs Juliette that she is to

marry Pâris. When she resists, he decides that Frère Laurent should persuade her of her duty. Instead, the friar offers a potion that will simulate death. But, a day later, she will reawaken to find Roméo at her side. Juliette fears waking up beside Tybalt's corpse, but she finally takes the potion ♂.

"Amour, ranime mon courage"

Dressed in her bridal gown, Juliette is about to marry Pâris when she collapses and is pronounced dead.

ACT FIVE Frère Laurent learns that his letter explaining Juliette's "death" never reached Roméo. Believing Juliette to be dead, Roméo breaks into the Capulet vault and finds her inert body. Devastated, he kisses her, then drinks poison. Suddenly, Juliette stirs and, briefly, they imagine fleeing together. But Roméo confesses that, thinking her dead, he took poison ♂. As

"Console-toi, pauvre âme"

he grows weaker, Juliette stabs herself with a dagger. Begging God for forgiveness, the lovers die in each other's arms.

"*What else is "opéra comique", in fact, but sung vaudeville?*"

Jacques Offenbach

JACQUES OFFENBACH

Born: 20 June 1819, Cologne, Germany
Died: 5 October 1880, Paris, France

Jacques Offenbach, the son of a cantor at Cologne's synagogue, became the master of French operetta. With their farcical plots and witty scores, Offenbach's *opéras-bouffes*, as they were also known, were the toast of mid-19th-century Paris. *La belle Hélène* was his biggest success, but *Les contes d'Hoffmann*, which was first performed a year after his death, is considered his operatic masterpiece.

Offenbach was just 13 when he moved to Paris, first to study, then to join an orchestra as a cellist, finally to compose. In this, he looked to Mozart and Schubert for inspiration, yet instinct and a need to survive led him to write vaudeville and salon pieces. To reach a wider audience, he founded the Bouffes-Parisiens, where he presented 30 of his one-act operettas before the triumph of *Orphée aux enfers* in 1858. Over the next decade, thanks to *La belle Hélène*, *La vie parisienne*, and other crowd-pleasers, his fame also spread across Europe, to London and Vienna. Immensely prolific, he wrote over 600 works of music, 130 of them for the theatre.

The 1870–1871 Franco–Prussian War disrupted his life. A Catholic convert and member of France's Légion d'Honneur, a man known for his wit and generosity, he was suddenly vilified as a German Jew. After briefly leaving Paris, he returned to an unwelcoming city. In 1873 he became director of the Gaîté Lyrique, but it soon went bankrupt. His own situation was increasingly desperate. In 1876, he toured the United States to raise some money, but his health was failing him. His last unfinished work, *Les contes d'Hoffmann*, completed by friends, reflects the pessimism of his final years.

Jane Rhodes in the title role of *La belle Hélène*, one of Offenbach's best-loved operettas, in a 1976 production at the Bouffes-Parisiens in France.

FIRST PERFORMANCES

1850

1858
Orphée aux enfers

1860

1864
La belle Hélène

1866
Barbe-bleue

1867
La Grande-Duchesse de Gérolstein

1870

1868
La Périchole

1880

1880
Death

1881
Les contes d'Hoffmann

1890

ORPHÉE AUX ENFERS
(Orpheus in the Underworld)

⚐ Opéra-bouffon in four acts, 1¾ hours
(rev. 2¾ hours)
⌛ 1858 (rev. 1874)

♄ 21 October 1858, Bouffes-Parisiens,
Paris, France
📖 Hector Crémieux and Ludovic Halévy

Orphée aux enfers, Offenbach's first major success, created the Paris fashion for full-evening operettas. A delicious parody of both Antiquity and Baroque opera, it also pokes fun at the Orpheus myth so beloved of 17th- and 18th-century opera-goers. With catchy tunes and absurd situations, it also captured the fun-loving spirit of the times, even ending with the famous Cancan, *"Ce bal est original"*.

⊰ Such was the popularity of *Orphée aux enfers* that a gala performance was organized for Emperor Napoleon III and Empress Eugénie, no small honour for the composer of operettas for popular audiences. ⊱

➤ PRINCIPAL ROLES ◄

Orphée (Orpheus) *tenor*
A musician

Eurydice *soprano*
Orphée's wife

Jupiter *baritone*
King of the gods

Aristée/Pluton (Pluto) *tenor*
God of the underworld

John Styx *tenor*
Prison guard in Hades

Mercury and Mars *tenor*
Gods

PLOT SYNOPSIS

Thrace, Mount Olympus, and Hades

ACT ONE Eurydice is bored with her husband, Orphée, whose flute-playing no longer amuses her. Annoyed, Orphée threatens her with a violin concerto. Pluton, in the guise of the shepherd Aristée, has won Eurydice's heart and leads her to the underworld. She leaves a note informing Orphée of her death. At the insistence of Public Opinion, Orphée follows her.

ACT TWO On Mount Olympus, Jupiter is not pleased that Pluton has abducted Eurydice. Other gods defend Pluton and mock Jupiter for his tyranny and ugliness. Accompanied by Public Opinion, Orphée comes

Madame Méaly was a striking Eurydice in a 1902 production at the Théâtre des Variétés in Paris.

in search of his wife. Jupiter offers to look for Eurydice in the underworld. All the gods follow him.

ACT THREE Eurydice is being held in the underworld's prison when Jupiter arrives to court her. To enter the locked cell, Cupid turns Jupiter into a fly who immediately charms Eurydice ♘. Confident of his conquest, Jupiter identifies himself.

"Il m'a semblé sur mon épaule"

ACT FOUR Jupiter turns Eurydice into a revelling Bacchante and, after she entertains with a song, everyone dances the Cancan ♘. While Pluton and Jupiter compete for Eurydice, Orphée arrives and is told he can recover his wife if he leads her away without glancing back. But when Jupiter throws a thunderbolt, Orphée looks around. With that, Eurydice remains a Bacchante and the gods celebrate.

"Ce bal est original"

LA BELLE HÉLÈNE
(Beautiful Helen)

⚜ Opéra-bouffe in three acts, 3 hours   Paris, France
⏳ 1864   📖 Henri Meilhac and Ludovic Halévy
🎭 17 December 1864, Théâtre des Variétés,

La belle Hélène echoes *Orphée aux enfers* by parodying the Greek classics. While using all the tricks common to farces, Offenbach also satisfies the 19th century's appetite for sweet melodies, starting with Hélène's opening paean to love, *"Amours divins"*. Choruses are important as lyrical cheerleaders to the romantic action. *La belle Hélène* was an immediate success, so popular that it was soon the one operetta regularly performed in mainstream opera houses.

> **✦ PRINCIPAL ROLES ✦**
>
> **Paris** *tenor*
> Prince of Troy
> **Hélène (Helen)** *mezzo-soprano*
> Queen of Sparta
> **Ménélas (Menelaus)** *tenor*
> King of Sparta
> **Calchas** *bass*
> Jupiter's high priest

⚜ In Hortense Schneider, who created Hélène, Offenbach not only found a mistress but also a talented soprano who contributed to the success of later operettas, including *La Grande-Duchesse de Gérolstein*. ⚜

PLOT SYNOPSIS

Sparta, Greece, in mythological Antiquity

ACT ONE Hélène has joined a ceremony at the Temple of Venus, but her mind is on Venus's vow that Paris, Prince of Troy, will win the most beautiful woman in the world. A shepherd learns that he has won the contest. Recognizing the shepherd as Paris, Calchas the high priest asks him to praise Venus *"Au mont Ida"* ♪. Hélène is attracted to the shepherd, but their flirtation is interrupted by Ménélas, Hélène's husband. A game of charades follows and the "shepherd" wins Hélène. To further Venus's scheme, Jupiter orders Ménélas to leave for Crete.

ACT TWO Paris asks to see Hélène in her chambers and, after very brief hesitation, she agrees. While she is sleeping, Paris arrives disguised as a

Felicity Lott as Hélène is courted by Yann Beuron's Paris in Laurent Pelly's hit production at the Théâtre du Châtelet, Paris, in 2003.

slave and, thinking she is dreaming, Hélène welcomes him warmly ♪. Ménélas arrives unannounced and protests wildly, but Hélène turns the tables on him, complaining that husbands should always give warning before returning.

"Oui, c'est un rêve"

ACT THREE Taking a holiday by the sea, Ménélas and other kings complain of the crowds and worry about Venus's influence over their women. Ménélas, who feels cuckolded by Hélène, summons a priest to restore order. Paris arrives disguised as the priest. He orders Hélène to accompany him to Cythera to honour Venus. After Paris reveals himself, a chorus wishes them bon voyage.

LA GRANDE-DUCHESSE DE GÉROLSTEIN
(The Grand Duchess of Gerolstein)

✍ Opéra-bouffe in three acts, 2¾ hours
☷ 1866–1867
♛ 12 April 1867, Théâtre des Variétés,

Paris, France
📖 Henri Meilhac and Ludovic Halévy

A mischievous parody of war and politics, *La Grande-Duchesse de Gérolstein* was timed to coincide with the 1867 Universal Exhibition in Paris. Censors demanded a few cuts to avoid offending visiting royalty, but the operetta proved a great success. In fact, it finally won over Britons and Americans to Offenbach and *opéra-bouffe*. Banned after the 1870–1871 Franco–Prussian war for its jocular treatment of war, it was revived to acclaim in 1878.

⚹ Typical of the demands that Offenbach makes on performers, the role of the Grand Duchess requires a voice of great stamina, agility, and lyricism as well as a comedienne's instinct for timing and character acting. ⚹

✧ PRINCIPAL ROLES ✧

La Grande-Duchesse *soprano*
Ruler of a principality

Fritz *tenor*
A soldier

Wanda *soprano*
A peasant girl

Général Boum *baritone*
The army commander

Baron Puck *baritone*
The chamberlain

Prince Paul *tenor*
The Grand Duchess's suitor

PLOT SYNOPSIS

A German principality around 1720

ACT ONE Général Boum mobilizes the Grand Duchy's ragtag army, ordering Private Fritz to stand guard. Fritz kisses Wanda, his girlfriend, but they flee when shots are heard. Baron Puck tells Boum he wants the Grand Duchess to marry Prince Paul. The Duchess arrives to rally her troops with the regiment's song ♫, but falls for Fritz and promotes him first to captain, then to general.

"Ah! C'est un fameux régiment"

ACT TWO Baron Grog encourages the Duchess to marry Prince Paul, but she awaits Fritz. Prince Paul, Boum, and Puck decide to kill the upstart private. The victorious Fritz is summoned to live with the Duchess, but he does not grasp her intentions ♫. Instead, he says he wants to marry Wanda. Furious, the Duchess decides that he must die.

"Oui, Général, quelqu'un vous aime"

ACT THREE As assassins gather, the Duchess takes a fancy to Grog. He agrees to join her court if she marries Prince Paul. She accepts and cancels orders to kill Fritz. Boum explains that Fritz was sent on a surprise mission. When Fritz returns looking dishevelled, the Duchess strips him of his rank. She then learns that Grog is already married. In resignation, she concludes that "when you can't get what you like, you must like what you get".

Frederica von Stade (the Duchess) and Rodney Gilfry (Prince Paul) at the Los Angeles Opera, 2005.

LES CONTES D'HOFFMANN

(The Tales of Hoffmann)

✍ Opéra fantastique in a prologue, three acts, and an epilogue, 2¾ hours
🕮 1877–1880

🏛 10 February 1881, Opéra-Comique, Paris, France
📖 Jules Barbier, after the play by Barbier and Michel Carré, based on several tales of ETA Hoffmann

Les contes d'Hoffmann, Offenbach's final and finest work, recounts an old poet's four ill-fated love affairs. The opera has a complex theatrical structure, with the same singers ideally used for each of the four soprano and four bass roles to underline the idea that the same love affair keeps repeating itself. The music is at once glittering and melancholic, notably with its most famous song, the lilting barcarolle in Act III.

⌖ Unfinished at the time of Offenbach's death, *Les contes d'Hoffmann* was completed by several different hands with the result that no definitive version of the opera exists, above all for Act III and the Epilogue. ⌖

> **→ PRINCIPAL ROLES ←**
>
> Hoffmann *tenor*
> A poet
>
> La Muse/Nicklausse *mezzo-soprano*
> Hoffman's muse and protector
>
> Stella/Olympia/Antonia/Giulietta *soprano*
> Women loved by Hoffmann
>
> Lindorf/Coppélius/Miracle/Dapertutto *bass*
> Hoffmann's enemies

PLOT SYNOPSIS

A tavern in Nuremberg, Germany, in the late 18th century

PROLOGUE Lindorf, an unscrupulous politician, lusts after Hoffmann's mistress, the singer Stella. At the urging of drinking students, Hoffmann tells the stories of his unhappy love for three other women, who all exist in Stella.

ACT ONE In Paris, Hoffmann falls for Olympia, a mechanical doll made by Spalanzani. At the touch of her shoulder, she sings ♫ and dances. "Les-ois-eaux-dans-la-char-mille" Coppélius, who has provided her eyes, feels cheated by Spalanzani and destroys Olympia. Only then does Hoffman realise she is an automaton.

ACT TWO In Munich, Crespel forbids his daughter, Antonia, from singing for fear she will die of the same disease as his opera-singer wife. In love, Hoffmann

Natalie Dessay's Olympia is coached by Sergio Bertocchi's Spalanzani in the Paris National Opera's production in 2000.

and Antonia decide to marry. Dr Miracle comes to treat Antonia and has a portrait of Antonia's mother tell the girl to sing. When she does, she expires. Dr Miracle vanishes and Crespel blames Hoffmann.

ACT THREE In a Venetian bordello, Giulietta sings of love ♫, but the evil Dapertutto has other plans. In exchange for a diamond ring, she is to capture Hoffmann's reflection. Easily seduced, the poet surrenders his reflection. He then kills Dapertutto, but he loses Giulietta anyway.

"Belle nuit, ô nuit d'amour"

EPILOGUE With his stories told, Hoffmann is by now quite drunk. Stella returns and finds him fast asleep. While Lindorf leads her away, she looks back sadly at Hoffmann.

"As a musician, I tell you that if we were to suppress adultery, fanaticism, crime, evil, the supernatural, there would no longer be the means of writing one note."

Georges Bizet

GEORGES
BIZET

Born: 25 October 1838, Paris, France
Died: 3 June 1875, Le Bougival, outside Paris, France

Georges Bizet's extraordinary celebrity as an opera composer is the fruit of just one work, *Carmen*. He wrote other operas, with one or two still occasionally performed. But none has come close to enjoying *Carmen*'s enduring popularity around the world. His early death, at 36, cut short a blossoming career.

A child prodigy, Bizet was just nine when he entered the Paris Conservatoire and only 17 when he wrote his fine *Symphony in C*. After three years in Rome, where he focused on *opera buffa*, his return to Paris brought frustration. He won a competition for a comic opera with *Le Docteur Miracle* and it was presented at Offenbach's Bouffes-Parisiens in 1857. This brought commissions for other operas, which were not produced in his lifetime. Eventually, in 1863, *Les pêcheurs de perles* reached a major stage.

Four years later, *La jolie fille de Perth* earned him some plaudits, but success still fell short of his talent. He kept busy writing orchestral music and piano works, with his incidental music to Daudet's Provençal tragedy *L'arlésienne* still proving popular today. But many of his operatic projects were never completed.

After the disruption of the Franco–Prussian War of 1870–1871, Bizet wrote an Orientalist comic opera, *Djamileh*, but soon he was absorbed by *Carmen*. With it he hoped to answer critics who had accused him of being complicated and obscure. "Well, this time I have written a work that is all clarity and vivacity, full of colour and melody," he remarked. But the premiere was a flop and, although *Carmen* was soon hailed as a masterpiece, Bizet did not live to savour his achievement.

Yevgeny Alexiev as Zurga, leader of the pearl fishers, in an atmospheric scene from Antoine Bourseiller's production of *Les pêcheurs de perles* staged at the Opéra National du Rhin in France.

FIRST PERFORMANCES

1860

1863
Les pêcheurs de perles

1867
La jolie fille de Perth

1870

1872
Djamileh

1875
Carmen

1880

LES PÊCHEURS DE PERLES
(The Pearl Fishers)

🎵 Opera in three acts (four tableaux), 2 hours
☙ 1863
⚜ 30 September 1863, Théâtre-Lyrique,

Paris, France
📖 Eugène Cormon and Michel Carré

Les pêcheurs de perles launched Bizet's operatic career, although it was not enthusiastically received at its premiere. The composer himself described it as "an honourable, brilliant failure". Today, however, it is "the other" Bizet opera – not *Carmen* – that is still regularly performed. Written when he was only 25, *Les pêcheurs de perles* shows Bizet influenced by Gounod and Verdi and still searching for his own voice. Thus, while this opera's story is set in Ceylon, the music offers no local colour. Rather, through wonderfully melodic arias, duets, and choruses, Bizet evokes a dreamlike world of pure romance, one presided over by a virgin priestess and convulsed by human passions. The opera is considered difficult to stage because of its minimal action, but the lush score is a permanent delight.

> ➤ **PRINCIPAL ROLES** ➤
>
> *Zurga baritone*
> The leader of the pearl fishers
>
> *Nadir tenor*
> Pearl fisher and Zurga's childhood friend
>
> *Leïla soprano*
> A mysterious virgin priestess
>
> *Nourabad bass*
> The high priest

⚜ This opera's loveliest melody, the tenor–baritone duet *"Au fond du temple saint"*, becomes a leitmotif that returns, at times echoed only by the orchestra, whenever the friendship between Zurga and Nadir is recalled. ⚜

PLOT SYNOPSIS

A beach in Ceylon (now Sri Lanka)

ACT ONE Gathered on a beach, pearl fishers choose Zurga as their leader while they await the virgin priestess who will protect them. Nadir, Zurga's childhood friend, arrives unexpectedly. They recall when they saw a beautiful veiled woman and both fell for her. But to avoid conflict, they renounced their love for her and swore eternal friendship ♫. The priestess is received by Nourabad, the high priest, while Zurga reminds her to remain veiled and to take no

"Au fond du temple saint"

lover. Suddenly Nadir recognizes her as his beloved Leïla. That night, he remembers how he betrayed Zurga and followed her ♫. In his sleep, he hears Leïla singing ♫. Following her voice, he finds her on a rock. As her face is briefly revealed, he rejoices.

"Je crois entendre encore"

"O Dieu Brahma"

ACT TWO The boats return safely and Nourabad tells Leïla she can sleep peacefully if she has kept her vow to remain pure. Leïla recalls that she once saved the life of a man who gave her a necklace in thanks. Alone, Leïla senses Nadir's presence ♫. When he

"Me voilà seule dans la nuit"

An ornate costume designed by Umberto Brunelleschi for a production of Bizet's opera at La Scala, Milan.

ALFREDO KRAUS

Less renowned outside the opera world than Luciano Pavarotti and Plácido Domingo, the Spanish lyric tenor Alfredo Kraus was considered the post-war master of *bel canto*. One of his earliest recordings was as Nadir in *Les pêcheurs de perles*, a role that also suited his high tenor voice and refined artistry. Famous for conserving his voice, he was 70 years old when he sang *"La donna è mobile"* at the reopening of Madrid's Teatro Real in 1997, two years before his death.

appears, they are both overwhelmed by love 👂.

"Leïla! Leïla!"

Leïla begs him to leave, as they are both at risk. Shots sound and Nourabad identifies Nadir as the stranger who violated the sacred sanctuary. The pearl fishers are enraged, vowing to kill Leïla and Nadir. Zurga, declaring that only he can decide their fate, tells the couple to flee. But as Nourabad tears off Leïla's veil, Zurga understands the depth of Nadir's betrayal.

ACT THREE Zurga regrets ordering Nadir to die at dawn but, when Leïla appears, his passion for her is rekindled 👂.

"Je frémis, je chancelle"

Leïla begs him to punish only her, saying she met Nadir by chance. But Zurga says he cannot reprieve his friend because she loves him. Admitting that he too loves her, he is torn by jealousy. Cursing him, Leïla defies him to take her life. Light in the sky announces the hour of execution.

Saying she is ready to die, Leïla asks a fisherman to give her necklace to her mother. Zurga seizes the necklace and runs after her. At the foot of the pyre, Nadir bids emotional farewell to Leïla. Zurga suddenly arrives, saying that the light in the sky is a fire sent down from heaven. As the people scatter in fear, Zurga reveals that he lit the fire to allow the lovers to escape. Showing the necklace that he once gave Leïla, he says he will now save both their lives. As they flee, Zurga feels he has done his duty.

Russell Braun as Zurga menaces Leïla (Isabel Bayrakdarian) and Nadir (Michael Schade) at the San Diego Opera, 2004.

CARMEN

🎵 Opéra comique in four acts, 2¾ hours
🕮 1873–1875
⚜ 3 March 1875, Opéra-Comique, Paris, France

📖 Henri Meilhac and Ludovic Halévy, after Prosper Mérimée's 1845 novella

Carmen ranks high among the world's most beloved operas. Yet, as so often with such favourites, it was not instantly recognized as a masterpiece: at its premiere, its indecency shocked the Opéra-Comique's conservative audience. Soon, though, *Carmen* worked its seductive magic through the charm of its melodies, Spanish "exoticism" of the score, and strength of its characters. The work is described as an *opéra comique* because it has spoken dialogue but, beneath its exuberance, it always hints at a tragic dénouement. Here, the rich colour of the choruses and orchestration plays a central role. But while Don José, Escamillo, and Micaëla have fine arias, Carmen is the fickle Gypsy diva of this opera, nowhere more brilliantly expressed than in her Act I *habanera*.

> **PRINCIPAL ROLES**
>
> **Carmen** *mezzo-soprano*
> A rebellious cigarette girl
>
> **Don José** *tenor*
> A corporal in
> the dragoons
>
> **Escamillo** *baritone*
> A matador
>
> **Micaëla** *soprano*
> A peasant girl
>
> **Zuniga** *bass*
> A captain
>
> **Moralès** *baritone*
> An officer
>
> **Lillas Pastia** *spoken role*
> An inn-keeper

⊶ Bizet may have modelled Carmen on Celeste Venard, a nightclub singer and former prostitute known as "La Mogador". After a chance meeting on a train, they became close friends in the mid-1860s, although in her memoirs Celeste Venard denied that they were ever lovers. ⊷

PLOT SYNOPSIS

Seville, Spain, in the early 19th century

ACT ONE In a square crowded with soldiers, a peasant girl seeks out a corporal, Don José, but cannot find him. Don José arrives afterwards, guessing it is Micaëla. Meanwhile, new to Seville, Capt Zuniga learns that hundreds of women work in the tobacco factory. When a bell rings, the women spill out noisily, while Carmen sings of her untamed love ♪. She then tosses a flower at Don José. Micaëla delivers a letter which Don José reads aloud. His mother says it is time he married and suggests Micaëla as a bride. Suddenly, a fight erupts in the factory and Carmen is blamed. After Zuniga orders her tied up, she flirts with Don José, proposing a tryst and persuading him to loosen the rope ♪. As she is led away, she escapes.

"L'amour est un oiseau rebelle"

"Près des remparts de Séville"

Spanish mezzo-soprano Teresa Berganza, seen here in a 1981 production at the San Francisco Opera, carried her sensuous interpretation of Carmen around the world.

ACT TWO Two months afterwards, Carmen is entertaining officers in a tavern ♪ when she learns that Don José has served his prison term for freeing her. Escamillo the toreador arrives and boasts of his exploits ♪. He tries to win over Carmen, but she brushes him off. As the tavern empties out, smugglers seek help to distract border guards. Carmen refuses, saying she is in love. Don José appears and Carmen dances for him. But when he hears bugles calling him back to the barracks, she mocks him. To prove his love, he shows the flower she threw at him ♪. Zuniga arrives to woo Carmen and is disarmed. Don José now realizes he must flee.

"Les tringles des sistres tintaient"

"Votre toast, je peux vous le rendre"

"La fleur que tu m'avais jetée"

CARMEN REVISITED

In 1943, Oscar Hammerstein Jr, turning *Carmen* into an African-American story, set it around a Southern military base and renamed it *Carmen Jones*. It was made into a popular film by Otto Preminger in 1954. Recently, a South African *Carmen* was brought to the screen as *U-Carmen eKhayelitsha*. Set in a poor township, it won the Golden Bear for best film at the 2005 Berlin film festival.

Dorothy Dandridge as Carmen Jones plays up to Harry Belafonte's Joe in Otto Preminger's screen adaptation.

ACT THREE At the smugglers' hideout, Carmen is losing interest in Don José. The Gypsy girls read their fortunes in cards; when it is Carmen's turn, the cards predict death for herself and Don José. Don José is left on guard. Nearby, Micaëla is building up courage to enter the camp ♪. Escamillo appears, announcing he has come for Carmen. Don José challenges him. In the fight, Escamillo has the upper hand at first, but he then falls. After Carmen saves his life, he invites her to his next bull-fight. Don José is furious but, learning from Micaëla that his mother is dying, he leaves. He vows to meet Carmen again.

"Je dis que rien ne m'épouvante"

ACT FOUR Outside the bull-ring, children welcome Escamillo, accompanied by Carmen. Her friends warn her that Don José is also there. When Don José finds her, he begs her to return to him, insisting that he loves her. Carmen rebuffs him, declaring that she was born free. Finally, he stabs her. When a triumphant Escamillo appears, Don José tearfully confesses to having killed his "beloved Carmen".

The American mezzo-soprano Denyce Graves, one of the most exciting Carmens of her generation, reaches out to the audience at the Arena di Verona in Italy in 1999.

JULES
MASSENET

Born: 12 May 1842, Montaud, France
Died: 13 August 1912, Paris, France

Jules Massenet, the dominant French opera composer of the late 19th century, wrote over 30 operas in styles ranging from intimate tragedy and *verismo* to *opéra comique* and *grand opéra*. Of these, only *Manon* and *Werther* are regularly performed. Yet both are so popular that they have carried the French flag to theatres around the world.

Like Gounod and Bizet before him, Massenet won the Prix de Rome, which took him to Italy. There, he developed a strong interest in religious music and he composed several sacred works when he returned to Paris. Still, opera literally consumed his life: he wrote his first in 1867 and his last in 1912. And he did so for Vienna, Brussels, London, and Monte Carlo as well as Paris, where he was viewed as Meyerbeer's successor.

His two finest works came in the middle of his career – *Manon* in 1884 and *Werther* in 1892 – but many others were popular in their day, including *Le roi de Lahore*, *Hérodiade*, *Le Cid*, *Thaïs*, and *Sapho*. Massenet often found inspiration in beautiful sopranos, while he wrote *Don Quichotte* for the great Russian bass Feodor Chaliapin. During his lifetime, he was viewed sceptically by some of his peers, above all after he published his memoirs, considered by many as highly inventive. Nonetheless, a century later, his reputation rests comfortably on his gift for fine tunes and touching stories.

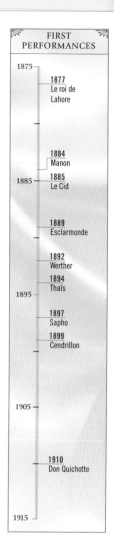

FIRST PERFORMANCES

1875

1877
Le roi de Lahore

1884
Manon

1885

1885
Le Cid

1889
Esclarmonde

1892
Werther

1894
Thaïs

1895

1897
Sapho

1899
Cendrillon

1905

1910
Don Quichotte

1915

Jules Massenet working in the study of his Paris home in the early years of the 20th century.

MANON

❧

🎼 Opéra comique in five acts (six tableaux),
2½ hours
🎵 1882–1884

🏛 19 January 1884, Opéra-Comique, Paris, France
📖 Henri Meilhac and Philippe Gille, after Abbé Provost's 1731 novel.

Manon, Massenet's most popular opera, daringly explores a young woman's sexuality. Only nine years earlier Bizet's *Carmen* was considered scandalous, but this work won public approval. Termed an *opéra comique* for its spoken dialogue, *Manon* is notably tragic, with a fast-paced story accompanied by exceptionally beautiful music. The score, with its famous arias and duets, is above all a gift to singers and audiences.

▸ One year after Puccini wrote his *Manon Lescaut*, Massenet returned to the story in a one-act opera called *Le portrait de Manon*, in which Des Grieux relives his love for Manon through his nephew. ▸

> **✦ PRINCIPAL ROLES ✦**
>
> **Manon Lescaut** *soprano*
> A fickle young woman
>
> **Le Chevalier des Grieux** *tenor*
> A young noble
>
> **Le Comte des Grieux** *bass*
> Le Chevalier's father
>
> **Lescaut** *baritone*
> A soldier and Manon's cousin
>
> **Guillot de Morfontaine** *tenor*
> A rakish financier
>
> **Brétigny** *baritone*
> A rich noble and farmer-general

PLOT SYNOPSIS

France in the early 18th century

ACT ONE Guillot, a financier, is drinking with an aristocratic friend, Brétigny. Outside the tavern, Lescaut receives his cousin, Manon, who is on her way to a convent ♪. Guillot starts wooing the girl, but Lescaut chases him away. Le Chevalier des Grieux falls for Manon and persuades her to live with him in Paris.

"Je suis encore tout étourdie"

ACT TWO Des Grieux wants his father's consent to marry Manon. Their hideaway is discovered by Lescaut and Brétigny, who warn Manon that her lover will be abducted. Brétigny reassures her that, if she says nothing, she can then live in luxury with him. Alone, Manon bids farewell to her little table ♪. On his return, Des Grieux is kidnapped.

"Adieu, notre petite table"

ACT THREE Now Brétigny's mistress, Manon learns that Des Grieux is to enter a seminary and hurries to see him. Des Grieux's prayers show he has not forgotten Manon. When she reiterates her love, they flee together.

Roberto Alagna as Le Chevalier des Grieux reads out a letter to Alexia Cousin's Manon in a 2004 production at the Opéra Bastille, Paris.

ACT FOUR Manon encourages Des Grieux to gamble. He wins but Guillot accuses him of cheating and summons the police. Des Grieux is released, but Manon is ordered to be deported to Louisiana.

ACT FIVE Des Grieux and Lescaut still hope to free Manon. Guards are bribed and the lovers are reunited. But Manon is too exhausted to move. And as they remember their happiness together, she dies in Des Grieux's arms.

WERTHER

✍ Drame lyrique in four acts, 2 hours
☙ 1885–1887
♆ 16 February 1892, Hofoper, Vienna (Austria)

📖 Édouard Blau, Paul Milliet and Georges Hartmann, after Goethe's novella *Die Leiden des jungen Werthers* (1774)

Werther, although less frequently performed than *Manon*, is Massenet's finest opera. Adapted from Goethe's novella, itself a pillar of the Romantic movement, it portrays a hopeless love story which ends in the most tragic of ways: a man's suicide with pistols provided by his beloved. Indeed, *Werther* was initially rejected by the Opéra-Comique in Paris as too depressing. As a result, one of the most celebrated French operas was first presented at the Vienna Opera. Massenet himself seemed eager to match Goethe's novella in opera. Thus he offers no relief from the emotional voyage through, say, choruses. Instead, with continuous music evocative of Wagner, Werther's desperate love and Charlotte's emotional disarray are portrayed through the poetry of recitatives and the lyricism of intense arias and duets.

> ⚏ The role of Charlotte is popular among woman singers, not least because, for once, they do not expire on stage. "Charlotte reverses the roles," Victoria de los Angeles noted, "It's the man who dies for her." ⚏

> → PRINCIPAL ROLES ←
>
> **Werther** *tenor*
> A 23-year-old poet
>
> **Le Bailli** *bass*
> A bailiff
>
> **Charlotte** *mezzo-soprano*
> The bailiff's 20-year-old daughter
>
> **Albert** *baritone*
> Charlotte's betrothed
>
> **Sophie** *soprano*
> The bailiff's 15-year-old daughter
>
> **Schmidt** *tenor*
> The bailiff's friend
>
> **Johann** *baritone*
> The bailiff's friend

PLOT SYNOPSIS

Frankfurt (Germany), around 1780

ACT ONE The bailiff, a widower, is rehearsing Christmas songs with his younger children – in July. His friends Johann and Schmidt wander by and learn that his 20-year-old daughter, Charlotte, is dressing for a ball. Talk turns to Werther, a melancholy young man. There is also praise for Albert, Charlotte's fiancé, who is away on business.

A poster for *Werther* at the Opéra-Comique in Paris, although the theatre initially rejected the opera, which premiered in Vienna instead.

Werther arrives, cheered by the children's singing. The bailiff introduces him to Charlotte and they go together to the ball, leaving 15-year-old Sophie caring for the smaller children. Hoping to surprise Charlotte, Albert arrives unexpectedly. Hours later, Charlotte and Werther return, arm-in-arm. Werther declares his love, but Charlotte does not respond ♋. Hearing that Albert is back, Charlotte says she promised her dying mother to marry him. Devastated, Werther tells her to keep the promise.

"Mais vous ne savez rien de moi"

ACT TWO Now married three months, Charlotte and Albert enter the town church. From afar, Werther watches them in despair ♋. As he slumps on a bench, Albert arrives to

"Un autre est son époux"

console him by acknowledging how he once felt for Charlotte. Werther insists that he no longer suffers, but Sophie remarks on his troubled spirit. Werther decides to leave town, but then sees Charlotte and again pours out his feelings. She tells him to go away and not to return before Christmas 🔊. Seeing him go, Sophie tells Charlotte and Albert, who now knows that Werther still loves Charlotte.

"Lorsque l'enfant revient"

ACT THREE It is Christmas Eve and Charlotte cannot forget Werther, constantly re-reading his letters. Seeing her sister's red eyes, Sophie says she knows her sadness began when Werther left. Finally, Charlotte bursts into tears 🔊. Sophie begs her to join the family. Suddenly Werther arrives. Charlotte says nothing has changed. He recognizes the case of pistols. She points to the love poem he was translating before he left. But when he reads it aloud 🔊, Charlotte begs him to stop. He tries to kiss her and she faints. When he embraces her, she flees. A servant brings Albert a letter from Werther, asking to borrow his pistols for a long

"Va! Laisse couler mes larmes"

"Pourquoi me réveiller"

Sophie Koch as Charlotte resists Massimo Giordano as Werther in Sebastian Baumgarten's production at the Deutsche Oper, Berlin, in 2002.

IN WAGNER'S SHADOW

In adapting Goethe's 1774 narrative fiction *The Sorrows of Young Werther*, Massenet assumed no small risk. By the late 19th century, Wagner's *Tristan und Isolde* had redefined tragic love and even French composers were being measured against the great operas of German Romanticism. Nonetheless, *Werther* was warmly received in Vienna in 1892 as "not too French" and, within a year, it was presented in Paris. Although the music is often unabashedly sentimental, Massenet considered the opera his greatest achievement.

journey. Albert orders Charlotte to hand them to the servant. As he storms out, Charlotte grabs her cloak.

ACT FOUR Charlotte finds Werther mortally wounded. He opens his eyes and asks for forgiveness. She wants to seek help, but he prefers to die, telling her of his love. Finally, she confesses her love for him and, for the first time, they kiss. Gradually, Werther loses consciousness 🔊. As he dies, children can be heard singing, "Jesus is born".

"Ah! Ses yeux se ferment"

GUSTAVE
CHARPENTIER

Born: 25 June 1860, Dieuze, France
Died: 18 February 1956, Paris, France

Gustave Charpentier's renown rests on a single opera, *Louise*. The son of a baker, he was a talented young musician who studied under Massenet at the Paris Conservatoire and won the coveted Prix de Rome. In Rome in his late twenties, he composed two applauded orchestral works, *Impressions d'Italie* and *La vie du poète*, as well as Act I of *Louise*. The opera was an immediate success, its working-class setting even earning Charpentier the tag of the "Émile Zola of music". But, unlike Zola, he was not a social reformer and he did little more worthy of note. His 1913 opera, *Julien*, flopped and he spent the rest of his long life collecting honours earned by *Louise*.

LOUISE

✍ Roman musical in four acts (five tableaux), 2¼ hours
☎ 1896–1899

♀ 2 February 1900, Opéra-Comique, Paris, France
📖 Gustave Charpentier

Set in 1900, the very year of its creation, *Louise* not only depicted "real" Parisians but, more daringly, it also addressed class differences and a young woman's yearning for the freedom to love. While the score is romantic, melodic, and naturalistic, even including cries from the streets of Montmartre, the opera represents no musical watershed, with echoes of Berlioz, Wagner, Gounod, and Massenet to be heard throughout. However, having spent more than a decade working on the libretto and score, Charpentier created a powerful theatrical event, with no fewer than 19 female soloists, 20 male soloists, and a large chorus. The accessibility of the music and the story ensure *Louise*'s popularity: it reached its 1,000th performance in 1956, the year of Charpentier's death.

→ **PRINCIPAL ROLES** ←

Louise *soprano* A seamstress
Louise's mother *mezzo-soprano*
Julien *tenor* A Bohemian poet
Louise's father *baritone*

⇥ Such was the success of *Louise* that Charpentier's peers could not ignore it: Saint-Saëns, Massenet, and Poulenc were full of praise, but Richard Strauss thought it derivative and Debussy dismissed it as "idiotic art". ⇤

A poster from the first production of *Louise* captures the young lovers against a background of Paris by night where they had spent their happiest times.

PLOT SYNOPSIS

Paris, France, in 1900

ACT ONE On a spring evening, Julien, a young poet, serenades Louise. She rushes to her window and they exchange vows of love 🔊. Hearing their exchanges, Louise's mother calls her away and warns her against falling for a worthless poet. The women are arguing when Louise's father arrives with a letter from Julien, in which he asks for Louise's hand. Her mother is furious and her father counsels patience, reminding Louise of the importance of her parents' love. He asks her to read the newspaper aloud. As she reads about Paris, she bursts into tears.

"O coeur ami! O coeur promis!"

ACT TWO In Paris at dawn, late-night revellers are mixing with the first workers. Julien searches for the little shop in Montmartre where Louise works as a seamstress 🔊. He sees her arrive with her mother and, once she is alone, he begs her to leave home and share freedom with him. Upset, she rushes into her shop. From outside, Julien serenades her. The other shopgirls tease her until, saying she feels ill, she leaves. The girls then see Louise with Julien.

"Elle va paraître"

ACT THREE Now living together, Louise speaks of her happiness 🔊. With Paris in festive mood, Julien's friends crown Louise as Muse of Montmartre. As they celebrate, Louise's mother arrives to beg her to return home, saying that her father is dying and is asking for her. Julien is suspicious, but allows Louise to leave.

"Depuis le jour"

ACT FOUR Three weeks later, as Louise sews in her parents' modest home, her father's health is returning. But he feels bitter about his own life and his child's ingratitude. His mood then changes and, taking Louise on his lap, he speaks again of his love for her. Seeing the distant lights of Paris, she asks for her freedom, for her life of love with Julien 🔊. Furious, her father throws open the door of their home and tells her to leave. As she runs off, he calls her back, but it is too late. Looking towards Paris, he curses the city that has taken his daughter.

"Tout être a le droit d'être libre"

Renée Fleming as Louise (*right*) tries to persuade her fellow seamstresses she is not in love in Lofti Mansouri's 1990 production at the San Francisco Opera.

CLAUDE
DEBUSSY

Born: 22 August 1862, Saint-Germain-en-Laye, near Paris, France
Died: 25 March 1918, Paris, France

Claude Debussy marked his era with sensuous and inventive music in all styles. While he is best remembered for his piano compositions and symphonic poems, his *Pelléas et Mélisande* stands as a monument in the history of opera, a work that broke with 19th-century tonal structures and harmonies, and paved the way for 20th-century modernity.

Debussy entered the Paris Conservatoire at the age of 11, and, at 18, he was hired as an accompanist by a widowed Russian millionairess. From then on, his life was a constant adventure. He won the Prix de Rome in 1884 but, pining for his married mistress, he returned to Paris early. Indeed, until he was 40, his personal life was stormy: both a later mistress and his first wife attempted suicide. Still, he remained productive, creating such memorable works as *Clair de lune* (1890), *Prélude à l'après-midi d'un faune* (1894) and *La Mer* (1905). *Pelléas et Mélisande* was his only opera, although *Le Martyre de Saint-Sébastien*, with his incidental music, is occasionally staged. Debussy's premature death from cancer at 55 cut short a remarkable career.

A MAN OF MANY ARTS

Debussy found musical inspiration in Wagner and Mussorgsky, but he also reached out to other arts, viewing creative expression as a whole. He has been called a "musical Impressionist" because of the influence of Monet and JMW Turner on his music, while he also composed works triggered by Pre-Raphaelite paintings. "I love painting almost as much as music itself," he once noted. Literature too intrigued him: he set Symbolist poems to music, while – ever curious – he long hoped to adapt two Edgar Allan Poe stories as operas.

Claude Debussy sitting at the piano beside Jeanne Chausson, wife of his composer friend, Ernest Chausson, at the Chaussons' Paris home.

LE MARTYRE DE SAINT-SÉBASTIEN
(The Martyrdom of Saint Sebastian)

❧ Drame sacré in five windows, 2 hours   📖 Gabriele d'Annunzio
⏳ 1910–1911
♈ 22 May 1911, Théâtre du Châtelet, Paris, France

Le Martyre de Saint-Sébastien expressed Debussy's ideal of total art: D'Annunzio's mystery play had Ida Rubinstein dancing Michel Fokine's choreography to Debussy's music in décor painted by Léon Bakst. The one-hour score includes solos, choruses, and accompaniment. While poorly received at its premiere, interest has been maintained by St Sebastian's homoerotic image as Emperor Diocletian's lover.

⚞ Before the premiere, the Archbishop of Paris warned Christians against a semi-pagan show in which a Jewish woman danced the role of Saint-Sébastien and, when killed by arrows, cried out, "More, more, more!". ⚟

⇢ PRINCIPAL ROLES ⇠

Narrateur *spoken role*
A narrator

Sébastien *spoken and danced role*
A Roman army officer

Dioclétien *spoken role*
Emperor of Rome

Marc *soprano*
A sacrificial victim

Marcellien *contralto*
A sacrificial victim

La Vièrge Erigone *soprano*

PLOT SYNOPSIS

Rome around 288

WINDOW ONE LA COUR DES LYS/THE COURT OF LILIES
The narrator invites the public to view Sébastien's life as if studying five stained-glass windows. The first shows the twins Marc and Marcellien being tortured in the public place while Sébastien calls for a sign from God. As he dances on hot embers, lilies emerge from the ground.

WINDOW TWO LA CHAMBRE MAGIQUE/THE MAGIC CHAMBER Sébastien overturns the false idols, enters the Temple of the Virgin Erigone, and defeats pagan forces. Another virgin sings a lament ♂.

"Qui pleure mon enfant si doux"

Vu-An Eric, in the spoken and danced role of Saint-Sébastien, faces death by arrows in this 1986 production which toured Milan, Salzburg and Brussels.

WINDOW THREE LE CONCILE DES DIEUX/THE COUNCIL OF FALSE GODS In the council of false gods, Emperor Dioclétien hails Sébastien as a "beauteous youth" whom he wants crowned. Sébastien claims he carries a crown, one forged by faith and prayer. The infatuated Dioclétien still wants to make Sébastien a god. When the young man dances the Lord's Passion and refuses the emperor's lyre, Dioclétien orders him put to death ⚰.

"Il est mort, le bel Adonis"

WINDOW FOUR LE LAURIER BLESSÉ/THE WOUNDED LAUREL In Apollo's laurel grove, Sébastien receives each arrow crying "Encore!" Alone, he sees stigmata appear on his hands, and surrenders to holy ecstasy.

WINDOW FIVE LE PARADIS/PARADISE Saint-Sébastien's soul is received in heaven by choirs of martyrs, virgins, apostles, and angels singing in unison.

PELLÉAS ET MÉLISANDE
(Pelleas and Melisande)

✍ Drame lyrique in five acts (12 tableaux), 3¼ hours
☠ 1893 (rev. 1900–1902)

♇ 30 April 1902, Opéra-Comique, Paris, France
📖 Hector Berlioz, after the 1891 play by Maurice Maeterlinck

Pelléas et Mélisande enjoys a unique place in the history of opera as the gateway to the 20th century. Although Debussy fought to escape Wagner's shadow, there are echoes of *Tristan und Isolde* and *Parsifal* in this work. But, inspired by Maeterlinck's play, a landmark work of Symbolist theatre, Debussy went further, creating a timeless world in which the characters communicate in the symbolic language of restrained passion. Indeed, as a lover of poetry, Debussy allows the flow of words to lead the uninterrupted music. Thus, in place of set-piece arias, the lyrics become an exquisite blend of declamatory chant and recitative, with the score playing the role of "musical scenery", as Debussy put it. The effect is a sensual, dreamlike, almost hypnotic atmosphere, one perfectly suited to the slow-motion tragedy that unfolds.

⚔ Maurice Maeterlinck tried unsuccessfully to sabotage Debussy's adaptation of his play after the Scottish soprano Mary Gardon was cast as Mélisande at the premiere, instead of Maeterlinck's mistress, Georgette Leblanc. ⚔

➔ PRINCIPAL ROLES ◆

Mélisande *soprano*
A mysterious and fragile young woman

Golaud *baritone*
A prince who marries Mélisande

Pelléas *tenor* or *baritone*
Golaud's half-brother

Arkel *bass*
King of Allemonde and grandfather to Pelléas and Golaud

Geneviève *mezzo-soprano*
Arkel's daughter, mother to Pelléas and Golaud

Yniold *soprano*
Golaud's young son from an earlier marriage

Un médecin *bass*
A doctor

Un berger *baritone*
A shepherd

PLOT SYNOPSIS

The imaginary kingdom of Allemonde

ACT ONE Lost in a forest, Prince Golaud comes across a weeping girl. He offers to recover her crown from a pool, but the terrified girl no longer wants it. Finally, giving her name as Mélisande, she nervously follows Golaud out of the forest. Six months later, Geneviève learns that Golaud, her widowed son, has married Mélisande and wants to make peace with Arkel, his grandfather. Golaud asks his half-brother Pelléas to light a lantern on the castle tower signalling if he can return. Later, residing in the castle, Mélisande is walking with Geneviève when Pelléas joins them. He is disturbed to meet her. As they watch a ship set sail, Pelléas announces that he too will soon leave.

ACT TWO Pelléas leads Mélisande to an old well. When she tries to touch the water, her ring, given to her by Golaud, falls into the well. At the same moment, Golaud is thrown from a horse. As Mélisande nurses

Mireille Delunsch as Mélisande and José van Dam as Golaud in Robert Wilson's production at the Opéra Bastille, Paris, in 2004.

305

him in bed, he notices her ring is missing. When she says she lost it in the cave by the sea, he tells her to find it and instructs Pelléas to accompany her. Mélisande is afraid, but Pelléas insists they enter the dark cave.

ACT THREE Mélisande is combing her hair by her window when Pelléas calls

"Mes longs cheveux descendent"

to her . He wants to kiss her hand, but cannot reach it. Suddenly her long hair tumbles down and Pelléas wraps himself in it passionately. Golaud appears and chides them. Outside the castle vaults, Golaud warns Pelléas to stay away from Mélisande, who is pregnant and fragile. Golaud questions his son, Yniold, about Mélisande and Pelléas. He then holds the boy to peer into Mélisande's room. Yniold sees her with Pelléas, but they are looking at a light in silence.

ACT FOUR Pelléas must see Mélisande alone and they agree to meet by the well. Arkel is trying to lift Mélisande's spirits. Golaud bursts in and, insulting her to her face, drags her across the floor by her hair. Pelléas finally tells

"On dirait que ta voix"

Mélisande of his love. "I love you too," she responds . They hear a noise and realize that they are doomed. As they kiss, Golaud kills Pelléas.

ACT FIVE Mélisande lies wounded in bed and asks to see the setting sun through the window

"Ouvrez la fenêtre"

. She calls Golaud to her side and he asks for her forgiveness . He then interrogates her.

"Est-ce vous, Golaud?"

"Did you love Pelléas?" he asks. "Why yes," she replies. Was it "forbidden" love? Mélisande assures him it was not, but he does not believe her. Her baby is brought to her, but she is too weak to hold it. And without a sound, Mélisande dies. Arkel takes the child, saying, "It must live now, in her place."

Russian Opera

R USSIAN OPERA EMERGED in the 1830s as a nationalist reaction to domination by imported European culture. To compete with Italian opera in particular, young composers mined Russian history, religion, and folklore for stories and melodies. The result was opera with a distinctly Russian sound and style, at once patriotic and mournful, dramatic and romantic.

IMPERIAL ROOTS

In 1712, Peter the Great moved his capital to St Petersburg from Moscow in order to open up Russia to Europe's modernizing influence. This process was accelerated by the German-born Catherine the Great, who modelled her court – its architecture and its culture – on Versailles. In 1783, with opera all the rage in Western Europe, she ordered the new Bolshoi Theatre in St Petersburg to perform opera – inevitably Italian – as well as drama.

LITERATURE LEADS THE WAY

A first response came when early 19th-century poets like Vasily Zhukovsky, Konstantin Batyushkov, and the towering figure of Aleksandr Pushkin discovered a native Russian voice in folklore and pre-Romanov history. These writers in turn paved the way for the emergence of Russian-language opera, set to Russian themes. Indeed, from the time of Mikhail Glinka, who pioneered the new nationalist school of music, Russian opera used literature as its primary source.

Glinka himself became the acknowledged "father" of Russian opera thanks to just two works: *Zhizn' za tsarya*, or *A Life for the Tsar*, also

The sumptuously ornate Mariinsky Theatre in St Petersburg, the cradle of Russian opera, has followed the example of the Royal Opera House in London by renovating its backstage areas.

known as *Ivan Susanin* (1836), a patriotic story about a peasant who saved a Tsar; and *Ruslan i Lyudmila*, or *Ruslan and Lyudmila* (1842), a fairy-tale opera based on a Pushkin poem. Both became immensely popular, not least because they echoed the musical traditions of folk melodies and Russian Orthodox sung liturgies.

A declamatory style of singing, which blended aria and recitative and would become a key trait of Russian opera, was developed by Aleksandr Dargomyzhsky in *Rusalka*, which premiered in 1856, and *Kamenny gost*, or *The Stone Guest*, staged posthumously in 1872. Although neither was successful, Dargomyzhsky reinforced the idea that Russian music owed nothing to Italy or Germany. This spirit inspired the opening of the Mariinsky Theatre in St Petersburg in 1860, and of music conservatories in St Petersburg in 1862 and in Moscow in 1866.

Valery Gergiev, artistic director of the Mariinsky Theatre in St Petersburg, has been an influential promoter of Russian opera in the West.

THE MIGHTY FIVE

Promoted by Dargomyzhsky, Romantic nationalism became the leitmotiv of a group of young, self-taught composers known to the West as "The Five", and in Russia as *Moguchaya Kuchka*, literally "The Mighty Five". Mily Balakirev, the group's authoritarian leader, and César Cui, also a music critic, gave political voice to the movement, while the others – Modest Mussorgsky, Aleksandr Borodin, and Nicolay Rimsky-Korsakov – played a central role in transforming Russian opera. Of these, Mussorgsky became the

An avant-garde poster announces the Leningrad premiere of Shostakovich's *Lady Macbeth of the Mtsensk District* in 1934, but the opera was later banned.

unchallenged "Verdi" of Russia: indeed, the 1862 premiere of Verdi's opera, *La forza del destino*, in St Petersburg may have influenced Mussorgsky's *Boris Godunov*, the first of his two landmark "national musical dramas", which premiered in 1874. His other great work, *Khovanshchina*, was completed by Rimsky-Korsakov and staged in 1886, five years after the composer's death. To this day, these vast historical tableaux, rich in choruses and spectacle, stand as monuments to the Russian soul.

Similarly stirring, though less performed, is Borodin's *Knyaz' Igor'*, or *Prince Igor*, a political drama set in the 12th century, which was also unfinished when he died in 1887; it was completed by Rimsky-Korsakov and Aleksandr Glazunov, and staged in 1890.

Rimsky-Korsakov was the most prolific of the group, composing not only operas, but orchestral music. In the spirit of The Five, he turned in 1873 to Russian history for his first opera, *Pskovityanka*, or *The Maid of Pskov*, also known as *Ivan the Terrible*.

In later operas, though, he often favoured Russian folklore for his material. His most popular work, *Zolotoi petushok*, or *The Golden Cockerel*, a fairy-tale about a foolish Tsar, can readily be interpreted as political satire.

TCHAIKOVSKY'S LUSH ROMANTICISM

In contrast, Pyotr Tchaikovsky was a student of Anton Rubinstein, a renowned pianist and composer who was openly critical of the nationalists. And while Tchaikovsky could hardly ignore The Five, he found a more cosmopolitan voice of his own, composing deeply romantic ballet and orchestral music as well as "tragic

love" operas of universal appeal. Two won worldwide acclaim: *Yevgeny Onegin*, or *Eugene Onegin*, first performed in 1879, and *Pikovaya Dama*, or *The Queen of Spades*, which premiered in 1890, three years before his death.

Still, it was Rimsky-Korsakov who kept alive a more Russian tradition through two of his students, Igor Stravinsky and Sergey Prokofiev. Both composers left Russia in their early thirties and absorbed other influences, but a strong Russian colour was always perceptible in their music.

Stravinsky joined Diaghilev's Ballets Russes in Paris and, after the 1917 Russian Revolution, he made his home there until he left for the United States in 1940. His early vocal works were radically modernist and not conventional operas: *Solovyei*, or *The Nightingale*,

Throughout the Soviet era, the government controlled culture, as evidenced by propaganda decorating the Bolshoi Theatre, Moscow.

ДА ЗДРАВСТВУЕТ КОММУНИСТИЧЕСКАЯ ПАРТИЯ СОВЕТСКОГО СОЮЗА !

RUSSIAN OPERA

	1836 Glinka's *Zhizn' za tsarya*	**1842** Glinka's *Ruslan i Lyudmila*		**1856** Dargomyzhsky's *Rusalka*		**1862** Premiere of Verdi's *La forza del destino* in St Petersburg		**1879** Tchaikovsky's *Yevgeny Onegin*	**1886** Mussorgsky's *Khovanshchina*
1825				**1850**				**1875**	
	1837 Death of Pushkin			**1860** Opening of Mariisnky Theatre in St Petersburg		**1873** Rimsky-Korsakov's *Pskovityanka*	**1874** Mussorgsky's *Boris Godunov*		

was described as a lyrical story, while *Oedipus Rex* was an opera-oratorio. Yet when he wrote a full-length opera, *The Rake's Progress*, it was unabashedly Mozartian in its lyricism.

STALIN'S SHADOW

Prokofiev left Russia in 1917, more for professional than political reasons. And, while away, he wrote several operas, including *Igrok*, or *The Gambler*, for Brussels; *Lyubov k trem apelsinam*, or *The Love for Three Oranges*, for Chicago; and *Ognenny Angel*, or *The Fiery Angel*, for Paris. Although he never broke with Moscow, his return home in 1936 proved disastrous. "Socialist realism" had just been declared the regime's artistic doctrine, while executions and disappearances of Stalin's perceived enemies were threatening the artistic world.

In 1936, Dmitry Shostakovich, who had earlier made his mark in opera with *Nos*, or *The Nose*, saw his avant-garde second opera, *Ledi Makbet Mtsenkovo Uyezda*, or *Lady Macbeth of the Mtsensk District*, denounced by the regime. Soon, only melodic "Russian" music was acceptable. Even Prokofiev's highly patriotic adaptation of Tolstoy's great novel, *Voina i mir*, or *War and Peace*, was considered politically suspect. Then, in 1948, in the infamous *Zhdanov Decree*, Prokofiev and Shostakovich were among the composers attacked for neglecting beauty in favour of "formalism". Intimidation suffocated creativity:

ALEKSANDR PUSHKIN

Russian opera's secret weapon has been its close association with popular literature. Thus, since the 19th century, Russian opera-goers have usually been familiar with the stories being staged to music. Some plots were borrowed from Gogol, Dostoevsky, and Tolstoy, but the Russian writer who inspired most operas – no fewer than 23 – is Aleksandr Pushkin, Russia's most beloved poet. Indeed, it is a measure of Pushkin's extraordinarily eclectic oeuvre that composers as different as Glinka, Mussorgsky, Tchaikovsky, Rimsky-Korsakov, and Stravinsky all turned to him for their material.

in the four decades that followed, no new Russian opera of importance was composed. And while Soviet opera houses continued to produce 19th-century classics, only *Boris Godunov* and *Yevgeny Onegin* held their ground around the world. Since the collapse of the Soviet Union in 1991, however, opera has again become a flag-carrier for "Russianness". And even long-neglected Russian operas are now entering the repertory of companies and theatres around the world.

1900			1925		1950	
	1917 Bolshevik Revolution	1924 Death of Lenin			1945 Prokofiev's (incomplete) *Voina i mir*	1953 Death of Stalin
	1909 Rimsky-Korsakov's *Zolotoi petushok*	1921 Prokofiev's *Lyubov k trem apelsinam*		1934 Shostakovich's *Ledi Makbet Mtsenkovo Uyezda*	1951 Stravinsky's *The Rake's Progress*	

MIKHAIL IVANOVICH
GLINKA

Born: 1 June 1804, Novospasskoye, Russia
Died: 15 February 1857, Berlin (Germany)

Mikhail Ivanovich Glinka is the acknowledged father of Russian opera. After studying music in St Petersburg, he travelled to Italy where he came under the sway of Bellini and Donizetti. But when he returned home, he set out to write an opera in Russian, about Russia, with echoes of Slavic folk songs and church music. The result, *Ivan Susanin*, or *A Life for the Tsar*, was an immediate success. Glinka's next opera, the fairy-tale *Ruslan i Lyudmila*, took five years to write and was initially poorly received. Yet the Russian colour of its arias, choruses, and orchestration came to define Russian "nationalist" music for the 19th century.

RUSLAN I LYUDMILA
(Ruslan and Lyudmila)

✍ Opera in five acts, 3¼ hours
♨ 1837–1842
♟ 9 December 1842, Bolshoi Theatre,

St Petersburg, Russia
📖 Konstantin Bakhturin, Valerian Shirkov, and others, after the poem by Aleksandr Pushkin

Ruslan i Lyudmila is considered the cornerstone of Russian opera. In truth, it was neither Russia's nor Glinka's first opera, yet its influence on later Russian composers was fundamental. Until Glinka, Italian opera dominated St Petersburg's musical taste. Indeed, echoes of Italian *bel canto* can still be heard in this score. Yet, along with its fairy-tale plot and richly attired cast, the opera's melancholic arias, stirring choruses, riotous dances, and Oriental colour all conspire to place *Ruslan i Lyudmila* firmly in Russia. The libretto, written by five amateurs, is famously uneven, but this does not detract from a succession of delightful arias. One of the finest is *"I zhar, i znoi smenila nochi ten"*, sung by a contralto in the "trouser role" of Ratmir.

> → PRINCIPAL ROLES ←
>
> Svetozar *bass* Grand Prince of Kiev
> Lyudmila *soprano* His daughter
> Ruslan *baritone* A warrior and Lyudmila's beloved
> Ratmir *contralto* A suitor to Lyudmila
> Gorislava *soprano* Ratmir's slave
> Naina *mezzo-soprano* An evil fairy

⚜ Pushkin's untimely death in a duel prevented him from turning his poem into an opera libretto. Another reason for the confused plot, however, is that Konstantin Bakhturin reportedly sketched the scenario in three hours while drunk. ⚜

An elaborate set designed by Boris Bilinsky for a 1930 Paris production represents the castle of the Grand Prince of Kiev, the setting for Lyudmila's suitors to court her in Act I.

PLOT SYNOPSIS

Russia around the 9th century

ACT ONE Svetozar, Prince of Kiev, has summoned his court to celebrate the betrothal of his daughter, Lyudmila. She has chosen the warrior Ruslan over Ratmir, an oriental prince, and Farlaf, another warrior, who are also present. After the minstrel Bayan sings of the travails of love, Lyudmila tells of her sadness to leave home, ♫ and her happiness to marry Ruslan.

"Grustno mne, roditel' dorogoi"

Suddenly the court is plunged into darkness and, when light returns, Lyudmila has disappeared. Distraught, Svetozar offers her hand – and half his kingdom – to the man who rescues her.

ACT TWO The good magician Finn tells Ruslan that Lyudmila has been abducted by Chernomor, an evil dwarf. Finn also warns Ruslan against the sorceress Naina. After Naina orders Farlaf to wait, Ruslan finds himself on a desolate battlefield and is consumed by melancholy ♫.

"O pole, pole"

Suddenly a giant head appears, identifying itself as Chernomor's brother. In a brief combat, Ruslan recovers a sword, which will enable him to defeat the dwarf.

ACT THREE Arriving in Naina's palace, Ratmir is wooed by Naina's dancing maidens ♫

"I zhar, I znoi smenila nochi ten"

and quickly loses interest in Gorislava, a slave who loves him. Instead, under Naina's spell,

Ruslan falls for her. Finally, Finn restores Ratmir to Gorislava and sends Ruslan in search of Lyudmila.

ACT FOUR In captivity in Chernomor's castle, Lyudmila yearns for Ruslan and laments her fate ♫. When Ruslan approaches, Chernomor puts her to sleep and rushes out to fight the warrior. Ruslan enters, holding Chernomor's long beard triumphantly in his hand. But Lyudmila cannot be awoken. Ruslan worries that she has betrayed him, then decides to take her home to Kiev.

"Vdali ot milogo"

ACT FIVE Ratmir, again with Gorislava, is now Ruslan's ally. On the way to Kiev, Farlaf steals Lyudmila, but she sleeps on. Finn then gives Ratmir a ring that will break Chernomor's spell. And when Ruslan finds Lyudmila in Kiev, the ring works its magic. As they finally marry, the court rejoices.

Yevgeny Nikitin as Ruslan waits for Svetozar (Gennady Bezzubenkov) to give Lyudmila (Lyudmila Dudinova) away, at St Petersburg's Mariinsky Theatre.

"*Enough of writing for pleasure. You must give your whole self to the people. That is what art needs.*"

Modest Petrovich Mussorgsky

MODEST PETROVICH
MUSSORGSKY

Born: 21 March 1839, Karevo, Russia
Died: 28 March 1881, St Petersburg, Russia

Modest Petrovich Mussorgsky, the most nationalistic of Russian composers, is best known for his operatic epic *Boris Godunov*, and for song cycles depicting ordinary life. Rejecting "art for art's sake", he wrote vocal music that echoed the inflections and intonations of the spoken language. He did this through declamatory arias and choruses shaped by the Orthodox church and popular tradition.

Mussorgsky was destined for a military career and, at 17, entered the Imperial Guard. From childhood, though, his mother gave him piano lessons and his wealthy father encouraged his love of music. Later, the composer Mily Balakirev helped him, but he was largely self-taught. At 19, after a nervous breakdown, he left the army.

A first visit to Moscow, the discovery of Mikhail Glinka's music, and his encounter with Balakirev awakened Mussorgsky's patriotic feelings for Russia. This led to his song cycle, *Detskaya*, and the immense challenge of *Boris Godunov*. After initial rejection and extensive revision, *Boris Godunov* finally premiered to popular – though not critical – acclaim in 1874.

By that time, his life was increasingly disrupted by alcoholism. Periods of temperance allowed him to compose his major works before his final years were again dominated by drinking. In early 1881, he was diagnosed with alcoholic epilepsy. He died just one week after his 42nd birthday. He planned *Khovanshchina* as the second in a trilogy of historical operas. But it was unfinished at his death and was completed by Rimsky-Korsakov. Mussorgsky's legacy includes the popular piano suite, *Pictures at an Exhibition*, but it was *Boris Godunov* that secured his place in opera history.

Vladimir Matorin conveys both the power and anguish weighing down Boris Godunov in a lavish production by Moscow's Bolshoi Opera, presented at the Royal Opera House, London, in 1999.

FIRST PERFORMANCES

1870 —

1874
Boris Godunov

1886
Khovanshchina

1880 —
1881
Death

1890 —

1900 —

1909
1910 — Zhenit'ba

1913
Sorochinskaya
Yarmuka

1920 —

BORIS GODUNOV

✍ National music drama in a prologue and four acts, 3¼ hours
☰ 1868–1869 (rev. 1871–1872)

♇ 8 February 1874, Mariinsky Theatre, St Petersburg, Russia
📖 Mussorgsky, after Pushkin's historical drama

Boris Godunov is in many ways the most Russian of operas, a sombre and grandiose spectacle in which the Russian people, both long-suffering and invincible, play the central role. Mussorgsky devoted great energy to this work, not only writing its libretto, which involved condensing Pushkin's drama, but also totally revising the score after it was first rejected by the Mariinsky Theatre. The opera's plot was acceptable to the Romanovs because it described Russia's disorder in the early 17th century, well before their rise to power. It was also patriotic since it portrays resistance to a Polish invasion. Above all, with Russian folk songs and Orthodox chants echoing through choruses and melancholic arias, *Boris Godunov* evokes a vast *tableau vivant* of Russia's troubled history and anguished soul.

✦ PRINCIPAL ROLES ✦

Boris Godunov *bass*
Tsar of Russia

Fyodor *mezzo-soprano*
His son

Xenia *soprano*
His daughter

Grigory *tenor*
The Pretender Dimitry

Marina Mniszek *mezzo-soprano*
Daughter of a Polish governor

Prince Shuysky *tenor*
Adviser to Boris Godunov

Pimen *bass*
A monk

Simpleton *tenor*
A Holy Fool

⚎ Mussorgsky extracted his libretto from Pushkin's play, but he was also influenced by Shakespeare's *Macbeth*, the story of another tyrant who murdered his way to power and provoked a foreign invasion of his land. ⚏

PLOT SYNOPSIS

Russia and Poland between 1598 and 1605

PROLOGUE Guards outside the Novodevitchy Monastery order the crowd to beg Boris Godunov to accept the nomination to succeed Tsar Fyodor. In Moscow, bells ring as a procession moves into the cathedral. The crowds cheer when the newly-crowned Tsar appears, but Boris is filled with foreboding.

ACT ONE Six years later in the Chudvov Monastery, Father Pimen is writing his chronicle of Russian history

"Yeshcho odno" | ♪. Grigory, a fellow monk, wakes and Pimen reminisces about Ivan the Terrible and his son, Fyodor. Pimen says the murderers of Dimitry, Fyodor's young half-brother, confessed they were sent by Boris. He notes that Dimitry would now be Grigory's age. At an inn near the

A set design by Alexander Golowin shows the sumptuous staging long associated with Russian productions of this ever-popular opera.

Lithuanian border, Grigory arrives with two mendicant monks. Police appear with a warrant for his arrest, and he escapes.

ACT TWO Boris comforts his sad daughter and tells his son to study hard. He then despondently contemplates his destiny,

"Dostig ya vysshei vlasti" | his sleep haunted by images of a bloodied child . Shuysky brings news of a false Pretender to Boris's throne called Dimitry, who is supported by Rome and Lithuania. Boris says a dead child cannot challenge a crowned Tsar, but then wonders if the murdered boy really was Dimitry. When Shuysky describes the wounds on his body, Boris sees Dimitry's ghost. In panic, he begs God's mercy for the "guilty Tsar Boris".

ACT THREE In a castle in Poland, Marina, the governor's daughter, dreams of

"Skuchno Marine, akh kak skuchno-to!" | becoming Tsarina . The Jesuit Rangoni urges her to convert Orthodox Russia to Catholicism. For that, he says, she must seduce the Pretender Dimitry. Marina objects, but Rangoni rebukes her. Nearby,

FEODOR CHALIAPIN

Feodor Chaliapin, the great Russian bass, made the title role of *Boris Godunov* his own (*below*). Still in his early twenties when he first sang the part in 1895, he returned frequently to it over the next three decades across Europe and the United States. Acclaimed for his remarkable voice and great stage presence, he was also famous for his interpretation of operas by Rimsky-Korsakov, Verdi, Rossini, and Mozart. Chaliapin left the Soviet Union in 1922 and died in Paris in 1938.

Dimitry yearns for Marina . Marina announces that only the | "V polnoch', v sadu, u fontana" | Russian throne tempts her. Angered, Dimitry responds that, once crowned, he will laugh at her. Suddenly Marina pledges her love.

ACT FOUR When urchins steal the Simpleton's last kopek, he asks Boris to kill the urchins, just as he killed young Dimitry. Boris asks for his prayers, but the Simpleton says he cannot pray for Herod. A deranged Boris appears at the boyar's council, imagining little Dimitry alive. Pimen the monk recounts a miracle at the child's tomb. Suddenly suffocating, Boris names his son the new Tsar and dies | "Ostav'te nas! Ujdite vse" | . In a forest, the Pretender calls on the people to follow him. As the mob leaves, the Simpleton weeps bitter tears | "Leytes, leytes, Slyozy gor'kiye" | for Russia .

Evgeny Akimov as the Simpleton sings his lament for Russia's future in the Kirov Opera's production, presented at London's Royal Opera House in 2005.

KHOVANSHCHINA

(The Khovansky Uprising)

♫ National music drama in five acts, 3 hours
🗓 1872–1880 (completed by Rimsky-Korsakov 1884–1886)

🏛 21 February 1886, Kononov Auditorium, St Petersburg, Russia
📖 Modest Petrovich Mussorgsky

Khovanshchina, inspired by the success of *Boris Godunov*, plunges into the late 17th-century turmoil that accompanied Peter the Great's rise to power and the birth of modern Russia. Planned as the second in a trilogy, this spectacle interweaves individual passions with political and religious disputes central to the Russian identity. Mussorgsky spent eight years on the opera and died before finishing it. It was completed by Nikolay Rimsky-Korsakov and was re-orchestrated by Dmitry Shostakovich in 1960. It nonetheless retains Mussorgsky's distinct musical colour, with declamatory arias driving the narrative and powerful choruses evoking Russia. Mussorgsky took most of his characters from history, but he invented the pivotal role of Marfa.

⚜ One of this opera's peculiarities is that its principal hero never appears: at the time, no Romanov could be portrayed on stage, so the young Peter the Great plans his victory out of public view. ⚜

> ✦ PRINCIPAL ROLES ✦

Prince Ivan Khovansky *bass*
Leader of the Streltsy militia

Prince Andrey Khovansky *tenor*
His son

Prince Vasily Golitsyn *tenor*
A Tsarist ally

Shaklovity *bass* or *baritone*
A boyar, or nobleman, and Tsarist ally

Dosifey *bass*
Leader of the Old Believers

Marfa *mezzo-soprano*
An Old Believer who loves Prince Andrey

Susanna *soprano*
An Old Believer

Emma *soprano*
A girl from the German quarter pursued by Prince Andrey

PLOT SYNOPSIS

Moscow, Russia, between 1682 and 1689

ACT ONE After the death of Tsar Alexis, his daughter, Sophia, is acting as regent for the young Tsars Ivan and Peter. Sophia and her former lover, Prince Golitsyn, are fighting the Old Believers who oppose religious reforms. Some Old Believers support the Streltsy militia, headed by Prince Ivan Khovansky, which defends feudalism. Shaklovity, a nobleman, warns Sophia anonymously of Khovansky's plot to put his son, Andrey, on the throne. As a scribe reads out graffiti describing Streltsy atrocities, Khovansky arrives and, to cheers,

"Deti, deti moi" | denounces the Western ideas assailing Russia ♫.

Andrey is pursuing Emma, a German girl. When he tries to kiss her, he is stopped by Marfa, his former mistress and now an Old Believer. Khovansky also desires Emma, but Dosifey, the

Ornate costumes designed by the Russian artist Leon Bakst in 1913 reflect the religious and historical importance of this opera to Tsarist Russia.

leader of the Old Believers, protects the girl and calls on Khovansky to save the true faith.

ACT TWO Golitsyn reads a letter from Sophia recalling their passion and seeking his help. Marfa then tells his fortune and predicts disgrace and exile for him. Enraged, he orders her

drowned. Khovansky and Dosifey arrive and the three men argue over Russia's destiny. Marfa returns, claiming a Golitsyn servant tried to kill her. She is followed by Shaklovity, who announces that Tsar Peter is investigating the Khovansky conspiracy.

ACT THREE Marfa relives her love for Andrey ♫, but Susanna, another Old Believer, accuses her of heresy. Dosifey tells Marfa to gain comfort by fighting to save her country. As Shaklovity mourns Russia's unhappy lot ♫, drunken Streltsy arrive, chased by their wives. The scribe brings word that Streltsy families are being attacked. Recognizing Tsar Peter's new power, Khovansky orders the militiamen home.

"Iskhodila mladyoshen'ka"

"Spit streletskoye gnezdo"

ACT FOUR Dancing girls are entertaining Khovansky when he learns he is in danger. He dismisses the threat. Shaklovity invites him to a Council of State convened by Sophia, then kills him. Dosifey watches Golitsyn head for exile and learns of orders to destroy the Old Believers. When Andrey comes looking for Emma, Marfa tells him that she has left Moscow and that Khovansky is dead. At first furious,

John Tomlinson as Dosifey, leader of the Old Believers, summons his followers in Francesca Zambello's production at the English National Opera in 2003.

Andrey then begs Marfa to save him. As she hides him, a herald announces that the Tsars have pardoned the Streltsy.

ACT FIVE Dosifey summons the Old Believers. Andrey and Marfa recall their love ♫. As trumpets announce Tsar Peter's troops, the Old Believers build a funeral pyre and Dosifey, Marfa and Andrey are consumed by flames.

"Ya ne ostavlyu teby"

BELIEVERS, OLD AND NEW

Written in the 1880s about events two centuries earlier, *Khovanshchina* has assumed fresh topicality. In the opera, the Old Believers oppose secular power and political reform, just as today religious fundamentalists in many countries continue to resist modernization. Just three months after the terrorist attacks of 11 September 2001, a new Paris production explored these parallels.

Andrei Serban's 2001 production at the Opéra Bastille, Paris, underlined religious fanaticism.

"Truly there would be reason to go mad were it not for music."

Pyotr Ilyich Tchaikovsky

PYOTR ILYICH
TCHAIKOVSKY

Born: 7 May 1840, Kamsko-Votkinsk, Russia
Died: 6 November 1893, St Petersburg, Russia

Pyotr Ilyich Tchaikovsky is best known for his symphonies, concertos, and ballet music, but he paid enormous attention to operas and, with *Eugene Onegin* and *The Queen of Spades*, he wrote two masterpieces, both inspired by Aleksandr Pushkin. He composed several other operas that were popular in his lifetime, but they are now rarely performed outside Russia.

Tchaikovsky was eight when his family moved to St Petersburg, the centre of court and musical life in Russia. Only six years later, his beloved mother died, a loss which may have contributed to his difficulty in loving another woman. He was 22 by the time he entered the St Petersburg Conservatory and was quick to try his hand at opera. His first, *The Voyevoda*, went largely unnoticed, while his second was never staged. But *The Oprichnik* then won him plaudits in St Petersburg.

His fourth opera, *Vakula the Smith*, was influenced by the "nationalist" school of music, but he turned back to a more European style for *Eugene Onegin*, which would become Russia's most popular opera. While instrumental music was earning him fame abroad, he continued writing operas for Russia, including *Mazeppa* and *The Enchantress*. Meanwhile, his personal life was often complicated and unhappy. In 1877, he was persuaded to get married with disastrous results. At the same time, his letters suggest he felt guilty about his homosexuality. Still, with *The Queen of Spades*, an unusual work which dwells on the obsessions of a man rather than the loves of a woman, Tchaikovsky again achieved operatic greatness. Completed three years before his death, it soon joined *Eugene Onegin* in the standard opera repertoire.

Marina Ivanova as Chloe in Graham Vick's production of *Pikovaya Dama* (*The Queen of Spades*) at the Glyndebourne Festival in 1995.

FIRST PERFORMANCES

1860

1870

1869
Voyevoda
(The Voyevoda)

1874
Oprichnik
(The Oprichnik)

1876
Kuznets Vakula
(Vakula the Smith)

1880

1879
Yevgeny Onegin
(Eugene Onegin)

1881
Orleanskaya
Deva (The Maid of Orleans)

1884
Mazepa (Mazeppa)

1887
Charodeika (The Enchantress)

1890

1890
Pikovaya Dama
(The Queen of Spades)

1892
Iolanta (Iolanthe)

1900

YEVGENY ONEGIN
(Eugene Onegin)

🎵 Lyrical scenes in three acts and seven scenes, 2½ hours
🕮 1877–1878

🏛 20 March 1879, Maliy Theatre, Moscow Conservatory, Russia
📖 Pyotr Tchaikovsky and Konstantin Shilovsky

Yevgeny Onegin is considered Russia's most popular opera, inspired by one of Pushkin's most beloved poems. Yet while it evokes bourgeois country life under the Tsars, its music is decidedly Western, with little of the spectacle and none of the religious and folk colour preferred by other Russian composers of Tchaikovsky's era. Indeed, with its numerous introspective arias, this is essentially an intimate opera. It is also a love story which is stained by tragedy and ends unhappily. Tatyana's famous and lengthy "letter scene" captures the dreams of a young woman whose imagination is shaped as much by literature as by the yearning for love. Onegin's callous response to her love then establishes the dark tone of the opera.

> ### → PRINCIPAL ROLES ←
>
> **Mrs Larina** *mezzo-soprano*
> The estate owner
>
> **Tatyana** *soprano*
> Her eldest daughter
>
> **Olga** *contralto*
> Her youngest daughter
>
> **Yevgeny Onegin** *baritone*
> Tatyana's beloved
>
> **Lensky** *tenor*
> Olga's fiancé
>
> **Prince Gremin** *bass*
> A retired general and Tatyana's husband
>
> **Filipyevna** *mezzo-soprano*
> Tatyana's nurse

⊹ Tchaikovsky's fear of failure led him to premiere *Yevgeny Onegin* with students from the Moscow Conservatory, although in practice their young voices were not equipped to meet the emotional challenges posed by its central roles. The opera's success soon attracted more mature singers. ⊹

PLOT SYNOPSIS

The Larin country estate near St Petersburg, Russia, in the late 18th century

ACT ONE As her daughters Tatyana and Olga sing about love and sorrow, Mrs Larina reminisces with her maid, Filipyevna. Peasants arrive to dance and sing for Mrs Larina. Tatyana says the songs make her dream, but Olga says she prefers to dance to them. Tatyana attributes her own pallor to the sad love story she is reading.

Olga's fiancé, Lensky, arrives with a friend, Yevgeny Onegin, who tells Lensky he chose the wrong sister. Tatyana is excited 🔊. Onegin wonders if life is not boring in the country, but she says she reads and dreams. That evening, Tatyana tells Filipyevna that she is in love. She then takes pen and paper and, between hesitations and fears, writes a

"Skazhi, kotoraya Tatyana?"

LOVE, IN LIFE AND ART

Tchaikovsky had already begun work on Tatyana's "letter scene" in May 1877 when he received a passionate love letter from Antonina Milyukova, a former student at the Moscow Conservatory. Shaken by the coincidence, Tchaikovsky accepted Antonina's marriage proposal, saying he would not play Onegin to her Tatyana. The marriage, perhaps intended to conceal the composer's homosexuality, lasted barely three months and drove Tchaikovsky to attempt suicide. Somehow, through all of this, *Yevgeny Onegin* was completed.

"Puskai pogibnu ya" long love letter to Onegin . Sealing it, she notes, "It's too frightening to read over." The following morning, it is delivered. A few days later, Tatyana awaits Onegin in her garden. Promising frankness equal to hers, he says that he is not made for marriage and predicts that she will soon turn

"Kogda bi zhizn domashnim krugom" her ardour elsewhere. Tatyana is shattered.

ACT TWO Guests at a party for Tatyana include Lensky and Onegin, who decides to break the tedium by flirting with Olga. Lensky is irritated, but Olga scoffs at his jealousy. A Frenchman toasts Tatyana's beauty and health but, as the dancing resumes, Lensky broods. When Onegin suggests he is mad, they start arguing.

"V vashem dome!" Finally, to everyone's horror, Lensky challenges Onegin. He then bids Olga farewell forever. The following morning, as he awaits

"Kuda, kuda, kuda vi udalilis" Onegin, Lensky again dreams of Olga. Finally Onegin arrives and the two men ask themselves why they are fighting not laughing. In the duel, Onegin fires and Lensky falls dead.

ACT THREE Years later, Onegin is bored at a ball in St Petersburg. Prince Gremin enters with his wife and Onegin recognizes Tatyana. The elderly Gremin sings of his great love for Tatyana and introduces Onegin to her. She recalls having previously met Onegin, then asks to leave. Onegin realizes he loves her. In Gremin's house, Tatyana feels her passion for Onegin returning. When Onegin appears, she wonders if he is now attracted by her new status. Onegin declares his love for her, but she asks him to leave. She admits she still loves him, but will never betray her husband. Onegin is left alone with his remorse.

"Onegin! ya togda molozhe"

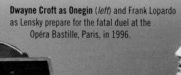

Dwayne Croft as Onegin (*left*) and Frank Lopardo as Lensky prepare for the fatal duel at the Opéra Bastille, Paris, in 1996.

PIKOVAYA DAMA

(The Queen of Spades)

⚜ Opera in three acts, 2¾ hours
♫ 1890
♆ 19 December 1890, Mariinsky Theatre,

St Petersburg, Russia
📖 Modest Tchaikovsky, after Pushkin's novella
Pikovaya Dama (1834)

Pikovaya Dama reached the stage almost by accident. Tchaikovsky's brother, Modest, wrote the libretto in 1886 for a different composer, who then lost interest. Finally, four years later, Tchaikovsky was persuaded to take it on. Written in 44 days during a sojourn in Italy, it became his own favourite opera. The libretto presents a less cynical hero than in Pushkin's novella: Herman shows genuine affection for Liza, rather than simply using her. Tchaikovsky also sets the action some 40 years earlier than Pushkin so that he can introduce Mozartian dance music. Finally, while Pushkin's Herman ends up in a mental asylum, here Herman chooses suicide. The opera's music is unabashedly romantic even as its story grows ever darker.

➤ PRINCIPAL ROLES ➤

Herman *tenor*
An army officer
The Countess *mezzo-soprano*
Liza *soprano*
Her granddaughter
Pauline *contralto*
Liza's companion
Prince Yeletsky *baritone*
Liza's betrothed
Count Tomsky *baritone*
An army officer
Chekalinsky *tenor*
An army officer
Surin *bass*
An army officer

⚜ Tchaikovsky wrote this opera with a particular singer in mind. But he then worried whether the tenor Nicolai Figner could handle the demanding role of Herman, who appears in every scene. ⚜

PLOT SYNOPSIS

St Petersburg, Russia, in the late 18th century

ACT ONE In St Petersburg's Summer Gardens, army officers discuss their colleague, Herman, and his obsessive gambling. Nearby, Tomsky remarks on Herman's gloominess. Herman explains

"Ya imeni yeyo ne znayu" | he is in love with a woman but does not know her name ♣.

Prince Yeletsky is congratulated on his engagement to Liza, who arrives with her grandmother, the Countess. Herman recognizes Liza as his beloved, while she is intrigued by Herman as a mysterious stranger. As the women leave, Tomsky tells how, years earlier, having gambled away all her money, the Countess gave herself to Count St Germain in exchange for the secret of three winning cards. Then, after sharing the secret with her husband and a young man, an apparition warned her that she would die by the hand of the next person she told. Girlfriends entertain Liza, who insists she is not sad. But, alone, she bursts into tears ♣,

"Otkuda eti slyozy"

realizing she has fallen for the stranger. Suddenly

A 1999 set design by the Russian artist Sergei Alimov injects a Surrealist idiom to this strange story.

Vitali Taraschenko as the obsessive Herman is visited by the skeletal ghost of the Countess in a 2000 production at the New Theatre, Cardiff.

"Prosti, nebesnoye sozdanye" | Herman arrives. When she begs him to leave, he proclaims his love for her ♪. He takes her in his arms and they declare their love.

ACT TWO At a masked ball, Yeletsky and Liza enter and, noticing her sadness, the

"Ya vas lyublyu" | prince reiterates his love for her ♪. After a pastoral *intermezzo*, a masked Liza slips Herman the key to her grandmother's bedroom, which leads to her own. In her bedroom after the ball, the Countess dozes off. She awakens to find Herman demanding the secret of the winning

"Yesli kogda nibud' znali vy chuvstvo lyubvi" | cards ♪. When she remains silent, he draws a revolver and she dies of shock.

Hearing Herman complain that the Countess did not reveal the secret, Liza feels betrayed and expels him.

ACT THREE At his army barracks, Herman receives a letter from Liza absolving him of her grandmother's death. Distraught, Herman recalls that the dead Countess winked at him from her coffin. Her ghost then appears and, telling him to marry Liza, finally shares the gambling secret. Awaiting Herman, Liza is plunged in sorrow ♪. When he arrives, they fall into each other's arms. But before

"Akh! Istomilas ya gorem"

eloping, he says, he must test the Countess's secret. When Liza accuses him of killing the Countess, he mocks her. As he leaves, Liza drowns herself in a canal. At the gambling table, Herman raises the stakes. He calls out three – and wins. He calls out seven – and again wins. But when he calls out ace, the Queen of Spades instead appears in his hand. Seeing the Countess's ghost, a terrified Herman stabs himself. With his dying breath, he begs for forgiveness.

A LIKEABLE VILLAIN

Although Herman, this opera's anti-hero, is a manic obsessive, Tchaikovsky described him as "a real, alive, and even likeable person" and wept when he scored the character's death. One reason may be that, to the end, Herman remains true to his belief that gambling is more important than love. Thus, he becomes fixated with extracting the secret of the winning cards from the old Countess. But while he succeeds, their dramatic confrontation leads to the dénouement which Tchaikovsky so lamented.

NIKOLAY
RIMSKY-KORSAKOV

Born: 18 March 1844, Tikhvin, near Novgorod, Russia
Died: 21 June 1908, Lyubensk, near St Petersburg, Russia

Nikolay Rimsky-Korsakov was a prolific composer of lushly melodic music as well as an influential teacher who shaped a generation of Russian composers, including Prokofiev and Stravinsky. Outside Russia, he remains best known for his orchestral pieces, *Capriccio espagnol* and *Sheherazade*, but he was also active in opera. He edited *Boris Godunov* and completed *Khovanshchina*, both by his friend Mussorgsky, and he wrote 15 stage works of his own, starting with *Pskovityanka*, or *The Maid of Pskov* a tragic love story set in the time of Ivan the Terrible. But *Zolotoi petushok*, or *The Golden Cockerel*, a satire on war, is Rimsky-Korsakov's only opera regularly performed outside Russia.

ZOLOTOI PETUSHOK
(The Golden Cockerel)

✍ Opera in three acts, with prologue and epilogue, 1¾ hours
☒ 1906–1907

♔ 7 October 1909, Solodovnikov Theatre, Moscow, Russia
📖 VI Belsky, after the 1834 fairy-tale by Pushkin

Zolotoi petushok, or *The Golden Cockerel*, is a fairy-tale with a political message critical enough for Russian censors to demand cuts. Since Rimsky-Korsakov refused to comply, the opera was performed only after his death – with cuts required by officials. The libretto, adapted from a Pushkin fairy-tale in verse, fits into a Russian folk tradition, but the score is

> ❖   **PRINCIPAL ROLES**   ❖
>
> Tsar Dodon *bass* The ruler of Russia
> Prince Gvidon *tenor* The Tsar's son
> Prince Afron *bass* The Tsar's second son
> General Polkan *bass* The Tsar's chief of staff
> The Astrologer *very high tenor*
> The Queen of Shemakha *soprano*
> The Golden Cockerel *very high soprano*

nonetheless sophisticated, notably in its orchestration. The vocal parts are particularly testing because of the high register of the Astrologer and Golden Cockerel roles and the requirement that king and queen dance while they sing in Act II. This work's best-known aria is the queen's "hymn to the sun" in Act II, while the bridal procession in Act III is a musical *tour de force*.

⊰ This opera mocks a monarch who attacks a neighbouring country and is defeated. Understandably, Russian authorities were upset: two years earlier, the Russo–Japanese War proved to be equally disastrous for Tsar Nicholas II. ⊱

The stage design for an early production of Rimsky-Korsakov's opera uses architecture to suggest a fantasy world that is not too distant from Russia itself.

PLOT SYNOPSIS

A land which could be Russia in no specific period

PROLOGUE The Astrologer announces that his fairy-tale has a moral.

ACT ONE Tsar Dodon summons his chief of staff, General Polkan, and his sons, Gvidon and Afron, for advice on fighting the country's enemies so that he can retire to bed. Gvidon and Afron make suggestions, which Polkan dismisses. The Astrologer presents a Golden Cockerel who will perch on a steeple and warn if an invasion is imminent ♌.

"Slaven bud', velikiy tsar'!"

Delighted, the tsar offers payment, but the Astrologer says he will name his price later. After the tsar's maid sings him to sleep ♌, he

"Veshnim dnyom sosnut' zdorovo"

dreams of an Oriental princess. Shaken from his slumber by the Cockerel, he dispatches his sons to the war front and goes back to sleep. But the Cockerel again sounds the alarm. This time, Dodon reluctantly dons his rusty armour and sets off with his army to save the country, cheered on by his people.

ACT TWO On a foggy night, Dodon discovers that his army has been defeated and that his sons have killed each other. As dawn breaks, a richly decorated Oriental tent comes into view. Emerging from it, the Queen of Shemakha celebrates the rising sun ♌. She then proclaims her desire to

"Otvet' mnye, zharkoye svetilo"

conquer Dodon's kingdom and orders the tsar to sing and dance until he collapses in exhaustion. Now in the queen's sway, the tsar proposes to her. While the queen's servants mock him, she prepares to take over his land.

In a 2002 production at the Théâtre du Châtelet in Paris, Olga Trifonova as the Queen of Shemakha sings to dawn.

ACT THREE Dodon returns home, accompanied by the queen and a procession of slaves, dwarfs, giants, and bizarre animals. The Astrologer arrives and, reminding the tsar of his promise to pay any price for the Cockerel, he says he wants to marry the queen ♌. Dodon tries

"Tsar' velikiy, eto ya!"

to dissuade him, then kills him with his sceptre. As the queen laughs, the Cockerel flies down and, with one peck, kills the tsar. A fierce storm erupts and, when it passes, the queen, the Astrologer and the Cockerel have vanished. The people lament.

EPILOGUE The Astrologer announces that only he and the queen were real and that everyone else was an illusion.

IGOR FYODOROVICH
STRAVINSKY

Born: 17 June 1882, Lomonsov, Russia
Died: 6 April 1971, New York, US

Igor Fyodorovich Stravinsky had a major influence on modern music. He came out of a Russian musical tradition, but spent most of his life in France and the United States. The son of an opera singer, he studied under Rimsky-Korsakov before composing numerous scores for Diaghilev's Ballets Russes. Of these, *The Firebird* and *The Rite of Spring* caused a shock with their fierce rhythms and lively orchestral colouring. Although Stravinsky remained close to the stage throughout his life, three of his four operas – *The Nightingale*, *Mavra*, and *Oedipus Rex* – were short. *The Rake's Progress*, written after he fled France for the United States in 1940, is his only full-length opera.

THE RAKE'S PROGRESS

✍ Opera in three acts and an epilogue, 2¼ hours
⊠ 1947–1951
♔ 11 September 1951, La Fenice, Venice, Italy

📖 WH Auden and Chester Kallman, after William Hogarth's etching and engraving series, *A Rake's Progress* (1735)

The Rake's Progress took Stravinsky on an unlikely journey. Having discovered Hogarth's prints in Chicago in 1947, he met the poet WH Auden and his partner, Chester Kallman, a playwright. From the eight engravings in *A Rake's Progress*, the couple created a brilliant verse libretto. Around this 18th-century plot, Stravinsky decided to write a pastiche of a late 18th-century opera in his own Neo-Classical style. For this, he unabashedly took inspiration from Mozart, notably *Così fan tutte*. Mozartian touches include accompanying the recitative with a harpsichord, inserting a coloratura soprano aria and ending the opera with a *Don Giovanni*-like epilogue. The result is Stravinsky's most lyrical score, a far cry from the pulsating rhythms of *The Rite of Spring* 40 years earlier.

> ➔ **PRINCIPAL ROLES** ←
>
> **Trulove** *bass* A country gentleman
> **Anne Trulove** *soprano* His daughter
> **Tom Rakewell** *tenor* A rake loved by Anne
> **Nick Shadow** *baritone* Tom's servant
> **Mother Goose** *mezzo-soprano* A brothel-keeper
> **Baba the Turk** *mezzo-soprano* Tom's wife

Show business glamour drew Stravinsky to Hollywood after he fled Europe in 1940, yet *The Rake's Progress* might never have been written if he had succeeded in his ambition to compose movie scores.

The final plate of Hogarth's morality tale, *Scene in Bedlam*, is reflected in Act III of this opera when Tom Rakewell goes mad.

In a production designed by David Hockney, Victoria Vergara shows her face as Baba the Turk at the San Francisco Opera in 1988.

PLOT SYNOPSIS

England in the 18th century

ACT ONE Anne Trulove is to marry Tom Rakewell. Her father has found work for him, but Tom prefers to live off his wits. When he wishes for money, Nick Shadow appears, announcing that Tom has been left a fortune by a mysterious uncle. As he hurries to London, Tom promises Anne that she will soon follow ♬. At Mother Goose's brothel in London, Tom and Shadow are discussing beauty, pleasure and love. Tom wants to leave, but Shadow persuades him to join the drinking and dancing. Mother Goose then takes him to bed. Meanwhile, with no word from Tom, Anne leaves for London ♂.

"Laughter and light"

"I go, I go to him"

ACT TWO Tom has tired of wine and women ♂. When he yearns for happiness, Shadow shows him a picture of Baba the Turk. Tom scoffs at the idea of marrying her, but quickly changes his mind. Anne sees Tom arriving in a sedan chair. He tells her to return home, but she refuses. A veiled Baba emerges from the sedan chair and is introduced as Tom's wife. As Anne leaves, the crowd asks Baba

"Vary the song"

to remove her veil and show her long beard. Tom's room is crowded with strange gifts collected by Baba. When he tires of her, she starts breaking them in rage. Tom silences her by putting her wig on her back-to-front. Shadow arrives with a machine to resolve the world's problems.

ACT THREE The contents of Tom's house are being auctioned. When the auctioneer tears off Baba's wig, she expels everyone except Anne. She tells Anne to rescue Tom and announces her return to her life as an entertainer. Shadow says he now expects payment for his services. And since Tom is broke, the payment is Tom's soul – unless he can correctly identify three hidden cards. When he succeeds, a furious Shadow makes him insane. Now in a mental asylum, Tom believes he is Adonis. When Anne arrives, he sees Venus and asks her to sing a lullaby ♂. As he sleeps, Anne bids him farewell. Awakening, Tom begs the other madmen to weep for Adonis.

"Gently, little boat"

EPILOGUE The players warn: "For idle hands/ And hearts and minds/ The Devil finds/ A work to do."

SERGEY
PROKOFIEV

Born: 11 April 1891, Sontsovka, Ukraine
Died: 5 March 1953, Nikolina Gora, near Moscow, Russia

Sergey Prokofiev wrote memorable music in many genres: sonatas, symphonies, film scores, and ballet music, including *Romeo and Juliet* and *Cinderella*. He also wrote a dozen operas. Of these, *War and Peace* is now judged the most significant, but only his fairy-tale, *The Love for Three Oranges*, was a success in his lifetime.

Prokofiev studied under Rimsky-Korsakov at the St Petersburg Conservatory, where his talent as a pianist led to his first compositions. While there, he also wrote five operas, although none was immediately staged. After the 1917 Revolution, he left for a lengthy tour of the United States. Later, living in Europe, Prokofiev wrote magical symphonies and ballet music, although a new opera, *The Fiery Angel*, was not performed until 1954. He returned to Moscow in 1936, but difficult times lay ahead. During World War II, his "patriotic" opera, *Semyon Kotko*, was poorly received. He spent years composing *War and Peace*. In 1948, he was attacked by the regime. Even his death went largely unnoticed because Stalin had died a few hours earlier.

IN AMERICA

To escape the disarray of post-revolutionary Russia, Prokofiev travelled to the United States in mid-1918. His American sojourn would prove tumultuous. While he was well received in Chicago, where the Lyric Opera commissioned *The Love for Three Oranges*, New York critics labelled him the "Bolshevik pianist" and criticized his "orgy of discordant sounds". In fact, even after he settled in Europe, his American tours followed this pattern: a hit in Chicago and a flop in New York. Had he felt more appreciated in the United States, Prokofiev might have made his home there and averted the pain of his return to Moscow.

***The Fiery Angel* is a** provocative opera about religious hysteria in 16th-century Germany. Nuns try to calm a sister possessed by spirits in this 1965 production at Sadler's Wells Opera, London.

LYUBOV K TREM APELSINAM
(The Love for Three Oranges)

🎵 Opera in a prologue and four acts, 1¾ hours
📅 1919
🏛 30 December 1921, Chicago Lyric Opera, US

📖 Sergey Prokofiev, after Carlo Gozzi's 1761 play
Fiaba dell'amore delle tre melarance

The Love for Three Oranges is a delightful fairy-tale inspired by *commedia dell'arte*. While the story could not be sillier, it is a response to the bombast of 19th-century opera. First performed in French in Chicago, its huge cast and fast pace leave little room for arias or set pieces, although the score is full of life and humour. The opera's most famous melody is provided by the "March" in Act II.

⚜ The idea that love can cast a magic spell takes on a whole new meaning in this opera: the Prince falls madly in love with three large oranges, unaware that each contains a princess. ⚜

✦ PRINCIPAL ROLES ✦

King of Clubs *bass*

The Prince *tenor*
His melancholic son

Princess Clarissa *contralto*
The king's ambitious niece

Leandro *baritone*
Clarissa's henchman

Truffaldino *tenor*
The court clown

Fata Morgana *soprano*
An evil sorceress

PLOT SYNOPSIS

The court of the King of Clubs and Creonte's palace

PROLOGUE Tragedy, Comedy, Lyric Drama, and Farce are boasting when the audience (The Ridiculous People) chases them off.

ACT ONE The king learns that his son's hypochondria can be cured only by laughter, but Leandro wants the prince to die so Princess Clarissa can be queen.

ACT TWO The prince finally laughs when Fata Morgana slips and tumbles ♂. Furious, she makes him fall in love with three oranges.

"Kha-kha Kha-kha-kha"

Martial Defontaine as the prince sleeps while François le Roux's Truffaldino opens two oranges in a 2005 production at the Netherlands Opera.

ACT THREE Tchelio helps the prince steal the oranges. When the prince falls asleep, Truffaldino the clown cuts open two of the oranges and finds two princesses. When they die of thirst, he flees. The prince awakens, opens the third orange and falls in love with Princess Ninetta ♂. Fata Morgana turns Ninetta into a rat.

"Truffaldino, Truffaldino"

ACT FOUR As Tchelio turns the rat back into Ninetta, the king orders Clarissa and Leandro put to death. But Fata Morgana helps them escape. The Ridiculous People then toast the happy prince and princess.

VOINA Y MIR
(War and Peace)

◭ Lyric dramatic scenes in two parts, 4¼ hours   (heavily cut concert version)
⛉ 1941–1943 (rev. 1946–1952)   ▭ Sergey Prokofiev and Myra Mendelson, after
♇ 7 June 1945, Conservatory, Moscow, Russia   Leo Tolstoy's novel (1863–1869)

Adapted from Tolstoy's monumental novel, *War and Peace* is Prokofiev's operatic masterpiece. Planned as a small-scale work focused on the vagaries of love, it assumed a patriotic dimension after Nazi Germany invaded the Soviet Union in June 1941. As a result, a romantic "peace", which dwells on Natasha's fickle love, is followed by a "war" which exalts the suffering and heroism of the Russian people in the tradition of Mussorgsky's *Boris Godunov*. This is reflected in the score: Part I offers a Tchaikovsky-like lyricism, while Part II evokes "eternal" Russia through rousing choruses that were designed to please the Kremlin. To add authenticity, Prokofiev researched military music of the era. However, although he imagined it being performed over two evenings, this opera is rarely produced because of its prohibitive length and the need for 70 soloists.

⌐ Tolstoy might not have welcomed Prokofiev's opera: in his final years, the increasingly irascible novelist proclaimed Russian folk songs to be superior to classical music and dismissed opera as absurd. ⌐

⇴ PRINCIPAL ROLES ⇴

Natasha Rostova *soprano*
The daughter of an impoverished landowner

Prince Andrey Bolkonsky *baritone*
Natasha's betrothed

Prince Nikolay Bolkonsky *bass-baritone*
His father

Count Pyotr Bezukhov (Pierre) *tenor*
Prince Andrey's friend

Hélène Bezukhova *mezzo-soprano*
His wife

Prince Anatol Kuragin *tenor*
Lover of Natasha

Lieutenant Dolokhov *baritone*
Prince Anatol's friend

Field Marshal Prince Mikhail Kutuzov *bass*
Russian army commander

Napoleon Bonaparte *baritone*
French emperor

PLOT SYNOPSIS

Russia between 1809 and 1812

PART ONE PEACE The widowed prince, Andrey Bolkonsky, is moved by hearing Natasha Rostova sing of the joys of spring ♪. Months later, at a New Year's Eve ball, they fall in love and become engaged. But Andrey's father, objecting to their marriage, sends his son away for a year in the hope that Andrey will forget her. Natasha worries that their love may not survive the separation. In May, during a party at Count Pierre's house, Natasha meets Prince Anatol Kuragin, who declares his love for her and kisses her ♪. Natasha's cousin warns her of Anatol's

"Ja ne budu, ja ne magu spat'"

"Chudo, kak khorosha ona, krasavitsa takaya"

disrepute, but she has been won over. The next night, before eloping with Natasha, Anatol visits his friend, Dolokhov. When Dolokhov reminds him that Natasha is engaged and that he is married, Anatol laughs that he cannot resist young women. Natasha's plan to elope has been discovered by Madame Akhrosimova, in whose house she is residing. The grande dame chastizes Natasha for her foolishness and recruits Pierre to tell her that Anatol is married ♪. Suddenly remorseful,

"Natalya Ilyinishna"

At the start of Part Two, peasants and volunteers prepare to defend Mother Russia against Napoleon's invading forces at the Paris National Opera in 2000.

A PAINFUL BIRTH

Once Communist Party officials grasped the parallels between Napoleon/Hitler and Kutuzov/Stalin, meddling in Prokofiev's operatic project was inevitable. A heavily-cut concert version of Part I ("Peace") was performed in 1946. But after the dress rehearsal of Part II ("War") in 1947, officials cancelled the production, saying it lacked heroism. It was only in 1959, six years after Prokofiev's death, that the opera was finally staged as written (*below*).

Natasha begs Pierre to ask Andrey to forgive her. Pierre, in turn, wishes that he could marry someone like Natasha. He then orders Anatol to give up Natasha and leave Moscow. As word arrives that Napoleon has advanced on Russia, volunteers prepare to join the army.

PART TWO WAR It is August 1812 and Russia's army of peasants and volunteers is confident of defeating Napoleon in the Battle of Borodino. Aware of Natasha's betrayal, Andrey is ready to die, even refusing a safe post at Field Marshal Kutuzov's headquarters. As the battle begins, Napoleon is impressed by Russian resistance, but he wins the day. Kutuzov debates whether to defend Moscow or to withdraw and regroup. Reluctantly, he decides to abandon Moscow ♫. After Napoleon's forces take Moscow, Muscovites set fire to the city ♫. Pierre learns that Natasha's family has fled with some wounded Russian soldiers, including Andrey. Pierre sets out to assassinate Napoleon, but is arrested. Meanwhile, a delirious Andrey recalls his love for Natasha. She recognizes him and begs him for his forgiveness ♫, but his life cannot be saved. Forced to retreat by the fierce Russian winter, the French army escorts Russian prisoners along the Smolensk road. Armed partisans free some prisoners, including Pierre. Hearing of the death of Andrey and his own wife, Pierre believes he can now love Natasha. As Kutuzov announces Russia has been saved, the people sing the glory of the motherland.

> "Kogda zhe, kogda zhe reshilos' eto strashnoye delo?"

> "Pred vragom Moskva"

> "Neuzheli tol'ko lish zatem sud'ba segodnya"

Olga Guryakova as Natasha meets Irina Bogatcheva's Madame Peronskaya (*left*) in Francesca Zambello's 2000 production of *War and Peace* at the Opéra Bastille, Paris.

DMITRY DMITREVICH
SHOSTAKOVICH

Born: 25 September 1906, St Petersburg, Russia
Died: 9 August 1975, Moscow, USSR

Dmitry Dmitrevich Shostakovich was the most important composer to emerge from the Soviet era. While he was forced to adapt to the regime's changing artistic diktats, his music engaged Russian tradition even as it forged Russian Modernism. His best-known work was orchestral, notably his *Fifth Symphony*, but he also wrote ballet and movie music as well as one major opera.

Born into a cultivated St Petersburg family, Shostakovich's teenage years were accompanied by both political turmoil and artistic ferment. At 19, he was acclaimed for his *First Symphony*. And, just four years later, in 1929, he presented his first opera, *Nos*, or *The Nose*. His next opera, *Ledi Makbet Mtsenkovo Uyezda*, or *Lady Macbeth of the Mtsensk District*, was initially well received. But after it was attacked by the official press in 1936, Shostakovich largely abandoned opera. He was hailed as a patriot for his *Seventh Symphony*, written during Nazi Germany's siege of Leningrad. But in 1948 he was attacked for "formalism". Then, after Stalin's death, he was again treated as a Soviet hero.

BRAVE OR COWED?

Decades after his death, Shostakovich's political views remain a topic of heated debate: admirers note that he was denounced by the Soviet regime in 1936 and 1948, while critics recall that he joined the Communist Party in 1960 and accepted state honours, such as the Lenin Prize. The fairest assessment may be that, unwilling to defect, he became a survivor: to enjoy any artistic freedom led him to find ways of coexisting with the dictatorship.

Shostakovich (*left*) joins firemen on the roof of the Leningrad Conservatory in 1941 during the prolonged siege of Leningrad in World War II.

NOS
(*The Nose*)

✍ Opera in three acts, 1¾ hours
🕮 1927–1928
🎭 18 January 1930, Maliy Opera Theatre,

Leningrad, Russia
📖 Dmitry Shostakovich, after the short story by Gogol (1835)

Nos, or *The Nose*, is a decidedly eccentric work, above all for a young composer writing his first opera. Combining the avant-garde influence of Berg, Schoenberg, and Hindemith with a bizarre libretto inspired by Gogol, this work at times verges on the anarchic. With a huge cast swarming the stage and over 70 named roles squeezed into a fast-paced score, ensembles take precedence over arias, expressionism over lyricism.

⌦ While this opera is clearly allegorical, Shostakovich shielded himself from criticism by suggesting it recounted a genuine human misfortune. "Why laugh at a poor wretch who has just been so disfigured?" he asked. ⌫

> ✦ PRINCIPAL ROLES ✦
>
> **Platon Kuzmich Kovalyov** *baritone*
> A civil servant
>
> **Ivan Yakovlevich** *bass-baritone*
> A barber
>
> **Police Inspector** *very high tenor*
>
> **Nose** *tenor*
>
> **Madame Podtochina** *mezzo-soprano*
>
> **Her daughter** *soprano*

PLOT SYNOPSIS

St Petersburg, Russia, in the 1830s

ACT ONE Kovalyov, a civil servant, is being shaved. The next morning, Yakovlevich the barber finds a nose in his bread roll and is ordered by his wife to dispose of it. He drops it in the river, but is spotted by the Police Inspector, who arrests him. Kovalyov discovers that his nose is missing and, after a fruitless search, decides to report the loss to the police. At the St Isaak Cathedral, he sees that his nose has become a state councillor, but it escapes.

ACT TWO Unable to find the inspector, Kovalyov tries to place an advertisement in the local newspaper, but the clerk suspects it contains a coded message and refuses him 🎵. He returns home in despair.

"Ya ne mogu vam skazat', kakim obrazom"

ACT THREE The inspector believes that the nose may flee town. As a coach prepares to leave, the nose tries to stop it. The crowd beats the nose. Finally, it reverts to its nasal shape and is taken to Kovalyov. But the nose refuses to return to its proper place, persuading Kovalyov that Madame Podtochina has cursed him for rejecting her daughter 🎵. Meanwhile, amid scenes of confusion, the entire town is still looking for the nose. Kovalyov wakes up with his nose back on his face. When a young woman responds to his advances, he is sure that he is again whole.

"Vinoyu etogo dolzhen byt' nikto drugoy"

Jeremy Huw Williams as Kovalyov tries to reattach his nose in the Opera Group's 2001 production.

LEDI MAKBET MTSENKOVO UYEZDA

(Lady Macbeth of the Mtsensk District)

✍ Opera in four acts and nine scenes, 2½ hours   ☞ 22 January 1934, Maly State Opera and
⚱ 1930–1932 (rev. 1935; and as *Katerina*   Ballet Theatre, Leningrad, Russia
Ismailova 1956–1963)   ☐ Dmitry Shostakovich and Alexander Prei

Ledi Makbet Mtsenkovo Uyezda was a daring venture for a composer in his mid-twenties. It may even have verged on reckless for Shostakovich to present the Lady Macbeth-like murderess of Nikolay Leskov's original story as "an affectionate woman, a deeply sensitive woman, by no means lacking in feeling". Certainly, by giving Katerina moments of both passion and reflection, he tries to explain her crime. The Shabby Peasant, an Old Convict, and Boris,

Katerina's father-in-law, all sing lively arias, but they are generally parodied in Shostakovich's orchestration. Although some critics found the opera coarse, it had over 100 performances in the two years before it was banned. Shostakovich later revised it as *Katerina Ismailova*. Today, opera houses prefer *Ledi Makbet*.

✄ The famous love-making scene between Katerina and Sergey need not be staged explicitly since the orchestration in the final scene of Act I, which makes heavy use of the brass section and includes suggestive trombone slides, portrays sexual passion with unusual vividness. ✄

PLOT SYNOPSIS

Kursk Gubernia, Russia, in the mid-19th century

ACT ONE Katerina is weary of life

"Akh, nye spitsa bol'she"

♫. Boris, her father-in-law, complains she has produced no heir, but she blames her husband, Zinovy. Boris orders her to find rat poison. As he leaves on business, Zinovy introduces a new labourer, Sergey. Boris tells Katerina to swear to be faithful to her husband. Aksinya, the maid, warns Katerina that Sergey is a skirt-chaser. Labourers, Sergey, and the Shabby Peasant molest Aksinya. Katerina mocks them for pretending to be brave. Sergey suggests wrestling with her. Boris discovers them on the floor and threatens to inform Zinovy. Naked in her bedroom, Katerina wishes someone would come to her. Sergey arrives and makes a pass at her. At first, she resists, then surrenders to wild love-making.

ACT TWO Boris reminisces about his philandering youth and imagines satisfying Katerina ♫.

"Pod oknami u chuzhikh"

When he spots Sergey leaving her room, his servants beat Sergey and lock him in a store-room. Katerina serves Boris mushrooms with rat poison. Feeling ill, he summons a priest. Boris tells the priest that Katerina has poisoned him – then dies. Unconcerned, the priest sings a quick requiem. In bed with Sergey, Katerina demands more passion, but he says their affair must end when Zinovy returns because he cannot share her ♫. She promises to marry him. Katerina

"Katerina Lvovna"

is awakened by Boris's ghost, who curses her. She then hears noises in the house. As Sergey hides, Zinovy appears, accuses her

STALIN AS MUSIC CRITIC

Ledi Makbet Mtsenkovo Uyezda was popular until Stalin attended a performance in December 1935. The following month, the Communist Party daily paper called it "Muddle instead of music", and complained that "singing is replaced with screaming". As for the work's popularity abroad, "is it not explained by the fact that it tickles the perverted tastes of the bourgeoisie with its fidgety, screaming and neurotic music?"

of infidelity, and beats her. She cries out for Sergey, who kills Zinovy with a candle-stick and hides him in the cellar.

ACT THREE The Shabby Peasant sings the praises of vodka and sets out looking for

"U menya byla kuma" | more drink ♪. Breaking into the cellar, he finds Zinovy's rotting corpse.

The police sergeant is annoyed that he was not invited to Katerina's wedding party. When the Shabby Peasant brings word of the body, the police rush off to fill up on food and drink at the wedding. Everyone is drunk except Katerina. Noticing that the cellar's door is open, she prepares to flee with Sergey when the police arrive. She promptly invites them to handcuff her.

ACT FOUR In a labour camp, an old convict laments his unhappy lot. Katerina finds Sergey, still yearning for his love, but he

"Nye legko posle pochota da poklonov" | rejects her ♪. Instead, he desires

Sonyetka, but she at first rejects him, saying she wants stockings as

proof of his love. Claiming he is ill, Sergey borrows Katerina's stockings and disappears with Sonyetka. Then, seeing Sonyetka standing on a bridge, Katerina pushes her into the river, and jumps in herself. An officer announces they have drowned and the prisoners move off, singing.

Larissa Gogolevskaya interprets Katerina opposite Viktor Lutsyuk as her lover Sergey in a 2002 production at the Mariinsky Theatre in St Petersburg.

c.1860–1940

Czech Opera

A S NATIONALISM SPREAD through 19th-century
Europe, opera played a key role in preparing the Czechs
for independence. Centuries of rule by the German-speaking
Habsburgs had smothered the Czech identity. But, as part of a
cultural renaissance known as the Czech National Revival, opera
gave pride of place to the Czech language, history, and folklore.

A FOLK LEGACY

After the ancient
kingdoms of Bohemia,
Moravia, and Slovakia
were absorbed into the
Austrian Empire in 1526,
Prague and Brno came
under the sway of
Viennese culture and the
German language. Music,
though, was an exception.
While Czech folk music
survived in rural
communities, Italian opera
came to dominate urban

The cover of the first edition
of Leoš Janáček's *Jenůfa* already
suggests a dark story.

musical taste. The first Italian opera
was heard in Prague as early as 1627.
Within a century, Venetian opera
companies were installed there. Even
the two operas that Mozart premiered
in Prague – *Don Giovanni* in 1787 and *La
clemenza di Tito* in 1791 – were in Italian.

THE RISE OF CZECH CONSCIOUSNESS

The French Revolution and the
Napoleonic wars shook European
monarchies by spreading liberal ideas
and encouraging rebellion. Although
the Habsburgs outlasted the convulsion,
it inspired Czech aristocrats, artists, and
intellectuals to start forging a sense of
nationhood. In 1826, František Škroup
presented *Dráteník*, or *The Tinker*, the first
Czech-language opera, although at the
time the lingua franca of Czech culture
was still German. For instance, when
František Palacky began publishing his

monumental history of
the Czech nation in 1836,
he did so in German.

Then, in 1848,
accompanying new
political unrest across
Europe, a failed Czech
uprising gave fresh
impetus to the Czech
National Revival.
With the abolition
of serfdom, migration
from rural areas began
swelling Prague's Czech-
speaking population.
In 1853, publication of Karel Jaromír
Erben's *Garland of National Tales* gave
new respectability to Czech folk
stories. Božena Němková's 1855
novel, *Babička*, or *The Grandmother*,
also stirred national pride. Soon the
Czechs were united behind the goal
of building a National Theatre, paid
for by contributions from citizens.

In the interim, the Czech-language
Provisional Theatre opened in 1862
to compete with the official Estates
Theatre, which still presented
German-language plays and
Singspiels. And it was at the
Provisional Theatre that Czech
opera as such was born. One of
the first works to make an impact in
1866 was Bedřich Smetana's *Braniboři
Čechách*, or *The Brandenburgers in Bohemia*,
which daringly portrayed the horrors
of foreign occupation, albeit before
the Habsburgs. A few months later,

Smetana staged *Prodaná nevěsta*, or *The Bartered Bride*, a rural romance filled with folk melodies and dances.

SMETANA AS FATHER FIGURE

These two works – a historical opera and a "village opera" – provided the basic models for a new Czech form. Smetana himself also came to personify cultural nationalism, which, in musical terms, meant turning his back on Wagner and other German influence. Curiously, like other artists of his generation, Smetana was more fluent in German than in Czech. Yet he found a way of using the inflections of the Czech language to create a distinctively Czech musical sound. In 1868, his new historical opera, *Dalibor*, again set in pre-Habsburg times, included a song to freedom that became an informal Czech anthem.

The long battle to build the National Theatre was finally won in June 1881 when it opened beside the River Vltava with yet another Smetana opera, *Libuše*. But just two months later, it was destroyed by fire. This was considered such a national catastrophe that money was quickly collected for its reconstruction, aided by the popularity of Smetana's patriotic symphonic poem, *Ma Vlast*, or *My Country*. When the National Theatre reopened in November 1883, again with *Libuše*, Czech opera, drama, and ballet had at last a permanent home.

By the time Smetana died in 1884, Prague enjoyed a lively and increasingly autonomous cultural life. The Czech Philharmonic was founded in 1894, when many younger composers were at work. One who gained popularity was Zdeněk Fibich, a prolific composer of instrumental music, who also wrote nine operas, including *Nevěsta messinská*, or *The Bride of Messina*, *Bouře* and *Šárka*. Fibich is little-known

New pride in traditional peasant costumes and folk dances, such as this Bohemian polka, played an important role in the Czech National Revival.

abroad today, but he took part in the Czech National Revival, and was another composer who came to personify "Czechness".

In contrast, Antonín Dvořák was acclaimed across Europe and in the United States, where he wrote his ever-popular *Symphony for the New World*. But his reputation as an opera composer was always challenged at home by Smetana loyalists. His sin, in their view, was to echo "old" French and Italian influence, while Smetana was modern and authentically Czech. These attacks, which grew after Smetana's death, left Dvořák embittered. Nonetheless, even among Czechs, his

Prague's National Theatre on the banks of the Vltava River has long been a monument to Czech nationalism.

wonderfully melodic fairy-tale *Rusalka* eventually matched the popularity of Smetana's *Prodaná nevěsta*.

JANÁČEK THE MORAVIAN MAESTRO

Dvořák died in 1904, the same year that a little-known Moravian composer, Leoš Janáček, staged the first of his operatic masterpieces, *Jenůfa*, in the provincial city of Brno. Janáček's problem was that he did not belong to the cultural and political elite of Prague. Further, *Jenůfa* was adapted from a play which had provoked moral outrage in 1890. As a result, the opera did not reach the National Theatre in

CZECH OPERA

1787 Premiere of Mozart's *Don Giovanni* in Prague	1836 Volume I of František Palacký's history of the Czech nation	1853 Publication of Karel Jaromír Erben's *Garland of National Tales*	1866 Smetana's *Prodaná nevěsta* in Prague
1785	1800	1825	1850
	1815 Czech National Revival begins	1848 Czech uprising	1855 Publication of Božena Němková's *Babička*

Prague until 1916 when, belatedly, Janáček was finally recognized as a major Czech composer.

Then, in 1918, following the defeat of Germany and the Austro-Hungarian Empire in World War I, Czechoslovakia finally became an independent republic. Its freedom would last barely two decades before it was crushed by five years of Nazi occupation and 41 years of Communist dictatorship. But the 1920s were a period of cultural ebullience, with Janáček the undisputed leader of Czech opera, a reputation he consolidated through a series of ground-breaking operas, including *Kát'a Kabanová*. These also enjoyed a following in Germany and Austria, although Janáček's fame only spread further afield from the 1950s.

Since Janáček, no Czech opera composer has matched his stature. Bohuslav Martinů, best

known for *Řecké pašije*, or *The Greek Passion*, and *Julietta aneb Snář*, moved to France in the 1920s and spent World War II in the United States. Other post-war composers turned from the traditional Czech musical language towards electronic and experimental music. But Czech opera-goers continued to prefer music rooted in their past. And to this day, even after the separation of the Czech Republic and Slovakia in 1993, the people of the region still look to Smetana, Dvořák and Janáček as guardians of their nationalist sentiments.

A FOREIGN PROPHET

In 1947, Charles Mackerras, an Australian musician in his early twenties, studied conducting in Prague and, almost immediately, discovered Janáček's *Kát'a Kabanová*. Thanks to this meeting, Janáček and other Czech opera composers still unknown in the West became popular around the world. In 1951, Mackerras conducted the first British performance of *Kát'a Kabanová*. And in the years that followed, Janáček's other major operas all had their British premieres. In time, Mackerras also brought works by Smetana, Dvořák, and Martinů into the standard opera repertory. Between 1997 and 2003, he was principal guest conductor of the Czech Philharmonic.

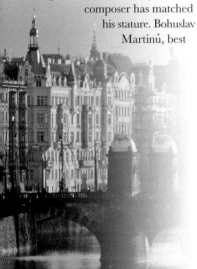

1875			1900			1925			1950
	1883 National Theatre reopens	**1894** Czech Philharmonic founded	**1904** Janáček's *Jenůfa* in Brno		**1918** Foundation of Czechoslovak Republic		**1938** Martinů's *Julietta aneb Snář*		
	1881 National Theatre opens in Prague; destroyed by fire		**1902** Dvořák's *Rusalka*	**1916** Janáček's *Jenůfa* in Prague	**1924** Janáček's *Kát'a Kabanová*		**1939** Nazi Germany occupies Czechoslovakia		

BEDŘICH
SMETANA

Born: 2 March 1824, Litomyšl, Bohemia (Czech Republic)
Died: 12 May 1884, Prague (Czech Republic)

Bedřich Smetana was the first great Czech opera composer, although he struggled to win recognition in his lifetime. In his twenties, out of frustration, he moved to Sweden. Then, in 1862, he returned home to write opera for Prague's new Provisional Theatre, starting with *The Brandenburgers in Bohemia*. This was followed by *The Bartered Bride*, the village opera that made him famous. His next work, *Dalibor*, was criticized as too Wagnerian, but is now considered a patriotic epic. In 1882, Smetana wrote his great symphonic tone poem, *Ma Vlast*, or *My Country*. Soon afterwards, chronic syphilis brought on lunacy and he died in a mental institution in 1884.

PRODANÁ NEVĚSTA
(The Bartered Bride)

🎵 Comic opera in three acts, 2¼ hours
🕮 1863–1866 (rev. 1869–1870)
♇ 30 May 1866, Provisional Theatre, Prague
(now Czech Republic)
📖 Karel Sabina

Prodaná nevěsta, or *The Bartered Bride*, is a delightful pastoral opera, but it took time for its distinctly Bohemian character to be accepted in a Prague still under Italian, French, and German musical influence. Indeed, the opera's initial lukewarm reception prompted Smetana to carry out a drastic revision, which he presented four years later, with three acts instead of two and sung voices replacing spoken dialogue. This version won over the Czechs. Its polka dances, rousing choruses, and traditional costumes evoke an idyllic and bucolic past, while its charming love story deftly captures the intrigues of village life. Musically, a succession of fine duets and Mařenka's "broken heart" aria in Act III provide lyrical stepping-stones through twists and turns in the plot.

> ✣ **PRINCIPAL ROLES** ✣
>
> Mařenka *soprano* Village girl
> Jeník *tenor* Mařenka's beloved
> Mícha *bass* His father, the wealthiest villager
> Vašek *tenor* Mícha's son
> Kecal *bass* A scheming marriage-broker
> Esmeralda *soprano* An acrobat

⚔ Operas traditionally travelled from Vienna to Prague, but *The Bartered Bride* reversed this practice when it reached Vienna in 1892. From there, its popularity quickly spread, with productions in Chicago in 1893 and London in 1895. ⚔

This frontispiece of a piano score of the ever-popular "People's March" from *Prodaná Nevěsta* shows traditional costumes and dancing.

PLOT SYNOPSIS

A Bohemian village fair in the 19th century

ACT ONE Mařenka reassures Jeník of her love, but reveals that her father wants her to marry Mícha's son, Vašek. She asks Jeník about his past and he recounts that, after his mother's death, his father remarried and he was driven from his home by his stepmother. He then wandered the world. Mařenka and Jeník vow undying love . Kecal, the local marriage-broker, tells Mařenka's parents that, while Mícha's son from an earlier marriage has disappeared, Mícha's other son, Vašek, would make a fine son-in-law. But Mařenka declares she only loves Jeník. As the villagers dance the polka, Kecal plots his next move.

"věrné milování"

ACT TWO Vašek, a stammering simpleton, builds up courage to woo Mařenka by reminding himself of his mother's warning: the entire village will mock him if he does not marry Mařenka . But he does not recognize her when she sweetly warns him against marrying the dreadful Mařenka, who will be the death of him. She makes Vašek swear not to marry this

"Má-ma-ma-matička"

Mařenka . Meanwhile, Kecal offers Jeník a bribe if he renounces Mařenka. Jeník takes the money on condition that Mařenka marry only "Mícha's son" and that her father's debts to Mícha be cleared. The villagers condemn Jeník for "selling" Mařenka, while Jeník is amazed that Kecal has been so easily duped.

"Známť já jednu divčinu"

ACT THREE The circus comes to town, but the "dancing bear" is hopelessly drunk and Esmeralda, an acrobat, persuades Vašek to play the role. Vašek worries that marrying Mařenka will kill him, but when he recognizes her, he wants to wed her. Mařenka is stunned by Jeník's betrayal . But Jeník presents himself as Mícha's missing son and claims his right to marry Mařenka. Mařenka understands the ruse and forgives him: Jeník keeps the bribe and wins the bride. Panic erupts because the bear has escaped. But when Mícha recognizes the foolish Vašek, he approves Jeník's marriage to Mařenka.

"Ten lásky sen"

Tomáš Černý as Jeník makes peace with Mária Haan as Mařenka in a production of this beloved Czech opera at the National Theatre in Prague in 2005.

ANTONÍN
DVOŘÁK

Born: 8 September 1841, Nelahozeves (Czech Republic)
Died: 1 May 1904, Prague (Czech Republic)

Antonín Dvořák is the Czech composer with the widest international following, thanks mainly to his symphonic work, notably his *Symphony for the New World*. But he met with less success as an opera composer. While he wrote ten operas, both comic and serious, his only lasting triumph was the romantic fairy-tale, *Rusalka*, presented three years before his death. More ambitious was *Dimitrij*, written 20 years earlier, in which the composer continues the story of Mussorgsky's *Boris Godunov*. But, except for *Rusalka*, Dvořák's operas were viewed by many Czechs as dramatically weak. In that sense, he failed in his lifelong ambition to be recognized as Smetana's heir.

RUSALKA

✍ Lyric fairy-tale in three acts, 3 hours
⚱ 1900
♇ 31 March 1901, National Theatre, Prague

(Czech Republic)
📖 Jaroslav Kvapil, after *Undine*, by FHC de la Motte Fouqué and folk-tales compiled by KJ Erben

Rusalka, a dreamily melodic opera about a water nymph who falls in love with a real prince, has its roots in northern European forest lore. The tale had already been used by La Motte Fouqué in *Undine*; by Hans Christian Andersen in *The Little Mermaid*; and by Pushkin in *Rusalka*. Kvapil then included some Slavonic features of the myth in his libretto. Dvořák's beautiful score occasionally evokes both Wagner and Debussy, but it too has earthier passages which underline its Czech identity. As a love story, it remains unusual: since Rusalka cannot speak to her prince, there is no conventional love duet. Nonetheless, the opera's finest arias – including the famous "Song to the Moon" – belong to Rusalka.

This set design for *Rusalka* perfectly captures the opera's distinctive underwater fairy-tale ambience.

> ➜ **PRINCIPAL ROLES** ◆
>
> Rusalka *soprano* A water nymph
> Water goblin *bass* The "father" of the water nymphs
> Ježibaba *mezzo-soprano* A witch
> Prince *tenor*
> Foreign princess *soprano*

⚜ Dvořák came to write *Rusalka* by chance: after three of Jaroslav Kvapil's composer friends turned down his libretto, it was recommended to Dvořák, who agreed to set it without even reading the text. ⚜

PLOT SYNOPSIS

A fairyland lake and castle

ACT ONE Rusalka rests in a willow tree while three wood nymphs tease a water goblin. She confides in the goblin that she has fallen for a man who swims in the lake and whom she embraces as a wave. If she were human, she says, he could kiss her too. Alarmed, the water goblin suggests she consult the witch Ježibaba. Alone, Rusalka asks the moon to shine on her beloved . She then tells Ježibaba why she wants to become human. The witch warns that she will have no voice and, if betrayed, will be forever damned. Rusalka drinks a magic potion. At the lake, the prince finds Rusalka standing before him and is overwhelmed by her beauty . When he questions her, she falls into his arms. Incredulous, he leads her to his palace.

"Měsíčku na nebi hlubokém"

"Ustaňte v lovu, na hrad vrat'te se"

ACT TWO Servants gossip about the prince's infatuation with the mysterious mute woman and hope a visiting foreign princess can distract him. The prince enters with Rusalka, complaining of her cold embraces. When the new princess presents herself, the prince tells Rusalka to dress for the ball. Upset to see the prince courting the princess, Rusalka finds the water goblin and pours out her sorrows. She returns to embrace the prince, but he pushes her aside. The water goblin tells him that he can never escape Rusalka. As Rusalka vanishes into a pond, the prince collapses at the feet of the princess.

ACT THREE Rusalka lies by the lake, dejected . Offering her a dagger, Ježibaba says she can save herself if she slays the man

"Necitelná vodní moci"

who seduced her, but Rusalka throws the weapon into the lake. Furious, Ježibaba leaves her to her fate. Rusalka plunges into the water, but her nymph sisters ignore her. Meanwhile, the prince's servants inform Ježibaba that their master is under Rusalka's spell. The prince arrives, asking for Rusalka's forgiveness and begging for a kiss . She warns that it will doom him, but he insists. She kisses him and he dies happily. As the water goblin laments that her sacrifice was in vain, Rusalka again kisses the prince and disappears into the lake.

"Milakču, znáš mne, znáš?"

The Czech soprano Gabriela Benackova as the love-struck water nymph Rusalka in Otto Schenk's 1993 production at the Metropolitan Opera in New York.

"*To deny the development of opera is to deny the development of the human spirit.*"
Leoš Janáček

LEOŠ
JANÁČEK

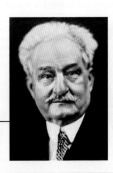

Born: 3 July 1854, Hukvaldy (Czech Republic)
Died: 12 August 1928, Moravská Ostrava (Slovakia)

Leoš Janáček, the most widely performed Czech opera composer, is now ranked among the giants of 20th-century opera. While his music often embraced folk traditions, his operatic scores were strikingly modern. He was 62 before he won national recognition, but his final years were enormously productive and included his masterpiece, *Kát'a Kabanová.*

Janáček attended musical conservatories in Prague, Leipzig, and Vienna before settling in the Moravian city of Brno. There he taught at a teachers' training college and the Brno Organ School, of which he became director. In 1884, the opening of the Brno Provisional Theatre awakened his interest in writing for the stage, but his first operas were either failures or not produced.

Finally, in 1904, after the success of *Jenůfa* in Brno, he devoted himself entirely to writing opera scores, using his own librettos. Even so, because of political intrigues and jealousies, *Jenůfa* only reached Prague in 1916. In the decade that followed, with a young married woman as his muse, he reached his prime, moving Czech opera far beyond the patriotic model established by Smetana. His music was notable for echoing the "speech melody" of the Czech language, while his often-sombre librettos touched on universal emotions.

His reputation quickly spread to Austria and Germany, but he was largely ignored in the rest of Europe and the United States until the 1960s. Since then, however, his operas have entered the repertory of lyric theatres around the world. In fact, rare is the opera house today that does not include one Janáček work in every season.

The Ukranian-born soprano Elena Prokina sings the tragic role of Kát'a, the ill-fated heroine of *Kát'a Kabanová,* Janáček's best-known opera, in a 1994 production at the Royal Opera House in London.

FIRST
PERFORMANCES

1890

1894
Počátek románu
(The Beginning
of a Romance)

1900

1904
Jenůfa

1920
Výlety páně
Broučkovy (The
Excursions of
Mr Broucek)

1910

1921
Kát'a Kabanová
(Katya Kabanova)

1924
Příhody lišky
bystroušky (The
Cunning Little
Vixen)

1920

1926
Věc Makropulos
(The Makropulos
Affair)

1928
Death

1930
Z mrtvého domu
(From the House
of the Dead)

1930

1934
Osud (Fate)

1940

JENŮFA

♫ Opera in three acts, 2 hours
☰ 1894–1903 (rev. 1907–1908)
⚖ 21 January 1904, National Theatre, Brno, (now
Czech Republic)
📖 Leoš Janáček, after Gabriela Preissová's 1890
play, Její pastorkyňa (Her Stepdaughter)

Jenůfa, the opera that made Janáček's name, was ten years in the making. Adapted from a bleak play by Gabriela Preissová, it borrows from Italian *verismo*, or realism, to portray a calamitous family conflict in a remote Czech village. To evoke rural life, the opera includes folk dances and choruses, but a dark mood gradually engulfs the work. Its most tragic figure is the Kostelnička, who commits murder to "save" Jenůfa. The opera's violent subject partly explains the refusal by Prague's National Theatre to present it until 1916.

⚞ *Jenůfa*'s sad story had echoes in Janáček's life. Having already lost an infant son, his 21-year-old daughter died while he was composing this opera. Devastated, he vowed to tie the score with black ribbons. ⚟

✦ PRINCIPAL ROLES ✦

Jenůfa *soprano*
A village girl

The Kostelnička Buryjovka *soprano*
The female sacristan and Jenůfa's stepmother

Grandmother Buryjovka *contralto*
Jenůfa's grandmother

Števa Buryja *tenor*
Jenůfa's cousin and lover

Laca Klemen *tenor*
Jenůfa's cousin and suitor

Karolka *mezzo-soprano*
The mayor's daughter

PLOT SYNOPSIS

A village in Moravia

ACT ONE Jenůfa loves the mill-owner, Števa, and worries that, if he is drafted into the army, they cannot marry before her pregnancy is discovered. Laca, Števa's half-brother, who loves Jenůfa, is unhappy when Števa is not conscripted. Jenůfa's stepmother, known as the Kostelnička, "the female sacristan", decrees Števa and Jenůfa cannot marry for one year. Crazed with jealousy, Laca slashes Jenůfa's face.

ACT TWO Jenůfa has borne a son. While she sleeps, the Kostelnička shows Števa the baby and begs him to marry Jenůfa, but he refuses. Laca, who believes Jenůfa is in Vienna, still wants to marry the girl. But he is put off when the Kostelnička reveals Jenůfa gave birth to a baby who died. Alone, the Kostelnička grimly decides she must drown the infant ♫. Jenůfa awakens and prays to the Virgin ♫. The Kostelnička announces that the baby has died of fever, leaving Jenůfa saddened but willing to marry Laca.

"Co chvíla, co chvíla"

"Zdrávas královno"

ACT THREE As the Kostelnička prepares to bless the couple, a boy brings news that a baby's frozen body was found in the mill-stream. The crowd blames Jenůfa, but the Kostelnička confesses her crime. At first stunned, Jenůfa forgives her stepmother. As the woman is led away, Laca says he still wants to marry Jenůfa.

Karita Matilla as Jenůfa fights off Jorma Silvasti's Laca in a 2001 production at the Royal Opera House.

PŘÍHODY LIŠKY BYSTROUŠKY
(The Cunning Little Vixen)

◈

⌂ Opera in three acts, 1½ hours
☷ 1922–1923
♇ 6 November 1924, National Theatre, Brno, (now

Czech Republic)
🕮 Leoš Janáček, after the 1920 novel by Rudolf Těsnohlidek

Příhody Lišky Bystroušky is a delight, for both its poetic music and its fairy-tale world where human and animal lives are entwined. Inspiration for the opera came from a serialized novel, itself built around 200 sketches about an adventurous little vixen. Using his own libretto, Janáček then created singing and dancing roles for countless animals, who are in turn given human attributes – in the case of the vixen, the need to love. Thus, through them and a half-dozen countryfolk, Janáček evokes the cycles of rural life. Long instrumental passages set different moods – comic, erotic, nostalgic, and tragic – while the melodies echo the rhythms of the human voice and animal sounds. In this way, Janáček gives the forest its own musical language.

> ⚜ Janáček was so fond of this opera that the final scene was performed at his funeral in August 1928, sung by his friend Arnold Flögl. ⚜

PLOT SYNOPSIS

A forest in Moravia

ACT ONE On a warm afternoon, as animals bustle around him, the Forester takes a nap. He wakes when Bystrouška the vixen cub chases a frog onto his nose. He grabs the cub to raise as a pet. Locked up with other animals, Bystrouška learns to defend herself. She also calls on the hens to mutiny. When they ignore her, she kills them and escapes.

ACT TWO Back in the woods, Bystrouška evicts the Badger from his home. At the inn, the Forester passes the time 🎵 teasing the Schoolmaster for not conquering his beloved Terynka. Later, the tipsy Schoolmaster takes Bystrouška for Terynka. The Forester fires at the vixen, but misses. Bystrouška then falls in love with Zlatohřbítek the fox. All the animals celebrate their marriage.

> "Ano, ve Stráni bude daleko lépe"

Dawn Upshaw as Bystrouška, the cunning little vixen, at the Royal Opera House in 2003.

ACT THREE Harašta the poacher is to marry Terynka. The Forester sets a trap for Bystrouška, but she and her cubs dance around it. She attracts Harašta's attention. When he trips, the foxes eat his chickens. He fires a shot and Bystrouška is killed. The Forester leaves the Schoolmaster weeping over Terynka and walks home through the wood. He sits down to rest and reminisces on the cycles of life 🎵. Falling asleep, he imagines chasing a little vixen, but instead he catches a frog.

> "Hoj! Ale neni to Bystroušky!"

→ PRINCIPAL ROLES ←

Animals
Bystrouška *soprano*
A vixen cub

Zlatohřbítek *soprano*
A fox

Lapák *mezzo-soprano*
A dog

Humans
The Forester *bass-baritone*

The Schoolmaster *tenor*

Harašta *bass*
A poacher

KÁŤA KABANOVÁ

(Katya Kabanova)

🜋 Opera in three acts, 1¾ hours
🜊 1919–1921
🜉 23 November 1921, National Theatre, Brno,

(now Czech Republic)
📖 Leoš Janáček, after Alexander Ostrovsky's 1859 play *Groza* (*The Storm*), translated by V Cervinka

Káťa Kabanová is considered Janáček's greatest opera. Its story is Russian in both setting and mood, with Káťa's impossible love and uncontainable guilt leading her irrevocably towards suicide. Janáček, himself a devoted Russophile, fell in love with his tragic heroine, imagining her to be as pure and gentle as his own muse, Kamila Stösslová. The opera is often viewed as a natural successor to *Jenůfa*, but in fact Káťa is a far more developed character, one whose solitude and unhappiness are expressed with almost painful realism. Although the score is through-composed, Janáček underlines his emotional attachment to Káťa through the flowing lyricism of her role, as if she alone had true feelings.

⚓ Long an admirer of Puccini, Janáček was struck by the parallel between Káťa's fate and that of *Madama Butterfly*'s heartbroken Cio-Cio-San, who also prefers suicide to living in shame. ⚓

PLOT SYNOPSIS

Kalinov, a Russian town on the Volga, around 1860

ACT ONE Kudrjáš asks his friend Boris why he tolerates the insults of his uncle, Dikoj. Boris explains glumly that Dikoj controls his inheritance. Now, adding to his troubles, Boris says, he loves Káťa Kabanová. Káťa arrives with her husband, Tichon, and her mother-in-law, Kabanicha, who as always is complaining. This time, Kabanicha warns Tichon that Káťa will never respect him if he keeps proclaiming his love. Alone with her friend Varvara,

"Viš, co mi napadlo" | Káťa reminisces on her sweet life before marriage 🜋. But now she is anxious.

At night, someone whispers lovingly to her, but it is a sin to love another man.

Marie Ordnerová as Kabanicha (*left*) berating Jana Hvranová as Káťa Kabanová in a 1996 production staged at the Prague State Opera.

Alarmed, she begs Tichon not to go on a trip. Kabanicha demands Kát'a's obedience while he is away.

ACT TWO Preparing for a tryst with Kudrjáš, Varvara gives Kát'a the key to the garden gate. At first terrified, Kát'a persuades herself that it is not a sin to talk to Boris. As she leaves for the garden, a drunken Dikoj arrives, hoping to seduce Kabanicha. Kudrjáš sings a love

"Nikohu te není!" | song while waiting for Varvara 🔊. Boris arrives

and Varvara brings word that Kát'a will soon be there. When she appears, Boris

"Jste to vy, Katěrino Petrovno?" | immediately declares his love for her 🔊. She asks if he is leading her to sin, but he promises

to obey her wishes. Throwing herself into his arms, she says she is now ready

"To jste si vymslili pěknou věc" | to die. Soon, Kát'a and Boris can be heard singing of their love in the darkness 🔊.

ACT THREE Sheltering from a storm, Kudrjáš notes that there are no lightning conductors to absorb the electric charges, but Dikoj insists that lightning is punishment from on high. Varvara warns Boris that Tichon has returned and that Kát'a is distraught. Kát'a herself arrives and asks Boris if he is satisfied with her suffering. When Kabanicha and Tichon appear, Kát'a

JANÁČEK'S YOUNG MUSE

During a long marriage, Janáček had many passions, but none was more important than his love for Kamila Stösslová, a married woman 38 years his junior whom he met when he was 63. Overnight, she became his muse and, while it is thought that their relationship was never consummated, Janáček remained obsessed with her until his death. Kamila excited his romantic imagination and inspired the principal female roles in his late operas. After completing *Kát'a Kabanová*, he wrote: "You know it's your opera."

throws herself at her husband's feet, crying that she sinned from the first night he left. When Kabanicha demands the identity of her lover, Kát'a blurts out Boris's name and flees into

the storm. Hours later, Kát'a now regrets her confession 🔊. Hearing her voice, Boris runs into her arms 🔊. But he has been ordered to leave town by his uncle. Devastated,

"Vidět se s ním rozloučit"

"Svedl nás Bůh"

Kát'a leaps into the Volga. Dikoj brings in her body and Tichon angrily blames his mother. Kabanicha is unmoved.

VĚC MAKROPULOS
(The Makropulos Case)

⚜ Opera in three acts, 1½ hours
🎼 1923–1925
♛ 18 December 1926, National Theatre, Brno

(now Czech Republic)
📖 Leoš Janáček, after the 1922 comedy
by Karel Čapek

Věc Makropulos is a strange and powerful opera. Its central character is a woman who was born in Crete in 1575 as Elina Makropulos and who, at the age of 337, appears in Prague in 1912 as an arrogant opera diva called Emilia Marty. In between, to conceal that an elixir extended her life by 300 years, she adopted different names, always using the initials EM. Karel Čapek called his play a philosophical comedy, but Janáček's opera is a far darker meditation on life.

⚓ The opera has long provoked speculation that Janáček created the cold and distant character of Emilia Marty out of frustration that his own muse, Kamila Stösslová, refused to reciprocate his love. ⚓

> ❖ **PRINCIPAL ROLES** ❖
>
> Emilia Marty (Elina Makropulos) *dramatic soprano*
>
> Dr Kolenatý *bass-baritone*
> A lawyer
>
> Albert Gregor *tenor*
> A Makropulos descendant
>
> Jaroslav Prus *baritone*
> A nobleman
>
> Janek *tenor*
> His son
>
> Kristina *soprano*
> Janek's girlfriend

PLOT SYNOPSIS

Prague, Czech Republic, in 1912

ACT ONE Gregor has a century-old claim to an estate owned by Jaroslav Prus. Emilia Marty, an aloof opera singer, arrives with the lawyer Kolenatý, who has just lost the case. Emilia says a document in Jaroslav's house could reverse the verdict. Emilia explains that in 1827 Baron Prus left the estate to his illegitimate son with Ellian MacGregor. Gregor is descended from that son. Kolenatý finds the document.

ACT TWO At the opera house, a crowd is congratulating Emilia, who treats everyone rudely except for an old man who recognizes her as Eugenia Montez. Jaroslav says Gregor cannot claim the estate ♛

"Dovolte mi dříve otázku"

because the mother of Baron Prus's illegitimate son was recorded as Elina Makropulos. Emilia asks Janek, Jaroslav's son, to steal another document. But Jaroslav offers it in exchange for a night with Emilia.

ACT THREE At dawn, Jaroslav hands over the envelope before learning that Janek has killed himself for love of Emilia. In Emilia's bags, Kolenatý and others find her many names, all with the initials EM. Emilia declares she is Elina Makropulos. She has lived 337 years thanks to an elixir of life which her father tested on her ♛, but she now believes a long life is pointless. As she dies, the elixir's formula is burned.

"Pro lékaře"

German soprano Anja Silja, won acclaim as Emilia Marty at the Glyndebourne Festival in 1997.

Z MRTVÉHO DOMU

(From the House of the Dead)

⚓ Opera in three acts, 1½ hours
🎵 1927–1928
🏛 12 April 1930, National Theatre, Brno

(Czech Republic)
📖 Leoš Janáček, after Dostoevsky's *Memoirs from the House of the Dead* (1862)

Z mrtvého domu, Janáček's final opera, is a work of heavy atmosphere and little plot. Adapted from Dostoevsky's own account of his time in a labour camp, it evokes the tedium and violence of prison life as well as the elusive dream of freedom. A wounded eagle becomes a symbol of hope: it lives with the prisoners until it can fly away. Perhaps unfinished when Janáček died, the opera was given a more cheerful ending by friends. But his original libretto and score are used today.

⇥ Even for an opera set among prisoners jailed for life in a Siberian labour camp, Janáček looked for the humanity in the story, noting that there are "bright places in the house of the dead". ⇤

➤ PRINCIPAL ROLES ➤

Prison Governor *bass*

Alexandr Petrovič Gorjančikov *baritone*
A nobleman

Skuratov *tenor*
A jailed cobbler

Luka Kuzmič (alias of Filka Morozov) *tenor*
A jailed murderer

Šiškov *bass*
A jailed murderer

Aljeja *mezzo-soprano*
A Tartar boy

PLOT SYNOPSIS

A Siberian labour camp in the early 19th century

ACT ONE Gorjančikov, a deported politician, arrives at the camp. When he protests, the prison governor orders him whipped. An inmate teases an injured eagle, but others proclaim the eagle to be tsar of the jungle. As prisoners leave for work, singing mournfully ♫, Skuratov recalls his life as a cobbler. Luka Kuzmič then recounts how he murdered a prison officer. Gorjančikov returns, barely able to stand.

"Neuvidí oko jiz tech kraju"

Šiškov recognizes the dead Luka as Filka Morozov in a scene from Act III of a Brno production in 1958.

ACT TWO One year later, Gorjančikov offers to teach young Aljeja to read and write. Skuratov explains that he is in Siberia because he loved a German girl ♫. When she married a rich relative, he was heartbroken and killed the man. The inmates improvise two plays, which provide brief respite from the boredom. As a prostitute arrives for a young prisoner, Gorjančikov and Aljeja drink tea. A prisoner attacks Aljeja and wounds him.

"Presel den, druhy, treti"

ACT THREE Gorjančikov cares for Aljeja. Luka is also ill. Šapkin recalls how a police officer tortured him by pulling his ears. Šiškov says he killed his fiancée because she still loved Filka Morozov. When Luka dies, Šiškov recognizes him as Filka. Gorjančikov is summoned and the governor apologizes to him. As Gorjančikov leaves, the eagle is released. The prisoners are ordered back to work.

BOHUSLAV MARTINŮ

Born: 8 December 1890, Polička (Czech Republic)
Died: 28 August 1959, Leistal, Switzerland

Bohuslav Martinů was a prolific and eclectic composer, not only writing in many genres music, but also absorbing influences from Bach to Stravinsky. While his early work echoed Dvořák, his music became more experimental after he moved to Paris in 1923. He wrote several of his 14 operas there, including *Julietta aneb Snář*, one of the few Surrealist operas. In 1941, he fled the Nazi occupation of France for the United States and only returned permanently to Europe in 1957, although not to Czechoslovakia, now under Communist rule. Among his final works was *Řecké pašije*, or *The Greek Passion*. This opera and *Julietta aneb Snář* are still occasionally staged.

JULIETTA ANEB SNÁŘ
(Julietta, or The Book of Dreams)

♒ Lyric opera in three acts, 2¼ hours
☷ 1936–1937
♇ 16 March 1938, National Theatre, Prague

(Czech Republic)
📖 Bohuslav Martinů, after Georges Neveux's novel, *Juliette, ou La clé des songes* (1930)

Julietta aneb Snář is Martinů's excellent adaptation of Neveux's Surrealist play, *Juliette, ou La clé des songes*, which was given a stormy reception when it opened in Paris in 1930. At first, the plot seems straightforward: a man returns to a seaside town where three years earlier he fell for a young woman. But when he discovers that neither she nor anyone else has any memory of the past, a complex game of fantasy and reality unfolds. Written in Czech, Martinů's fast-paced libretto names 25 roles and comprises 28 scenes, with the Central Office of Dreams in Act III providing the key to the story. Rather than reinforcing the notion of a dream, however, Martinů's score treats events at face value, with lyricism, drama, and even satire.

> ✦ **PRINCIPAL ROLES** ✦
>
> **Julietta** *soprano* A mysterious woman
> **Michel** *tenor* A Paris bookseller
> **A Policeman** *tenor*
> **A Fortune-teller** *contralto*
> **Man in helmet** *baritone*
> **Old Arab** *bass*

⚟ When Martinů travelled to Prague for this opera's premiere in March 1938, Hitler was already threatening Czechoslovakia. It would be the composer's last trip home: in 1948, Prague came under Communist rule. ⚞

The programme for a new production of the opera at the Palais Garnier, Paris, in 2002 announces its French-language title, *Juliette ou la clé des songes*.

Paul Nilon as Michel is received by Jessica Walzer's Little Arab in David Pountney's production at Italy's Ravenna Festival in 2005.

PLOT SYNOPSIS

A small port on France's Côte d'Azur in the 1930s

ACT ONE Arriving in a small French port, Michel finds everyone behaving strangely. He looks for the Sailor's Inn, but is told it does not exist. When he complains that an Old Arab demanded his life's story at knife-point, a Policeman explains 🔊 that, since no one can remember anything, visitors are required to speak of the past. Since Michel alone has a memory, he is given a pistol and is named mayor. He recounts that, on an earlier trip, he saw a beautiful girl singing at a piano. He has now returned to find her. Suddenly, he hears Julietta's voice 🔊 and she seems to recognize him. They agree to meet at a crossroads in the forest.

"Ztratil paměť'!"

"Moje láska v dálce se zratila"

ACT TWO Michel is awaiting Julietta when three gentlemen arrive, calling her name 🔊. A Fortune-teller reads Michel's hand, but only predicts the past. Julietta appears 🔊 and declares her love for Michel. A Memory-vendor offers mementoes, which remind Julietta of

"A nyní když jsme se"

"Ach, konečně! Konečně!"

trips with Michel that she never made. When she laughs at his account of how they met, they quarrel. Julietta runs off and Michel fires a shot at her. The villagers put him on trial, but he distracts them with a story. Michel tells some sailors to look for Julietta, but they return only with her scarf. A boat is leaving. Hearing Julietta's voice, Michel steps on board.

ACT THREE At the Central Office of Dreams, which sells dreams every evening, an official tells Michel that he is dreaming and it is time to wake up. As others come in to collect their dreams, the official warns Michel that he will remain trapped in his dream unless he leaves. But he wants to see Julietta once more. As the bureau prepares to close, Michel fears that she will be lost forever if he leaves. Suddenly, she reappears, but Michel is locked inside. The night-watchman wants to expel him, but Julietta begs him not to leave. Finally he steps outside, calling out to her, ready to relive his dream, but she is gone. And again Michel finds himself arriving in the little port, looking for the Sailor's Inn.

Modern Opera

T HE MODERN ERA sent opera in two fresh directions. Innovations in technology carried the melodies of earlier opera to mass audiences, and turned charismatic singers into recording stars. At the same time, opera began to address the complexities of modern life, its fragmented nature, its rush towards change, and the new sounds of its urban landscapes.

MODERN TIMES FOR OPERA

Opera's modern epoch began with recording technology. For 300 years, great singing was enjoyed in live performances. But, in the 20th century, the gramophone brought Enrico Caruso, Rosa Ponselle, and other opera stars into family drawing rooms. The thrill of a dynamic vocalist's live sound and stage presence was sacrificed for the pleasure of a recorded rendition, often in the form of popular arias by Verdi, Bizet, or Puccini. Simultaneously, opera itself was responding to a fast-changing world. For the first time, voices crackled with electricity over telephones, radios, and monitors. In cars, underground trains, and aeroplanes, life sped up to blur sights and sounds in burgeoning metropolises. And when Sigmund Freud discovered hidden depths to the unconscious, the human mind appeared less coherent as well. Composers responded by abandoning old definitions of music and drama to make way for operas about the alarming pace and disturbing isolation of modern life.

SCHOENBERG AND EUROPEAN SERIALISM

The modern era entered opera houses as Arnold Schoenberg rewrote the rules of tonality. Until then, "beautiful"

A crowd in Queen's Park in Manchester, England, in the early 20th century is captivated by an Auxeto Gramophone amplifying the voices of Enrico Caruso and Antonio Scotti singing a duet from Verdi's *La Forza del destino*.

music remained loyal to a basic key anchoring the notes. But in works like his 1909 *Erwartung*, Schoenberg placed the centre of gravity on relationships between notes, rather than on a single grounding one. His breakthrough, made just as artists pursued abstract painting, was akin to Einstein's theory of relativity, which described laws of physics beyond earthbound space and time. With his "12-tone method", Schoenberg effectively proposed the $E=MC^2$ of modern music, and established the Second Viennese School. Its most important opera composer was Alban Berg. His *Wozzeck* and *Lulu* explored the human condition in a newly configured, modern universe. In Berlin, atonal music interacted with jazz as Kurt Weill collaborated with playwright Bertolt Brecht on works including *Die Dreigroschenoper* (*The Threepenny Opera*). Experimentation rippled through Europe's opera capitals, only to be stopped in the 1930s, when Schoenberg, Weill, Brecht, and a generation of opera creators fled the rise of Fascism in Europe.

In 1945, America's atomic bombs exploded in Japan, finally ending World War II. Composers struggled to adapt inherited musical palettes to a much-changed world. In Europe, Romanticism was bypassed by serialism, a practise extending the relativity of Schoenberg's method from tone to other musical variables such as tempo and dynamics.

Die Dreigroschenoper (*The Threepenny Opera*) by Kurt Weill introduced American jazz elements into European atonal music.

Emerging composers headed to Paris, or to Darmstadt, in Germany, to study with rigorous serialists. But with the Berlin Wall erected in 1961, academic concepts of music gave way to the earthier human issues of listening and being heard in a divided world. By the early 1980s, Olivier Messiaen's opera *Saint François d'Assise* expressed unshakable faith in mystical divinity. And Luciano Berio's *Un re in ascolto* urgently searched for meaning in the fractured Cold War era.

BRITTEN'S BRITAIN

In contrast to the Continent, England welcomed a one-man Renaissance of opera in 1945. It was then that London discovered *Peter Grimes* by the young Benjamin Britten. He was England's first operatic master since Henry Purcell 250 years earlier. Britten was a deeply human composer, melding influences as diverse as Romantic

In 1948, designer **Tanya Moiseiwitsch** works with a miniature model for an opera set while the British composer Benjamin Britten looks on.

opera, atonal compositions, sacred music, and Asian music theatre. His 15 operas ranged from the tragic *Billy Budd* and comic *Albert Herring* to the festive Shakespearean *A Midsummer Night's Dream* and meditative *Curlew River*. Together, they placed him alongside Richard Strauss as the century's most significant opera composer. Britten's influence was greatest in Britain: composers John Tavener and Judith Weir, and the more recent Mark-Anthony Turnage and Thomas Adès, would find themselves indebted to Britten no matter how broad their operatic reach.

OPERAS MADE IN AMERICA

American opera took a different course. With no indigenous classical music tradition, the United States first embraced imported opera. Immigrants from England, Italy, and Germany added to opera's melting pot. Not until the first half of the 20th century did American composers find their own voices. With librettist Gertrude Stein, Virgil Thomson tuned his music to the rhythms of American speech in *Four Saints in Three Acts*. And for his triumphant opera of 1935, George Gershwin travelled from New York to the Carolinas to absorb the music and speech of the African–American communities depicted in the novel *Porgy and Bess* by Dubose Heyward. Both composers linked new American opera to the Broadway musical, even as European operas were given at New York's Metropolitan Opera. Indeed, Gershwin was Broadway's top composer for a decade from the late 1920s. After the war, Leonard Bernstein continued to defy Old World distinctions between opera and popular entertainment. Less than a year separated the Broadway premieres of his 1956 operetta, *Candide*, and his most cherished musical, *West Side Story*. In recent decades, the eclectic form of American opera has been kept alive by composers William Bolcom, John Harbison, and Tobias Picker.

But there was also a reaction against the Broadway style. In the 1960s, composers like John Cage joined European experiments, while others found a natural idiom in minimalism. Partly influenced by Indian classical music, minimalism shaped music through variations on repetition and

IN SEARCH OF AN OPERA

America's top opera houses – in New York, Chicago, Santa Fe, Houston, and San Francisco – have made it their business to show works likely to reverberate nationwide. After all, opera is inseparable from grand-scale themes. Creators have mined the country's literary treasures, such as Tennessee Williams's *A Streetcar Named Desire* and F Scott Fitzgerald's *The Great Gatsby* (right). Inspiration has also come from celebrity figures like Jackie Onassis, or history, such as the Civil War. But America's music theatre pulse is perhaps best taken on Broadway.

Penguin Modern Classics

F Scott Fitzgerald
The Great Gatsby

MODERN OPERA 1900–PRESENT DAY

| 1890 | 1900 | 1902 Enrico Caruso records for the first time | 1902 Debussy's *Pelléas et Mélisande* | 1905 Strauss's *Salome* | 1909 Schoenberg composes *Erwartung* | 1914 World War I begins | 1920 | 1925 Berg's *Wozzeck* | 1930 Weill's *Aufstieg und Fall der Stadt Mahagonny* | 1931 First live opera broadcast on American radio | 1935 Gershwin's *Porgy and Bess* |

Italian mounted police form an honour guard in front of La Scala, Milan, in 2004, during the inauguration of the reopened opera, restored to its former glory.

symmetry in works such as Philip Glass's *Einstein on the Beach* and John Adams's *Nixon in China*. Leading American stage directors were also drawn to opera: Robert Wilson worked with Glass and Peter Sellars teamed up with Adams. And although they received more recognition overseas than at home, they reinforced the director as a central figure in the story of post-war opera around the world.

GLOBAL OPERA

Opera's global era began with the fall of the Berlin Wall in 1989, and the rise of the internet in the 1990s. Once again, popularization accompanied experimentation. For the first time in almost a century, talents of the former Soviet Bloc and the West intermixed freely in opera houses from Moscow to San Francisco. Newly unified, Berlin suddenly boasted three opera houses and St Petersburg again came alive

with opera. In 1990, Plácido Domingo, Luciano Pavarotti, and José Carreras teamed up as The Three Tenors to warm millions of hearts through a worldwide television broadcast. In turn, the internet provided new forums for diva worshippers and opera enthusiasts.

But the global era has also ushered in a new generation of creators. Opera's future relies on the promise of composers like the Hungarian Peter Eötvös; the Belgian Philippe Boesmans; the Frenchman Pascal Dusapin; the Finn Kaija Saariaho; and the Chinese–American Tan Dun. Tan's first major opera, *Marco Polo*, happened to honour a founding figure of global culture: like opera itself, Marco Polo set out from Venice to travel further than anyone could have guessed possible.

| 1945 Britten's *Peter Grimes* | 1951 Britten's *Billy Budd* | 1978 Stockhausen begins composing *Licht: Die sieben Tage der Woche* | 1979 Berg's *Lulu* | | 1984 Berio's *Un re in ascolto* | 1989 Berlin Wall dismantled | 1996 Tan Dun's *Marco Polo* |

1940 · · · · · · · · · · · · 1960 · · · · · · · · · · · · 1980

| 1945 World War II ends; the atomic era dawns | 1961 Berlin Wall erected | 1976 Glass's *Einstein on the Beach* | 1983 Messiaen's *Saint François d'Assise* | 1987 Adams's *Nixon in China* | 1990 The Three Tenors' TV broadcast |

ARNOLD
SCHOENBERG

Born: 13 September 1874, Vienna (Austria)
Died: 13 July 1951, Los Angeles, California, US

Arnold Schoenberg was the first composer to give voice to a modern idiom within the language of classical music. As the 20th century dawned, he paved the way for opera to express contemporary experience. He fashioned new musical building blocks with his 12-tone method, and established the Second Viennese School, whose chief opera composer would be Alban Berg.

At 19, Schoenberg played cello in an ensemble led by Austrian composer Alexander Zemlinsky, who became his teacher. Over the following decade, Schoenberg discovered that, when notes were given equal weight – rather than made to serve a musical key or chord, as in traditional harmony – the door to a new realm of "atonal" expression was opened. Among his short works for the stage were *Erwartung*, or *Expectation*; *Die glückliche Hand*, or *The Fateful Hand*; and *Von Heute auf Morgen*, or *From One Day to the Next*. His sole attempt at a full opera came with *Moses und Aron*, but it was never completed. Persecuted as a Jew while teaching in Berlin, Schoenberg fled to the United States in 1933.

DER BLAUE REITER

In Munich in 1911, Wassily Kandinsky heard Schoenberg's *Three Piano Pieces*, which inspired him to explore musical ideas through abstract painting. With other painters, Kandinsky formed a group known as *Der Blaue Reiter* ("The Blue Rider"). Schoenberg exhibited his own paintings with the group in Vienna, and corresponded copiously with Kandinsky about relationships between musical and visual art forms.

Wassily Kandinsky's artwork for a catalogue of Der Blaue Reiter *group.*

Arnold Schoenberg (*seated, second from left*) gathers with his wife Gertrud, the architect Adolf Loos (*left*), and the artist Oskar Kokoschka at a bar in Berlin.

MOSES UND ARON
(Moses and Aaron)

🎭 Opera in three acts (incomplete), 1¾ hours   📖 Arnold Schoenberg
🎼 1930–1932
♆ 6 June 1957, Stadthalle, Zurich, Switzerland

Moses und Aron, an incomplete opera, and challenging to stage, is rarely given. To convey the frustrations of a prophet who deems himself inarticulate, Schoenberg set the role of Moses in Sprechgesang or "speak-singing". The tenor voice of the eloquent Aaron is by contrast all the more penetrating. Choral passages and Act I's "Dance round the Golden Calf" are highlights of this intense opera based on the biblical Exodus. In the United States in 1945, Schoenberg's application for funding to complete the opera was rejected.

⇥ The name "Aaron" would normally have been spelled the same way in German. Schoenberg changed the spelling to Aron because he believed that the title *Moses und Aaron* would be inauspicious: it contains 13 letters. ⇤

> ✦ PRINCIPAL ROLES ✦
>
> **Moses** *spoken*
> A prophet of God
>
> **Aaron** *tenor*
> Interprets Moses's God
> for the Israelites
>
> **Young Girl** *soprano*
> She embraces the new god
>
> **Young Man** *baritone*
> He embraces the new god
>
> **Priest** *bass*
> He warns the Israelites
> against Moses
>
> **Naked virgins** *2 sopranos/*
> *2 contraltos*
> They are raped by priests

PLOT SYNOPSIS

Biblical Antiquity

ACT ONE God instructs Moses to lead the Israelites to the Promised Land. Moses claims himself incapable, but God promises that signs will aid him. In the wilderness, Moses meets Aaron. Israelites favour Moses's God, but a priest warns of Moses as a murderer. Moses and Aaron arrive. Aaron interprets the new god as infinite, but the Israelites reject God's invisibility. Aaron produces signs persuading the Israelites to challenge Pharaoh 👣. The people wonder what they will eat in the desert. Aaron reassures them. The Chosen People celebrate their seeking the Promised Land.

"Ein Wunder erfüllt uns mit Schrecken"

INTERLUDE The Israelites ask after Moses, who has been absent for 40 days.

ACT TWO The Israelites refuse to wait for Moses to return from the Mount of Revelation with the new law. The people are agitated 👣 and claim they will slaughter their priests. Aaron promises them an image of God. At Aaron's invitation, people worship the Golden Calf. Sacrifices are followed by orgiastic excesses, with virgins raped by priests. Moses descends from the mountain and the people flee. Aaron tries to justify the idol to Moses, claiming that the tablets are also "visible" forms of God. Moses smashes the tablets. Alone, Moses is anguished.

"Wo ist Moses?"

Frode Olsen plays the reluctant prophet Moses, a spoken role, at the Hamburg Staatsoper in 2004.

"*Berg's music is saying farewell to life.*"

The philosopher Theodor Adorno

ALBAN
BERG

Born: 9 February 1885, Vienna (Austria)
Died: 24 December 1935, Vienna, Austria

Alban Berg has since World War II been hailed a key figure of 20th-century art music. He wrote only two operas: *Wozzeck* was one, and the other, *Lulu*, remained unfinished at the time of his death. These works – atonal, passionate, and shocking – sent opera music on a startling new path.

Berg was born in Vienna and lived there until his death from blood poisoning at age 50. He showed early strength as a composer of songs, writing dozens of them in his teenage years. But Berg's formal music education was scant until 1904, when in the burgeoning arts scene of Vienna he met Arnold Schoenberg, originator of the 12-tone method of composition. He then studied with Schoenberg, whose rejection of Romantic definitions of music and beauty, along with the radical lyricism of fellow Viennese composer Gustav Mahler, strongly influenced Berg's distinct style. He moved freely among forms and effects, from folk music to tightly-wound dissonance. But Berg's life and work were hit hard by historical circumstances. Progress on the opera *Wozzeck* was delayed by World War I, when he worked for the War Ministry. And from 1933, as Berg was composing *Lulu*, Nazi authorities took steps to ban performance of his music in Germany and Austria. Berg is often remembered as the leading opera composer of the Second Viennese School led by Schoenberg; its other chief composer was Anton Weber. Both the music and themes of Berg's operas influenced composers throughout the 20th century. His inarticulate anti-hero Wozzeck in particular captured new problems of listening and being heard, and spawned tragic opera heroes of a distinctly modern kind.

Sets designed by Stefanos Lazaridis add a chilling realism to a 2002 *Wozzeck* for London's Royal Opera House, wth German baritone Matthias Görne as Wozzeck, and Swedish soprano Katarina Dalayman as Marie.

FIRST PERFORMANCES

1920

1925
Wozzeck

1930

1935
Death of Berg
1937
Lulu

1940

1950

1960

1970

1979
Lulu completed
1980

WOZZECK

🎵 Opera in three acts, 1½ hours
⏳ 1914–1922
🏆 14 December 1925, Staatsoper,

Berlin, Germany
📖 Alban Berg, from the play *Woyzeck* (1837) by
Georg Büchner

Wozzeck is a masterwork of the modern era, and its influence on subsequent composers is difficult to exaggerate. Based on Georg Büchner's 1837 play, itself based on a true story, the opera presents a disturbed murderer as a sympathetic man struggling to preserve his dignity. Musically, the opera is a *tour de force*. Each of its 15 scenes is built on forms such as the lullaby, the military march, the rhapsody, and the fugue. Berg's signature music creates maximum theatrical effect, as does his pacing. Indeed, a central subject in the opera is haste, and it exerts stress on the troubled Wozzeck from the first scene. The 1925 premiere of *Wozzeck* was a triumph and, until it was banned in 1933, the opera was a success in Germany.

⚞ The opera famously took Berg nearly eight years to write. Preparation for the premiere was also time-consuming. Conductor Erich Kleiber called 137 rehearsals, including 34 for the orchestra alone. ⚟

✣ PRINCIPAL ROLES ✣

Wozzeck *baritone*
A poor soldier

Andres *lyric tenor*
Wozzeck's friend

Tambourmajor *tenor*
(Heldentenor)
Drum Major

Hauptmann *tenor*
(buffo tenor)
Captain

Doktor *bass (buffo bass)*
Doctor

Der Narr *tenor*
The Idiot

Marie *soprano*
Mother to Wozzeck's child

Mariens Knabe *treble*
Their son

Margret *contralto*
Marie's neighbour

PLOT SYNOPSIS

In and around a military town

ACT ONE As Wozzeck shaves his Captain, the officer berates him for immorality for having a child out of wedlock with Marie. Cutting brush with Andres, his fellow soldier, Wozzeck believes the place is haunted. When night falls, the men depart fearfully. Margret, a neighbour, taunts Marie for admiring the Drum Major who leads a military band in the street. Slamming her window on Margret, Marie sings her child a lullaby ♫.
When Wozzeck appears, she holds | "Mädel, was fangst Du jetzt an?"
their son out to him. But, disturbed by visions, he leaves. Wozzeck complains of hallucinations to the Doctor, who grows ecstatic imagining his fame for treating Wozzeck's strange illness ♫. Marie eyes | "Oh! meine Theorie!"
the Drum Major as he marches before her. At first she resists his advances, then falls into his arms.

ACT TWO Admiring her new earrings, a gift from the Drum Major, Marie prevents her son from seeing them ♫. When Wozzeck asks | "Was die Steine glänzen!"

her how she obtained the jewellery, Marie lies to him. He gives her his earnings and leaves. In a street, the Doctor discusses his medical cases with the Captain. Wozzeck passes by, but rushes away when they needle him about the Drum Major. Wozzeck reaches Marie's home. Crazed, he lunges at her, but she takes refuge in her room. Wozzeck watches the Drum Major dance

"Ein Jäger aus der Pfalz" | gropingly with Marie in a garden. Andres joins others in song ♨, and a

"Jedoch, wenn ein Wanderer" | drunkard delivers a sour sermon ♂. An Idiot warns Wozzeck that he

smells blood. In the barracks, Wozzeck is sleepless. The Drum Major arrives drunk, bragging about his conquest. After they fight, Wozzeck is left bleeding on the floor as the Drum Major leaves.

ACT THREE Studying the Bible, Marie pushes her child away in self-disgust, then calls him back. At dusk, Marie and Wozzeck walk in the woods. With a red moon rising, he plunges a knife into her throat. Marie dead, Wozzeck hurries off. In a tavern, Wozzeck sings,

then watches others dance. Margret notices blood on his hand. Wozzeck rushes out. In the woods, Wozzeck stumbles on Marie's corpse while looking for his knife ♂.
He throws the knife into | "Das Messer?"
a pond, then wades in to throw it further. The Doctor and Captain hear a man drown as they pass, but they do nothing. Marie's son plays with other children. They tell him his mother is dead, but he does not understand. Hopping along on a toy horse, he follows the children as they go to inspect Marie's body.

At the Santa Fe Opera in 2001, Håken Hagegård's Wozzeck (*from left to right*), Michael Smallwood's Andres, and Anthony Laciura's Idiot perform in the opera's second act.

LULU

⚗ Opera in a prologue and three acts, 2¾ hours
🎼 1928–1935; Act III completed by Friedrich Cerha, 1974

🏛 14 January 1900, Teatro Costanzi, Rome, Italy
📖 Berg, from Frank Wedekind's plays *Erdgeist* (1895) and *Die Büchse der Pandora* (1903)

Lulu has been hailed a landmark atonal opera, although Berg had only scored the first two acts by the time of his death in 1935. The third and final act was supplied by the Austrian composer Friedrich Cerha some 40 years later. Formally precise and complex, but also seething with psychological luxuriance, *Lulu* has since Berg's day remained a shocking opera built around the sexually mesmerizing "black angel" Lulu. The subjects of obsession, lust, disfiguring disease, and violence have struck some as gratuitously outrageous. But Berg worked on the piece in Sigmund Freud's Vienna, where tight-laced hypocrisy fed on unspoken desires. The intrepid *Lulu* still takes to stages like a savage creature just released from its cage. Since 1979, the complete version has been given in major opera houses worldwide.

⚜ The Royal Riding School in the Christiansborg Palace of Denmark was the venue for Travis Preston's 1996 production. In the theatre dressing-room scene of Act I, American soprano Constance Hauman sang Lulu naked. ⚜

✢ PRINCIPAL ROLES ✢

Lulu *soprano*
A bewitching dancer

Dr Schön/Jack the Ripper *baritone*
An editor-in-chief/Murderer

Countess Geschwitz *mezzo-soprano*
Schön's lesbian fiancée

Alwa *tenor*
A composer, and Dr Schön's son

Schigolch *bass*
An old man who passes as Lulu's father

The Painter/Negro *tenor*
Lulu's second husband/Sex client

The Prince/Marquis *tenor*
Wooer of Lulu/Sex-trafficker who betrays Lulu

Animal Tamer/Acrobat *bass*
Presenter of the opera/Man in love with Lulu

PLOT SYNOPSIS

A painter's studio, drawing rooms, a theatre dressing-room, a Paris casino, and a London attic

PROLOGUE An Animal Tamer welcomes the audience to his tent, where he promises a show of wild rather than domesticated beasts.

ACT ONE Lulu poses for the Painter in his studio while her lover, Dr Schön, observes. Sexual tension coils when Schön departs

"Sie bekommen mich noch lange nicht"

👄. The Painter confesses love for Lulu just as her husband arrives; the husband dies on the spot. Married to her worshipful Painter, Lulu meets Schön at

home in secrecy. He aims to end their long affair and marry Countess Geschwitz. When the Painter discovers Schön with Lulu, he commits suicide. Three years later, in the dressing-room of a theatre where Lulu dances, she argues with Schön, still unmarried 👄. Taking dictation from Lulu, Schön, still as bewitched by

"Das hättest du dir besser erspart!"

Evely Lear and Dietrich Fischer-Dieskau in 1968 playing the leads at the Deutsche Oper, West Berlin.

her as ever, pens a letter renouncing his engagement. The task complete, he finally breaks down.

ACT TWO Married now to Schön, Lulu entertains her lesbian admirer, the Countess Geschwitz. When Schön enters the drawing room with a revolver, Lulu takes him to bed. She returns to flirt with visiting lovers, who hide when Alwa, Schön's son, woos her with passion. Discovering them, Schön urges Lulu to kill herself, but she refuses ♪. Instead, she fires on Schön, and promises

"Wenn sich die Menschen"

Alwa love. But, his father dead, Alwa has contacted the police. **ORCHESTRAL INTERLUDE** A silent film portrays Lulu spending a year in prison and contracting cholera. As the staged action resumes, the Countess leaves for the cholera ward to change places with Lulu. When Lulu

FRIEDRICH CERHA

Born in Vienna in 1926, Austrian composer Friedrich Cerha became a vibrant member of the city's avant-garde arts scene in the 1950s and 60s. Cerha used Berg's notes and partial score of Act III to complete *Lulu* in 1974. A full version of the opera was given for the first time in Paris in 1979, with Pierre Boulez conducting. Cerha's own operatic works include *Baal*, based on the 1923 play by Bertolt Brecht.

returns in the Countess's stead, the Acrobat who was to marry her is revolted by her diseased features. Alone with Alwa, Lulu rejoices in her freedom as he praises her body ♪. In a Paris casino, all are gambling when the Marquis, a sex-trafficker, warns Lulu: he will betray her unless she agrees to be sold. Others return from gambling, and Lulu quarrels with the Countess ♪. Lulu

"Durch dieses Kleid"

"Brilliant! Es geht brilliant!"

trades clothes with a Groom in order to escape, and departs with Alwa before the police arrive. In a London attic room, Lulu, now a prostitute, returns with a client, the Professor. When he leaves, the Countess arrives with Lulu's portrait by her dead husband. Terrified, Lulu returns to the street, and reappears with a violent Negro client who soon departs. With Lulu back on the street, the Countess, love-sick for her, toys with suicide. Lulu returns with a client, Jack. They wrangle about money, and prepare for moonlit sex ♪. From her room, Lulu shrieks wildly. Jack emerges with a bloodied knife and stabs the Countess, who dies calling for Lulu ♪.

"Wie sie meinen"

"Lulu! Mein Engel"

An exotically clad Lulu, sung by Lisa Saffer, at the English National Opera in London, 2002.

KURT
WEILL

Born: 2 March 1900, Dessau, Saxony (Germany)
Died: 3 April 1950, New York, US

Kurt Weill rejected distinctions between high and low art to write dozens of inspired works of music theatre. His masterpieces in German, *Die Dreigroschenoper* and *Aufstieg und Fall der Stadt Mahagonny*, created an earthier species of opera in Weimar Germany, while his later American pieces elevated the Broadway musical to new heights.

Weill was born to a cantor in the synagogue of Dessau and began composing music as a boy. He later studied under teachers including Wagner's protégé, Engelbert Humperdinck. By the late 1920s, he was writing operas marked by new European music as well as American dance music. Collaboration with writer Bertolt Brecht then generated *Die Dreigroschenoper* (*The Threepenny Opera*) and *Aufstieg und Fall der Stadt Mahagonny* (*Rise and Fall of the City of Mahagonny*). Both works found wide popularity in Weimar Germany, but Weill's operas of the early 1930s provoked riots. The Nazis' rise to power in January 1933 prompted him to flee, first to Paris, and then, in 1935, to the United States. There, Weill gained renown for his musicals, from *Johnny Johnson* and *Lady in the Dark* to *One Touch of Venus* and *Street Scene*.

At the Music Box Theater in New York, Weill plays tunes from his musical *Lost in the Stars*.

FIRST PERFORMANCES

1925

1926
Der Protagonist

1927
Royal Palace

1928
Der Zar lässt sich photographieren

Die Dreigroschenoper

1930
Aufstieg und Fall der Stadt Mahagonny

Der Jasager

1932
Die Bürgschaft

1933
Der Silbersee

Die sieben Todsünden

1935

1936
Johnny Johnson

1937
The Eternal Road

1938
Knickerbocker Holiday

1940

1941
Lady in the Dark

1943
One Touch of Venus

1945
The Firebrand of Florence

1947
Street Scene

1948
Down in the Valley
Love Life

1949
Lost in the Stars

1950

DIE DREIGROSCHENOPER
The Threepenny Opera

✍ Play with music in a prologue and three acts,
1¼ hours (music only)
🖩 1928

⚱ 31 August 1928, Theater am Schiffbauerdamm,
Berlin, Germany
📖 Bertolt Brecht, from J Gay's *The Beggar's Opera*

Die Dreigroschenoper became one of the most popular operas ever to hit the German stage. Irresistible numbers, such as the "Cannon Song" in Act I, and the "Song of Sexual Depravity" in Act II, pepper the opera, and each act ends in a show-stopping finale. Weill and librettist Bertolt Brecht mined the flexibility of the English ballad-opera, whose 1728 archetype, John Gay's *The Beggar's Opera*, was their chief source.

※ *Die Dreigroschenoper* was single-handedly responsible for introducing Weill to a wide American public when, in the monumental New York revival of 1954, its run lasted 2,611 performances. ※

→ PRINCIPAL ROLES ←

Polly Peachum *soprano*
Daughter to Mr and Mrs Peachum

Mrs Peachum *mezzo-soprano*
Polly's mother

Jonathan Jeremiah Peachum *baritone*
Polly's father

Macheath *tenor*
Also known as Mac the Knife

Jenny Diver *soprano*
A whore, and Mac's former lover

PLOT SYNOPSIS

London's Soho district in the Victorian era

PROLOGUE A street-singer introduces the opera with the "Ballad of Mac the Knife" ♪.

"Die Moritat von Mackie Messer"

ACT ONE Mr and Mrs Peachum, who head a gang of beggars and petty criminals, disapprove of their daughter Polly's eloping with Mac. Polly and Mac celebrate their marriage in Soho, but Polly's parents want the sheriff of London to arrest Mac.

ACT TWO Polly puts on a show of lamenting Mac's flight from the law. Mac takes up with Jenny, a prostitute bribed by Mrs Peachum to betray him to the police. In the law-courts, Mac escapes with help from Lucy, the sheriff's daughter. In a finale, the company sings of survival in a world where "Mankind is kept alive by bestial acts" ♫.

"Denn wovon lebt der Mensch?"

ACT THREE Mr Peachum threatens the sheriff: Mac must be arrested, or beggars will upset the imminent coronation. Mac, whoring again, is returned to court, where he is condemned to death by hanging. But Mr Peachum informs the audience that, since this is an opera, humanity will prevail over justice. The sheriff pronounces Mac free, bestows a peerage on him, and all propose that injustice be spared from persecution.

Bertolt Brecht's granddaughters Johanna and Jenny Schall directed and costumed this production at the Maxim Gorki Theater, Berlin, in 2004.

AUFSTIEG UND FALL DER STADT MAHAGONNY

(Rise and Fall of the City of Mahagonny)

⚎ Opera in three acts, 2¼ hours
☒ 1927–1929
♟ 9 March 1930, Neues Theater,

Leipzig, Germany
📖 Bertolt Brecht

Aufstieg und Fall der Stadt Mahagonny, Weill's landmark opera, redefined the sound of modernity. Weill and his librettist, Bertolt Brecht, had written *Kleine Mahagonny* (*Little Mahagonny*) in 1927, about an American city, and it formed the basis of the full opera that shocked and delighted audiences at its Leipzig premiere in 1930. Weill integrated music-hall tunes and existing music into a visionary score of classical structure that – like the modern experience – magically coheres even as it threatens to disintegrate. With its story of existential misery and political subversion, the opera's career was choppy in the 1930s, particularly as the Nazi regime gained footing. But it has since found its place as a major opera of the 20th century.

⊰ In Act I, men are recruited with music parodying the "Bridesmaids' Chorus" in Weber's *Der Freischütz* and, later in the act, a saloon entertainer hammers out Tekla Badarzewska's "The Maiden's Prayer" on an out-of-tune piano. ⊱

⇥ PRINCIPAL ROLES ⇤

Leokadja Begbick *mezzo-soprano*
A widow fleeing the police

Fatty the bookkeeper *tenor*
Begbick's associate

Trinity Moses *baritone*
Begbick's associate

Jenny Smith *soprano*
A Cuban bargirl

Jim Mahoney *tenor*
A lumberjack from Alaska

Jake Schmidt *tenor*
A lumberjack, Jim's friend

Bankroll Bill *baritone*
A lumberjack, Jim's friend

Alaska Wolf Joe *bass*
A lumberjack, Jim's friend

Tobby Higgins *tenor*
A defendant charged with murder

PLOT SYNOPSIS

An American desert

ACT ONE When their truck breaks down in the American desert, Leokadja Begbick tells fellow outlaws Fatty and Trinity Moses that she wants to build Mahagonny, a city devoted to pleasure in an otherwise rotten world. "Sharks" drift into Mahagonny, starting with Jenny and six girls

Trude Hesterberg (*left*) plays Begbick to Lotte Lenya's Jenny in a 1931 production of Weill's opera staged in Berlin.

♘. Within a few years, the renowned city draws Jim Mahoney, Jake, Bill, and Joe from Alaska. Jenny tries to sell herself to Jack but, with his price too low, she settles for Jim. The city's economy then sours, and many depart. Jim nearly boards a boat,

"Oh show us the way to the next whisky bar"

but his pals take him to the saloon instead. When Jake praises the saloon entertainment as Eternal Art, Jim explodes in anger at the schmaltzy sound ♩ and the boredom he suffers in Mahagonny. But when a hurricane approaches Mahagonny, Jim's anger turns to happiness. Others panic, but he finds a new lease of life, passionately advocating that each do purely as he pleases. ♩

"Tief in Alaskas schneeweissen Walden"

"Denn wie man sich bettet so liegt man"

At the Saxony State Opera in 2005, the director Harry Kupfer updated Weill's work by having Begbick and her gang arrive not by truck but by helicopter.

ACT TWO The hurricane's path misses Mahagonny, where Jim's politics provide the town's new laissez-faire credo: "DO IT!" Jake becomes a glutton and dies from overeating; Begbick runs a brothel; Jim bets on Joe in a boxing match against Moses, who kills Joe; and, finally, Jim is arrested for debt to the saloon, where he ordered drinks for everyone without being able to pay.

"Wenn der Himmel hell wird" | Chained up at night, Jim hopes that day will never come ♫.

ACT THREE Awaiting justice in the law-courts, Jim watches as Tobby Higgins bribes Judge Begbick for acquittal on a murder charge. Jim asks Bill to lend money for a bribe, but Bill refuses him. With Moses now his prosecutor, Jim is charged with never paying for whisky; raping Jenny; singing an illegal song on the night of the hurricane; and destroying happiness in Mahagonny. He is sentenced to death. All consider moving to Benares, but learn that it has been

"Liebe Jenny, auch ich habe" | demolished by an earthquake. Jim bids Jenny goodbye ♫

and assures all that he has no regrets. He urges the citizens of Mahagonny

to live fully since there is no afterlife. With Jim in the electric chair and execution underway, the others portray God's visit to Mahagonny, with Moses in the role of God. News blasts through a loudspeaker: mass protests against the high cost of living in Mahagonny destroyed the city. In a final procession, former citizens of Mahagonny determine "We cannot help ourselves, or you, or anyone" ♫.

"Können uns und euch und niemand helfen!"

BERTOLT BRECHT 1889–1956

The German Bertolt Brecht was a dominant force in 20th-century theatre. Librettist to Weill, he was also a poet and playwright. From 1926, he was a Communist Party member, but fled Fascism in 1933 to live in Scandinavia and the US. In 1949, he directed his celebrated play, *Mother Courage and her Children*, in East Berlin, where he founded the Berliner Ensemble. As an influential Marxist theatre reformer, Brecht maintained that audiences should remain detached from, rather than absorbed by, staged illusions.

BÉLA
BARTÓK

Born: 25 March 1881, Nagyszentmiklós, Hungary (now Sînnicolau Mare, Romania)
Died: 26 September 1945, New York, US

Béla Bartók is now recognized as a major 20th-century composer, although in his lifetime he was better known outside Hungary as a concert pianist. Today, his most popular work is instrumental, although his only opera, *A kékszakállú herceg vára*, or *Duke Bluebeard's Castle*, has also earned a place in the repertory. As a young man, Bartók explored folk music, and this is echoed in his work. But he was also influenced by Debussy, Liszt, and Richard Strauss. Then, in the 1920s, he recognized Stravinsky and Schoenberg by including dissonance in some quartets. In 1940, he took refuge in the United States, where he wrote his monumental *Concerto for Orchestra*. He died there in 1945.

A KÉKSZAKÁLLÚ HERCEG VÁRA
(Duke Bluebeard's Castle)

✍ Opera in one act, 1 hour
🎵 1911 (rev. 1912, 1918, 1921)
♔ 24 May 1918, Budapest Opera, Hungary

📖 Béla Balázs, after Charles Perrault's story *Barbe Bleue* (1697)

A kékszakállú herceg vára, Bartók's only opera, is a Gothic tale set to a masterful score. For the libretto, Béla Balázs adapted Charles Perrault's *Barbe Bleue*, itself a retelling of a popular folk tale. But he added a dark ending – Bluebeard's latest wife joins the others in death – and used the stark, emotional language of Symbolist poets to create a mood of permanent tension. The powerful score combines the harmony, melody, and *parlando rubato* rhythm of Hungary's folk music with nods to Wagner, Richard Strauss, Debussy, and Ravel. The result, notably the "tone poem" orchestration, is highly original. Bluebeard and Judith are engaged in dialogue throughout, leaving no room for traditional arias, yet their vocal parts vividly capture the ever-changing colours of the opera.

> ➤   **PRINCIPAL ROLES**   ◄
>
> The Storyteller *spoken*
> Duke Bluebeard *baritone* A baron
> Judith *mezzo-soprano* His newest wife
> Three murdered wives *silent*

Béla Bartók is photographed with his composer friend Zoltan Kodaly (*far right*) and a quartet of folk musicians. Both men were inspired by Hungary's music traditions.

⊱ After the socialist Béla Balázs was driven into exile by a rightist regime in 1919, Bartók refused to take Balázs's name off this opera. It was not presented again in Budapest until 1955. ⊰

PLOT SYNOPSIS

Europe in the late Middle Ages

The Storyteller announces that "old is the castle, and old the tale that tells of it". Duke Bluebeard leads his new wife, Judith, into his castle. She wonders why it is "always icy, dark, and gloomy" and vows to let in warmth and light. For this, she points to seven bolted doors, which she must open. Bluebeard discourages her, recalling rumours about his sinister past, but she insists, saying she loves him. The first door reveals daggers, racks and branding irons, all covered with blood: it is Bluebeard's torture chamber. As a crimson sunrise brings the first rays of light into the castle, Judith asks for another key. The next door leads to the armoury, where spears are also splashed with blood. Judith presses on, ignoring Bluebeard's warnings. The third door opens to gold,

"Oh, be sok kincs!"

diamonds, and pearls, again blood-stained ; it is Bluebeard's treasury.

A fragrant garden stands behind the fourth door, and still more light pours in. Judith asks about white roses spotted with blood, but Bluebeard will answer no questions. The fifth door leads to Bluebeard's sunny

"Ah!"
"Lásdez az én birodalman"

kingdom , but even here

clouds are streaked in blood red. Bluebeard says the castle glitters with light now that Judith has achieved her aim. But if she continues, he cautions that darkness will return. "Though I perish, I fear nothing," she replies. Opening the sixth door, she sees a white sheet of

water . "Tears, my Judith, tears, tears," says Bluebeard. He tries to

"Csendes fehér tavat látok"

distract her with a kiss, but she asks about his former lovers. When he again refuses to answer, she says she can explain all the blood: as long rumoured, he killed all his former wives. He gives her the key to the seventh door and announces his former lovers . As three finely-attired women emerge, Judith

"Lásd a régi aszszonyokat"

is stunned by their beauty. The first wife, Bluebeard explains, he found at daybreak; the second at noon; the third in the evening. And, turning to Judith, he adds, the fourth at midnight – and darkness will be hers forever. Suddenly terrified, Judith is dressed in diamonds as the "queen of all my women". And, still pleading for her life, she passes through the seventh door. "Henceforth," he says, "all shall be night, night, night."

Willard White, who has often sung the macabre role of Duke Bluebeard, is seen here in 2002 at the Royal Opera House.

VIRGIL
THOMSON

Born: 25 November 1896, Kansas City, Missouri, US
Died: 30 September 1989, New York, US

Virgil Thomson was a leading American composer of the 20th century. His two non-narrative operas to librettos by Gertrude Stein were *Four Saints in Three Acts* in 1933 and *The Mother of Us All* in 1947. While Europeans wrote Neo-Classical or atonal operas, Thomson's example inspired American composers to take musical cues from spoken language.

Thomson exhibited strong passions for music as a child growing up in Kansas City, Missouri. Home to a major river and a railway line cutting through America's heartland, Kansas City exposed him to a wealth of popular and traditional songs alongside the secular and sacred music he absorbed in his church-going Welsh-Scottish family. His talents were shaped at Harvard College, where he was introduced to Gertrude Stein's poetry and Eric Satie's music. Conductor Archibald Davison then also trained Thomson to work with vocalists of the Harvard Glee Club. In 1925, Thomson travelled to Paris to study with the celebrated Nadia Boulanger, and to hold his own in the city's exhilarating arts community. He remained true to his roots, writing from musical experience and personal conviction, rather than adopting theoretical precepts or new fashions. His compositions ranged from choral and symphonic music, to songs and film scores.

In 1983, Virgil Thomson (*centre*) was among Americans honoured at the Kennedy Center, Washington DC, for work in the performing arts.

GERTRUDE STEIN

In Paris in 1926, Thomson met Gertrude Stein (*below*), a poet whose work he had come to revere. The encounter proved to be pivotal, since Thomson went on to collaborate with Stein on numerous projects, including two operas. Stein's approach to language, and especially to American rhythms of speech, perfectly suited Thomson's musical sensibilities. She and her partner Alice B Toklas hosted legendary salons in their home, where Jean Cocteau, Pablo Picasso, and others influenced Thomson.

FOUR SAINTS IN THREE ACTS

⚐ Opera in a prologue and four acts, 1½ hours

☷ 1927–1928

♇ 8 February 1934, Wadsworth Atheneum,

Hartford, Connecticut, US; concert reading 20 May 1933, Ann Arbor, Michigan, US

📖 Gertrude Stein

Four Saints in Three Acts enjoyed a run of 60 performances when, in 1934, it opened on Broadway with an all-African-American cast. Called a "choreographic spectacle", this through-composed opera with dialogue celebrated its freedom to engage audiences with motion-packed staging, vocal virtuosity, and Stein's lyrics. A highlight is the powerful choral music informed by hymns that Thomson heard as a child in Missouri.

⚑ The playful character of Thomson's work with Stein begins with the opera's title: *Four Saints in Three Acts*. The opera in fact features 16 saints in four acts ⚑

→ PRINCIPAL ROLES ←

Saint Teresa of Avila
soprano and contralto
(two singers used for this role)

Saint Settlement *soprano*
Teresa's confidant

Saint Ignatius Loyola *baritone*

Saint Chavez *tenor*
Ignatius's confidant

Compère *bass*
Male presenter

Commère *mezzo-soprano*
Female presenter

PLOT SYNOPSIS

16th-century Spain

PROLOGUE In the company of a chorus of saints, the Compère and Commère introduce the idea of four saints.

ACT ONE In Avila, a Sunday School entertainment unfolds on the steps of the cathedral. Saint Teresa presents scenes from her life, observing as a second Saint Teresa portrays her courted by
"Ten saints can" | Saint Ignatius ♫; in ecstasy; and with child.

ACT TWO From an opera box, Saint Teresa and Saint Ignatius attend the action of a garden party near Barcelona: a Dance of Angels; a love scene; and party games. Both Saint Teresas see a Heavenly Mansion in the sky through a telescope. All saints kneel in awe of the vision, and rejoice.

ACT THREE In a monastery garden, Saint Ignatius tells other saints of his vision of the Holy Ghost. They believe him upon hearing a celestial chorus. After a Spanish dance by women and sailors, saints dispel fear of darkness in hymnal singing.

ACT FOUR Before the house curtain, the Compère and Commère debate whether there is to be a fourth act. Finally, the curtain rises on all the saints gathered in heaven. They recall happy memories of life below. Finally, they sing a hymn of communion ♫.
"When this you see remember me"

Robert Wilson's staging of *Three Saints in Four Acts* for the Houston Grand Opera in 1996.

GEORGE
GERSHWIN

Born: 26 September 1898, Brooklyn, New York, US
Died: 11 July 1937, Hollywood, California, US

The leading Broadway composer of the 1920s and 30s, George Gershwin teamed up with his lyricist brother, Ira, to create unforgettable songs that America would adopt as its own. *Porgy and Bess*, his only opera, changed the sound of stage music in the United States, where composers are still under its jazzy spell.

George Gershwin became a professional pianist at age 15, and as a young man began composing songs absorbed into musicals signed by other talents. His career soon skyrocketed. He composed a string of Broadway hits, from musical comedies like *Strike up the Band*, to his sole operatic work, *Porgy and Bess*. From 1924 on, George and Ira Gershwin created countless numbers whose very titles, like "'S Wonderful" from *Funny Face*, and "I Got Rhythm" from *Girl Crazy*, still trigger popular recollection of entire songs. The dance team Fred and Adele Astaire were among America's top stage talents who appeared repeatedly in Gershwin's musical comedies. Many of these works were influenced by the operetta form, but Gershwin's masterpiece, the opera *Porgy and Bess*, was most indebted to traditional African-American music. Gershwin was inspired by DuBose Heyward's novel *Porgy*, and his resulting "folk opera" was meant to premiere at the Metroplitan Opera in New York. But when those plans fell through, it opened at the Alvin Theater, where it enjoyed a run of 124 performances. Less than two years after the 1935 premiere of *Porgy and Bess*, Gershwin's blossoming career was cut tragically short. He died of a brain tumour at age 38.

The front cover of the programme for Gershwin's well-loved masterpiece *Porgy and Bess* from the Everyman Opera production that toured the world in 1952.

PORGY AND BESS

🎼 Opera in three acts, 3 hours
📅 1934–1935
🏛 10 October 1935, Alvin Theater, New York, US

📖 DuBose Heyward, from the play *Porgy* (1927) by DuBose and Dorothy Heyward based on DuBose Heyward's 1925 novel; additional lyrics by Ira Gershwin

Many hit songs from Porgy and Bess – "A Woman is a Sometime Thing", "It Ain't Necessarily So", "Bess, you is my woman now" – have been recorded by great jazz and blues singers. Gershwin travelled to South Carolina to take in the atmosphere and music of the opera's setting. His score integrated African-American gospel music, blues, and jazz to create worlds of sound that Broadway had never heard the likes of before 1935.

🎵 The first Porgy, Todd Duncan, recalled George and Ira Gershwin singing through the opera to interest him in the role. In spite of their "awful, rotten voices", Todd was seized by the melodies 🎵

→ PRINCIPAL ROLES ←

Porgy *bass-baritone*
A cripple in love with Bess

Bess *soprano*
A loose woman

Crown *baritone*
Her boyfriend

Robbins *tenor*
A gambling patron

Serena *soprano*
His wife

Sportin' Life *tenor*
A drug dealer

PLOT SYNOPSIS

Charleston, South Carolina, in the early 1920s

ACT ONE The mood in the tenement on Catfish Row is trance-like 🎵. Porgy, a cripple, is in love with Bess, whose boyfriend, Crown, joins other men to gamble. When Robbins gets lucky with the dice, Crown stabs him in a burst of anger. As police close in, Crown flees, and Bess finds refuge with Porgy. Serena and others mourn Robbins's death in her room. A detective questions them, then detains a guiltless suspect.

"Summertime"

ACT TWO Porgy and Bess fall in love. But during a picnic on an island where Crown is in hiding, Bess is again seduced by her old lover. Back on Catfish Row, a distraught Bess assures Porgy of her love for him. As a hurricane threatens, all sing for the Lord's protection. Suddenly, Crown returns for Bess, but then risks his own life to save a fisherman in the storm.

ACT THREE All console the dead fisherman's wife. When Crown reclaims Bess, Porgy stabs him. The detective leads Porgy away to identify Crown's body. Returning from jail-time, Porgy learns that Bess has run off to New York with the drug dealer Sportin' Life. Porgy has no idea where New York is, but begins his journey to find Bess 🎵.

"Oh Lawd, I'm on my way"

In 1985, American tenor, Simon Estes was the first Porgy ever to appear at the Metropolitan Opera in New York.

CARL
ORFF

Born: 10 July 1895, Munich, Bavaria (Germany)
Died: 29 March 1982, Munich, Germany

Carl Orff, a leading German composer of the mid-20th century, has long moved classical music lovers the world over with his early masterpiece, the staged cantata *Carmina Burana*. While fellow European composers pursued atonal music and concepts, Orff wrote melodious operatic works fuelled by seemingly archaic, ritual forces.

Orff's training at the Munich Academy was interrupted by military service during World War I. Then, after studies in early music, he was influenced by the earthy, elemental energies of modern dance. Indeed, in 1924, he co-founded a Munich school devoted to exploring music, language, and physical expression. His own works often treated the voice as an instrument of primordial emotional urgency. Early success came with his renowned setting of medieval poems, *Carmina Burana*. Latin poetry was used again for the erotic *Catulli Carmina*, for which he set love lyrics by Catullus. Orff was also moved by Ancient Greek drama. His tragedies *Antigonae* and *Oedipus der Tyrann* were based on plays by Sophocles that he had read in startling translations by the Romantic poet Friedrich Hölderlin. Orff's most popular opera remains *Die Kluge*, an intense, charming work. Like his lesser-known *Der Mond (The Moon)*, it was inspired by a German folk tale.

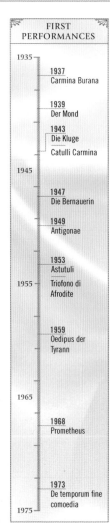

FIRST
PERFORMANCES

1935

1937
Carmina Burana

1939
Der Mond

1943
Die Kluge

Catulli Carmina

1945

1947
Die Bernauerin

1949
Antigonae

1953
Astutuli

1955   Triofono di
Afrodite

1959
Oedipus der
Tyrann

1965

1968
Prometheus

1973
De temporum fine
comoedia

1975

Carl Orff (*right*) watches dancers rehearse one of his works at the Bayerische Staatsoper in Munich in 1963.

DIE KLUGE
(The Clever Girl)

⌂ Märchenoper, 1½ hours
🗓 1940–1942
♇ 20 February 1943, Städtische Bühnen,

Frankfurt am Main, Germany
📖 Carl Orff, loosely based on a German folk tale collected by the brothers Jacob and Wilhelm Grimm

For *Die Kluge*, Orff turned an old folk-tale into a modern parable pitting wisdom and love against mindless power. This one-act opera hypnotizes with its mixture of sweet and sour sounds, characters, and story threads. Mischievous vagabonds lighten the mood with their antics, even as the clever girl's untiring commitment to truth creates solemn entrancement.

⚜ Born in Germany in 1915, the diva Elisabeth Schwarzkopf's soprano voice was perfect to play characters like Alice Ford in Verdi's *Falstaff*, the Marschallin in Strauss's *Rosenkavalier*, and the lead in *Die Kluge*. ⚜

✦ PRINCIPAL ROLES ✦

Der König *baritone*
The king

Der Bauer *bass*
The farmer

Der Bauern Tochter *soprano*
The farmer's daughter

Der Mann mit dem Esel
tenor Man with a donkey

Der Mann mit dem Maulesel
baritone Man with a mule

PLOT SYNOPSIS

A land from fairy-tale

A peasant laments: had he listened to his daughter, the king would not have imprisoned him. The king marries her and frees her father when she correctly answers three riddles. But he offers no justice to a man with a donkey whose foal is claimed by a man with a mule. The queen offers the donkey-man help. The donkey-man fishes on dry land, but claims this is normal in a world where mules give birth. Suspecting his wife of coaching the donkey-man, the king instructs her to leave. First, though, she may fill chests with whatever she most treasures. Dosing his wine with poppy seeds, she sings the king sweetly to sleep with a lullaby 🎵.
The king awakens inside a chest and peers about in wonder. His wife explains: she was to fill the chests with whatever her heart most desired.

"Schuschuschu, schuschuschu"

The two look at one another and smile.

Peter Edelmann as the king and Bettine Kampp as his wife perform at the Carl Orff Festival in Andechs, Germany, in 2003.

FRANCIS
POULENC

Born: 7 January 1899, Paris, France
Died: 30 January 1963, Paris, France

Francis Poulenc, the reigning *enfant terrible* of French music
in the 1920s and 30s, following World War I, was drawn into
the Surrealist movement. He set poems by Paul Élouard, Jean Cocteau,
and Guillaume Apollinaire, whose play *Les Mamelles de Tirésias*, or *The Breasts
of Tiresias*, also served as the source for his first opera, in 1947. A decade later,
Poulenc's operatic masterpiece, *Dialogues des Carmélites*, showed that his youthful
piquancy had given way to genuine sentimental depth. It and his final opera,
La voix humaine, or *The Human Voice*, struck some contemporaries as too Romantic,
but both have entered the repertoire as major 20th-century works.

DIALOGUES DES CARMÉLITES
Dialogues of the Carmelites

✍ Opera in three acts and twelve scenes, 2½ hours
📖 1953–1955
♜ 26 January 1957, Teatro alla Scala, Milan, Italy

📖 Francis Poulenc, after the play by Georges Bernanos

To capture the intimacy of dialogue,
Poulenc resists luxurious textures in favour
of a lean, focused sound that cuts to the
heart of the drama. The music's searing
clarity owes more to Stravinsky than
Massenet, though Poulenc retains Massenet's
elegant way with a melody. For the finale,
one of the opera's few ensembles, nuns
sing a lyrical hymn, *"Salve Regina"*, with
voices dropping out one by one to the
sound of a falling guillotine.

→ **PRINCIPAL ROLES** ←

Blanche de la Force *soprano* A timorous woman

Chevalier *tenor* Her brother

Madame de Croissy *contralto* Prioress of the Carmelite Convent

Mère Marie (Mother Mary) *mezzo-soprano* Assistant Prioress

Madame Lidoine *soprano* The new Prioress

Soeur Constance (Sister Constance) *soprano* A very young nun

⚜ Blanche and de Croissy share the ambitious name "Sister of the Agony of Christ", referring to the moment when Jesus expressed fear of death in Gethsemane. De Croissy capitulates to her fear, but Blanche transcends it ⚜

PLOT SYNOPSIS

Paris and Compiègne, France, at the time of the French Revolution of 1789

ACT ONE SCENE 1 Blanche tells her father she wants to become a nun and escape the fearful excitement of the world. SCENE 2 Blanche tells the mother superior, Madame de Croissy, she wishes to take the name "Sister Blanche of the Agony of Christ". SCENE 3 Blanche chastizes Constance for her irreverence on the subject of death. SCENE 4 De Croissy blasphemes as she suffers a horrible, tedious death. She asks Mère Marie to watch over Blanche. She bids Blanche goodbye ♫ and dies.

"Relevez-vous, ma fille"

ACT TWO SCENE 1 De Croissy lies in state, as Blanche minds her. Blanche fearfully tries to leave the room, but Marie arrives and chides her. Later, Constance muses that someone else will receive the graceful, unafraid death God intended for de Croissy. SCENE 2 The new mother superior, Madame Lidoine, greets the order. SCENE 3 The Chevalier bids his sister Blanche goodbye before going to war and asks her to care for their father. She refuses, citing her duty to God. SCENE 4 A commissioner arrives and orders the Convent to disband.

ACT THREE SCENE 1 The Carmelites vote anonymously whether to take a vow of martyrdom. After Constance

Francis Poulenc (*left*) reads through the libretto of *Dialogues des Carmélites* with two members of the cast at a rehearsal for a 1958 production at the Royal Opera House, London.

retracts her initial objection, they take the vow. Blanche then flees. SCENE 2 Marie urges Blanche to return. She declines. SCENE 3 Jailed, the Carmelites await execution. SCENE 4 The nuns chant as they advance to the guillotine. As Constance awaits her turn, a serene, accepting Blanche joins them ♫.

"Salve Regina"

A scene from Poulenc's opera in a spare and moving production staged by Francesca Zambello for the Opéra Bastille in 2004.

"It is cruel that music should be so beautiful. It has the beauty of loneliness and of pain, of strength and freedom."

Benjamin Britten

BENJAMIN
BRITTEN

Born: 22 November 1913, Lowestoft, Suffolk, England
Died: 4 December 1976, Aldeburgh, Suffolk, England

Benjamin Britten was the first major English opera composer since Henry Purcell almost three centuries earlier. He was also the first ever to demonstrate the full operatic potential of the English language. In 1945, post-war England discovered new cultural life in his landmark opera, *Peter Grimes*. But it was only the beginning of a career that would dominate late 20th-century opera.

Britten was born in 1913 in Suffolk, where his father was a dentist. He began composing at six, and at 15 studied with Frank Bridge before attending the Royal College of Music in London. His career blossomed amidst the political upheavals that scarred Europe in the 1930s. Still a teenager, he was recognized as an exceptional talent and by age 22 was employed with the Government Printing Office, where he worked as a composer with the Film Unit. During the late 1930s, he met the poet WH Auden, and the tenor Peter Pears. Pears remained Britten's muse, collaborator, and partner throughout the remainder of his life. A committed pacifist, Britten travelled with Pears just before the outbreak of World War II to live in exile in the United States. There, with Auden his librettist and Pears his lead tenor, he created *Paul Bunyan*, an opera about the American folk-hero. The work was largely ignored after its New York premiere in 1941, yet Britten himself was noticed. That same year, he was awarded a Library of Congress Medal for his services to chamber music in the United States, and received a commission from the library's Koussevitsky Music Foundation to write an opera. The result, *Peter Grimes*, proved to be Britten's first masterpiece, and cause for celebration in England.

At the historical premiere of Benjamin Britten's *Peter Grimes* in 1945, the tenor Peter Pears (*left*) held London audiences spellbound in the unsettling title role.

FIRST
PERFORMANCES

1940

1941
Paul Bunyan

1945
Peter Grimes

1945

1946
The Rape
of Lucretia

1949
The Little Sweep

1950

1951
Billy Budd

1953
Gloriana

1955

1954
The Turn of
the Screw

1958
Noye's Fludde

1960

1960
A Midsummer
Night's Dream

1964
Curlew River

1965

1966
The Burning
Fiery Furnace

1968
The Prodigal Son

1970

1971
Owen Wingrave

1973
Death in Venice

1965

EARLY OPERAS
1945–1955

When Britten returned with Peter Pears to England in 1942, they were already at work sketching *Peter Grimes*. The country was at war, but both young men were recognized as conscientious objectors and were exempted from military service. *Peter Grimes* premiered in London in 1945 mere weeks after VE-day in Europe, with Pears singing the title role Britten had written for him. The opera was instantly embraced as a work heralding a new era for the war-tattered country. The following years brought *The Rape of Lucretia*, based on the poem by Shakespeare; *Albert Herring*; and *The Little Sweep*, a children's opera. But of all operas from this period, many today consider *Billy Budd*, which premiered in 1951, to be the composer's finest. Subsequent operas were the controversial *Gloriana*, about Queen Elizabeth I, and *The Turn of the Screw*.

LATER OPERAS 1956–1976

In 1956, Britten and Pears travelled to Bali and Japan, where new horizons in sound and drama marked the composer for subsequent operas.

Benjamin Britten appeared on the cover of *Time* magazine in 1948. Fishing nets in background suggest his opera *Peter Grimes*.

Noye's Fludde, a miracle play, and *A Midsummer Night's Dream*, based on Shakespeare's play, sparkle with Eastern effects, as do the three "church parables" of the 1960s: *Curlew River*, *The Burning Fiery Furnace*, and *The Prodigal Son*. In this era, too, Britten's legendary pacifism grew more explicit in his music. The much-loved *War Requiem* of 1962 was followed by *Owen Wingrave*, an anti-war opera of 1971 based on a story by Henry James. Britten's final opera, *Death in Venice*, was written as he struggled with a heart ailment. He was too sick to attend the premiere at the Aldeburgh Festival, which he and Pears had founded in 1948. But he did hear his beloved Pears give a *tour-de-force* interpretation of the extraordinary role of Aschenbach at Covent Garden in London. By the time of his death in 1976, the composer was Baron Britten of Aldeburgh, a Life Peer named by Queen Elizabeth II. By then, too, his operatic oeuvre was formidable and sure to be enduring.

Benjamin Britten (*second from right*) on a boating expedition with friends including the novelist who was his librettist, EM Forster (*left*), in 1949.

ALBERT HERRING

✍ Comic opera in three acts, 2½ hours
🗓 1946–1947
♔ 20 June 1947, Glyndebourne, Sussex, England

📖 Eric Crozier, after the Guy de Maupassant short story *Le rosier de Madame Husson* (1888)

Albert Herring has been called a comical version of the tragic *Peter Grimes*, Britten's earlier opera about a man stripped of his dignity. Here, the man prevails. Filled with strong characters, *Albert Herring* is often moving, as when Albert struggles against his overbearing mother, or when townspeople mourn his presumed death. The work suffered a poor premiere in 1947, but has since been hailed a comic opera of painfully real dimensions.

⊰ The opera abounds in quotations from other operas. One takes place early in Act II, when Albert's lemonade is heavily spiked with rum. The orchestra cites Wagner's motif for the love potion in *Tristan und Isolde* ⊱

→ PRINCIPAL ROLES ←

Albert Herring *tenor*
A grocer of Loxford

Mrs Herring *mezzo-soprano*
Albert's mother

Lady Billows *soprano*
A bossy autocrat

Florence Pike *contralto*
Her housekeeper

Sid *baritone*
A butcher's delivery boy

Nancy *mezzo-soprano*
Sid's girlfriend

PLOT SYNOPSIS

the fictional town of Loxford, Suffolk, England, in the early summer of 1900

ACT ONE Lady Billows receives townspeople to discuss who shall be the town's May Queen. All suggested girls are discredited on moral grounds by the housekeeper, Florence. When a May King is proposed – Albert Herring, the upstanding grocer – Lady Billows finally accepts. In his grocery shop, Albert is goaded by Sid, a delivery boy, about his domineering mother. The committee arrives to declare Albert the May King of Loxford. Mrs Herring forces her reluctant son to accept "the crown" and cash prize.

ACT TWO On the big day, Sid spikes Albert's lemonade. Lady Billows presents the May King. But Albert, drunk, has an attack of hiccups. Alone in the shop, Albert hears Sid and his girlfriend Nancy

outside. This fills him with resentment of his mother ♂. Albert slips out into the night.

"Heaven helps those who help themselves!"

ACT THREE In the shop the next day, the townspeople presume Albert dead. As they mourn him ♕, Albert returns to report his disorderly pub crawl. All are outraged. Albert lashes out against his mother; receives a kiss from Nancy; and takes command of his shop.

"In the midst of life is death"

For the 1947 premiere at Glyndebourne, Peter Pears (*left*) played the title role, and Betsy de la Porte (*centre*) was his mother.

PETER GRIMES

⚐ Opera in a prologue and three acts,
2¼ hours
⚰ 1944–1945

♔ 7 June 1945, Sadler's Wells, London, England
📖 Montagu Slater, after the poem *The Borough*
(1810) by George Crabbe

Peter Grimes is Britten's first operatic masterpiece. He was living in the United States during World War II when he read George Crabbe's *The Borough*, a poem from 1810 about a fisherman and his community in Britten's beloved Aldeburgh. Work on adapting the poem began before his return to Britain, where the opera premiered after the war. It would become the first major opera written in English since Purcell's 17th-century *Dido and Aeneas*. With Peter Pears singing the title role, *Peter Grimes* proved a tremendous success. The threads of its dark and stirring story – of injustice, hatred, dashed hopes, and a man's struggle with his poisoned fate – are woven into a musical net of heart-rending orchestral beauty and vocal transcendence.

⌁ The opera company of the Sadler's Wells Theatre was initially hostile to the idea of premiering *Peter Grimes*. Company members, who found the work grim and unmusical, were astounded by its success. ⌁

➤ PRINCIPAL ROLES ◄

Peter Grimes *tenor*
A fisherman

Ellen Orford *soprano*
A widowed schoolmistress

Captain Balstrode *baritone*
Retired merchant sea-captain

Auntie *contralto*
Owns The Boar, a tavern
and brothel

Bob Boles *tenor*
A righteous Methodist
fisherman

Mr Swallow *bass*
Mayor, coroner, and lawyer

Mrs Sedley *mezzo-soprano*
An unpopular widow

Reverend Horace Adams
tenor The parson

Ned Keene *baritone*
The apothecary

PLOT SYNOPSIS

A coastal borough in England

PROLOGUE At a coroner's inquest, Peter Grimes gives evidence about the death of his most recent apprentice. He is warned not to take another, and gossip instantly shapes his reputation.

ACT ONE Several days later, fishermen work on their boats. Ned Keene, the apothecary, has found Grimes a new apprentice from an orphanage. The Borough responds with fear, but Ellen Orford, the schoolmistress, vouches for Grimes. Balstrode, a retired captain, spies a gale force storm approaching, and the Borough prepares 🎵. | "Now the flood tide"

Grimes tells Balstrode that he hopes to become rich fishing, to gain respect and marry Ellen. Grimes enters The Boar tavern, thinking aloud about fate 🎵. The Methodist Boles, drunk, tries to strike him, but | "Now the Great Bear and the Pleiades"

Balstrode blocks the effort. When John, the new apprentice, is delivered, Grimes takes him home directly.

Benjamin Britten (*left*) and the opera's producer Eric Crozier examine a model for the stage set of the 1945 premiere of *Peter Grimes*.

Eerie staging by David Pountney marks a 2005 production of *Peter Grimes* at the Opernhaus in Zurich, Switzerland, with Christopher Ventris as Peter Grimes.

ACT TWO Villagers sing hymns in church while Ellen sits outside with John. Seeing

"Let this be a holiday"

his wounded neck, she realizes that Grimes has hurt him ♿.

Grimes arrives in a state of excitement, eager to profit from waters teeming with fish. When Ellen objects, Grimes strikes her. They part ways, and villagers soon form a mob to head to

"In dreams I've built myself some kindlier home"

Grimes's hut. In the hut, Grimes reflects on his life's plans ♿. Hearing the mob, he

leads John to the back door, where a landslide caused by the storm has created a precipice over the sea. The boy falls out of sight, and Peter rushes after him. The villagers burst in, but realize that their search is pointless. All leave as they came, save Balstrode, who follows the route Grimes took.

ACT THREE A few evenings later, villagers dance in the town hall. But Mrs Sedley leaves to sit on the shore. She listens unnoticed as Balstrode then discovers

"Embroidery in childhood was"

Grimes's boat, and as Ellen recognizes the missing boy's jersey ♿.

Mrs Sedley gives the news to Swallow, who gathers a posse. The Borough erupts with hatred and disperses in search of Grimes ♉.

Hours later, Grimes returns to an empty

"Who holds himself apart"

town. He rehearses the accidental losses of his apprentices and accepts his fate. Ellen and Balstrode arrive to offer solemn help. Balstrode instructs Grimes to take his boat out to sea and sink it. As the town comes to life the next day, Swallow notes that a boat is sinking at sea, but is too far off to be rescued.

A MARGINAL HERO

Peter Grimes is an anti-hero, but Britten made him a sympathetic and deeply human one. When Grimes adds his voice to those of villagers singing together in Act I, they break off to leave his voice alone. Emotional impact is heightened by Grimes's exclusion, and by his urgent desire to be accepted. The rapport between Grimes and his community is a central concern in the opera's score.

Peter Pears played Peter Grimes numerous times after he created the role in 1945.

BILLY BUDD

⚖ Opera in four acts (revised version two acts with prologue and epilogue), 2¾ hours
☷ 1950–1951; rev. 1960

♔ 1 December 1951, Royal Opera House, London
☐ EM Forster and Eric Crozier, from the story *Billy Budd, Foretopman* (1891) by Herman Melville

Billy Budd is widely considered the finest opera of the 20th century, a flawless work about human flaws. Tension builds from the outset as an English warship enters enemy waters to fight the French. But the real war occurs among the English. Whether outwardly or internally, seamen are in perpetual conflict. Further, alluring ideas about "the rights of man" lead officers to fear that their own crew plots mutiny, inspired by the revolutionary French enemy. Tension was no less present in the opera's creation. Britten wrestled with his librettists, EM Forster and Eric Crozier, until he was satisfied with the work.

⚓ The opera calls for three principals, a full male chorus, and a children's chorus, also male, who form part of the crew aboard the *Indomitable*. With all the action set on a warship in 1797, there are no female roles. ⚓

→ **PRINCIPAL ROLES** ←

Billy Budd *baritone*
Able seaman

Captain Vere *tenor*
Captain of
HMS Indomitable

Claggart *bass*
Master-at-arms

Mr Redburn *baritone*
First Lieutenant

Mr Ratcliffe *bass*
Second Lieutenant

Mr Flint *bass-baritone*
Sailing Master

Dansker *bass*
An old seaman

Squeak *tenor*
Ship's corporal

PLOT SYNOPSIS

Aboard the Indomitable, *during the Napoleonic Wars of 1797*

PROLOGUE Captain Vere recalls the French wars of 1797, when he commanded the warship *Indomitable*. He searches for meaning in the balance of Good and Evil, and notes that even good is always marred by imperfection.

ACT ONE Mr Flint, the Sailing Master, treats his crew harshly. When three recruits arrive, Claggart, Master-at-arms, interrogates them. Only the third appears promising. He declares himself to be Billy Budd, able seaman. But he stammers helplessly when asked about his home. Officers find this a flaw, but Claggart sees Billy as goodness incarnate. Assigned to the foretop, Billy rejoices, and bids a spirited farewell to his

previous ship, the *Rights o' Man* ♪. Officers fear that Billy's evocation of the "rights of man" could incite mutiny. Meanwhile, fellow crew members warn Billy against Claggart, and praise Captain Vere ⏱. A week later, Vere invites Redburn and Flint to his cabin, where they note that a new recruit cheered the "rights of man". But Vere has no fears about Billy Budd. Ratcliffe reports that the *Indomitable* has entered enemy waters. On the berth-deck, Squeak provokes Billy to fight.

"Billy Budd, king of the birds!"

"Starry, Starry Vere"

The American Theodor Uppman created Billy Budd at the Royal Opera House in London in 1951.

"O beauty, o handsomeness, goodness" | Claggart puts Squeak in irons but, alone, aims to destroy Billy ♻. Under Claggart's orders, the Novice offers Billy money to wage mutiny. When Billy's anger produces stammering, the Novice flees.

ACT TWO Captain Vere worries about enveloping mists as his men grow impatient for battle. Suddenly, a French frigate is sighted, and the crew excitedly prepares for action ♻.

"This is our moment! The moment we've been waiting for!" | But exhilaration wanes when Vere gives orders to abandon the chase. Claggart informs Vere that mutiny is being fomented by Billy Budd. Dismayed, Vere summons Billy. In Vere's cabin, Claggart accuses Budd of mutiny. Billy stammers and, in frustration, strikes the officer. When Claggart proves to be dead, Vere realizes

"The mists have cleared" | he has no choice but to put Billy on trial ♻. After speaking in his own defence, Billy is taken away, crying for Captain Vere to save him. But the law requires Billy's execution, and Vere reluctantly accepts his officers' verdict. Billy explains to Dansker that Fate has determined his death. But, alone, he

"And farewell to ye, old Rights o' Man!" | discovers an inner strength – stronger than Fate – that allows him to embrace death ♻.

At first light, Billy blesses Captain Vere, then is hanged. The crew reacts with groaning sounds, and tension builds until the officers cause the men to disperse.

EPILOGUE Years later, the elderly Captain Vere reflects that he could have saved Billy from death, but that instead Billy saved him, and blessed him.

The crew aboard the *Indomitable* becomes restless in Tim Albery's production of *Billy Budd* for the English National Opera in London in 1991.

Francesca Zambello's staging of Benjamin Britten's *Billy Budd* was visually striking and charged with symbolism at the Royal Opera in London, 2002.

THE TURN OF THE SCREW

🎵 An opera in a prologue and two acts, 1¾ hours
📅 1954
🏛 14 September 1954, Teatro La Fenice,

Venice, Italy
📖 Myfanwy Piper, after Henry James's story

In this chamber opera, a governess attempts to save two children haunted by a dead man. Music associated with the governess is stark, percussive, and neurotic. But the ghost's hypnotic vocal lines and dreamy music thread through the opera, and even dominate at the end of Act I. The prologue establishes a musical theme, and orchestral interludes return in increasingly demented variations to create ever-deepening suspense.

⚜ The libretto borrows a line from poet WB Yeats, "The ceremony of innocence is drowned", which not only refers to the abused children, but also illuminates the governess's shattered idealism. ⚜

→ PRINCIPAL ROLES ←

The governess *soprano*
Cares for the children

Miles *treble*
Boy in her charge

Flora *soprano*
His sister, also in her charge

Mrs Grose *soprano*
The housekeeper

Quint *tenor*
A former valet

Miss Jessel *soprano*
A former governess

PLOT SYNOPSIS

In and around Bly, a country house in the East of England, in the mid-19th century

PROLOGUE A governess has agreed to care for two children who live in a country mansion. Their handsome guardian insists that she not contact him.

ACT ONE Riding in a coach, the governess anxiously anticipates her arrival at Bly. Mrs Grose and the children, Miles and Flora, welcome her. Later, the governess receives notice of Miles's dismissal from school, but she and Mrs Grose do not believe that Miles could be bad. The governess sees the figure of a man upon a tower. Hearing the description, Mrs Grose verifies it is Peter Quint, who had abused the children and former governess, Miss Jessel. Both Quint

Mireille Delunsch portrays the overwhelmed governess in Luc Bondy's production at Théâtre des Champs Élysées, 2005, with haunting sets by Richard Peduzzi.

"Malo, Malo, Malo" | and Miss Jessel are dead now. Miles rehearses Latin 🔊.

The governess and Flora sit on the lake, where the governess sees Miss Jessel and rushes Flora away. At night, Miss Jessel and Quint beckon to Miles and Flora. The governess hurries them inside.

ACT TWO Quint and Miss Jessel describe what they seek in the children 🔊. Mrs Grose and the children attend church, and | "I seek a friend" | the governess decides to write to their guardian. Miles steals the letter. Later, Miles plays the piano, and Flora sneaks off. The governess confronts Flora, who calls her cruel and hateful. She then questions Miles. Increasingly distraught and frightened, Miles blurts out "Peter Quint, you devil," then falls lifeless into the governess's embrace.

A MIDSUMMER NIGHT'S DREAM

🎵 Opera in three acts, 2½ hours
📅 1959–1960
🎭 11 June 1960, Jubilee Hall, Aldeburgh,

Suffolk, England
📖 Benjamin Britten and Peter Pears, adapted from Shakespeare's play (1595–1596)

The opera is divided into three distinct spheres. For the fairy realm, Britten makes extravagant use of celesta, glockenspiel, harps, and even harpsichord to achieve an orchestral texture of enchantment. The lovers constitute a balanced vocal quartet despite the improbable story unfolding onstage. But the show often goes to the rustics, who win over audiences with their comic timing, playful harmonies, and tight ensemble work.

✴ The rustics put on a play that parodies 19th-century *bel canto* style. At the premiere, Pears, as Flute, imitated the diva Joan Sutherland to perfection, leaving the assistant conductor, George Malcolm, in stitches. ✴

> ✦ **PRINCIPAL ROLES** ✦
>
> **Oberon** *countertenor*
> King of the Fairies
>
> **Tytania** *coloratura soprano*
> Queen of the Fairies
>
> **Lysander** *tenor*
> In love with Hermia
>
> **Demetrius** *baritone*
> In love with Hermia
>
> **Hermia** *mezzo-soprano*
> In love with Lysander
>
> **Helena** *soprano*
> In love with Demetrius

PLOT SYNOPSIS

A wood outside Athens

ACT ONE Oberon and Tytania quarrel over a changeling left in Tytania's care. Oberon instructs the trickster Puck to obtain a love potion. Hermia and Lysander pledge their love for each other, while Helena futilely pursues Demetrius. A simple group of men, the rustics, plan a play for the Duke's wedding celebration. Puck administers his potion to Lysander, making him fall in love with Helena. She interprets his attention as mockery.

ACT TWO As the rustics rehearse, Puck bewitches Bottom, the lead of their troupe, by fitting him with the head of an ass. Tytania, charmed with the same potion as Lysander, falls in love upon seeing the ass-headed Bottom. She instructs the fairies to dote on him

"Be kind and courteous to this gentleman"

♫. Puck lastly gives the potion to

Demetrius, who also falls in love with Helena. Helena and Hermia quarrel, as the men ally themselves with Helena.

ACT THREE Oberon releases Tytania from the spell and arranges the lovers into two suitable pairs. Upon waking, they celebrate their love ♫. The rustics perform their ridiculous play for the Duke's wedding festivities.

"Helena!"
"Hermia!"
"Demetrius!"
"Lysander!"

Director Simon Phillips gave the opera's Shakespearean action a fresh and modern feel for a 2006 production at the Staatsoper in Hamburg.

CURLEW RIVER

⚐ Parable for church performance, 1¼ hours
🎭 1964
⚑ 12 June 1964, Orford Church, Suffolk, England

📖 William Plomer, based on the Japanese Noh play *Sumidagawa* by Juro Motomasa (1395–1431)

Curlew River, one of Britten's three church parables, marries Eastern and Western cultures in both its music and its story. Basing his work on a Japanese Noh play about a mother searching for her child, Britten also harks back to medieval liturgical dramas. Latin plainsong hymns and Balinese gamelan music are among the distinct elements given new life in this short work about a miracle on a river that divides, connects, and heals. Aptly, it premiered in a church.

> ⤖ **PRINCIPAL ROLES** ⬅
>
> The Abbot *bass*
> The Ferryman *baritone*
> The Madwoman *tenor*
> The Spirit of the Boy *treble*

⤛ In the Japanese Noh tradition that inspired *Curlew River*, flutes and drums are used as accompaniment. Britten kept them in the foreground of the work, but also called for an organ and a harp in the ensemble. ⤜

PLOT SYNOPSIS

In a church by the Curlew River, in early medieval times

An Abbot and Monks process into the acting area as they praise God in a Latin hymn. The Abbot invites the congregation to attend a mystery. Monks assume roles in the following parable. A Ferryman on the Curlew River explains that he transports people to a shrine, where someone was buried exactly one year earlier. A weary male Traveller reaches the ferry. A Madwoman searches for her son, who was captured and taken to the East. She and the Traveller board the ferry. The Ferryman explains why people gather on the far bank: a year ago, a young Christian boy, taken as a slave by a Heathen, was abandoned there; the boy fell ill and asked to be buried there. All realize that the boy was the son of the Madwoman, whose search has ended on the Curlew River. The Madwoman laments at her child's tomb ♪. She and others offer a moonlit prayer. From inside the tomb, a voice joins them ♫. The Spirit of the Boy appears and, in a solemn but uplifting manner, affirms to the boy's mother that they will meet in heaven. As in the work's opening section, the Abbot addresses the audience as a congregation. He explains that a miracle occurred on the Curlew River. In a procession away from the acting area, the Monks praise God with the same Latin hymn sung in the initial scene.

"Hoping, I wandered on"

"Sanctae sit Triadi laus pia iugiter"

Toby Spence is the Madwoman and Tomas Baird is the Spirit of her dead son in a production at the Royal Lyceum Theatre in Edinburgh, Scotland, in 2005.

DEATH IN VENICE

⚔ Opera in two acts, 2½ hours
🕮 1971–1973
♛ 16 June 1973, Snape Maltings,

Aldeburgh, England
📖 Myfanwy Piper, based on the novella by Thomas Mann, *Der Tod in Venedig* (1912)

Death in Venice was Britten's last opera. Based on the novella by Thomas Mann, the subjects of this operatic masterpiece are inspiration, beauty, longing, wisdom, and sacrifice. Britten weaves these into music of deceptive simplicity and refined restraint, bringing all the maturity of his musical experience to bear on the score. The opera belongs to Aschenbach, perhaps the most demanding role in the English repertoire.

⇥ The role of Aschenbach was scored for the tenor Peter Pears, who for decades had been Britten's collaborator and lover. Britten was too sick to attend rehearsals, and struggled against death to complete the opera. ⇤

→ PRINCIPAL ROLES ←

Gustav von Aschenbach *tenor*
A famous writer

Tadzio *silent role*
A Polish boy

Hotel Clerk *bass-baritone*
He warns of cholera outbreak

Voice of Apollo *counter-tenor*
A voice Aschenbach hears

Voice of Dionysus *bass-baritone*
A voice Aschenbach hears

PLOT SYNOPSIS

The European cities of Munich and Venice

ACT ONE In Munich, Aschenbach, a famous writer, confronts his lack of

"My mind beats on and no words come"

inspiration ♂. He travels to Venice. A mysterious Gondolier deposits him at his hotel. At supper, noting a Polish boy with his family, he ponders the child's beauty. In a strange and hot wind on the beach, he watches the boy and, hearing his name, Tadzio, compares differences between beauty created and experienced. With Venice repulsing him, he tries to leave but, his luggage lost, he remains. On the beach, Aschenbach imagines Tadzio and other children as Olympians; he hears Apollo praising beauty. Alone, Aschenbach realizes that he is in love.

For the premiere at Snape Maltings, Aldeburgh, in 1973, Peter Pears (*in white suit*) played Aschenbach, and Robert Huguenin (*kneeling centre*) was Tadzio, the boy who possesses his imagination in Venice.

ACT TWO Aschenbach accepts his love for the boy. In town, he hears rumours of disease. In the hotel, he finds honour in being enslaved to Eros. When some strolling players entertain, he senses a bond with Tadzio. The Hotel Clerk reveals that cholera will grip the city. Aschenbach resolves to warn Tadzio's mother, but does not. Dreaming of Dionysus (who stands for the urge to die) vying with Apollo (who in contrast stands for the urge to thrive), he wonders where beauty leads ♂.

"Does beauty lead to wisdom, Phaedrus?"

Tadzio beholds the writer, his hair newly dyed. Aschenbach learns that the Polish family is soon to depart, then observes Tadzio on the beach. As the boy beckons him, the writer collapses in his chair, dead.

OLIVIER
MESSIAEN

Born: 10 December 1908, Avignon, France
Died: 28 April 1992, Paris, France

Olivier Messiaen was a maverick composer who followed a spiritual Muse. A church organist at La Trinité in Paris, he began in the 1930s to draw on diverse sources, from Gregorian chant to Indonesian gamelan music, to compose works inspired by Roman Catholic mysteries. He was also moved by natural sounds, such as birdsongs and breezes. After World War II, he systematized the 12-tone method – Schoenberg initially applied it to pitch – through all musical variables, including rhythm. This project launched the movement known as serialism, a major influence on composers beginning with Messiaen's students, Pierre Boulez and Karlheinz Stockhausen.

SAINT FRANÇOIS D'ASSISE
Saint Francis of Assisi

✍ Scènes franciscaines in three acts (eight tableaux), 4 hours
🎗 1975–1983

🎗 28 November 1983, Paris Opéra, France
📖 Olivier Messiaen

Saint François d'Assise, a masterpiece of the late 20th century, is a work of unparalleled musical and theatrical force. However, few are the opera-goers lucky enough to attend the work, since Messiaen called for rare resources – one being a chorus 150 strong – and a vocalist of superhuman stamina in the title role. Saint François's journey into the pain and love experienced by Christ during the Passion takes four hours. The intricate architecture of this ritualistic piece is carefully constructed: solo voices dominate until Saint François comes within reach of God's greatest mystery. Then, massive choruses express the Lord's responses to François's prayers. These reverberating voices lift François into a sphere of stunned divinity, and transfix audiences in an age all too bereft of spiritual intensity.

> ➧ **PRINCIPAL ROLES** ➧
>
> Saint François (Saint Francis) *baritone*
> L'Ange (The Angel) *soprano*
> Le Lépreux (The Leper) *tenor*
> Frère Léon (Brother Leo) *baritone*
> Frère Massée (Brother Masseus) *tenor*
> Frère Élie (Brother Elias) *tenor*

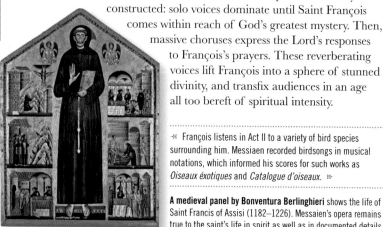

⊷ François listens in Act II to a variety of bird species surrounding him. Messiaen recorded birdsongs in musical notations, which informed his scores for such works as *Oiseaux éxotiques* and *Catalogue d'oiseaux*. ⊷

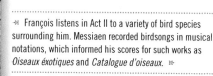

A medieval panel by Bonaventura Berlinghieri shows the life of Saint Francis of Assisi (1182–1226). Messiaen's opera remains true to the saint's life in spirit as well as in documented details.

PLOT SYNOPSIS

In and around Assisi, in Italian Umbria, prior to the death of Saint Francis in 1226

ACT ONE **TABLEAU 1: THE CROSS** Saint François and Frère Léon walk along a road. François explains how suffering brings perfect joy ♿. **TABLEAU 2: LAUDS** In a church, François asks the Lord to show him how to love what he so fears, the leper. **TABLEAU 3: LE BAISER AU LÉPREUX** In a hospice, a Leper angrily complains to François of his suffering. Unseen yet heard, an Angel visits them. François alone understands the Angel's message of God's Love. Embracing the Leper, François heals him. The Leper weeps, and both men are healed.

"S'il se met à pleuvoir"

ACT TWO **TABLEAU 4: L'ANGE VOYAGEUR** In the monastery of La Verna, Frère Massée welcomes a traveller, who is in fact the Angel. Élie refuses to answer the traveller's questions, but Bertrand is responsive. **TABLEAU 5: L'ANGE MUSICIEN** At prayer, François asks to be shown the abundance of God's tenderness. The Angel appears, carrying a viol. Recognized by François, the Angel responds to his prayer with music ♿. When Léon and Massée arrive, François, stunned by celestial music, has lost consciousness. They revive him. **TABLEAU 6: LE PRÊCHE AUX OISEAUX** At the Hermitage of the Carceri, François blesses birds, who respond in a concert of birdsong.

"Ah! Dieu nous éblouit par excès de vérité"

José Van Dam, seen here onstage in Paris in 1983, is the reigning baritone in the famously demanding role of Saint Francis.

ACT THREE **TABLEAU 7: THE STIGMATA** At La Verna, François asks the Lord to grace him with sensations of His pain during the Passion; and of the Love that allowed Him to endure pain. As François begins to taste Christ's suffering, the Lord, speaking through the chorus, tells François that no pain is too great to bear for Eternal Life ♿. François is motionless with ecstasy ♿. **TABLEAU 8: LA MORT ET LA NOUVELLE VIE** In the church of the Porziuncola, monks surround François, who is dying. François bids all farewell, and beholds a vision of the Angel and Leper. When François dies, the stage darkens. Then, light appears in his stead. The curtain down, the chorus praises God ♿.

"C'est Moi, c'est Moi, c'est Moi"

"Si tu portes de bon coeur la croix"

"Autre est l'éclat de la lune"

LEONARD
BERNSTEIN

Born: 25 August 1918, Lawrence, Massachusetts, US
Died: 14 October 1990, New York, US

Leonard Bernstein redefined American music theatre in much-loved works over a span of four decades from the 1940s. His unmistakable signature, at once declarative, life-loving, and sophisticated, galvanizes his comic operetta, *Candide*. Bernstein's two other operatic works, *Trouble in Tahiti* (1952) and its sequel, *A Quiet Place* (1983), portray life in suburban America.

Bernstein burst onto the American music scene as a conductor, with the same flair that came to characterize his compositions. On 14 November 1943, the New York Philharmonic required a conductor to fill in at the last moment. Only 25, Bernstein picked up the baton and stepped into American music history. His charisma enthralled New York, and he went on to dazzle audiences worldwide. From 1956 to 1966, he would serve as the first American-born conductor of the New York Philharmonic. By then, he had long established himself as a composer. His first musical comedy came in 1944 with *On the Town*, to a libretto by the legendary Broadway duo Betty Comden and Adolph Green. They teamed up again for the 1953 musical *Wonderful Town*. But it was the sensational *West Side Story*, in 1957, that would become the quintessential American musical. With all of his works for the stage, including the remarkable operetta *Candide*, Bernstein injected into American theatres and opera houses a fresh mix of classical and popular sound.

THE COMMUNICATOR

Leonard Bernstein reached audiences with his infectious enthusiasm for music. The first concert he conducted was broadcast nationally from Carnegie Hall. It mesmerized America, and captured worldwide interest. Within a decade, he would lead orchestras in London, Prague, Tel Aviv, and Milan, where he was the first American to conduct an opera at La Scala. From 1958, and for 14 years, his TV programme *Young People's Concerts* opened countless American ears to classical music.

Bernstein flamboyantly conducts Mahler in 1970 during the Tanglewood Festival in Lenox, Massachusetts, US.

West Side Story
A New Musical

A programme cover for Bernstein's *West Side Story* shows the hit musical's lovers, Maria and Tony, in happier times before tragedy strikes.

CANDIDE

⚎ Comic operetta in two acts, 2½ hours
🗓 1954–1956 (rev. 1973, 1988–1989)
♈ First performance 1 December 1956, Martin Beck

Theater, New York, US
📖 Lillian Hellman, based on the 1756 novel by
Voltaire; lyrics by Richard Wilbur

Candide has suffered a rocky production history, but since the 1970s has been regarded as one of Bernstein's greatest works. The French 18th-century novel by Voltaire is treated in high comedic style of a distinctly American stripe that joyfully mocks Old World ideas and musical traditions. Beloved numbers are "Glitter and be Gay" and "The Best of all Possible Worlds", but the most famous passage is the winsome overture.

⚎ The opera was so often revised that, after the final changes of the 1988–1989 version, the noted *Candide* conductor John Mauceri joked: "The last time I saw Lenny, I said, 'Now you've really screwed everything up!' " ⚎

→ **PRINCIPAL ROLES** ←

Candide *tenor*
Naïve young man

Cunegonde *soprano*
His wealthy foster sister

Max *baritone*
Brother to Cunegonde

Pangloss *baritone*
Tutor to the three children

Paquette *soprano*
A dissolute servant

Old Lady *mezzo-soprano*
A Parisian brothel-keeper

PLOT SYNOPSIS

A castle in Westphalia and throughout the world

ACT ONE Candide is an adopted boy living with his cousins, Cunegonde and Max, in Westphalia. He loves Cunegonde and she him. Their tutor, Pangloss, instructs them to find "the best of all possible worlds" in all situations. When the Bulgar Army brings war, all but Candide are slain. Candide sets out to wander the world. He discovers Pangloss, not dead after all and now a beggar. They witness atrocities, but Candide remains optimistic even when Pangloss

The Neue Oper
in Vienna put on a cabaret-influenced production of the opera in 2000.

is hanged. Candide wanders to Paris ♟, where Cunegonde has become a prostitute. When she inadvertently stabs a man, she and Candide flee with her brothel-keeper, the Old Lady, and eventually set sail for South America.

"It must be me"

ACT TWO Candide and the others discover Max and the former family servant Paquette miraculously alive and residing in Buenos Aires. Later, in a jungle, Candide stabs Max by mistake and, following extraordinary events, rediscovers Pangloss. Accompanied by the tutor, Candide, Cunegonde, and the Old Lady reach Venice. There, the group rediscovers Max and Paquette, and all throw themselves into Carnival gambling. Finally, in a farmhouse near Venice, Candide celebrates his love for Cunegonde and realizes that life is neither good nor bad ⚰.

"Make our garden grow"

BERND ALOIS
ZIMMERMANN

Born: 20 March 1918, Bliesheim, near Cologne, Germany
Died: 10 August 1970, Königsdorf, near Cologne, Germany

Bernd Alois Zimmermann was among the foremost
composers of Germany's avant-garde during the 1950s and
1960s. His background was eclectic. He trained in Cologne, Berlin, and
Darmstadt, but also studied literature, philosophy, and film. Having mastered
serial music under René Leibowitz, Zimmermann wrote pieces rippling with
jazz and pop as well as experimental electronic music. Among his important works
was the 1969 *Requiem für einen jungen Dichter*, or *Requiem for a Young Poet*. His only
opera, the probing yet disturbing *Die Soldaten*, set a new agenda for post-war opera
in Europe. Five years later, in 1970, Zimmermann committed suicide.

DIE SOLDATEN
The Soldiers

⚐ Opera in four acts, 1¾ hours
☎ 1958–1960; 1963–1964
♱ 15 February 1965, Opernhaus, Cologne, Germany

📖 Bernd Alois Zimmermann, from the 1776 play by
Jakob Michael Reinhold Lenz

Die Soldaten premiered to great success in
1965 as a profoundly German opera of the
post-war era. Although set in no particular
time, its story spoke urgently to audiences
with fresh memories of World War II:
soldiers abuse a young Everywoman in
militarized Flanders. Through its formal
and thematic links to Alban Berg's 1925
Wozzeck, Zimmermann's work also added
a new dimension to avant-garde opera in

→ **PRINCIPAL ROLES** ←

Wesener *bass* A fancy goods merchant in Lille
Marie *soprano* His daughter
Stolzius *baritone* A draper in Armentières
Desportes *tenor* A nobleman serving in the
French army
Countess de la Roche *mezzo-soprano*
The Young Count *tenor* Her son
Major Mary *baritone* He pursues Marie

German. *Die Soldaten*'s cinematic pacing combined with simultaneously
projected films in Act IV redefined the roles of time and place on opera stages.
Zimmermann's own musical idiom further upsets expectations of any linear
action; Bach chorales, jazz music, a
waltz passage, or recorded segments
remind audiences that no one world
of sound is independent of another.

⇥ Typical for a piece by Zimmermann, the opera
calls for atypical resources: an onstage jazz ensemble
works in tandem with an enormous orchestra that
includes five Wagner tubas. ⇤

The opera's ritual energies are captured on the
cover of a 1991 recording of a performance at
the Staatstheater in Stuttgart, Germany.

An innocently-costumed Marie is engulfed by menacing soldiers in a production at the Nederlandse Opera in 2003.

PLOT SYNOPSIS

French-speaking Flanders, yesterday, today, and tomorrow

ACT ONE At home in Lille, Marie Wesener writes to the mother of her beloved Stolzius, a draper. In Armentières, the love-sick Stolzius snatches the letter from his mother. In Lille, Marie would like to attend the theatre with Desportes, a baron who courts her. Her father, Wesener, will not allow it. In Armentières, Eisenhardt, an army chaplain, decries the effects of the theatre on soldiers' relations with girls. At home, Wesener urges Marie to reject neither the baron nor Stolzius. Alone, Marie worries about Stolzius, but dreaming of improving her lot in life, is attracted to Desportes ♂.

"Das Herz ist mir so schwer"

ACT TWO In a café in Armentières, officers gamble and drink. They goad Stolzius with comments about Marie and Desportes. At Wesener's house, Desportes seduces Marie ♨, who has received a punishing letter from Stolzius. Meanwhile, her grandmother foretells Marie's downfall. Stolzius resolves to take revenge on his romantic rival Desportes ♂.

"Ha ha ha"

"Ein Tag ist wie der andere"

ACT THREE Major Mary has moved to Lille, where Stolzius is now his orderly. With Stolzius, the major calls on Marie, who almost recognizes Stolzius. Elsewhere, the Countess de la Roche waits up for her son ♂. When she learns that he has fallen for Marie, the Countess orders him to leave town and, to save Marie's reputation, offers her a position in the la Roche home.

"Er fängt an, mir trübe Tage zu machen"

ACT FOUR In dream-like film sequences, Marie flees while Desportes plots from prison to be rid of her; Desportes's huntsman rapes Marie. On stage, people dance in a ballroom and Marie is seen as a prostitute. Various people note that she has fled ♨. Over supper in Major Mary's apartment, Desportes calls Marie a slut and Stolzius poisons him. Mary draws his sword on Stolzius, who reveals his true identity to the dying Desportes before killing himself with Mary's weapon. On the banks of the Lys river, Wesener shoos off a beggar. Thinking twice, he gives her a coin, not noticing that she is his daughter. Marie falls to the ground weeping.

"Marie fortgelaufen!"

HANS WERNER
HENZE

Born: 1 July 1926, Gütersloh, Westphalia, Germany

Hans Werner Henze emerged following World War II to become a major composer of the second half of the 20th century. While he has composed ballets and symphonies, his dozens of operas, spanning more than five decades, have established him as the greatest German opera composer since Richard Strauss.

Henze began composing at age 12. Having grown up under Fascist rule in Germany, he served in 1944–1945 as a soldier and was taken prisoner by the English before resuming musical training in Heidelberg. Like the Italian composer Berio, he studied in Darmstadt with the French exponent of serialism René Leibowitz. Serialism marked Henze's music until his career took the first of many turns. Following the premiere of his 1952 opera, *Boulevard Solitude*, he resided on the Italian island of Ischia, near Naples. There, his work was touched by a more lyrical, Italianate style. The first opera to register Henze's new sound was *König Hirsch*, "The King Stag", but *The Bassarids*, of ten years later, is widely held to be his operatic masterpiece. Residency in Cuba contributed to yet another new phase in the 1970s, when the composer wrote music of a decidedly political tenor. Literary sources for his operas have ranged from Shakespeare to a novel by the Japanese Yukio Mishima. Sensitive to his surroundings, social or natural, Henze has remained an inveterate artist, unafraid to change in a changing world.

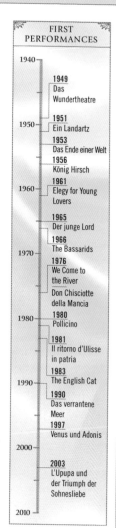

FIRST PERFORMANCES	
1940	
	1949 Das Wundertheatre
1950	**1951** Ein Landartz
	1953 Das Ende einer Welt
	1956 König Hirsch
1960	**1961** Elegy for Young Lovers
	1965 Der junge Lord
1970	**1966** The Bassarids
	1976 We Come to the River
	1976 Don Chisciotte della Mancia
1980	**1980** Pollicino
	1981 Il ritorno d'Ulisse in patria
1990	**1983** The English Cat
	1990 Das verrantene Meer
	1997 Venus und Adonis
2000	
	2003 L'Upupa und der Triumph der Sohnesliebe
2010	

Henze acts as both conductor and teacher in 1982 with young musicians at the Britten-Pears School, Snape Maltings, England.

DIE BASSARIDEN
The Bassarids

⚐ Opera seria with intermezzo in one act and four movements, 2½ hours

🕮 1965

🏆 6 August 1966, Grosses Festspielhaus, Salzburg

📖 WH Auden and Chester Kallman, after Euripides's *The Bacchae* (407 BCE)

Die Bassariden is a thoroughly modern opera fuelled by an Ancient Greek storyline. The tragedy pits Pentheus, the new king of Thebes, against the god Dionysus, who lures the Thebans into unbound sensual pleasures on Mount Cytheron. Responding to a lyrical libretto by WH Auden and Chester Kallmann, Henze's music is at once dramatic and otherworldly.

⇥ In 2005, the opera's French premiere was disrupted by a strike. With no orchestral instruments delivered to the opera house, conductor Kazushi Ono quickly adapted the score for three pianos. ⇤

→ PRINCIPAL ROLES ←

Pentheus *baritone*
King of Thebes

Kadmos (Cadmus) *bass*
His grandfather, founder of Thebes

Agaue (Agave) *mezzo-soprano*
Mother to Pentheus

Autonoe *soprano*
Her sister

Dionysus *tenor*
Son of Zeus and Semele

PLOT SYNOPSIS

Thebes and Mount Cytheron, in mythological Antiquity

FIRST MOVEMENT As Pentheus becomes their new king, the people of Thebes head to Mount Cytheron to meet the god Dionysus. Pentheus delivers a proclamation forbidding Thebans from accepting Dionysus. But his mother, Agaue, and her sister, Autonoe, are lured to the mountain to be entranced.

SECOND MOVEMENT Pentheus has those on Mount Cytheron taken prisoner. When they are delivered to him, he tries to awaken his mother from her trance and questions a Stranger among the prisoners. Threatened with death, the Stranger sings of Dionysus.

THIRD MOVEMENT Pentheus orders the Stranger tortured and, alone, expresses fear. Prisoners escape and return to Mount Cytheron. The Stranger offers Pentheus a vision. (**INTERMEZZO** In a mirror, Pentheus sees the Bassarids, followers of Dionysus, perform a charade.) Enchanted by the Stranger, Pentheus joins the Bassarids 🎵. Frenzied members of the cult discover Pentheus. He begs his mother to recognize him, but is hunted down.

"Nacht öffnet weit, was Tag verschloss"

FOURTH MOVEMENT Agaue presents "the head of a lion". Then, as she returns to normal, she realizes with horror that it is the head of her son. The Stranger presents himself as Dionysus 🎵; exiles the royal family; and orders the palace destroyed. Thebans worship Dionysus.

"Ja, ich bin er: Ich bin Dionysos"

Kristine Ciesinski delivered a blood-drenched Agaue at the Nederlands Opera in Amsterdam, in 2005

GYÖRGY
LIGETI

Born: 28 May 1923 in Dicsöszentmárton, Hungary (now Târnăveni, Romania)
Died: 12 June 2006, Vienna, Austria

György Ligeti injected a new world of sound into avant-garde music of the late 20th century. Fleeing Communist Hungary in 1956, he settled in Vienna, where in the 1960s his experiments with polyphony distinguished him from even the most innovative composers of the day. While Europeans like Luciano Berio, Karlheinz Stockhausen, and Pierre Boulez explored serialism derived from Arnold Schoenberg's 12-tone method, Ligeti was drawn to surrealism. His 1962 *Poème symphonique* was scored for 100 wound metronomes, its duration dependent on the time it took for all of the contraptions to unwind. *Le Grand Macabre*, his only full-length opera, is equally playful and provocative.

LE GRAND MACABRE

🎭 Opera in two acts (original version); opera in four scenes (revised version), 2 hours
🗓 1972–1976; revised 1996

🏛 12 April 1978, Royal Opera, Stockholm, Sweden; 28 July 1997, Festspielhaus, Salzburg (revised)
📖 György Ligeti and Michael Meschke

Le Grand Macabre is an intrepid, exuberant opera based on the 1934 farce by Michel de Ghelderode. Brimming with impish humour and coursing with shock, it pleads that life must not be lived in fear of death. Or lived in fear of anything. The opera's Terminator is in theory Nekrotzar, Lord Macabre, the Reaper, whose divine purpose is to annihilate the world. But

PRINCIPAL ROLES

Piet the Pot *buffo tenor* A life-loving drunk
Nekrotzar *baritone* Lord Macabre
Astradamors *bass* A transvestite court astrologer
Mescalina *mezzo-soprano* His sadistic wife
Go-Go *counter-tenor* Sovereign prince of Breughelland
Gepopo *soprano* His Chief of the Secret Police

even he is a clown, one of cosmic proportions. Whichever time-honoured operatic morsel the work devours, from the love duet to the death scene, it is

spat back out as rebellious entertainment. After the 1978 premiere, the opera was revised for 1997. Marks of its double life remain, not least in a mix of postmodern and Cold War era elements. But the music – by turns raucous, heart-grabbing, wizardly, and flip – makes the opera irresistible in any period.

Cover image taken from the CD of Ligeti's *Le Grand Macabre*, shows a rocking horse, a key image in stagings of the opera.

⊰ In the opera's otherworldly Breughelland, all is subject to musical mockery, including life after death. When Piet the Pot and Astradamors return as ghosts of their former selves in Scene 4, ironic harp music accents the action. ⊱

PLOT SYNOPSIS

Breughelland, an imaginary and surreal location

SCENE ONE In a graveyard, the drunken Piet praises the paradise that is Breughelland. Amanda and Amando, lovers, want to die together. Nekrotzar warns that all will perish at midnight ♂. Piet recognizes Nekrotzar as Lord Macabre, and begs his mercy. Spirits warn of destruction ♔. The lovers vow love unto death.

"Heute noch, um Mitternacht"

"Es naht schon das Verderben"

SCENE TWO Mescalina tortures her husband Astradamors. She petitions Venus for a night of sex, then falls asleep. Nekrotzar arrives, riding on Piet's back. In a dream, Mescalina asks Venus for a "well-hung" man. Nekrotzar has violent sex with the unconscious Mescalina; she comes to, then falls dead. Nekrotzar prepares for his mission ♂. He rides off atop Piet. Astradamors notes: "At last I am master in my own house."

"Feuer und Feuersnot"

SCENE THREE Two ministers exchange insults in alphabetical order. They place their sovereign prince, Go-Go, atop a rocking horse. He falls. Gepopo, Chief of the Secret Police, reports turmoil. The ministers court the people of Breugelland, but they hail Go-Go instead ♔. Informed of the comet, the ministers abandon Go-Go, who notes that he is finally master of his own house. Gepopo and others flee, fearing Lord Macabre. A siren sounds. Nekrotzar enters atop Piet. People panic. Piet, Astradamors, and Go-Go feast, drink, and mock Nekrotzar, who asks to sip human blood from a chalice ♔.

"Uns'ren Fürsten!"

"Ex! Trink! Ex!"

He drinks to excess, relishing his career of destruction. Lightning strikes, and Nekrotzar renews his motivation. But, when placed on the rocking horse, he falls off, drunk.

SCENE FOUR In the graveyard, Piet and Astradamors, now ghosts, float away. Ruffians massacre everyone, but Go-Go bounces back up. At sunrise, Nekrotzar melts into the earth. Amanda and Amando are heard making love in a tomb. The lovers explain that the world came to an end for them as well, only that they were in ecstasy. All praise life lived without fear of death.

Dutch mezzo-soprano Jard Van Nes as Mescalina and German soprano Sibylle Ehlert as Venus in Scene Two of the opera at the Théâtre du Châtelet in Paris, 1998.

LUCIANO
BERIO

Born: 24 October 1925, Oneglia (now Imperia), Liguria, Italy
Died: 27 May 2003, Rome, Italy

Operas by the Italian composer Luciano Berio galvanized international music circles over the second half of the 20th century. His experiments in electronic music plugged instruments and voices into a contemporary mode of expression and, with Italo Calvino, he wrote a landmark opera, *Un re in ascolto*.

Berio began his music education at home well before he entered the Milan Conservatory in 1945. He had hoped to be a pianist, but a hand injury spurred him to take up composition. Still at the conservatory, he met a fellow student, the American soprano Cathy Berberian, who became his wife in 1950. Berio's most influential works were responses to masterpieces – literary as well as musical – which he absorbed voraciously. First in Milan in the 1950s, and then in Paris in the 1970s, Berio founded electronic studios where his musical experiments redefined the contours of classical music. His six major works of music theatre include *La vera storia*, to a libretto by Italo Calvino, which premiered at La Scala in 1982.

ELECTRONIC MUSIC

In Milan in 1955, Luciano Berio and fellow composer Bruno Maderna co-founded the *Studio di fonologia musicale*, an electronic studio devoted to experimentation. The Italian composer Luigi Nono soon joined the group, but with guest composers like the American John Cage and the Belgian Henri Pousseur, the studio's impact was international. By cutting up and reordering recordings of vocal music he wrote for the soprano Cathy Berberian, Berio made *Thema (Omaggio a Joyce)* and *Visage*.

Luciano Berio and his wife Cathy Berberian, for whom he wrote his 1966 solo vocal masterpiece, *Sequenza III*.

UN RE IN ASCOLTO
A King Listens

⚟ Musical action in two parts, 1½ hours
▣ 1979–1984
♇ 7 August 1984, Kleines Festspielhaus,

Salzburg, Austria
📖 Luciano Berio, after Italo Calvino, WH Auden, and Friedrich Gotter

Un re in ascolto takes up a subject that preoccupied Berio throughout his career: listening, and what it means to listen. The opera works on many levels, not least as the mysterious quest of the character Prospero for a singular voice. In a work dwelling on sound, memory, and the meaning that may be gleaned from a sea of voices, the riveting solos and intense ensemble passages stand out like musical islands.

⚞ Berio operas typically use an operatic masterpiece or a literary classic as a point of reference. Shakespeare's *The Tempest* informs the action of this opera, and supplies the title role of the king with his name: Prospero. ⚟

✦ PRINCIPAL ROLES ✦

Prospero *bass-baritone*
A theatre impresario whose "kingdom" is his theatre

Producer *tenor*
He rehearses a play

Actor *spoken*
He rehearses the role of Friday

Soprano 1 *soprano*
She auditions for Prospero

Female Protagonist *soprano*
She embodies Prospero's quest for a voice

PLOT SYNOPSIS

Prospero's study and theatre

PART ONE Prospero recalls his dream of a theatre. Gradually, theatre personnel enter and rehearse a play set on an island. The Actor playing Friday practises lines. Prospero listens to a Singer and her accompanist, then argues with the Producer about the nature of listening. The Producer insists that the piece is about a king who must listen to save his kingdom. The Actor delivers lines about silence. Prospero retires to his room to reflect on the nature of sound as the stage is turned into a seascape. A second Singer delivers an aria ♫. Alone, Prospero confronts a voice that says "You are dying". Prospero faints.

"Oh notte grave, immensa chiara"

Georg Nigl as the Actor at the Grand Théâtre de Genève, Switzerland, 2002.

PART TWO Prospero revives and calls for Ariel. Artists return to the stage, but Prospero convulses on the floor. A Doctor and Nurse intervene. Prospero, seated in silence on a throne, auditions another Singer who is removed by armed men. Prospero realizes that his kingdom cannot be seen or touched, but resembles a flowing sea of music.

A Female Protagonist, dressed in tatters, informs Prospero that her voice is her own, and that her singing is a lament for him. All scatter; cry "Listen!"; remove costumes; and exit. Alone on the dark stage, Prospero recalls memories of oblivion, and, in high modern fashion, of the future ♫. He dies.

"C'è una voce nascosta tra le voci"

KARLHEINZ
STOCKHAUSEN

Born: 22 August 1928, Mödrath, near Cologne, Germany

Karlheinz Stockhausen, a towering composer of the late 20th century, has electrified the music world since the 1950s with his pioneering explorations of sound. His operatic cycle *Licht: Die sieben Tage der Woche*, or *Light: The Seven Days of the Week*, took 27 years to write, and requires 29 hours to perform.

Stockhausen was awakened to the boundless potentials of composition when, in 1948, he heard the "Concert of Noises" produced by Pierre Schaeffer for Radio France. Schaeffer manipulated recordings of natural and instrumental sounds to create *musique concrète*, or "concrete music". In 1952, while studying at the Paris Conservatory with Olivier Messiaen, Stockhausen joined Schaeffer's studio to experiment with taped sound. Within a year, his work would earn him a place in music history as the founder of electronic music. Stockhausen's unquenchable passion for pursuing the boundaries of music – its relationship to sound, noise, "soundless" vibration, and more – has since been unceasing. His curiosity led him into laboratories even as it has propelled him to tour Asia. His *summum opus* is the gargantuan operatic cycle *Licht*, which portrays musical and mythological interactions among the seven days of the week. The first production of the entire cycle, and the spiritual experience of sound it promises to offer, is keenly awaited by Karlheinz Stockhausen's fervent followers worldwide.

FIRST PERFORMANCES

1980	
	1981 Donnerstag aus Licht
	1984 Samstag aus Licht
1985	
	1988 Montag aus Licht
1990	
	1992 Dienstag aus Licht
1995	
	1996 Freitag aus Licht (Freitag – Versuchung)
	1998 composed Mittwoch aus Licht
2000	
	2003 composed Sontag aus Licht
2005	
	2008 projected Licht: Die sieben Tage der Woche
2010	

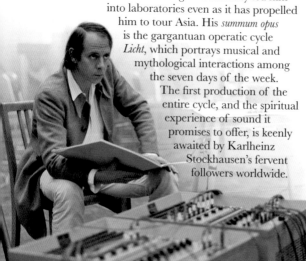

Karlheinz Stockhausen in a recording studio. From the outset, his work has welcomed innovative technology.

DONNERSTAG AUS LICHT
Thursday from Light

🎵 Opera in three acts, a greeting, and a farewell,
3¼ hours

📅 1978–1980

🏆 3 April 1981, La Scala, Milan, Italy

📖 Karlheinz Stockhausen

Donnerstag aus Licht was the first of seven operas Stockhausen composed between 1977 and 2003 for his cycle *Licht*, or *Light*. Three melodies structure the cycle, and each is linked to a character: Michael, and his parents Eva and Luzifer. This opera focuses on Michael. A highlight is the invisible chorus, which creates atmospheres of layered time and space as Michael takes a journey beginning with his childhood.

⚞ Five trumpet players delivered the opera's closing section, *Thursday Farewell*, from five exterior balconies between 11.30 PM and midnight at the end of each performance at La Scala in 1981. ⚟

PLOT SYNOPSIS

Michael's home and beyond

DONNERSTAGS-GRUSS/ THURSDAY GREETING An instrumental ensemble greets arriving audience members in the lobby of the opera house.

ACT ONE **MICHAEL'S YOUTH** *Childhood* Michael's mother, Eva, attempts suicide and is committed to an asylum. His father, Luzifer, drinks, then goes to war. *Moon-Eva* Michael falls in love with Moon-Eva, a bird-woman who visits him from the heavens.

Donnerstag aus Licht was performed in 1985 at the Royal Opera House in London, where striking sets were designed by Maria Bjørnson.

His mother is killed by a doctor and his father is shot. Moon-Eva disappears. *Examination* Michael is required to take the examinations to enter the High School of Music. While responding to his examiners, Michael does not recognize his parents in the jury. As a singer, trumpet player, and dancer, he describes his childhood, and is subsequently admitted to the school.

ACT TWO **MICHAEL'S JOURNEY AROUND THE EARTH** Michael climbs into a globe. As it rotates, he emerges from portals to converse on the trumpet with the orchestra. At the seventh station, he hears a basset horn. It is Eva, who plays with him and then dances away with him.

ACT THREE **MICHAEL'S HOMECOMING** *Festival* Michael returns home. Eva greets him, and Michael gives thanks as an invisible chorus sings ♆. But Luzifer inspires an argument. *Vision* Michael envisions seven moments of his life, the last of which is Light. Michael announces to his parents that he became human in order that God and humans may listen to one another ♂.

"Wunderbare Dinge erscheinen"

"Mensch geworden bin ich"

PHILIP
GLASS

Born: 31 January 1937, Baltimore, Maryland, US

Philip Glass became the most popular opera composer to emerge from among the American minimalist composers of the late 20th century. His *Einstein on the Beach*, a collaboration with director Robert Wilson, took opera to new conceptual heights in 1976.

Glass earned a master's degree from the Juilliard School of Music in New York and then studied with Nadia Boulanger in Paris. But the sitar-player Ravi Shankar and travels to India also marked Glass. In New York in the 1960s, he used electronic instruments to experiment with combinations of Western and Indian musical ideas. Among the distinctive features of his minimalist style is the deliberate, trance-like repetition of notes or chords. Glass has scored over 20 major works for the stage, including *Satyagraha: M. K. Gandhi in South Africa* and *Akhnaten* (operas completing the "Portrait Trilogy" begun with *Einstein on the Beach*); *the CIVIL warS*; *The Juniper Tree*; *The Fall of the House of Usher*; and *The Voyage*.

ROBERT WILSON

Born in 1941, Robert Wilson attended the Pratt Institute in Brooklyn, New York, and studied painting with George McNeil in Paris, France. Influenced by the choreography of Merce Cunningham and Martha Graham, Wilson applied visual ideas to on-stage movement. While his work with Glass has been legendary, Wilson has inspired numerous illustrious collaborators, including Susan Sontag, William S Burroughs, Lou Reed, David Byrne, Laurie Anderson, and Jessye Norman.

Robert Wilson (left) and Philip Glass formed a new approach to opera with Einstein on the Beach. *Wilson has since staged operas worldwide.*

Shown rehearsing in New York in 1993 with the Philip Glass Ensemble, Glass has also composed for films such as Errol Morris's *The Thin Blue Line*.

EINSTEIN ON THE BEACH

✍ Opera in four acts and five "knee plays", 4½ hours
🕮 1974–1975
♜ 25 July 1976, Théâtre Municipal, Avignon, France

📖 Philip Glass, Robert Wilson, Christopher Knowles, Samuel M Johnson, and Lucinda Childs

Einstein on the Beach is an avant-garde opera of wide influence. Electronically repeated at high speed, some musical passages can have a hypnotizing or disorienting effect. The opera's non-linear action keeps attention on its atmospheres, and on reverberating visual and musical motifs. Einstein, incarnated by a costumed on-stage violinist, presides loosely over the work's logic. His theory of relativity serves as a source of conceptual surprises, at once visual, musical, and ultimately theatrical.

> ✦ PRINCIPAL ROLES ✦
>
> Einstein *violinist*
> Author of the theory of relativity
> Ensemble *soprano, alto, tenor, actors, dancers*

⌁ Most opera composers initially respond to a libretto. Glass took a different starting point in his collaboration with Wilson, who engaged the composer's imagination with drawings and visual elements. ⌁

PLOT SYNOPSIS

No specific time or place

Einstein on the Beach is unusual for being a non-narrative opera. Its building blocks are visual, musical, and verbal repetitions rather than plot elements. The opera explores myriad ideas: Einstein's theory of general relativity, a railway train's motion as a metaphor for the theory, and law court exchanges as portals into concepts of

Robert Wilson designed the opera for a third time at the progressive MC 93 Bobigny theatre outside Paris in 1992.

prejudice and judgment. These are presented in lyrical juxtapositions rather than in narrative fashion. The work's atypical structure is reinforced in performance: with no intermission, the long piece invites audience members to come and go freely, and without missing key moments in any "story". The opera is partly shaped by what Glass and Wilson called "knee-plays", or "knees" for short. These appear between scenes requiring major set changes.

The opera opens with Knee 1: the ensemble builds a hypnotic web of effects by vocalizing digits 🎧.
Act I includes a train

"Two. Eight. Two, three, four"

scene and a trial scene with lyrics about Mr Bojangles, and concludes with Knee 2. Act II offers a dance, and revisits the train thread in a variation called "Night Train". After Knee 3, Act III revisits the trial thread in relation to the theme of "Prison". A Witness recites text by Lucinda Childs into a dense sound-cloud of mechanical choral chanting 🎧. A second dance is followed by Knee 4. Act IV visits themes of "Building", "Bed", and "Spaceship". And the opera concludes with Knee 5, in which a Bus Driver sings of "Two Lovers on a Bench".

"I was in this prematurely air-conditioned supermarket"

JOHN
ADAMS

Born: 15 February 1947, Worcester, Massachusetts, US

The American John Adams and his collaborator, the director Peter Sellars, have taken contemporary opera down a new path. Before Adams, minimalist composers such as Philip Glass built their opera music around interrelated concepts and images rather than on story threads. Working with Sellars, Adams pressed beyond the minimalist idiom of repetition and symmetry to embrace a narrative opera form replete with characters who feel and evolve. In 1985, Adams and Sellars captured attention with *Nixon in China*, arguably the first opera to address audiences raised on television culture. Subsequent operas include *The Death of Klinghoffer*; *El Niño*; and *Doctor Atomic*, to a Sellars libretto.

NIXON IN CHINA

✍ Opera in three acts, 2½ hours
☎ 1985–1987
♇ 22 October 1987, Brown Theater, Wortham

Center, Houston Grand Opera, Texas, US
📖 Alice Goodman

Nixon in China is about President Richard M Nixon's 1972 visit to Peking for meetings with the Chinese leader Mao Tse-tung. The opera benefits from a remarkable libretto by Alice Goodman. Spectacular ceremonial action is balanced by private exchanges. But attention is also paid to the subtler inner workings of political figures. Music moves fluidly and relentlessly forward, yet can be suddenly transformed by the drama of the moment, switching from the reflective to the explosive. *Nixon in China* awakened excitement in opera circles when it premiered in Houston in 1987. Like early operas, this one offered a story which audiences were likely to know and, since it was based on recent history, even find relevant to their own lives. The opera was an overnight success.

⊶ The opera's creative team – Adams, Sellars, Alice Goodman, and choreographer Mark Morris – remained intact for *The Death of Klinghoffer* in 1991. ⊷

→ PRINCIPAL ROLES ←

Richard Nixon *baritone* President of the United States
Pat Nixon *soprano* The First Lady
Henry Kissinger *bass* American National Security Adviser
Chou En-lai *bass* Chinese Premier
Mao Tse-tung *tenor* Chairman of the Party
Chiang Ch'ing *soprano* Wife of Mao Tse-tung

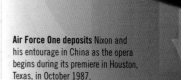

Air Force One deposits Nixon and his entourage in China as the opera begins during its premiere in Houston, Texas, in October 1987.

THE SPIRIT OF 7

PLOT SYNOPSIS

Peking (now Beijing), China, in February 1972

ACT ONE On an airfield in Peking, Chinese military personnel greet President Richard Nixon . As Premier Chou En-lai introduces key officials, Nixon privately thrills to the idea that "the world is listening" before descending into delusional fantasies . In Mao's study, Nixon struggles to bond with the philosophical Chairman. Dr Kissinger, National Security Adviser, adds awkward remarks. In the Great Hall, the Nixons are feeling light-hearted. Chou toasts the Americans , and Nixon the Chinese. A tide of goodwill washes over all . When the First Lady, Pat, reminds that it is George Washington's birthday, galvanized, Chou and Nixon reinforce their toasts.

> "The people are the heroes now"

> "It's prime time in the USA"

> "Ladies and gentlemen, Comrades and friends"

> "Cheers!"

ACT TWO Touring Peking, Pat pauses to foresee a time of simple virtues. That night, the Nixons and Chiang Ch'ing, Mao's wife, attend the premiere of a revolutionary ballet. Its heroine is whipped by a counter-revolutionary, Lao Szu, surprisingly performed by Kissinger. Upset by the action, Pat rushes onstage to alter its course. The president follows, consoling her in his way. But the heroine is beaten senseless. Following a storm scene, the now-armed heroine, prompted by Chiang Ch'ing from the audience, stuns the ballet ensemble by opening fire on Lao Szu and his lot ahead of her cue. Chiang Ch'ing joins the stage to deliver her revolutionary vision .

> "I am the wife of Mao Tse-tung"

ACT THREE On the President's last night in Peking, all save Chairman Mao are weary. When Chiang Ch'ing calls for music, a solo piano sparks Pat's nostalgia for California. The Maos dance. Chou directs Kissinger to the toilet. Nixon reminisces about World War II. In a searching final solo, Chou notes that "Everything seems to move beyond/ Our remedy."

TAN
DUN

Born: 18 August 1957, Si Mao, Hunan Province, China

The Chinese–American Tan Dun has become the most successful and outspoken composer to represent global opera culture in the new century. Following his first opera, *Marco Polo*, his works for the stage have combined classical and Asian resources and themes to explore a kind of opera unbound by any music tradition.

Tan grew up in rural China, where he was a rice planter during the Cultural Revolution. As a violin player and arranger, he worked for a provincial opera ensemble before entering the Central Conservatory of Beijing. In 1986, he travelled to New York to study at Columbia University with Chou Wen-Chung and Mario Davidovsky. Tan's operas integrate his diverse backgrounds into a singular realm of expression that explores Eastern and Western traditions alike. He scores for standard orchestral ensembles enhanced by Chinese instrumentalists and vocalists. Tan also intermixes Chinese forms, such as those of *kunju* opera with, say, European medieval chant. While Western composers like Britten and Glass have for decades injected Asian elements into native resources, Tan has made the intermarriage of East and West a musical priority. His first two operas, *Marco Polo* and *Peony Pavilion*, premiered in the West. His third, *Tea*, was first given in Tokyo's Suntory Hall. But wherever staged, Tan's operas have reopened definitions of music theatre for a global era.

Costumes and staging invite audiences into the ceremonial world of Tan Dun's third opera, *Tea*, at the Nederlandse Opera in Amsterdam in 2005.

EAST MEETS WEST

Like Bright Sheng, a fellow American opera composer born in China, Tan was influenced by the late Toru Takemitsu, the Japanese composer who freed Asian and Western instruments and musical idioms from the strictures of their independent traditions. Tan's operas call for such instruments as the Chinese pipa, the Indian sitar, and the Tibetan horn to augment Western orchestras. Sheng's most eclectic opera, *The Silver River*, employs Asian dancers as well as vocalists and instruments alongside Western resources.

MARCO POLO

⚐ An Opera within an Opera, 1¾ hours
🎞 1995
♅ 7 May 1996, Muffathalle, Munich, Germany

📖 Paul Griffiths, after his novel *Myself and Marco Polo* (1989)

Tan describes *Marco Polo*'s central theme of travel in his notes: "Paul Griffiths and I conceived of three journeys: Physical, Spiritual, and Musical." The central character, Marco Polo, is here split into two figures: Marco is the hero's active self, while Polo is his memory, a contemplative voice. Griffiths's libretto, with its literary allusions and sources, is in English, but Chinese and other languages are also used.

※ Tan Dun structured the opera so that its multi-layered journey would lead the music through distinct soundscapes: Medieval, Middle Eastern, Indian, Tibetan, Mongolian, and, finally, Chinese. ※

✦ PRINCIPAL ROLES ✦

Marco *mezzo-soprano*
Marco Polo's active self

Polo *tenor*
Marco Polo's memory

Rustichello *Chinese opera singer* A questioner

Water *soprano*
Lover of Marco Polo

Dante *baritone*
A guide

Kublai Khan *bass*
Mongol Emperor

PLOT SYNOPSIS

Venice, Italy, and locations to the East

THE BOOK OF TIMESPACE: WINTER Marco reads his past in his Book and, with Polo, his other self, finds the story incomplete. PIAZZA Dante and Shadows compel Polo to emerge again into light and life. Meanwhile, Kublai Khan prepares his own journey. Marco invites Polo, his memory, to take him on travels.

THE BOOK OF TIMESPACE: SPRING When Marco and Polo hesitate to depart, Shadows remind them of "gold" and "silk".

"Such a moment" | SEA Marco sets out on Water ♟, as Polo recalls past travels. A storm threatens, then recedes. BAZAAR Marco sees a market, and Dante fears it is dangerous. But, as Marco and Polo fuse, all proceed.

THE BOOK OF TIMESPACE: SUMMER Marco and Polo are speechless. Rustichello urges them on. DESERT Marco and Polo are separated as the desert seductress, Sheherazada, tries to win Polo. HIMALAYA In a ritual ambience, Polo is silent while others sing. Marco and Polo are bound with silk scarves. THE WALL Marco and Polo advance towards the Wall.

For the opera's premiere in Munich in 1996, director Martha Clarke responded to Tan's music by combining traditional and modernist elements in her staging.

THE BOOK OF TIMESPACE: AUTUMN Rustichello asks whether the Wall was in the Book. All attempt to recall the journey, and suggest that life is a dream. THE WALL Before the Wall, Polo sings to the Khan's Queen ♟. The Khan and Queen | "tsong gou feng" invite Marco and Polo to remain in their realm. But at Polo's prompting, Marco breaks through the Wall.

THOMAS ADÈS

Born: 1 March 1971, London, England

Thomas Adès burst onto the music scene in his native England as a teenager with his Chamber Symphony of 1990. A pianist and conductor as well as composer, Adès studied at London's Guildhall School of Music and with Hungarian composer György Kurtag. His first opera, *Powder Her Face*, premiered in 1994. To a libretto by Philip Hensher, it told the story of the scandal of Margaret Sweeny's divorce from the Duke of Argyll in 1955. But with *The Tempest*, Adès gained a calling card to an international audience. Alongside Mark-Anthony Turnage, composer of *The Silver Tassie*, Adès is the most promising British opera composer of his generation.

THE TEMPEST

✍ Opera in three acts, 2 hours
🕮 2002–2004
♟ 10 February 2004, Royal Opera House,
London, England
📖 Meredith Oakes, after the 1611 play by William Shakespeare

Shakespeare's *The Tempest*, an inherently musical play, has inspired instrumental music by great composers far and wide: Beethoven, Debussy, and Tchaikovsky are among them. Operas based on the play include Fromental Halévy's *La Tempesta* in 1850, and Luciano Berio's *Un re in ascolto* in 1984. Adès breathed new life into the beloved play with music that captured the story's scintillating magic while preserving its darker ambiences. His librettist, Meredith Oakes, aroused controversy by departing freely from the Bard's sacrosanct language and even introducing some plot twists. But Shakespeare is never far away, even when characters such as Prospero and Caliban express themselves in sing-song rhymes. A highlight is the spirit Ariel, whose high soprano vocal acrobatics shimmer at every turn in the opera.

⚐ *The Tempest*, Adès's second opera, premiered at the Royal Opera House in London when the composer was 32. Pressure soared before the opening night as critics noted that Britten's second opera was the masterpiece *Peter Grimes*. ⚐

PLOT SYNOPSIS

A remote island

ACT ONE Following a tempest depicted in the opera's overture, shipwreck victims cry out on a remote island. Moved by their voices, Miranda questions her father, Prospero. He explains that fate has delivered his enemies: his brother, Antonio, who usurped him as Duke of Milan, and the King of Naples. While Miranda sleeps, Prospero commands his captive spirit Ariel to retrieve the victims. Caliban, a monster native to the island, claims to be its king, but Prospero accuses him of lunacy 🜨. Ariel reports saving the victims, and reminds Prospero that he promised freedom 🜨. Miranda awakens to fall in love with a shipwreck survivor, Ferdinand, the king's son. Prospero uses magic to immobilize Ferdinand.

"Abhorrent slave"

"Five fathoms deep"

ACT TWO The shipwrecked rejoice to be alive 🜨. Prospero observes his enemies as Ariel sows confusion. Caliban meets the new arrivals and promises to show them the island's secrets 🜨. The king's entourage searches for Ferdinand while Caliban and his new friends, Stephano and Trinculo, imagine themselves siring "a nation" when the king dies. Elsewhere on the island, Prospero observes the power of love as Miranda frees Ferdinand.

"Alive, awake"

"Friends don't fear"

ACT THREE Caliban and Trinculo drunkenly cheer Stephano's reign as King. Elsewhere, Antonio and Sebastian, the real King's brother, nearly slay the sleeping King. Ariel awakens the court, and magically presents a feast, but, in harpy form, admonishes Prospero's enemies 🜨. Prospero savours the sight of the King and Antonio realizing they have wronged him. Miranda and Ferdinand announce their marriage. Prospero's hunger for revenge is sated. "King Caliban" returns, intent on Miranda as his Queen. Prospero grants Ariel freedom. Under Prospero's spell, the King marvels to behold his son and Miranda. The visitors anticipate sailing home in their magically restored ship; Prospero breaks his magic stave. Alone, Caliban wonders if he dreamed of humans.

"You are men of sin"

Ian Bostridge created Caliban (*left*) and Simon Keenlyside created Prospero for the opera's premiere at the Royal Opera House in London in 2004.

Index

Page numbers in **bold** refer
to main entries; *italic* numbers
denote illustrations

Picture credits

The publisher would like to thank the following for their kind permission to reproduce their photographs:

a = above; b = below/bottom; c = centre; l= left; r = right; rh = running head; t= top

AA = The Art Archive; AE = Agence Enguerand; AKG = akg-images; AL = Alamy Images; BAL = Bridgeman Art Library; Co = Corbis; GI = Getty Images; Leb = Lebrecht Music and Arts Photo Library; RJ = Robbie Jack Photography

1 Fondazione Teatro La Fenice: Michele Crosera; 2-3 Rex Features: Olycom Spa; 4 Co: Bettmann; 5 TopFoto.co.uk: Clive Barda; 6-7 TopFoto.co.uk: Clive Barda/PAL; 9 AL: Steve Sant (cl). AA: Bibliothèque des Arts Décoratifs Paris/Dagli Orti (br). DK Images: Judith Miller/Gorringes (c). Leb: Richard Haughton (t); 10 GI: Keystone/Stringer; 11 Rex Features: Nils Jorgensen; 12-13 Státní Opera Praha: Ondřej Kocourek; 14 AL: Jeremy Hoare; 15 Co: (t); 15-21 AL: image100 (rh); 16 Co: Bettmann; 17 BAL: Yale Center for British Art, Paul Mellon Collection, USA (b). Co: Christie's Images (tc); 18 Leb (tc); 19 Leb (t); 20 Co: RJ (bl). Leb (t); 21 AE: Marc Enguerand (b); 22 AL: Garry Gay; 23 Co: (t); 23-27 Photospin.com (rh); 24 AA: Museo Civico Modena/Dagli Orti (t). BAL: Private Collection, The Stapleton Collection (b); 25 AA: Hospital Institute Verona/Dagli Orti (A) br). Leb (tc); 26 Co: Bettmann (b). Leb (tc); 27 BAL: Private Collection, Archives Charmet (tr). Co: Wally McNamee (b); 28 Co: RJ; 29 Co (t); 29-33 AL: Steve Sant (rh); 30 BAL: Private Collection (tc). Co: Philippe Caron/ Sygma (b); 31 Co: Annebicque Bernard/Co Sygma (cl). Leb: Laurie Lewis (b); 32 Co: Annebicque Bernard/Co Sygma; 32-33 Bregenzer Festspiele: Karl Forster (b); 34 Rob Moore Photography; 35 Co (t); 35-42 DK Images: Eddie Gerald/ Rough Guides (rh); 36 BAL: Civica Raccolta Stampe Bertarelli, Milan, Italy (t). Co: Origlia/Pizzoli/Co Sygma (b); 37 Staatsoper Unter den Linden: bildTeam Berlin (b); 38-39 SuperStock: Photick; 40 Archiv der Salzburger Festspiele: Fritz Haseke (b); 41 Co: Gail Mooney (b); Patrick Ward (tc); 42 Co: Tim Graham/ Hulton-Deutsch Collection; 43-47 AL: Comstock Images (rh); 44 Leb (tr); Toby Wales (b); 45 GI: Johan Elbers/Time Life Pictures; 46 Empics Ltd: AP Photo/Uwe Lein (b); 47 Co: Reuters (tr). Mary Evans Picture Library: (b); 48-49 GI: Francesco Ruggeri; 50 Leb (t); 50-121 Fotosearch: Iconotec (rh); 50-51 AA: National Portrait Gallery Scotland/Dagli Orti (A) (t); 51 BAL: Private Collection, The Stapleton Collection (c); 52 Leb (tc, b); 53 Leb (c); 54 RJ; 55 Leb (tr); 56 RJ (b); 57 BAL: Private Collection, Archives Charmet © ADAGP, Paris and DACS, London 2006 (cr). Festival d'Aix-en-Provence: Elisabeth Carecchio (b); 58 BAL: Bibliothèque Nationale, Paris, France, Lauros (b); 59 AL: David Sanger Photography (b). RJ (t); 60 Staatsoper unter den Linden: Monika Rittershaus (b); 61 Leb: Colette Masson (b); 62 Bayerischen Staatsoper: Wilfried Hösl (b); 63 Staatsoper unter den Linden: Marion Schöne (b); 64 Leb (tl, b); 65 AE: Pascal Gely/Agence Bernand (cr); 66 AE: Tristan Jeanne-Vales (b); 67 Opera Atelier, Canada – The Elgin Theatre: Bruce Zinger (b); 68 Leb (tl); 68 AE: Agence Bernand (b); 69 Opera Atelier, Canada: Bruce Zinger (b); 70 Leb: Royal Academy of Music Coll (d), (b); 71 RJ (b); 72 RJ (b); 73 Alamy: Malcolm MacGregor (t); 73 Leb (b); 74 Leb (tl, b); 75 State Opera Prague: Frantisek Ortmann (b); 76 AA: Pinacoteca Civica Iesi/Dagli Orti (A) (tr). Leb (b); 77 Colette Masson (b); 78 AE: Tristan Jeanne-Vales; 79 Leb (tr); 80 Zurich Opera House: Peter Schnetz (b); 81 AE: Tristan Jeanne-Vales (cl). GI: George F Mobley (b); 82 TopFoto.co.uk: Clive Barda/PAL; 83 Colette Masson; 84 RJ; 85 Leb (tr); 86 BAL: Guildhall Library, City of London (tr). Birmingham Museums and Art Gallery (b); 87 Topfoto: Clive Barda/PAL (b); 88 GI: Johan Elbers/Time Life Pictures (b); 89 BAL: Louvre, Paris, France, Lauros/Giraudon (t). Leb (b); 90-91 Hamburgische Staatsoper: Brinkhoff/ Mögenburg; 92 AL: Ramon SENERA Agence Bernand (c); 93 Leb: Tristram Kenton (b); 94 Leb: Laurie Lewis (b); 95 Leb: Laurie Lewis (c); 96 RJ; 97 Leb (tr); 98 BAL: State Central A.A. Bakhrushin Theatre Museum, Moscow (b); 99 RJ (b); 100 RJ (b); 101 Leb (c); 102 akg images: Marion Kalter; 103 AA: Society Of The Friends Of Music Vienna/Dagli Orti (A) (tr); 104 Leb (tc); 105 Leb: ColouriserAL (cr), (b); 106 Leb (bl). RJ (b); 107 Leb: Tristram Kenton (c); 108 De Munt La Monnaie: Johan Jacobs (b); 109 Staatstheater Stuttgart, Opernhaus: A. T. Schaefer (b); 110 Teatro Massimo Palermo: Franco Lannino/ Studio Camera (b); 111 Co: Reuters (c); 112 AL: Beateworks Inc/Tim Street-Porter (br); 113 AE: Pascal Gely/Agence

Bernand (t). Co: RJ (b); 114-115 The Banff Centre: Donald Lee; 116 AKG: (b); 117 Leb: Laurie Lewis (b); Private Collection (tr); 118 Leb: (b); 119 TopFoto.co.uk: Keith Saunders/ArenaPAL (t); 120 AKG: Erich Lessing (b); 121 GI: Angelo Cavalli (b). Leb: Colette Masson (tl); 122-123 PunchStock: Image Source; 124 BAL: Collection, Roger-Violet, Paris (c). Leb (b); 124-201 Co: (rh); 125 BAL: Musee Conde, Chantilly, France, Lauros/ Giraudon (b); 126 Leb (b); 127 Leb: J. Massey Stewart (cr); 128 Leb: Tristram Kenton; 129 Leb: H.Weidner-Weiden Interfoto (tr); 130 Leb (tc, b); 131 Teatr Weikl Poland: Juliusz Multarzyński (cr); 132 Riccardo Musacchio & Flavio Ianniello: (cl); 133 Hamburgische Staatsoper: Karl Forster (b); 134 Riccardo Musacchio: (b); 135 De Nederlandse Opera: Hans Hijmering (tr). Leb: Private Collection (b); 136 Royal Danish Opera: Martin Mydtskov Rønne (b); 137 Co: Massimo Listri (t). TopFoto.co.uk: Clive Barda/ArenaPAL (cr); 138 Topfoto: Colin Willoughby/ArenaPAL (b); 139 Leb: Private Collection (b); 140 Ken Howard: San Diego Opera; 141 Co: Krause, Johansen/ Archivo Iconografico, SA; 142 Co: Mimmo Jodice (t); 143 Met, NY: (b); 144 Festival Della Valle D'itria; 145 RJ (b); 146 Teatro alla Scala: Erio Piccagliani (b); 147 Co: Raymond Gehman (b). Leb: HIS Interfoto (tr); 148 RJ; 149 Leb (tr); 150 AA: Donizetti Museum Bergamo/Dagli Orti (A) (b). Leb (tr); 151 Fondazione Teatro Regio di Torino: Ramella & Giannese (b); 153 Leb (tl). RJ (b); 154 Co: Sandro Vannini; 155 RJ (b). Leb (tl); 156 RJ (b); 157 Leb: Private Collection (b); 158 TopFoto.co.uk: Clive Barda (b); 159 Riccardo Musacchio: (b); 160 Leb (tr). Topfoto: Ron Scherl/Arena Images (b); 161 Leb (tr); 161Topfoto: ArenPAL (b); 162 BAL: Bibliotheque de L'Opera, Paris, France (b). Co: Hulton-Deutsch Collection (tr); 164 Riccardo Musacchio; 165 AA: Society Of The Friends Of Music Vienna/Dagli Orti (A)]; 166 Leb: ColouriserAL (cl); 166-167 Mary Evans Picture Library: (b); 167 Leb: TAL RA (cr); 168 Co: Ira Nowinski (cr); 169 Co: Bill Cooper/epa (b); 170 Leb (b); 171 Leb (b); O. Rotem; 172-173 Teatro alla Scala: Andrea Tamoni (b); 173 Co: RJ (tl). Leb: O. Rotem (tc); 174 Co: Leonhard Foeger/Reuters; 175 BAL: Bibliotheque de la Comedie Francaise, Paris, France, Archives Charmet (b). Teatro alla Scala: Andrea Tamoni (t); 176 Deutsche Oper Berlin: Bernd Uhlig; 177 Co: Bettmann; 178 Colette Masson; 179 Co: RJ; 180 Co: Ira Nowinski; 181 Teatro Regio Torino: Ramella & Giannese (t). GI: National Geographic/Kenneth Garrett (b); 182-183 GI: AMR NABIL/ AFP; 184 The Lordprice Collection: Tony Price; 185 TopFoto. co.uk: Clive Barda/ArenaPAL (b); 186 BAL: Private Collection (b); 187 GI: Patrick Riviere (t); Leb: Laszlo Vámos (b); 188 Co: Alinari Archives/Gaetano Puccini; 189 Leb (tr); 190 The Lordprice Collection: Tony Price (b). AKG (b); 191 Co: Eduardo Abad/epa (b); 192 AL: Mary Evans Picture Library (c); 193 Co: Vittoriano Rastelli (b). Leb: Private Collection (tr); 194 Leb: Private Collection (b); 195 Co: Gianni Giansanti/Sygma (b). Hulton-Deutsch Collection (b); 196 The Lordprice Collection: Tony Price; 197 Co: Bettmann (c); 197 Leb: Gilles Bouquillon (b); 198 Co: Tristram Kenton (c); 199 Leb: MetropolitanOpera Archives (b); 200 Topfoto: Clive Barda/ArenaPAL (b); 201 Ken Howard: San Diego Opera (b); 202-203 Co: Robert Matheson; 204 Mary Evans Picture Library: (c); 204-205 Leb (b); 205 AKG (cb); 207 Leb (tl). TopFoto.co.uk: Ron Scherl/Arena Images (br); 208 AA: Beethoven House Bonn/Dagli Orti (A) (tr). Co: Sandro Vannini (b); 209 Staatsoper Unter den Linden: Monika Rittershaus; 210 AKG (b). AA: Musée Bonnat Bayonne France/ Dagli Orti (A) (tl); 211 TopFoto.co.uk: Roger-Violet (br); 212 Science Photo Library: Mike Agliolo (b); 213 AKG (cr). Staatsoper Unter den Linden: (b); 214 Bildarchiv Preußischer Kulturbesitz, Berlin: 007081Willi Saeger (bl). Co (tr); 215 Theater Erfurt: (tc); 216 Colette Masson; 217 Leb (tr); 218 AL: nagelestock.com (b). Leb (tl); 219 AKG: Richard-Wagner-Museum (b); 220 Staatsoper Unter den Linden: Monika Rittershaus (b); 221 Leb: S.Lauterwasser (b); 222 GI: Bryan Peterson (b); 223 Co: Bettmann (b). Empics Ltd: Stephen Chernin/AP (t); 224 Leb (tl); 225 Leb (tl). Los Angeles Philharmonic: Kira Perov/Bill Viola (Artist, b); 226 TopFoto. co.uk: Clive Barda (b); 227 AKG: (bl). Staatsoper Unter den Linden: Monika Rittershaus (t); 228 Co: Christie's Images (b); 229 AA: Neuschwanstein Castle Germany/Dagli Orti (tc); 230 Leb (b); 231 Bayreuther Festspiele: Jorg Schulze (tr). Leb: S Lauterwasser (b); 232 Leb: Tristram Kenton (b); 233 Leb (b). The Metropolitan Opera: (r); 234 Leb: Private Collection (b); 235 Bayreuther Festspiele: (b). Leb (tc); 237 Bayreuther Festspiele (b). AE: Marc Enguerand (c); 238 GI: Beatriz Schiller/Time Life Pictures; 239 BAL: Bibliotheque des Arts Decoratifs, Paris, France, Archives Charmet (tr). Redferns: Ron Scherl (b); 240 Leb (tr). RJ (b); 241 Pat Bromilow: Cape Town Opera (tr); 242 Leb (tr), (b); 243 Deutsche Oper Berlin: Bernd Uhlig (br); 244

Co: Hulton-Deutsch Collection (tl). Leb (b); 245 TopFoto.co.uk: Ron Scherl/Arena Images (b); 246 Leb (tl), (b). Kobal: Warner Bros (cr); 247 GI: Andreas Schaad/AFP (b); 248 Leb: Laurie Lewis; 249 Leb (b); 250 GI: Hulton Archive (b); 251 AKG: Coll. Archiv f.Kunst & Geschichte (b). Leb: Private Collection (t); 252 Leb: Colette Masson (bl); 253 GI: Theo Allofs (t). TopFoto.co.uk: (b); 254 TopFoto.co.uk: Clive Barda/PAL (cr); 255 Co: Herwig Prammer/Reuters (b); 256 AE: Tristan Jeanne-Vales (b); 257 Leb (cr); 258 AE: Marc Enguerand (c); 259 Leb: Laurie Lewis (b); 260-261 Co: Nathalie Darbellay/Sygma; 262 Co: Gianni Dagli Orti; 262-305 PunchStock: Photodisc (rh); 263 Co: Swim Ink 2, LLC (tc); 264 Co: Patrice Latron (b); 265 Co: Alfredo Dagli Orti/Estate of Jean Beraud ADAGP, Paris and DACS, London 2006 (cr); 266 Co: Bettmann (b); 266-267 AE: Ramon Senera/ Agence Bernand (b); 268 AKG: (bl). Co: Bettmann (r); 269 Co: Austrian Archives (cr); 270 AL: Sami Sarkis (b); 271 RJ (bl). Leb (tl); 272 RJ; 273 AA: San Pietro Maiella Conservatorio Naples/ Dagli Orti (A) (tr); 274 Opéra national du Rhin: Alain Kaiser (b); 275 RJ (b); 276 GI: Beatriz Schiller/Time Life Pictures (b); 277 TopFoto.co.uk: ArenaPAL (tl); 278 Leb (tl). Réunion des Musées Nationaux Agence Photographique: Droits réservés/Musée d'Orsay, Paris (b); 279 Leb (t); 280 Leb: Private Collection (b); 281 Colette Masson: (tl). Co: Ted Spiegel (br); 282 Topfoto: Roger-Viollet (t); 283 Co: Hulton-Deutsch Collection (t); 284 Leb (b); 285 Leb: Colette Masson (b); 286 Los Angeles Opera: Robert Millard (b); 287 RJ (c); 288 AE: Agence Bernand; 289 AA: San Pietro Maiella Conservatorio Naples/Dagli Orti (A) (tr); 290 Leb (b); 291 Leb: Private Collection (tl); 291 Ken Howard: San Diego Opera (b); 292 TopFoto.co.uk: Ron Scherl/Arena Images (b); 293 Co: Bettmann (tr). Photolibrary: P Berchery (bl); 294-295 TopFoto.co.uk: Gianfranco Fainello/PAL; 296 Co: Gianni Dagli Orti (b). Leb (tl); 297 AE: Pascal Gely/Agence Bernand (cr); 298 Leb: Brian Morris (b); 299 Deutsche Oper Berlin: Bernd Uhlig (b); 300 Co: Michael Nicholson (r). AA: Bibliothèque des Arts Décoratifs Paris/Dagli Orti (b); 301 San Francisco Opera: Ken Friedman (b); 302 Leb (tl), (b); 303 Teatro alla Scala: Lelli & Masotti (cr); 304 GI: Bruce Forster (tr); 304-305 AE: Tristan Jeanne-Vales; 306-307 AL: Diomedia; 308 Co: Catherine Panchout (b); 308-338 Co: (rh); 309 Co: Helen Atkinson/Reuters (tr). Leb (c); 310 Co: Peter Turnley (b); 311 Co: Stefano Bianchetti (cr); 312 Co: Bettmann (tr). Mary Evans Picture Library: (b); 313 Mariinsky Theatre: Natasha Razina (b); 314 RJ; 315 Leb (b); 316 AKG (b); 317 Leb (tr). RJ: (bl); 318 AA: Bibliothèque des Arts Décoratifs Paris/Dagli Orti (b); 319 RJ (t). Opéra national de Paris: Eric Mahoudeau (t); 320 RJ; 321 Leb (tr); 322 AKG (b); 323 GI: Gary Holscher (t). RJ: (b); 324 AKG: (b); 325 RJ (t); 326 BAL: Pushkin Museum, Moscow, Russia/The BAL (b). Leb (tr); 327 Colette Masson: (b); 328 Co: Burstein Collection (b). Leb (tr); 329 San Francisco Opera: Ken Friedman (t); 330 Leb (tl).Topfoto: Zoe Dominic/Boosey & Hawkes Collection/ArenaPAL (bl). GI: Time Life Pictures (br); 331 De Nederlandse Opera: Hans van den Bogaard (b); 333 Leb (cl). RJ (b); 334-335 AE: Marc Enguerand; 336 Co: Bettmann (cr); Underwood & Underwood (tl). Leb (b); 337 The Opera Group (b); 339 Mariinsky Theatre: Natasha Razin (b). TopFoto.co.uk: (tr); 340-341 Co: Ladislav Janicek/Zefa; 342 Leb (c); 343 Leb (bl); 344-345 Co: Liba Taylor (b); 345 Leb: Jim Four (cr); 346 AA: Conservatoire Prague/Dagli Orti (b). Leb (tr); 347 Prague National Theatre: František Ortmann (b); 348 Leb (tr); 348 BAL:

Private Collection, RIA Novosti (b); 349 GI: Beatrz/ SchillerTime Life Pictures (r); 350 RJ; 351 Leb (tr); 352 RJ (b); 353 RJ (cr); 354 State Opera Prague (b); 355 GI: Terje Rakke (tr). Leb: Moravské Zemské (cr); 356 RJ (b); 357 Leb (cr); 358 Institut Bohuslava Martinu, o.p.s. (b). Leb: PB Martinu (r); 359 Ravenna Festival Foundation (r); 360-361 AL: OJPhotos; 362 Leb: Private Collection; 362-423 AL: Chris Ivin (rh); 363 GI: Denis De Marney/Stringer (b). Leb: Kurt Weill Foundation (tc); 364 Leb (br); 365 GI: AFP (tr); 366 BAL: Stadtische Galerie in Lenbachhaus, Munich, Germany © ADAGP, Paris and DACS, London 2006 (cr). Co: Sylvia Salmi/Bettmann (tl). Leb (b); 367 Hamburgische Staatsoper: Hermann und Clächen Baus (b); 368 RJ; 369 Co: Bettmann (tr); 370 GI: Marc Moritsch (b); 371 TopFoto.co.uk: Ken Howard/PAL (b); 372 AKG: Gert Schütz (b); 373 RJ (b); 374 Co: John Springer Collection (b). Leb: Kurt Weill Foundation (tl); 375 DRAMA. Agentur fuer Theaterfotografie: Iko Freese (b); 376 Leb: Kurt Weill Foundation (b); 377 AKG (b). GI: Norbert Millauer/AFP (t); 378 AA: (b). Co: Hulton-Deutsch Collection (t); 379 RJ (b); 380 Co: Bettmann (b). GI: Hulton Archive (cr). Los Angeles Philharmonic: Betty Freeman (t); 381 RJ (b); 382 Co: Bettmann (tl, cr). Leb (b); 383 Co: Jacques M. Chenet (b); 384 Leb (tl). Ullstein Bild (b); 385 Orff in Andechs e.V.: Stefan A. Schuhbauer-von Jena (b); 386 Leb: (t); 386-387 AE: Pascal Gely/Agence Bernand (b); 387 Co: Hulton-Deutsch Collection; 388 Co: Hulton-Deutsch Collection; 389 Co: Hulton-Deutsch Collection (tr). Mander & Mitchenson Theatre Collection: (b); 390 Co: Hulton-Deutsch Collection (b). Leb: Time Life Pictures (tc); 391 Mander & Mitchenson Theatre Collection: (b); 392 GI: Kurt Hutton/Picture Post/Hulton Archive (bl); 393 Zurich Opera House: Suzanne Schwiertz (tc). TopFoto.co.uk: Zimmermann/Boosey & Hawkes Collection/ArenaPAL (br); 394 Leb: Private Collection (b); 395 Leb: ArenaPAL (tr); B. Rafferty (b); 396-397 RJ; 398 AE: Pascal Gely/Agence Bernand (c); 399 Hamburgische Staatsoper: Brinkhoff/Mögenburg (br); 400 Leb: Drew Farrell (bl); 401 Leb: Nigel Luckhurst (cr); 402 BAL: San Francesco, Pescia, Italy (bl). Leb: Suzie Maeder (c); 403 AE: Agence Bernand (br). Neue Oper Wien: Peter Grubinger (b); 404 Co: Bettmann (cr). Leb (bl); Mike Evans (tl); 406 Leb (tr, bl); 407 Hans van den Bogaard: (t); 408 Leb: Richard Haughton (tl); Nigel Luckhurst (bl); 409 De Nederlandse Opera: Ruth Walz (bl); 410 Leb: Sony Classical (bl); Horst Tappe (tr); 411 TopFoto. co.uk: Clive Barda/PAL (r); 412 Leb (bc); Betty Freeman (tl); 413 Grand Théâtre de Genève: (cr); 414 Co: Hulton-Deutsch Collection (b). Leb: Laurie Lewis (c); 415 Leb: Laurie Lewis (c); 416 Co: Nubar Alexanian (bl). Leb: Betty Freeman (tl). TopFoto. co.uk: Richard Mildenhall/Arena Images (br); 417 Tilde de Tullio: (cr); 418 Leb: Betty Freeman (tl); 418-419 TopFoto.co.uk: Jim Caldwell/Arena Images (b); 420 De Nederlandse Opera: Hans van den Bogaard (b). Leb: Laurie Lewis (tl); 421 Regine Koerner: (cr); 422 AL: Patrick Medd (b). Leb: T. Martinot (tl); 423 Leb: Alastair Muir (b); Jacket images: Front: AL: Chad Ehlers (t); Leb (bl); Jeff Morgan (br; Leb (bl). Back: ArenaPAL: Clive Barda Co (l). Clarke (c); RJ (tl); Francis G. Mayer (br); Leb (cra); Spine: ArenaPAL: Clive Barda (t)

All other images © Dorling Kindersley
For further information see: www.dkimages.com

Authors' acknowledgements

The authors wish to thank Michael Berger-Sandhofer, James Conlon, Sergei Dreznin, Robert Minder, David Stern, and Augusta Read Thomas for their thoughtful readings and comments. They are grateful to EMI and Mariko Tada for research materials; Opera News for archival access in New York; Liza Vick and the staff of the Loeb Music Library of Harvard University; and John Varney and the Handel House Museum in London. For loving support and patience, Marlise, Alexander, Jordan, and Naira will never be forgotten.

Publisher's acknowledgements

DK would like to thank Robert Weinberg for reading the manuscript, and Liz Moore for additional picture research.

Studio Cactus would like to thank Lindsey Brown for proofreading, and Robbie Jack for access to his archives and expertise.